A LIFE OF SERVICE

GUY V. MOLINARI

CO-AUTHORED WITH
PATRICIA FEERICK-KOSSMANN

First Edition

PAGE PUBLISHING, INC.
New York, NY

First originally published by Page Publishing, Inc. 2016

ISBN 978-1-68409-168-3 (Paperback)
ISBN 978-1-68409-170-6 (Hard Cover)
ISBN 978-1-68409-169-0 (Digital)

Printed in the United States of America

To James
One never knows why paths cross, but in this situation it was clearly Destiny. We Both have clearly encountered Difficult Life Paths – but we persevere!! You are a Really nice and inquisitive person

It is with great pride that I dedicate this work to my two beautiful granddaughters, Susan and Katie. When you reach my age, having two granddaughters who show their love to mom and dad, as well as to their "Poppy" – well, that makes it all worthwhile.

Pat and I enjoyed putting this work together, knowing that my granddaughters would read every word cover-to-cover and keep these memories alive in their hearts.

I Look Forward to many "chats" yes "chats" in the Future. AND YES" YOU Are A Great man! Technology is great so we will Keep in touch ☺

Your Friend
Pat
(c) 516-376-8958

EMAIL

Back cover image- Photo by: Bill Paciello

CONTENTS

CHAPTER I

The King of Midland Beach

To GET A SENSE OF WHO I AM, YOU should first know from where I came. I was born in Booth Memorial Hospital on the Lower East Side of Manhattan on November 23rd, 1928. I was christened Gaetano Kenneth Molinari on April 7th, 1929 at the Church of St. John Nepomucene located on the Upper East Side of Manhattan.

It was a name that I myself changed during my early teen years because I just didn't like the way it sounded. My godfather was Victor Sotardi. As I was growing up, I liked the name Victor. It was a lot easier to say Guy V. Molinari. Guy K. Molinari just didn't roll off the tongue easily. It was as simple as that. Considering the name change, you can see that from my youth, I was always able to think outside of the box. It is my opinion that this ability is the key to being successful in achieving personal goals, no matter how difficult they may seem.

After reading the first paragraph of this book, people who have known me their entire life are going to say, "I didn't know that." That is why I am writing this book: to set the record straight, to ruffle a few feathers, and maybe have a little fun at my expense.

My grandfather, Gaetano Molinari, was born in Amantea, a small town located in the Calabria region of southern Italy. He married my grandmother, Marie Antoinette, in Amantea. Their first born, my father, Sigmund Robert Molinari, was born in Italy on February 22nd, 1898. Forever after in this book, my father will be referred to as "Bob" or "Robert" Molinari. He never referred to himself as Sigmund. Formally, he would write his name as S. Robert Molinari. That is how I knew him and that is how everyone else did. So like father, like son, we both naturally changed our names very early in our life.

In 1899, my grandfather and his nine siblings decided to leave Italy and immigrate to America. Poverty, crop failures, political unrest and unemployment, coupled with the myth that in America the "streets were paved with gold," and life was much easier, prompted this decision. Initially my grandfather came to America without his wife since she was pregnant with their second child. After she gave birth to their daughter, Ernoldina, in Italy, Antonetta immigrated to America with their two children.

When my grandfather Gaetano and his siblings were on the Norddeutscher Lloyd ship to America, they heard rumors about deadly diseases that were rampant in New York such as diphtheria and tuberculosis. The Molinari siblings had a heated discussion. On November 29th 1899 when the Norddeutscher Lloyd arrived in New York Harbor five of them decided to get off the ship and live their dreams. The other four said, "No, I didn't come on this hellish boat ride to die from disease." So, they stayed on the ship and immigrated to São Palo Brazil. As is typical of most any immigrant at the time, the Molinaris could not speak a word of English when they arrived in America.

In this time of vast immigration, every ship's captain was required to sign a notarized statement attesting to the fact that:

> ...I believe that no one of said passengers is an idiot or insane person, or a pauper or likely to become a public charge, or suffering from a loathsome or dangerous contagious disease, or a person who has been convicted of a felony or other infamous crime or mis-

> demeanor involving moral turpitude, or a polygamist [.][1]

So I can say for certain that I came from good blood since the ship's captain attested to this. Talk about political correctness, but given the time period, no one found these words offensive. Back then people were just thrilled to follow protocol in order to enter our great country.

When my grandfather arrived in New York, he first lived in Little Italy and then he rented an apartment at 1120 1st Avenue, Manhattan. My grandfather was a barber by trade, as was his entire family. So, naturally he opened a barbershop.

In the early 20th Century, the Mafia was at its apex. When I was growing up I remember being told the breathtaking story of how my grandfather boldly refused to pay the Mafia their weekly illegal extortion demand in order to continue operating the barbershop. One day the Mafia slipped a piece of paper with a black hand on it under the doorsill of the barbershop. The "Black Hand" was a notorious signal that they were going to blow up his barbershop, if he didn't pay the extortion demand. My grandfather was a stubborn guy, as all the Molinari men are. He said he would not pay and he didn't. At the time it was an amazingly bold action for this new immigrant from Italy to take. Incredibly, nothing happened to him.

My grandparents ultimately had fourteen children, five of whom died. Four died in childbirth, and one died at the age of sixteen when she choked on a piece of soft candy. As immigrants with no financial resources, struggling to survive, the children who died were all buried in Potters Field located on Hart Island, New York City, the largest tax funded cemetery in the world.

The surviving nine were Robert, Ernoldina, Arnaldo, Rosalba, Columbia, Giuseppe, Aurelio, Pia, and Elvira. As was the Italian tra-

---

1 *Required by the regulations of the Secretary of the Treasury of the United States, under Act of Congress approved March 3rd, 1893, to be delivered to the Commissioner of Immigration by the Commanding Officer of any Vessel having such passengers on board, upon arrival at any port in the United States.*

dition at the time, the family was large. Seeking more living space, the family eventually moved to 46-01 104 Street located in Corona, Queens.

During my childhood, we would visit my grandfather in Queens on Sunday after he closed the barbershop for the day. As you can surmise, I was named after my grandfather. Although my brother was older, my mother, not being Italian-American, didn't like the name Gaetano, so she refused to name her first born Gaetano. To my mother's credit, she did insist that her children were baptized in St. John Nepomucene Church, since it was founded by immigrants from Slovakia. When I came along two years later, my mother knew she could not win the name fight twice, so I was blessed with the name Gaetano. In the long run, it brought childhood blessings whenever I was with my grandfather.

For example, whenever I visited my grandfather he had a parlor that everybody gathered in. At the end of the night my grandfather would close the rolling doors to the kitchen and he would cook a couple pieces of meat that were hard to come by. My grandfather and grandmother would be sitting there, and then he would call out, "Gaetano, *veni ca, sediti.*" It was the only Italian I understood and it meant, "Gaetano, come here, sit down."

It always seemed like there were at least twenty of us outside the parlor. I would yell, "Yes, Grandpa. I'm coming." Since I was named after him, he treated me special. I was able to eat the precious meat. During the Depression, this was a big deal. I would sit at the kitchen table, thinking of the rest of my relatives who wished they were invited into the parlor.

On Sundays, my grandfather would walk around Corona shopping for the week's groceries. He had a Homburg hat and cane and I remember him walking around town like he was the king. The people would go, "Mr. Molinari, how are you?" I thought they treated him like royalty. I was very proud of him. From the way the people treated him you would never know that he was a barber. He generated respect from his neighbors and friends. As a child, I was always puzzled how my grandfather was able to do that. As time went on I understood that it is a person's overall character that makes the man, not the job he has.

The Molinaris were introduced to Staten Island during the "Roaring Twenties." My grandparents came to Staten Island with the summer crowd and they rented a bungalow in Midland Beach for the summer. My grandmother's sister, Marietta and other relatives rented bungalows as well. The bungalows offered shelter and that's it. The bungalows had no finished inside walls, the studs ever present. There was no heat, yet to the Molinaris it was luxury. The family was on vacation for the summer and they had the time of their life. My grandparents operated a grocery store for the summer crowd.

In the summer the population of Midland Beach and the surrounding area increased ten-fold. People from "The City" rented summer bungalows and vacationed at Midland Beach. Even though Staten Island is a borough in New York City, residents of Staten Island have always referred to the other four boroughs as "The City."

Midland Beach today has evolved into a residential community. Ironically, Midland Beach residents' today travel to the Jersey Shore and the Hamptons for their summer vacation. When I was growing up, Midland Beach was the place to be. It was considered one of the finest resort areas in the tri-state area. Tourism was a great source of revenue for the entire beach area of Staten Island.

My father eventually met my mother, Elizabeth Majoros. They fell in love and they were married on Valentine's Day, February 14th, 1926. After I was born in Manhattan in 1928, my parents decided to move to Corona, Queens, and then ultimately to the Midland Beach section of Staten Island. It was the same area where my grandparents rented in the summer. The area was full of immigrants from Italy and Ireland, and my parents happily joined the crowd. My parents were the first Molinaris to live year round on Staten Island. As a result, my entire life has revolved around my beloved Staten Island.

My father bought his first house on Midland Avenue in Staten Island. Within one year of my birth, the Great Depression occurred. Unfortunately, my father, like many others at the time, immediately lost the first house he bought due to the Depression. We then lived in a small apartment above a Ralston Store[2] in Midland Beach. Eventually we moved to a winterized bungalow style house that was located at 250 Oldfield Street. By that time our family had grown and I had three younger sisters: Elizabeth, Dolores, and Joan, and my older brother, Robert.

Unlike today, my father purchased the Oldfield house directly from the owners. There was no bank mortgage involved. After the disastrous stock market crash and closing of banks in 1929, everyone was very skeptical about utilizing the banks. I remember once a month the sellers would come to the house to pick up their monthly payment. It was a payment that my parents never missed. The sellers held my parent's mortgage until it was fully paid off.

My mother was of Czechoslovakian descent, but her father would get angry when we said that. Even though my mother's father came from Czechoslovakia he would not say that they were Czechoslovakian; rather they were Slovakian. He said the Czechs sold out to the Germans while the Slovaks fought them.

My mother's father Michael Majoros was a big burly guy who smoked a pipe. He came to America when he was sixteen or seventeen years old. A few years after he arrived, he sent for his brother John. He actually worked on the foundation of the Empire State Building as a digger. He was very proud of the fact that he worked in a foundry as an iron worker. He would talk about the hard work that he did while working in the foundry. He was honored that he helped to forge the tools that were necessary to continue to build and defend America. During this time period, a blue collar job was a fantastic way to make a living and serve your country. His wife, my grandmother, worked at night cleaning floors of offices. She helped her son, my Uncle Mike, pay for law school at the University of Indiana. He wound up being a prosecutor and a judge in Indiana.

Throughout my life the Italian part of my heritage would overpower the Czechoslovakian because in Staten Island, especially at the time, the Italian population trumped the Czechoslovakians. This was a simple fact in the hierarchy of various other immigrant populations

---

2 *These stores sold general merchandise, such as tools, kitchen utensils, firewood, etc.*

of Staten Island at the time.

My mother was an extraordinarily quiet lady. She rarely left the house, whereas my father was a very active man. He attended functions almost every night. My mother would always get very nervous about going out. She was a homebody. She enjoyed sitting at home with the children and tending to the housework. She was a wonderful mother yet she had one minor fault which we all took advantage of – she would let us do whatever we wanted to do.

Even though the Depression impacted everyone's life, Midland Beach was still considered a popular summer resort, attracting thousands of visitors on a single day. Many people came for day trips on excursion boats that ran directly from Manhattan, Brooklyn, and Newark. There was an open air train that ran from the ferry in St. George straight to Midland Beach.

There were amusement rides, bath houses, a long pier, a beautiful boardwalk with a bandstand, outdoor movie section, dancing area, and an in-ground pool. The beach was right in front of everyone as they sang, danced, and went on the rides. There were several hotels and hundreds of summer bungalows spread throughout the area. As such, in the 1930s, it was a wonderful area for a child to grow up in regardless of the fact that the Depression was in full force.

My father worked very hard to make ends meet. He was not an idle man. It was tough times and there were no hand outs. In order to survive tough times, you had to hustle. My father said soup kitchens were not a place that the Molinaris would visit. Family pride was extremely important. So from an early age, I was taught to work for what I wanted. There was no such thing as entitlements. If my father wasn't working, he was doing something for the community. He was actively involved in every aspect of life on Staten Island. I clearly remember one Christmas during the Depression, my mother said to my brother Bobby, "Santa won't be bringing any gifts this year." A lady showed up with a bagful of used boots. Those were our presents that year and we were extremely grateful for them.

He was always working several jobs at the same time to support his family. He was a real estate appraiser for the City of New York, as well as a real estate and insurance agent. He ultimately bought a few buildings in Midland Beach. He owned and operated a pizza and beer establishment during the summer season, which was called *MOLINARI'S. MOLINARI'S* was a nice place to eat and relax. Throughout the night during the summer season, pizza flowed out of the kitchen continuously. *MOLINARI'S* pizza was known throughout the island as one of the best—if not the best.

There were fights at *MOLINARI'S* every night. Across the street was *DAVIS'S* where the Irish hung out and there were fights there every night as well. I used to sit in the corner of my father's bar and just watch the fights spill out into the street. Summertime in Midland Beach was an adventure. In my teens, I waited tables and cleaned the restaurant for my father. The smell of stale beer on a Sunday morning is a smell I will never forget. I could keep my tips, but the rest went to the family.

In addition to his skills at supporting a family, my father was also a superb banjo player. He made my brother, Robert, and me take accordion lessons. Our accordion teacher was Omero Castelucci. I hated playing the accordion, but my brother loved it. My father loved music and wanted his children to embrace music as he had done. Because my father made me play the accordion, I was forced to perform at nursing homes, community concerts, and any other event my father deemed worthy. My father would play the banjo, my brother the accordion, and an uncle of mine the guitar. They were all accomplished. And then there was me. It was never a question of did I want to go. When my father said, "We're going," that's what we did. We went.

My father had a jazz band at the time call the "Merrymakers Band," or simply the "Bob Molinari Band." As a testament to his band's excellence they participated in a huge band competition in midtown Manhattan. The Paul Whiteman Band came in first and my father's band came in second. This was an incredible achievement at the time. In the 1930s, Paul Whiteman was a world famous American bandleader. Many people, even the great Duke Ellington, consider him to be the true "King of Jazz."

During the summertime on occasion, I would have to play the accordion with my brother Robert at the bandstand on the boardwalk of Midland Beach. Again, I wasn't very good at it, but my brother was fantastic. There was a dance arena on the boardwalk and everybody could dance right on the open waterfront. Hundreds of people would be swimming in the water, playing in the casinos and dancing on the boardwalk while we played. We also played the accordion at the World's Fair in 1939. The only perk of playing, to me, was that when we were done, we got free tickets to enjoy all the festivities.

Otherwise, like so many other boys my age, my thoughts drifted toward baseball. The New York Yankees ruled the world for me. Babe Ruth, Lou Gehrig, and Joe DiMaggio were heroes to every Staten Islander, but to me especially. I have been a devout Yankees fan for my entire life, and will continue to be one until my pinstriped heart stops beating.

Every summer night around 11:30 p.m., the businesses would shut everything down in Midland Beach. Midland Avenue was the focal point of Midland Beach. It would be impossible to drive a car up or down Midland Avenue because so many people were walking in the streets to go home for the night.

Labor Day weekend signaled the end of summer. It culminated with a great celebration which lasted for the entire Labor Day weekend. Part of the celebration included a parade. The King and Queen of the parade were the two kids who sold the most tickets for the festivities. When I was seven years old, I sold the most tickets to the festivities so I was the King of the parade. I fell in love with the Queen of the parade. She was about twelve years old, but it didn't matter that she was five years older than me; she was still my first true love. To this day, I don't know whether she reciprocated those feelings, but I still have a crush on her. She was so beautiful. As you can imagine to a child, it was a fantasyland in the summer.

So Midland Beach had two very different seasons: the summer and the winter. When the weather turned, the "city" people went back to their winter homes. Immediately after Labor Day, Midland Beach became very quiet and took on a different aura. It was almost like a ghost town.

When it got cold in the winter and nobody was out, I loved to walk up and down Midland Avenue. I used to imagine myself

"The King of Midland Beach" in the wintertime. I had these fantasies about working for the people of Midland Beach. Little did I know at the time that when I embarked on my political career it would come to fruition.

With the end of summer, the children also went back to school. I attended St. Margaret Mary's Catholic Grammar School. The school was run by the Presentation Sisters and they did a wonderful job of teaching. Father Martin Drury oversaw the nuns and ensured that "Love of Country and Church" were traditions to be followed. Every morning, Father Drury would stick his head into the classroom and ask, "Guy, do you want to serve mass with me?" I would always cower and cover my head and shamelessly answer, "No." At the time I was terribly afraid I would drop the host, or even worse, the Bible itself. So, the church was an extremely important part of my upbringing. Every Sunday our entire family would attend church. Unlike today, the Sundays of my childhood were days filled with church and family.

Prior to completing third grade, the nuns told me that I was going to skip the fourth grade completely and come back in the fall as a fifth grader. That set off a huge argument in my family. Some of my aunts thought it was a bad thing. My parents ultimately agreed with the nun's decision since I didn't have a problem with it. Looking back, I have no regrets about skipping a grade and in the long run I think it helped.

After I graduated from St. Margaret Mary's school, I went to St. Peter's Boys' High School located on Richmond Terrace in the St. George section of Staten Island. I had to take three buses to get to St. Peter's every day. The brothers who taught us did an excellent job, but as a young man, I felt that there was something missing. More importantly, I felt that I just didn't fit in. There were a lot of ethnic issues at the time between the Italian-Americans and the Irish-Americans.

When I was thirteen, my father decided that we were moving to a new home located at 116 Eighth Street, which was only a couple of blocks from New Dorp High School. This move and the fact that it was so close to New Dorp High was sort of a blessing since I was having some issues at St. Peter's Boys' High School. During my sophomore year, I was seriously thinking about leaving St Peter's. I went to visit one of the priests who worked there.

He said, "Why do you want to leave? You've got good grades, why are you thinking of leaving?"

I said, "I think that the other students would rather see me leave, so I'd rather leave too, maybe it's better for all of us." I explained that I wasn't comfortable there. There were more Irish at that school than Italians and I would hear "Guinea, Wop, Grease ball, etc." Vile ethnic slurs directed at me all the time. It angered me and I knew I was only going to get in trouble if I stayed.

At the same time that this was happening, my father was embarking on the only political election campaign he would be successful in. Throughout my entire youth, my father was very active in the Democratic Party. In the 1940s it was difficult for anybody to be elected on the Republican line in Staten Island. So what happened back then was the Republican Party wouldn't put forth a Republican for office but they would look for an independent Democrat who might be popular, like my father.

In 1942 the Republicans came to my father, who was an independent Democrat, and said they'd like to have him run on their line, and my father agreed to do it. Back then you had the American Labor Party which my father already had. He threw his heart and soul into the race.

On November 3rd, 1942 he was proudly elected to the New York State Assembly representing Richmond County's 2nd District for a two-year term. In the exuberance of the win his constituents scrawled their signatures and congratulatory messages in red, black, and blue ink on my father's starched white shirt. It was the first time I remember seeing my father in a disheveled shirt, and to a fourteen-year-old boy, he looked glorious.

The following day, my father's triumphant picture was on the front page of the *Staten Island Advance*. Pride spilled from the Molinari household. He was the first Molinari to hold public office. During the campaign, my father had promised that my siblings and me could stay home from school for one day if he won. When he made the promise we were all sure that he would lose since missing school was forbidden in the Molinari household.

Well, lo and behold, my father kept his first campaign promise. On Thursday November 5th all the Molinari children were given a holiday from school. It would be the first and last time that happened and we reveled in playing hooky because Bob Molinari was elected. The *Staten Island Advance* came to our house and took a family picture of us playing hooky from school. Obviously I was the envy of all my friends.

It was an awesome achievement for an Italian immigrant. It was my father's proudest moment of his life. He was the first foreign-born citizen to be elected to the New York State Legislature. I was thrilled to finally see one of his dreams come true. He was such a hardworking man and he deserved to win. My father loved being an assemblyman and threw himself into the job.

Regarding my father's tenure as an assemblyman, it came to an abrupt end in 1944 when he ran for re-election on the Democratic ticket because the Republicans threw their support to a Republican Edmund P. Radigan. He was defeated by Radigan. He lost by a slim margin. It was a crushing defeat to him.

Shortly after the election, I decided that I definitely wanted to go to a public high school rather than to the Catholic high school. My parents agreed when they heard my reasoning. Suddenly, I was a teenager in the public school system and I found it to be a totally different environment from the Catholic school. The biggest difference of course was that there were girls in the class. I had no idea that there was such a thing as female high school students until I got to New Dorp High School. If you will, the action was "on," and I enjoyed myself immensely while attempting to learn at the same time.

Looking back, I can see there were tremendous pressures placed upon students in Catholic high school. So, it was easy to transition from a Catholic school to a public high school. The learning process was completely different and I made a lot of new friends, many of whom would become lifelong friends. For me, this change helped me more than what I could have learned from Catholic high school.

It was the first time I was able to engage in totally adolescent behavior without the fear of being caught by the nuns or brothers. I had a newfound freedom. I did things I would have never dreamed of, and I am not proud of all of them today, but they were funny. For example, there was an older female teacher who was overseeing our recess time. She would go to the auditorium to supervise and made sure we didn't get into trouble. One day I snuck around her so that she couldn't see me. I placed a matchstick in her shoe and lit it. We used to call that in those days, "giving somebody a hotfoot" and she eventually started yelling. She thought that she stepped on a match and she gave us a lecture about being careful about what you throwaway. "See what happens? I stepped on a lit match and I burned myself." She never found out that it was me. We all had a great laugh at that.

High school was loads of fun. At the end of the school day instead of rushing home, we would go to the auditorium and put on our own skits since there was a piano there. Someone would play the piano and the rest of us would be singing. Those were wonderful get-togethers and I treasure them to this day.

When we weren't putting on skits at New Dorp High, my friends and I would go to Novena at Our Lady Queen of Peace Church after school and then we would hang out at Lemoles, the local ice cream parlor. At Lemoles, we'd meet girls. Afterwards we'd play handball, touch football, or whatever was fun and cheap. At the time table tennis or ping pong was a huge sport. Ping pong was and is a sport that poor people could play. It wasn't expensive like golf. We played the game all the time in Midland Beach and I became a ping pong whiz really quick. In my youth I was very agile so I wound up beating most of my opponents. As a teenager I actually came in second for the Staten Island championship.

I made so many friends while I was growing up in Midland Beach during my teenage years. When I think back to this time I realize how the friends that I made at that time played such a pivotal role when I first sought elected office.

CHAPTER 2

Road to Becoming a Republican

When I graduated from High School in 1945, my father was adamant that his sons would go to college. As an Italian immigrant, he believed that the key to success in America was obtaining a college education. Although he had attended some college classes he never graduated because he had to support his family by running the many business endeavors which he continually got involved in. As such, he vowed to ensure his sons would get the college education he was unable to obtain for himself.

Unfortunately for my sisters, my parents did not think that college was necessary for women. In 1945, careers were basically geared toward the men. The men were supposed to work and support the family and the women were destined to marry and raise a family. That is exactly the path followed by my siblings and myself.

With those family values, it was only natural that my brother Robert and I attended Wagner College on Staten Island. Wagner was a well-established institution. It was the logical and affordable choice for a family of modest means. Unlike today we paid for our own education. We worked, studied, worked, studied. You get the idea. I loved the fact that Wagner was a co-ed college. It may seem like an odd statement now, but in the 1940s many colleges prohibited the admission of women and minorities.

I was extremely proud to attend Wagner College. Our country had just emerged victorious from World War II and America was committed to rebuilding the internal structure of the country. The war had taken a tremendous toll on the country. The energy in the air was blowing toward revitalization and regrowth.

At the time Wagner College was located on fifty-seven meticulously maintained acres on Grymes Hill. When I first saw the view from the hill I was awestruck by the sweeping views of New York Harbor, Manhattan, and the Atlantic Ocean. The campus was located on the former country estate of Sir Edward Cunard, a 19th Century shipping magnate. His surname survives today as the Cunard/Carnival Cruise line that so many Americans are fortunate to vacation on.

In 1945 the center of campus life, especially for a commuting student like me, was the beautiful ivy covered Main Hall surrounded by an immense great lawn. We called it the "AD building." It housed our classrooms, faculty, and administrative offices, library, gym, etc. Basically the Main Hall made Wagner College the college it was. Many of the other structures that exist today did not exist in 1945. At the time many of the resident students were housed in temporary war-surplus buildings rather than in permanent residence halls.

When I started Wagner College in 1945, the enrollment was a mere 450 students. By the time I graduated in 1949, enrollment had soared to more than 2,000. The huge jump in enrollment was a result of the flood of young men returning from the war with G.I. Bill College funding. As a result, Wagner hastily constructed Veterans Village, which consisted of a half a dozen one-story Army barracks and a two-story war surplus dormitory.

At Wagner College, I joined the fraternity Kappa Sigma Alpha. It was founded in 1931 and is Wagner College's oldest fraternity. So in addition to learning, I was having fun. Sometimes too much. I remember one night, the fraternity boys and I went out on the town to have a few drinks. My good frat brother George Esposito said to me, "Hey Guy, have you ever ridden a horse?"

I said, "Nope, I've never ridden a horse."

He said, "Do you think you could ride a horse?"

So I said, "Yeah, I think I could ride a horse, what's so hard about riding a horse?"

With that he said, "Come on with me. Are you strong enough to come out and ride a horse now?"

It was about 1:30 in the morning and we had been drinking all night. For me, the timing was just about right, so I said, "Of course. What's the big deal?"

So, he takes me to the sheriff's mounted posse field. We threw on the lights, and there were the horses. We took the horse out to the corral, and I said, "What do we do? Where's the saddle?"

George said, "You're not going to have a saddle."

"What?"

"Do you think you need a saddle?"

By the way he asked the question I immediately said, "Of course, I don't need a saddle, no."

So, here we are in the middle of winter, it's freezing, and my good friend George gives me a boost to get on top of the horse. When I get on top of the horse I grab the mane. The other fraternity brothers start throwing rocks at the horse as it starts moving. They wanted the horse to go faster. So there I was, on top of the world. I made it around the circle a few times and I am proud of myself. To hell with them, I thought. I'm hanging in there.

Then, things took a turn for the worse. George was getting pissed that I was able to stay on so long, so he rushed up and jumped on the horse and landed behind me. He reached around and grabbed the mane that I was holding and he kicked the horse to make it really gallop. Off we went. As the horse galloped into a turn I started to fall. I had nothing to hold on to because George had the mane! The weight of me starting to go down pulled George down as well and I hit the ground, which was like concrete because it is frozen from the winter weather. As luck would have it, George landed on top of me. As drunken teenagers will do, we all laughed at the time and I thought I was no worse for the wear.

When I finally got home I reached into my pocket and realized I didn't have my keys! It is now 2:30 in the morning and I had to ring the doorbell and wake my father up to let me in. It was something I never wanted to do, but I had no choice. So, I rang the doorbell and my father opened the door and he yelled, "Who hit you?"

I said, "Nobody hit me."

"Your face is full of blood."

"Well, I didn't know that, nobody hit me."

"Don't lie to me! Somebody hit you."

"Nobody hit me."

"Well, then what happened?"

"I fell off a horse."

I could have mentioned anything else and he might have believed it, but telling him I fell off a horse was not something he believed. On that night, my father thoroughly believed I was lying, and looking back I can't blame him. It just sounded so stupid, but it was the truth. To make matters worse the next morning when I tried to get out of bed, I couldn't move. I was bed ridden for three solid days from body shock.

Looking back, if I had to do it over again, I certainly would have insisted on a saddle. I learned a life lesson from this. It's simplistic, but true. You really have to think before you act. This is especially true when you are an impetuous young college student who may or may not have had too much to drink.

At Wagner, ping pong became a very important part of my college life. I played it all the time, usually for money. In essence I was a ping pong hustler, as was my good friend, Frank Lynch. I would signal Lynch when he could give the opposition as much as a five-point spread. Nearly every time we would win and split the proceeds.

At the time there was a major ping pong tournament sponsored by an Irish bar on Staten Island. I said to my friends in the fraternity that I played ping pong with, "We should enter the tournament as 'The Wagnerians.'" They agreed and four of us entered the tournament as a team.

One team that was in the tournament had won for over a decade. During the tournament we played two doubles matches and then we played singles games. A player could play as many as three single games if they were good. If the player wasn't so good they would play one or two. I played three games, because the other players on my team acknowledged that I was the best player on the team.

The tournament went on for months and we ultimately made it to the finals. Nobody thought we had any chance of ultimately winning because the reigning ping pong champs were so good. I won my two doubles matches and then I won my first two single matches. It was a flat out tie and the winner would be determined by the final singles game. It was me against the reigning team's best ping pong player. The pressure was on.

I believed that best player on the opposing team had an illegal serve. So before the final match started I challenged the player and told him, "Before we play, your serve is illegal."

He said, "What are you talking about?"

I said, "You have to either throw the ball in the air when you hit it or you have to drop your hand away. You cannot hit the ball off your hand. When you do that it is an illegal serve. The ball jumps to the right or to the left and no one has a clue of where it is going."

I knew that was exactly what he was doing although he made you think that he didn't do that. He claimed that he let it go, and as he let it go he hit it. We had a big argument. Unfortunately, yet not unexpectedly, the judges from the bar ruled in his favor saying that it was not an illegal serve.

With that ruling the game started. When he served I could not even see the ball when it came over the net. Now, I'm thinking to myself, "How can I possibly win?" I was a very competitive son-of-a-bitch. I figured that the only thing that I could do was hit the ball immediately as it came up. I had to teach myself while I'm playing the match how to do that. It was tough, but I did it. Miraculously I won the match. I remember the headline the next day in Wagner College's paper was, "Molinari Leads Team to Huge Win." We were thrilled when we claimed our trophy at the bar since we were all college kids and we beat the seasoned ping pong players.

While at Wagner, I decided that I wanted to become a lawyer.

Although my father was not a lawyer, I had watched him for years giving free legal advice to the poor. Even though my father wasn't supposed to do wills, contracts, etc., he did it anyway. In essence he acted like a semi-lawyer to me. So I thought that I would like to be a real lawyer. I liked the fact that people would put their trust in me for legal advice. As a lawyer I would also be able to help people so it was almost a natural choice since I admired my father so much.

I pushed myself to fulfill all the requirements as quickly as possible, and in 1949, at the age of twenty, I graduated from Wagner College ahead of time with a Bachelor of Arts degree in Social Studies. My brother Robert was drafted during World War II, so his education was delayed two years. As such, I graduated with Robert and we were the first Molinari men to graduate from college. It was an extraordinarily proud moment for my parents, and they were even more thrilled with my decision to enroll in law school.

If you ask me how I picked New York Law School, I will give you three candidly honest reasons: convenience, high probability of acceptance, and affordability. When I was in Wagner, I heard that they were taking just about anyone who applied. So, I jumped on the bandwagon. It seemed the most practical and economical way to obtain a law degree. Obviously such is not the case today for anyone who desires to engage in the practice of law in New York State.

First and foremost, in 1949 New York Law School was located at 244 William Street in Lower Manhattan which was a short ferry ride from Staten Island, and just a stone's throw away from City Hall. So again, as a commuter student, taking the ferry was extremely convenient. Also, there were quite a few other Staten Islanders going to New York Law at the time, so I had plenty of company.

Second, New York Law was hit hard during the Great Depression and saw a serious decline in enrollment. In 1941, the school was closed completely due to the draft and World War II, but they reopened in 1947. As such, in order to operate they were forced to accept a lower quality of student than had been previously accepted. In essence, if you could pay you would get in, but that didn't necessarily mean you had the academic qualities necessary to be a successful law student. Finally, New York Law was affordable. As with undergraduate school I had to work while attending school. My father didn't have much money, but he gave me what he could. I took whatever job was available. One year I worked at Gulf Oil rolling drums for the summer. I made a pretty good penny. It was hard work, but I was anxious to make money to help pay for law school. The more I made, the less I owed. In the long run, I did not walk out of school with extraordinary debt that would take years to get out of. I believe I paid approximately five-hundred dollars a year in tuition and about fifty dollars for fees and books. The difference today is astronomical. Great buy, you betcha.

So, New York Law School was a great choice and it worked out extraordinarily well for me. I remember when the marks were posted for each semester and everyone would look at "the board." Every classmate would see how you did, and I kind of liked that, owning your own actions. Although I did well, the board also showed how many of the students were failing. Most of these students were ones who had previously failed out of other law schools and came to New York Law under the mistaken impression that, since New York Law was accepting nearly everyone, they would also be passing everyone. Unfortunately for those students, New York Law still expected their students to do the work. At the time, I felt that I wasn't a very good student, but my marks were great compared to all the other students. It certainly was a morale booster.

It would be at New York Law School in 1949 that I would officially register my political affiliation for the first time. Unlike today, in 1949 under the Constitution you could not vote until the age of twenty-one. Whereas most of my friends registered under their family's political affiliation, I did the exact opposite. I guess there's a part of me that always liked to make difficult decisions, yet they are always based on sound reasoning, at least in my own mind.

One of the main reasons why I chose to be a Republican was that I watched my father struggle within the Democratic Party for years. My father loved the world of politics, but made a lot of basic mistakes which taught me at a young age what not to do in certain situations. For example, if somebody said to my father, "We want you to run for office," he was off running. He never gave it a lot of forethought. Therefore, he never had the money to run a decent race and he never had the backing that he needed. He'd take on the challenge, but the majority of times it was wasted energy. I would argue with him to no avail. I watched him carefully on how he ran his campaigns and made up my own mind as to how I would do it if I ever decided to get into politics.

So, during these years, I analyzed what the Democratic Party stood for and what the Republican Party stood for. I thought way back then that I was more comfortable with what the Republicans were saying. I surmised that if you were a Republican you believed you had to work hard to get ahead. It was definitely not the Party of handouts. It was the Party that wanted you to work hard to get where you were going. I kind of liked that idea.

I felt that if you were going to open up a business, law practice or anything else, you'd be better served with the Republicans who had a fuller understanding of business. I thought very carefully of what makes everything tick and function well. So, after careful consideration, first time out of the box, I registered Republican. My father respected my views and never had any problems with my being a Republican.

Additionally, early on in my career, I started studying why Republicans were ineffective on Staten Island. Why couldn't we elect Republicans on the Republican ticket? Why did we have to go to the Democrats for candidates to run, as in the case of my father? I clearly concluded that it was the fault of the Republican Party leadership.

Unfortunately, the Korean War interrupted my law school education. It was another game changer for young American men, and as with my predecessors, my generation would now have their war. Yet unlike them, it was in a part of the world hardly anyone knew anything about – Korea.

CHAPTER 3

The Accidental Marine

When I was growing up, my life was filled with war. It was basically the talk of the town. My family served honorably in both World Wars. I was acutely aware that my family expected me to serve our country, if I was age eligible. That is exactly what happened to me with the Korean War. Our country needed men to fight the war and I was called. I did what was expected without question, because that was what American men did.

Immediately after World War II everyone wanted to get back to a normal life. Therefore, the size of our military decreased swiftly. As a result, when the issue of the Korean War surfaced, the draft age was lowered from nineteen to eighteen-and-a-half in order to increase the pool of eligible draftees. The outbreak of the Korean War on June 25th 1950 fostered the creation of the Universal Military Training and Service Act of 1951. As such the United States government again began drafting people into the services.

Today young men don't really think about the impact of the

Selective Service System.[3] The reinstatement of the draft in the near future is a realistic possibility in light of how things are going. Since the Vietnam War, we have not had an active draft, because the military has been able to survive on volunteers. Such might not be so if we get involved in another war of global proportions. It is a terrible thought, but it must be recognized especially since our current president, Barack Obama, is extremely weak in the area of foreign affairs. Without a strong and omnipresent vanguard for freedom it does not take much to tilt the tables against world peace in this day and age.

I was finishing my second year at New York Law School in Manhattan as I anticipated receiving my draft notice. The regulations at that time provided that you could try to volunteer with any branch of the armed services that you wanted to join until you received your actual draft notice. At that point your options were frozen, and you no longer had the luxury to look at any other branches. You just had to wait until duty called.

I was looking into the Air Force, because they had a place for special investigation officers with my background. The problem was you had to serve three years active-duty and two years inactive. The recruiting office was very honest with me and said it would be very difficult to get a replacement, so the odds were rather strong that I'd be asked to serve five years' active service.

Although I was ready to serve my country, I did not want to make a career out of the military. My goal was to serve honorably like my relatives had done and get out. My dream was to open my own law office in either Manhattan or Staten Island. I had worked very hard in law school to attain this dream and I was going to do everything I could to achieve it.

In 1950 there was an entirely different sentiment toward the

---

3 *The only citizens who have to register for the draft today are males over the age of eighteen, and they must do so within thirty days of their 18th birthday. As it is today, so it was back in the 1950s except the age was slightly higher. As much as things change, some things remain constant. We do not see women registering for the draft.*

The Selective Service System describes its mission as "to serve the emergency manpower needs of the military by conscripting untrained manpower, or personnel with professional health care skills, if directed by Congress and the President in a national crisis." Military conscription has played a part in our country's history since the Revolutionary War and has not been without controversy.

Korean War than there was toward World War II. World War II captured the attention of the entire country like no other foreign war because America had been attacked at Pearl Harbor. This was in stark contrast to the Korean War which concerned a country most Americans didn't even know existed. The majority of Americans were confused about what America was trying to accomplish in Korea. Strong nationalism was missing in the Korean War. My only hope was to serve honorably and come back alive.

Since I didn't want to commit to five years, I did not volunteer for any branch at the time. Therefore, I had to register for the draft. I went with my father to the old Army Building, located at 39 Whitehall Street, in Manhattan. The building itself was a near-fortress consisting of eight stories of red granite, sandstone, and red brick. The ground floor was marked by slit windows, as if to fend off mobs. Above the front entrance was a decorative granite panel carved with cannon, mortar, chainmail shirt, cannonballs, and a spear. Apropos for the military. This is where I left my father.

When I entered the Draft Building, I found myself in a huge room with hundreds of other young men. There were quite a few that I knew from Staten Island that day. When they opened up the session for the day they said they had openings for a dozen Marines. The military personnel yelled out, "If you guys want to volunteer for the Marines, we would be willing to accept you now." I was shocked that some of my Staten Island buddies put their hands up to volunteer for the Marine Corps.

I thought to myself, "That's a gutsy thing to do," but I knew I wasn't interested in being a Marine at the time. Shortly afterward, the military personnel started calling out names. Amid repeated reminders that they still needed two more bodies to fill out the quota that day for the Marine Corps, they handed out forms and we got on line.

As I approached the desk, there was a gentleman behind me who was supposed to be in front of me. When I got to the front desk there was a form there and the military guy stamped it. It said USMC.

I said, "What does that mean?" and he said, "You're a Marine."

I said, "Oh, great," and one of the military guys said, "Wait a second, there's a mistake. He's not supposed to be there. The guy behind him is supposed to be in front of him and he should be the Marine."

The answer that he was given was, "What the hell is the difference? A man is a man." I thought to myself it might have made a big difference to the two of us! With no choice in the matter I had just become a Marine. I was the last Marine picked and filled their quota for that day.

When I walked out of the Draft building I met my father, who was waiting for me, and he said, "How did it go?"

I said, "Congratulate me: I'm a Marine."

"Oh, that's wonderful," he said.

I said, "Yeah? What's so wonderful about it?"

He said, "Oh, it's a great outfit and you're going to be very proud."

And I said, "Okay." And that was that. In retrospect, it is amazing how right he was.

My father then proceeded to lecture me about honor and not disgracing the family. He said, "You have to serve honorably and make us proud. The family name is very important and if you're in combat, just please remember that." In other words, don't be a coward.

I said, "Dad you can be sure that I will make you proud, I certainly wouldn't forget something like that." There were an awful lot of my family members who had served during World War II so it was nothing new for us. My brother was in the Navy and my uncles all served, some as many as four years in World War II.

As I look back, I realize how easily one's fate can change. Although I had no interest in being a Marine, the life lessons I would learn from being a Marine would be immense and follow me forever. At the time, I felt cursed that I didn't have a choice, but as time went on I realized the gift I had been given. Being a Marine made me the man I am today and allowed me to do things I never dreamed imaginable.

Years later when my life was slipping through my hands after a tragic car accident, after my heart stopped beating on the operating table, it was my Marine Corp experience that pulled me through. Being a Marine was certainly the greatest gift that I've been given in my lifetime, other than my family. I learned to be PROUD to call myself a MARINE.

CHAPTER 4

Semper Fidelis

At the end of 1951, I left Manhattan on a train full of men prepared to become full blown Marines headed to Parris Island for boot camp. On the way down, the train stopped at Washington DC. About fifteen or twenty of us went to a bar to get a beer. There was an African-American man named Sampson with us. The bartender refused to serve him. Because he wouldn't serve Sampson, we all walked out of place and refused to drink there.

When we got back on the train, Sampson was talking to me and he suddenly became very sullen. I said, "What's the matter? You were happy and laughing and everything else?"

He said, "Oh, sir," he called me sir. "We're going to the south and I'm told that it's not going to be good for people who are black." I really did not know what he meant then, but as time went on I learned about racial segregation in the south.

The Marine Corps Recruit Depot Parris Island (MCRD PI) was a huge military installation located within Port Royal, South Carolina. In 1951 Parris Island was used for the training of enlisted Marines, specifically male recruits living east of the Mississippi River who were preparing for combat in Korea. Parris Island drill instructors trained more than 138,000 recruits for the Korean War. During the time that I was training at Parris Island there were almost 24,000 recruits. Needless to say it was an extraordinarily active place.

Unfortunately for me, I was very unpopular with the drill instructors at Parris Island, because when they saw on my résumé that I had two college degrees, I was screwed. At the time, believe it or not, in the Marine Corps, having a college education was not a good thing. We were not considered "Grunt" material. They considered us wiseasses. As a result, I was repeatedly given guard duty from midnight till two in the morning. This was during the six hours that we were allowed to sleep from 10:00 p.m. to 4:00 a.m.

Marine Corps training life was physically draining to begin with, but worse for me because of guard duty. Guard duty entailed getting up at 11:30 p.m. to get dressed, working from midnight till 2:00 a.m., and then waiting for the next guy to take your post, which is another half hour. I was getting a maximum of three hours sleep and then working hard all day long. After four days of that, I was a zombie. I actually went down to sick bay to tell them that I just couldn't do it anymore. The sick bay was packed. They said if I wanted out of the duty I would have to start all over again. With that information, I told them to forget it and I immediately left.

So, in addition to working all day with the drilling and the training they put you through, I was doing it on very little sleep. Boot camp was made to weed out the weak ones. Even though it was tough, if you could survive under those circumstances, it made you a tougher person and a good Marine.

Of course being a Marine one would think I knew how to swim. Nothing could be further from the truth. Even though I grew up in Midland Beach, right next to the water, I was afraid of the water. I never learned how to swim! So, once I joined the Marines, I figured, "This is great, I'm finally going to learn how to swim."

In boot camp as they were kicking the hell out of me all day and night, those who couldn't swim had to go down for swim instruction. Of course I was included in that group. As I did the first session, I found I was doing better than anybody else. All of a sudden they said, "Okay, this is it: swim to the end and back." I thought to myself, "Aren't there another ten lessons? This is it?"

They had these muscular Marines with big poles and as you came out of the pool, they'd push you back in.

So, after the fifth or sixth time that they pushed me back in, there was this big guy from New Jersey, who said to me, "Molinari, I'm not going to let them push me back in without fighting. How about you?"

I said, "Alright, I'd rather fight than drown."

So, we got out of the pool, and these Marines looked at us as we put up our fists and advanced on them.

The Marines called it off, figuring that these two nuts were going to fight them over swimming. That was the end of that. Nothing further happened, but I never learned how to swim. And to this day for the record, if you asked me if I could swim, I'd tell you right now I would sink straight down and set a record while doing it.

When we finished our Parris Island stay, they had a parade at the end, and your platoon was graded. My platoon was not marked as an honor platoon. The reason why we didn't make the roster as an honor platoon was because the Drill Instructor in charge of our platoon made a mistake in calling us as we were marching. Immediately afterward, we lined up outside our Quonset huts anxious to go home for a couple of days. We thought we were finished with boot camp.

Not so.

One of our superiors came walking through inspecting us for reasons that we didn't understand. He stopped in front of me, stared at me for a moment, and moved on. He then saw another Marine that had a college degree and grabbed him and said, "Come with me." They went inside the Quonset hut with some other superiors and beat the hell out of the private. They actually put him in the hospital. We could hear the beating taking place. They picked three other privates with degrees and did the same thing to them as well.

I guess when the guy was looking at me, he was sizing me up, trying to figure out if he could take me or not. I realized later on how close I came to getting a beating. After the fourth guy was beaten, we all got together and said, "Look, every one of us is going to take a hell of a beating. Why? Because the D.I. made a mistake? That's why we didn't make honor platoon. Why in the hell should we get beat up because he made a mistake?"

The D.I. that made the mistake was not even there. While we were having this meeting he came back. He had gone to town to have a couple of drinks. He saw the beatings that his men got. He was pissed and we could hear him challenging the guys doing the beatings to fights one by one. We thought, "He is a good man, if he was here this would never have happened." He told them that if there was going to be any beatings, it would be him doing it.

By that time, we had decided that we were going to march on to Headquarters and report them. We went to our head D.I. and told him what we were going to do. He said, "If you're going to report them, you're going to have to report me as well, because I'm not going to submit your report. If you want to report me, fine." We didn't want to report him. Although he was tough on us, we liked him and we didn't want to report him, so we didn't go further with it. We felt at least he did what he had to do to stop this crap from going on.

When I finished basic training on October 31st, 1951, we were given a ten-day break to go home, with one day for travel, and then I was ordered to report to Quantico, Virginia on November 11, 1951, to await further orders. I was assigned to Casual Company. We were instructed to look at the bulletin board every morning to see if your name was on the list. The list would indicate what your assignment was going to be, and where you would go next. We were told, "You may be here for weeks, months, whatever." With two college degrees, some of my fellow marines were telling me that I was sure to be assigned to a school in the Marine Corps. It was very likely that I would never serve in combat.

When I looked at the bulletin board the very first morning I was surprised to see my name at the top of the list. It said "19th Draft" on top. I yelled out to one of the guys, "What's the nineteenth draft?"

He said, "That means you're going to Korea."

I said, "What?" He said, "Yeah. The nineteenth draft is the next group that's going to go to Korea."

So, I called my folks and said, "Congratulate me; I'm part of the nineteenth draft and we're going to go to Korea."

Of course my family was worried. There was always a possibility that you would not return.

The next stop for me was Camp Pendleton, California for Advanced Basic Training. Here I would get training that was unique to where I would be stationed, specifically Korea. The first thirty days at Camp Pendleton entailed Mess Duty and then there was cold-weather training for a week, and then the necessary training for combat in Korea.

Believe it or not, Mess Duty was really difficult stuff in the Marine Corps because it was so degrading. You were assigned to cleaning plates, scrubbing pots and pans, etc. The superiors put Joe Lombardi, from New Dorp Heights, Staten Island, in charge of our entire group on Mess Duty. Joe would stand at the doorway and watch what was going on. One day it was really busy and we were all working really hard and Joe comes up to me and says, "Hey Molinari. You're whistling and singing. How can you be so happy doing this kind of crap?" I said, "Well, what the hell am I going to do? Crack up?"

Well, there was this young guy next to me, and all of a sudden he explodes and he starts taking trays and flinging them. All the while he's screaming and yelling, and he continued to scream and yell while they carried him out. That was the end of him; the kid cracked up. I learned throughout life that sometimes you just have to make the best of a bad situation. Mess Duty is tough, but it's something you have to do. It's very humiliating, and that's why that guy cracked up: he should have just gone with the flow, like I was doing.

After Mess Duty, we then had cold weather training in Nevada. They told us that nobody could survive the bitter cold there. The Marine Corps said that's exactly what they were looking for, so we got used to that kind of thing. You were expected as a Marine to be able to do things that nobody else could do, and you were very proud of that. In a combat situation you make friends and your job is to protect them in combat and vice versa.

Crazy things happened during training, but you were expected to go with the flow and deal with it. One day we were marching on a twenty-mile hike with a full pack on our backs, and after marching many miles we were allowed a short break. A Corporal, who was a big guy, confronted the fifty or so Marines now sitting down on the ground. The Corporal said, "I'm a judo expert and I want to challenge any two guys in this outfit. I will demonstrate how judo works and how I can take on any two guys and be victorious. I don't care if they're big or whatever."

A friend of mine, Newmann, yelled out, "Molinari and I will take you on."

I was one of the smallest guys in the outfit and I yelled out, "Why me?" Since Newmann was a friend, I said, "What the hell are you doing?"

He said, "Look, one guy can't beat two guys, especially Marines. Here's what you do: You get on one side and I'll get on the other side. When I give you a signal, you run at him and tackle him, but when you tackle him hold on to his legs." Newmann was bulky and he said, "I'll hit him up top and knock him down, all you have to do is hold onto his legs and we'll win."

I was basically stuck with the situation, so I said, "Okay I'll give it a shot."

As we were getting ready, I thought to myself how foolish we were. I could see myself flying through the air and ending up with a broken neck, but I did what Newmann suggested. Surprisingly, we made the Corporal look awfully bad. I tackled him and held on for dear life, and Newmann hit him on the shoulders and knocked him down and we just held on. That was the last time I ever saw that Corporal. It was an ego booster for Newmann and me.

There were so many incidents similar to that where guys would challenge each other. It was not unusual for guys to have fistfights. If you were challenged, you had to accept it since it was the Marine Corps. If you didn't accept the challenge you were going to pay a price.

There was one fellow from New York who was an obnoxious S.O.B. who wouldn't do anything. When we got to cold weather, you would take your shelter half and you would take the next guy's shelter half and build a little tent so that you could sleep during the night and not freeze to death.

This guy would refuse to help me make the tent. I screamed at him, "You better fucking help make the tent or you're out of the tent."

He was a semi-pro fighter before he joined the Marine Corps. So, words led to words and we got out the gloves. Of course I didn't last very long, but at least I defended my actions. He took a few shots and hit me in the solar plexus and I collapsed and lost the fight.

I didn't learn from that experience though. It happened two more times, same guy, we got the gloves out again and he went through this little jig that he did and hit me in the solar plexus and down I went. I was furious, but I was also paying attention to how he was kicking my ass. I noticed that right before he was getting ready to throw the punch at my solar plexus he went into the jig.

The final time I fought him, as soon as he started his jig, I brought my elbows close together and protected my chest. Every time he did the jig I just pulled my elbows together and that's all he had. I then proceeded to beat the hell out of him. He refused to fight me thereafter, but better yet, he actually started doing his job. Looking back, it was a fun experience for me, since I got to experience the thrill of victory after so many agonizing defeats.

As grueling as the training was, we all knew we were in the best physical shape of our young lives. We knew this was ever so important for combat. Back in those days, there was talk about doing away with the Marine Corps and folding it into the Army. This would have been a terrible, terrible mistake. There is no outfit in the entire world of any country that can match the United States Marine Corps. They are the best, their training is the best, and their esprit de corps makes them do things that people—mortal people—are not supposed to be able to do. By the time we left for war, we felt like we were the very best of the best because we were Marines. Fortunately, even now, witnessing current combat activities, it's always the Marine Corps that are out front in almost every military action.

Finally, after all the training, in March of 1952, the big day came and we went aboard a "liberty ship." There were over 2000 Marines aboard that ship and we were all part of that "19th draft" headed to Korea. No one knew if we would ever return again to our great nation, but we did what was expected of us because that is how we were brought up. We were willing to lay down our lives for our country.

CHAPTER 5

Off to Korea

For a war that virtually no one cared about, it would make a dramatic impact on the rest of my life. As with almost any soldier who has been sent to war, the esprit de corps would be imprinted in my moral fiber for eternity.

Around March 22, 1952, the nineteenth replacement draft sailed from Camp Pendleton, California. It took over two weeks to make the crossing across the pacific. The ship transported thousands of Marines from the 1st Marine Division. As a result, there wasn't enough room for everyone to go up for fresh air on the deck during the day. So, they brought up one group at a time to do exercises on deck, and then you had to go back downstairs to wherever your cot was. There were two cots on top of each other, and I was in the lower cot.

Tensions could get high, especially since the quarters were so restricted. One day I had an encounter with another Marine who was across the way from where I was sleeping. He was a Southerner. I passed some silly remark about his being a rebel and the next thing

I knew, he screamed, "You fuckin' Yankee," and grabbed his bayonet off his pack and came charging at me with the full intention of stabbing me. There was another Marine above his bunk who was from Florida. He jumped down on top of the Southerner. They were both large men. Luckily he knocked the Southerner down to the ground, pinned his arm, and grabbed the bayonet. My life was spared.

So, I quickly learned that for some people the Civil War was still on, and it was not a joking matter. It was quite an experience, especially since I was only a few days away from going into combat. It would have sucked to be killed by a fellow Marine for passing a stupid remark.

At the same time, we had a seasoned Marine that was on the ship coming over with us that had his own specially tailored knife. He had been in the Marine Corps for a long time. All day long he would take out this knife and continuously sharpen it on his own honing tool. He would repeatedly say, "I can't wait to shove this knife in a Gook and kill him." Of course that kind of language is derogatory, but we were less concerned about being P.C. than we were about conjuring up all the tenacity required to go into war. We all said we would love to be in combat with him. He would definitely be a survivor because he was rough and tough.

The trip across the Pacific was difficult for everyone because almost everybody got seasick. Those of us that didn't get seasick, such as myself, always felt nauseous due to the terrible odor from the people that were vomiting. The environment was definitely not conducive to eating. We survived on candies and things of that nature and most of the guys lost a lot of weight. We finally landed in Kobe, Japan, on Saturday, April 5th, 1952. We docked for one day, and my buddy Ed Mieskoski and I got to stretch our sea legs out in Kobe, Japan, for a brief time, and then we left immediately for Korea.

When we arrived in Korea and climbed down the netting to get to shore they started calling out names. When your name was called you were told go to the rear and stay there for further orders. I noticed that all the Marines that were called were Black; nothing was said further. The rest of us were directed to get on an old train that was all shot up and looked like a casualty of war. It was packed with men. After a long train ride, we got out and they start calling names again. Again, these Marines were Black.

So, I asked one of the Marines who had been there for a while what was going on. He said, "They are going to be chefs, truck drivers, or likewise: basically they stay behind the lines." I was surprised that they were keeping the Blacks from going into combat. I was under the impression that President Truman's Executive order 9981, which was instituted after World War II, would have erased segregation in the military. This order was enacted by Truman in order to forbid military segregation because of race, color, religion, or national origin. As with many things in life, the best intentions are not always followed through by those assigned with the task to implement them.

Next we were loaded onto the six-ply's, or military trucks, and we drove for hours and hours. All of a sudden we looked around and you could see that the surrounding woods were on fire. We didn't know where we were or where we were going, but we were pretty sure that we had arrived in the war zone.

Then we heard a mysterious singing that sounded like, "ASAHI, ASAHI, ASAHI." We looked at each other in the truck and wondered what the hell it was. It sounded mystical. We had no idea who was singing, we were all very nervous. I had no idea if we were going to be attacked or whatever. We then arrived at the camp compound and were dumped into a large clearing.

We learned immediately that the Marines were singing "Asahi" which was the Japanese beer that the military served. Apparently the Army had received 10,000 cases of Asahi beer and all the soldiers got drunk. The General was livid and to get the men upset, said, "You guys can't hold your beer, so I'm sending all this beer over to the Marines in reserve. I know they can handle it. They can take care of it without doing what you guys have done."

I was dying to have a beer after a long journey of being deprived of alcohol. Unfortunately, I learned quickly I wasn't eligible; the Marines who were already there had first dibs, so I would have to wait. I would make up for it later on.

We were told that we were part of the outfit that was not going into immediate combat. We all breathed a sigh of relief. We were in reserve. We learned that we would rotate usually two months in combat, one month in reserve, subject to other things happening in the interim.

I was assigned to the HMS company which was a company attached to the Seventh Marine Regiment. It was our responsibility to make sure that our regiment was fully prepared and had all the necessary supplies for any combat situation that would break out.

Our command post was in what they called at that time a defilade position, if at all possible. In other words, if the enemy is out there and fired missiles toward us, you would be on the side of a mountain where they couldn't possibly hit you with missiles, because you were shielded by the height of the mountain. Common sense—it was a safer position.

My very first night there I was told that I was going to be on guard duty at the entrance to the compound that I was assigned to. It was raining heavily and the poncho that I had was leaking. I was by myself, out of sight, and I couldn't see anybody else from where I was. I didn't know where I really was. That was probably the longest and loneliest night of my entire life.

In the middle of the night I heard something, and as we were trained, I dropped to the ground and put my M1 at the ready and aimed it in the direction in which I heard a noise. At first I saw what I thought was the enemy creeping in, stooped over. There were clouds coming up from the ground, my heart was beating rather heavily, there was nobody else to call upon. Much to my shock and surprise, the enemy closing in on me was nothing more than a pack of wild dogs.

A short time later, there was a male voice that yelled out, "Private First Class Molinari!" I challenged the voice, the man gave me the proper password and he stepped forward and said, "Colonel Luck wants to see you." I asked where to go, and he gave me directions. Everything was muddy and wet. I got to his tent, knocked on the outside framework, and he called me in.

He was very kind. He was holding my resume when he said, "You have two college degrees?"

I answered, "Yes, sir."

"What are you doing here?"

I thought to myself that I asked myself the same exact question often. I said, "I'm following orders. I was told to come here."

He showed me some forms and said, "We're in desperate need of legal officers back home. Where you are attached, there were six legal officers in a row that were killed, so we're very much short staffed. There are things that happen here all the time that require legal minds. If you would sign these forms I'll have you in New York by this weekend."

It was a very tempting offer. I had over six months in the Marine Corps at the time, but I thought to myself, "Well, I have a year and a half to go and I kind of liked the idea of serving as a grunt rather than an officer who would be responsible for the lives of a lot of others. Also, it would retard the date that I would get out. I would have to sign up for a longer term." And so again, my dream to become a lawyer and practice law would be put off. I declined the tempting offer and went back to my guard duty spot.

In the first four days in Korea I was lucky that I was in the reserve. I was trained, for example, for "Night Noises." You would hear a noise and you would have to identify if it was friendly or enemy, what kind of a weapon was it, trigger sounds, grenades and that kind of thing. There would be incoming artillery fire from the enemy, but since we were in a protective position, it really didn't pose much of a threat to us. Surprisingly though, the guy on the ship that kept on saying "I can't wait to shove this knife in a Gook and kill him," bugged out and went crazy from the incoming artillery shells. It shocked the hell out of all of us. He was relieved of his duties and sent back Stateside.

We had another experience similar to that. There was an officer who earned the Medal of Honor during World War II. We all knew that the Medal of Honor was the highest military decoration that a soldier or Marine could receive, so he was a real hero to all of us. We were thrilled that he was going to join us. We all looked forward to having a decorated Medal of Honor war veteran in combat with us. However, during the very first combat situation we were involved in, he took a bullet to the arm. The bullet didn't go in very far, since, you could actually see it was protruding. He went into a state of total shock and we were told ultimately that he was sent back home. We quickly realized that being in combat as a single young man was much different. The hero in this case was now married and had several children. So, facing possible death represented an entirely different circumstance than when he was a single young carefree kid, such as me, just joining the Marine Corps.

At about the same time another Marine approached me and said, "I don't want to go to combat. I need help to get out of it." I said to him, "I'm going to combat myself. Nobody wants to go, but that's what we have to do. How am I going to help you?" He said, "I'm not gonna go. I'm not gonna go." I said, "Okay."

The next day I learned that he shot himself and was dead. It was nothing that I could have anticipated at the time. How somebody would commit suicide rather than take their chances in combat was beyond me.

April 13th, 1952, Easter Sunday was my very first religious holiday spent abroad. My family now was my fellow Marines. All of us were in a foreign country almost 7,000 miles from home, so we relished the camaraderie of being together and told stories of our holiday get-togethers back home.

The day was crystal clear, the weather was beautiful, and yet, the countryside was completely foreign. It really didn't matter if you were Catholic or not; all the Marines that could attend an outdoor mass were present at 2:00 pm. The priest that celebrated the mass gave everyone in attendance general absolution. I thought, "Great, absolution during wartime."

As we sat on the hill overlooking the priest the backdrop of the mass was filled with tents, weapons and armored vehicles. The mass was comforting, but somehow it was in total contradiction to why we were there. Looking back, I know I was lucky to have my good friend Ed Mieskoski sitting next to me. In Korea he was my family.

If you think that war is glamorous, in my opinion, nothing is further from the truth. You live under the daily threat of death to yourself and your buddies, many times under deplorable situations. For us the seasons of Korean weather were dramatically different. Disgustingly hot and humid weather permeated the summer season. Monsoon rains wreaked havoc on our daily lives June through September. The winter was surprisingly bitter cold, what I imagine a Siberian winter would be. Living in tents didn't help much to alleviate the extreme weather. So, between the hot and humid weather, monsoon seasons, and finally agonizing polar conditions, my life as a Korean War Marine was ever-changing but incredibly stagnant. The seasons themselves were nothing more than a monotonous regime of punishing weather.

I would learn very quickly that my legal skills would be in high demand almost immediately upon my arrival in Korea. When we were in reserve, they had an area called "Officer's Country." Just as the name implied, only officers were welcomed. Well this one grunt walked up a little hill where the officers were and stole a case of beer. He was caught coming down and he was lucky that they were pretty lenient. They told him to bring it back. He brought it back, but by then he had already imbibed more beer than he could handle. He foolishly stole another case of beer and was caught again. This time the officers were rightfully pissed, so he was brought up on charges.

He asked me to represent him. I agreed because it was something different, it involved military law and I thought I could do a good job. I enjoyed it a lot, but I made my comrades in arms unhappy because of my training. I successfully defended the grunt and fortunately the officer that actually tried the case against me was a Colonel. After the trial was completed, the Colonel told me he was going to put me in for a battlefield promotion because he was impressed with my trial strategy.[4] Unfortunately for me, the Colonel was not able to follow through since I was told he cracked up during a military mission and was sent back to the States.

Initially I was assigned to communications because my MOS (Military Operations Specialty) was in communications since I scored high in that area back in the States. However, as word of my legal skills got out, I was told to report to the legal officer who was in charge. When I entered the tiny tent, which barely held the three people and an old desk, there was a legal officer who was leaving within a day or two. The only person left to replace him was the Sergeant who had requested my presence. He was a Tech Sergeant and he asked me if I could help him because he thought he was in over his head. I said, "If I have the time, I'd be happy to do it. You know I am assigned to communications, so in between, if I can help you, I will."

So, I found myself working with the communications outfit and at the same time I was helping the legal officer who really wasn't an officer, but a Tech Sergeant. A month later when he finished his tour of duty in Korea and went home, the only one left to do any legal work was PFC Molinari. Many cases were very challenging and this is where I applied common sense and what I considered an appropriate moral standard when analyzing the merits of the case.

There were very serious charges that occurred in combat situations. Obviously there were many cases of military personnel exhibiting cowardice by refusing to go into combat or worse yet going to

---

4 *On August 24th, 1952 in a letter to home I wrote "I have to get out that kid I defended last April for stealing a case of beer. He may be sent up to the lines or left here. I pity the guys that get him. He is a habitual thief and actually no good."*

combat and then fleeing when the action started. The Marines called this "bugging out."

"Bugging out" originated during the Korean War but it was nothing that a Marine would be associated with. Some military units were directed to "bug out" when their current position was no longer considered defensible and likely to be overrun by hostile forces. Basically it was a retreat. It was not something that was looked upon with favor in the Marine Corps. I had seen my fair share of it by this time as well as heard the incredible story of the Chosin Reservoir battle.

Before I had arrived in Korea, the Chinese had entered the war and sent hundreds of thousands of troops across the borders into North Korea, and nobody knew they were coming. There was a huge battle at the Chosin Reservoir. It is not in a Marine's blood to retreat. So when the Marines were being overrun by large numbers of Chinese, General Oliver P. Smith said, "Retreat? HELL. We're attacking in the opposite direction." There would be no "bugging out." The Marines that were involved in the battle went through hell being attacked by overwhelming numbers and suffering severe frostbite, shortages of ammunition, food, gas, etc. The ones that survived were known as the "Chosin Few" because they beat the odds and showed everyone why a Marine was a different type of fighter. The Chosin Reservoir battle became legendary.

I remember one freezing winter night when we were in reserve status, there were about eight of us huddled around the pot belly stove in order to keep warm in the tent. In Korea every soldier had to carry his weapon around 24/7/365. Well, there was one fellow who kept on playing with his weapon. As a Marine, one of the first rules you learn is to take care of your weapon, but you never play with your weapon. A couple of the guys told him to stop playing with the weapon, but he ignored them. In the tent next door to us there was a group of Marines watching a movie.

Suddenly a life changing tragedy occurred. His weapon accidently discharged and he shot his best friend in the head who was sitting right next to him. His best friend was killed immediately. The bullet went through the next door tent as well. As soon as he fired the shot he threw the weapon to me. We were all in shock at what had happened. I was like, "What the fuck?" and I threw it in a drawer.

Everybody that was next door came flying in, and a Lieutenant was screaming, "Who shot that shot?" Nobody would talk. The Lieutenant said, "Molinari, did you see what happened?" I said, "No, sir, I didn't see anything."

It was up to the Marine that did the act to take responsibility for the act. Ultimately he did and the case was sent to Division Rear. The Navy Admiral was in charge of Division Rear and had the cream of the crop regarding personnel, specifically legal and medical.

You also had the cases of Friendly Fire during combat. Friendly Fire is often seen as an inescapable result of combat. Friendly Fire was, and always will be, a tragedy for the victim and a mentally devastating event for the survivor that leaves lifelong scars. A Marine is dead, and in many case it would be your buddy.

Another case involved a Marine who snuck out of our outfit during the night. He went to a tent where there were female prostitutes. When he entered the tent there were no lights on and he stumbled over something. His weapon accidently discharged. He tragically shot an innocent civilian. The Marine was brought up on charges. These cases would be handled by Division Rear after our preliminary investigation.

When I became the acting legal officer, I ran into some problems with a superior. I felt I had a duty to tell people that did an investigation that they made a mistake if I found one, even if I was only a lowly PFC. I always recommended that the mistakes be corrected before we sent the reports back to Division Rear. The majority of the time the drafter of the report would be grateful for my insight.

Yet one day, this crusty old Colonel calls up and barks, "Let me talk to the legal officer on the phone."

I said, "You're speaking to him, Colonel."

He says, "Who are you?" I said, "PFC Molinari."

"I want the legal officer," he said. My response was, "I am the legal officer."

He started cursing up a storm and said, "What the fuck are you doing, sending this thing back to me?" I said, "Sir, there's mistakes there and I'm offering a chance to correct it. I'll show you how to correct it and we'll send it on to Division Rear."

As I said, usually an officer would appreciate it because it makes them look better. It was late in the day and the Colonel said, "The first thing in the morning, I want you to bring that report back to me and I don't want to ever talk to you again. Don't ever, ever send back anything like that again or I'm going to bring you up on a court-martial."

Well, the next morning, I promptly arrived at his tent at 0600 hours. There was this old guy shaving in zero-degree temperature outside his tent. I couldn't believe what I was seeing. To make matters worse, he was in his underwear. I thought that guy had to be a really tough man. Well, he reamed me out pretty good and proper.

It was kind of funny and at the same time, I was a little upset because I was trying to work with him and help him. It was clear he didn't appreciate it. But this is the Marine Corps. Its combat, tough people, so you learn every day who you can talk to, and who you can't. Although I thought I was attempting to do the right thing, it wasn't always appreciated by those above.

When we were busy we were busy, but many times boredom could be overwhelming, especially during the monsoon season. So to pass the time I would diligently write letters home to my parents, relatives and friends. On August 24th 1952 I wrote home as follows:

> It's a Sunday morning and a really dismal day. It rained all day yesterday and all night long and looks as though it will all day today. Last night I went out to the area where those boys who flew in by plane were located and were they a sorry sight. They were in shelter half's with the rain coming in on them and

> they really looked down-in-the-mouth. In such case, they usually take away their ammunition every night so that they don't go blowing a hole in their leg, as often happens.

On August 27th 1952, I wrote to my family as follows:

> ...It rained again all day today for about the 5th or 6th straight day. The roads are out; bridges down and the gooks are acting up. There were two gook attacks last night on Bunker Hill. Incidentally, Dad you mentioned the fact that the news has been censored. I'll tell you why. This is the worst beating the Reds have taken in over a year and it's all Marine action. The publicity was all Marines and we only have 1 division over here. The Army has 6 and got trounced and lost Baldy Hill. So they now call it a UN action etc. Well here is the tip off. Bunker Hill is held only by the Marines. We control the whole area around Panmunjom. Whenever you hear of activity around Panmunjom you will know it is us. There is supposed to be some activity tonight, I believe by the gooks [.]"

Looking back, I can see that in less than five months in combat, I had become the proud Marine that we were told we would be.

On September 13th, 1952, I wrote:

> It is Saturday afternoon and a quiet day. I am always amazed when I write that it is a Saturday or Sunday on a letter. Back home such days had an extra significance but here they are the same as any other day and I never know what day it is until I look at a calendar...

> Yes, Dad, I would appreciate seeing a few pictures of the office as it now looks. I probably will spend most of my time there when I get back. Lately, I have been looking through magazines, books etc. for office furniture etc. There are three things I believe I will need when I get out that will be necessary at once. First, I will need a wardrobe. I have almost nothing at home that I'll be able to use. Secondly, I will need to outfit my office and I intend to spend every available cent on it. A beautiful office is a big asset to any business or professional man. I will try to get a set of draperies and venetian blinds on the windows. Then there will be a desk, the extra-large type; filing cabinets a rug, chairs, and possibly a sofa set in the waiting room. Then I will have to buy a new car. On Staten Island, it is a necessity for a lawyer…
>
> P.S. Going to try and catch the Yankee game on the radio in a little while. It is certainly a tight race.

You can see that I had a burning desire to practice law, and it was never far from my thoughts, even in combat. I was realistic about my finances and how my dream could come true. My mind was never really idle in war. I always tried to think about the future. And yes, the New York Yankees were always on my mind.

On September 27th, 1952, I started my fourteenth month in service. I wrote:

> So Ike will speak on the Island. I didn't think that there were enough voters on the Island to attract a Presidential candidate. The election coverage we get is pretty good and we usually have quite a few arguments over it. It looks right now that the Demos are having that money deal bouncing right back in their

> faces. Most of the guys around here are voting for Ike even the Southern Democrats who are still mad about that Tidewater deal. This Korean deal seems to be a main issue and I think the election may end this affair sooner or later.

The way we were set up in combat we had the MLR (Main Line of Resistance). Out in front of the MLR, a good distance away, were small hill positions called outposts. A couple dozen men go out in the evening to take these outposts and stay there all night. When the Koreans hit them we would have to help them quickly. They served a critical function in detecting enemy movement and alerting the camp.

I will always remember the day that I myself could have been involved in a friendly-fire incident, which would have resulted in a disastrous international incident. While on guard duty with two other fellows at one of the assigned outposts, we were told to be on the alert because the enemy had infiltrated our lines the night before.

What would normally happen was one guy would be outside in a trench line on high alert and the other two would be in the bunker. If the one outside heard or saw anything suspicious, a second man would exit from the bunker. On this night there was a fellow named Martin who was a strong stocky Marine outside and two of us were inside the bunker. We were writing letters home and all of a sudden Martin yelled, "Molinari, get out here!" I ran out and asked, "What's up?" He said, "We're being overrun. Take a look."

Oh my God. I looked down and I saw scores of men sneaking through the area. We called up our base and asked if we had anybody in the area that's a friendly and we were told, no. They were shocked when we asked that because every Marine knew not to come up during the night to an outpost that was on high alert. You would wind up getting shot.

We were told that they must be the enemy, so we told them to put out notice that we were about to be overrun. As these guys approached, Martin yelled out, "Cover me." This man walked up toward Martin, even as Martin yelled for him to put his hands up. The guy wouldn't put his hands up and Martin says, "I'm going to knock him down. Cover me."

Well, I had my M1 pointed at the infiltrator's heart with the trigger half pulled, because it looked like we were going to be attacked, and then all of a sudden we heard his voice cry out in the dark in a very distinct British accent, "I say, what's going on up there?" Martin said, "Who are you?" He identified himself as part of a Scottish outfit, The Black Watch.

The soldiers that we saw were stringing wire for communications for their camp that they were setting up for the following day since they were going to take over our position. We were stunned that they could be so stupid, but breathed a sigh of relief that we had not shot them. But, by the grace of God, no lives were wasted that night.

I've always thought back to that day thinking to myself that if I had pulled that trigger it would have been an international incident. I would have had to carry that for the rest of my life, and it would have been devastating. It would have been legal hearing after hearing after hearing on an unforeseen tragic incident. It was an experience that I wouldn't wish on anybody.

At about that time, we had a combat operation that was called, "The Hook." The hook was an area that was surrounded on three sides by the enemy, specifically the Chinese. If the Chinese got control of "The Hook," disastrous results would follow. The Hook held the key to controlling the Simochon and Imjin valleys. Its capture would leave the 1st Marine Division exposed, thereby causing us to move back two to three miles for a new defensive position. The enemy attacked us unyieldingly.

On October 4th, 1952, there was a Marine observation plane that was flying over the combat area. Major Robert A. Owens was a super nice guy, and was the intelligence officer for the regiment. Major Owens had already won the Silver Star. He was shot down with our Captain Arthur R. Morin. When they were shot down they were trying to locate the exact position of the enemy. Their plane crashed a short distance in front of the MLR line behind enemy lines in gook territory. It was a terrible situation. They were listed as Missing in Action.

Lieutenant Taylor was appointed the investigating officer to try to find out whether these officers were killed in action or if they were captured. It made a big difference in terms of notification to families. Lt. Taylor asked me if I would volunteer to go with him to the front line, an exposed area, and question the Marines that were in the combat positions that were overrun. Of course I agreed to do it. We were all grief stricken with this incident. We went to the front line and questioned quite a few Marines who had witnessed the crash. We did an extraordinarily thorough job and even went to the VMO-6, which was a small airport where their flight originated.

Eventually, we determined that the Koreans hit their aircraft with anti-aircraft fire and knocked it down. From witnesses account, it looked as though one Marine survived the crash and fought the Koreans off with his bare hands, but the Koreans eventually subdued him by sheer numbers. Where the plane actually crashed was only about 300 yards from the MLR. At the time of our inspection, it was riddled with the corpses of dead Marines who had attempted to rescue the Marines from the crash. It was a horrendous site.

Afterwards, Lt. Taylor was asked to go to Japan, where all the wounded Marines who witnessed the crash were taken. He asked his superiors if I could go with him. The officers in charge refused to allow that to happen. We were a good team, but unfortunately, due to lack of manpower and time, many of our efforts were cut short. This never had a good effect on the investigations. In December of 1953, the status of both Morin and Owens was changed to that of killed in action and their remains were determined to be non-recoverable.

There was another incident that happened during the Battle of the Hook that affected me rather deeply. When the Chinese broke through there was a machine gun outpost manned by a young man and two supporting Marines. They were responsible for feeding the machine gun ammunition. It was an impossible position to be in, looking at thousands and thousands of enemies pouring across the border. There were only three Marines there. They could only survive for so long, so the two Marines that were feeding the ammo got up and said, "Come on. Let's go." The young Marine manning the machine gun said, "We can't. We were ordered to stay until we are relieved." The other Marines retreated and the young Marine stayed.

The next morning, the regiment took a head count of everybody. This young Marine that was on the machine gun was missing. When they went to the outpost where he was last seen, there he was, sitting by the machine gun, with dead enemy surrounding him. He was completely shell shocked. He couldn't speak a word.

An investigation was conducted regarding the actions of the two Marines who retreated. I was asked to review it. When the brave young Marine was able to speak, I had an opportunity to talk to him. I remember him telling me, "I come from an Italian-American family. Before I came over my father told me not to do anything that would cause shame to be borne by the family."

It reminded me of the exact conversation I had with my father when I was drafted. The young Marine said, "All I could remember was his words when the two other Marines were leaving, and I said to myself, 'I promised my father that I would never do anything like that,' so that's the reason why I stayed." He was a true American hero.

One day, when I was in reserve on guard duty, I had a hunting disaster that could have turned deadly. The area that I was assigned was beautiful. There were a lot of interesting flowers; the landscape was actually stunning, minus the obvious signs of war. To my amazement, I suddenly saw a pheasant. As for animals, I would occasionally see deer and fox, but this pheasant was the first one I saw. I would later learn that it was a common bird in Korea.

Every day, we would be forced to eat liver. Liver, liver, liver. The liver was something that you couldn't cut. It tasted awful. The Navy was in charge of us in terms of food. The Admiral came and said,

"You have to think of this not as food, but as medicine, because it is. You guys can't eat candy all day."

He was right, that's what we relied upon to keep us going: junk food, since the food they served us was barely edible.

When I saw this damned pheasant I said to myself, "If I could bag a pheasant, we all could have a nice little supper. Something different, it would boost our morale and appetites." The next day, I wasn't on guard duty, so I check out a shotgun and I went to the area where the pheasant was. Sure enough, there was the pheasant. The pheasant started running up the side of the mountain, and I raced after him. There I was, trying to get the bastard, and he's running, not flying, and I'm running trying to catch him up at the top.

All of a sudden, shit, I hit a tripwire and I froze. I didn't know what else to do. Another step and I might have been dead. You can't stay there for the rest of your life, so I dove off the mine. Boom! It triggered off the dreaded Willie Peter, slang for white phosphorous. It is a deviously horrendous chemical that would burn everything in its path, including clothes, and more importantly, flesh. I was lucky to come away unscathed, but the other purpose of white phosphorous mines was to mark areas where artillery fire could strike.

As soon as the mine went off a highly visible explosion erupted with a trail of smoke visible for miles that identified a target area for the enemy. As luck would have it, the next thing I knew, the enemy saw the smoke and they started striking our area with artillery.

I heard the company Sergeant screaming, trying to figure out who was up in the hill and triggered the Willie Peter. I ran down the other side of the hill and hid the shotgun. The Sergeant came up to me and asked if I saw who did it. I responded, "No, sir, I didn't." So, the woods were on fire, the artillery was coming in. It was an interesting day at the shop. Fortunately, there were no casualties, and unfortunately I didn't get to kill the damn pheasant either.

Back in Division Rear there were some nice compliments being passed about the work that I was doing. There were times when it got rather difficult. We had an incident where a young man, Louie

Damers, from New York was on guard duty at the ammunition dump. The temperature at the time was about twenty-degrees below zero. In Korea it could hit as much as thirty below zero in winter months.

While on guard duty you were not permitted to walk into the ammunition dump tents where the men slept who weren't on duty. Louie was freezing, so he sat down next to the potbelly stove they had and was warming his hands up and fell asleep. The officer of the day came by and noticed Louie was sleeping. Following protocol, the officer picked up the Louie's gloves and his weapon. He then woke Louie up and told him he was under arrest.

The next day the head of the 7th Regiment called me in to see him and said he wanted me to convene a court-martial. He wanted Louie Damers to receive capital punishment. I was terribly distraught. Louie was one of the few that shouldn't have been in the Marine Corps. He was a very sickly person and didn't intend to fall asleep.

I tried to talk the Colonel out of it, but he said, "No, this is the way it is. I have the lives of all these men on my hands and this is one of the most sensitive areas in Korea, the ammunition dump. Pvt. Damers is going to be punished as he could have cost the lives of all those people that were in the ammunition dump area."

I was aghast, just terribly distraught at the thought that we would put somebody to death for that. But the Colonel wanted it that way, and he had a report that I actually had to prepare for him sent to Division Rear.

The head Naval Officer was in charge of matters like this and sent it back. He said that he did not agree that capital punishment was warranted. Much to my happiness, they sent it back for a lesser court-martial without capital punishment being applied. The Colonel said all right, convene the court-martial.

Then I got to work my legal magic. I appointed for the Colonel's signature, the best, smartest Marine in our outfit to be the defense lawyer. I then appointed the officer that I felt was the dumbest as the prosecuting attorney. I had what I considered the nicest officers in our regiment put down for jury duty. That was the best that I could do. I knew that, while the Marine Corps would never find anybody innocent during a court martial, I gave Pvt. Damers the best shot at minimal punishment.

After the trial was over, as expected, Pvt. Damers was found guilty. When I was writing up the officer's recommendation, I highlighted every little mistake that I could find, and I documented it in the report. The Colonel in charge called me up to Officer's Country and said, "Is this true? This guy made all these mistakes?"

"Yes sir. It's all true," I said. He said, "Well, gee whiz. I'll tell you what. What do you think we should do? I don't want to sign this thing."

I said, "Well, sir, I think he has already learned his lesson with that capital punishment thing. I think at this point, if you find him guilty, and just take away his stripe, and let him forfeit his pay and allowances for a term, that would be adequate punishment." Much to my shock and surprise, he agreed.

Here was Louie, who was facing capital punishment, who now was getting what basically amounted to a slap on the wrist. After that Louie followed me all over Korea. He would take ammunition boxes and make a chair for me. He just couldn't do enough to thank me. It turned out to be a wonderful and fulfilling experience for me.

I was lucky because my father wrote to me almost every single day while I was in Korea. I will never know how he made the time, since he was working three jobs. He would also send packages filled with dried meats such as salamis, pepperoni, canned goods, candies and things that I could share with my friends. Every package was like a birthday present. If he couldn't afford to send me something he would get a relative to chip in and send a package. Mail call was always the highlight of the week.

It was really hard to obtain basic essentials. They had a commissary truck come around every couple of months. Many times you just couldn't buy the things outright. You had to win a drawing for the privilege of buying items. If I needed a comb or something easily mailed, I would just ask my father to try and send it. It was easier than winning the lottery with the commissary.

I remember one day I was lucky enough to buy a watch from the commissary. I thought that the watch was just too beautiful to wear into combat. It would just get destroyed, so I put it into a box and mailed it to my father. I kept writing to my father asking him if he got the watch. He kept writing back that he never received it.

Finally, after several months, my father wrote to me and said, "By the way, I came to the office today and I was cleaning up in front of the building, and I saw a crushed box by the curb. I opened it, and there was the watch." It was still in the box that I mailed it in and it was fine. Not broken or anything. I was extremely pleased that he got the watch and in one piece as well.

A few weeks before I was scheduled to go home, there were ten of us in our immediate outfit. We were called upon to quickly get our gear together and fill a hole that was breached by the enemy. Eight out of the ten had to go. I was not one of those eight because I was scheduled to go home on the next draft, so I was exempt. There was one other fellow who was hit in the head and physically not able to go.

Much to my surprise, our officer in charge came to me and said one of the fellows refused to go. I said, "Well, you've got to write him up then. Bring him up on charges." And he said, "I don't want to do that. Would you go and take his place?" I stopped dead in my tracks because I had heard all the stories about how guys were killed when they were just ready to go home in a few days. It was every Marine's nightmare to get killed right before you are ready to go Stateside. But the officer was a great officer, and I respected him, so I agreed to go with the others. As luck would have it though, at the last minute, it was all called off. Another act of divine intervention.

I've mentioned before that my closest friend during the war was Ed Mieskoski. We both went to Korea as PFC's, and then like everybody else with the time served, we became Corporals. Before we were scheduled to come back to the States, Ed and I were the two finalists in line to get a battlefield promotion. Only one of us could get it. I was the one selected, so I was promoted from Corporal to Sergeant. I was kind of sorry because I wanted my friend to win it, but at the same time I did want to win it myself. I could use the money. He was a great guy and just laughed at it. In the long run we were just happy to get the hell out of there alive.

On April 5th, 1953, my buddy Ed Mieskoski and I had survived combat and we happily left for the States. When we arrived back in the States, I only had about four months left to serve. I was stationed at Quantico, VA., which is the base of the Marine Corps where all the officers are trained. It is a spit-and-polish kind of operation. Since I wasn't an officer I had some innocuous position and bided my time. I didn't have any outfits to do parades, and by this time, I had no interest in spending money on the uniforms. I just had the stuff that I wore while in combat.

Several months after I came home, on July 27th, 1953, an armistice was signed which ended the war. Korea remained divided along approximately the same boundaries as in 1950 before we had entered the war. These boundaries remain in effect today with American soldiers stationed there to guarantee it. From a military perspective there were no winners.

One of my regrets is that when I came back from Korea and assimilated back into society, I never really had the time to keep in touch with my war buddies. It wasn't until recently that I had the time to reach out and unfortunately in one situation it was too late.

About five years ago, around Memorial Day, I was sitting around thinking about combat and my friends. I felt a little maudlin about the fact that I never really kept in touch with Ed Mieskoski. He was from Ohio, so I got the operator on the phone that day and said, "I'm a Korean War veteran and I'm trying to reach a friend of mine, but I don't have much information as to where he lived in Ohio." She was a very nice lady and said, "Let me try to help you. The good news is he doesn't have a very common name." She gave me a phone number for Ed Mieskoski, and I said, "Well, now I'm hopeful that it would be either him or relatives with that name."

I called the number and there was nobody home. I left a message, "This is Guy Molinari. I served with Ed Mieskoski during the Korean War, and I'm looking to say hello to him." At about ten o'clock that night the phone rang and he said very formally, "Hi, Mr. Molinari, this is Ed Mieskoski." I said, "This doesn't sound like the Ed Mieskoski that served with me in Korea, you sound much younger."

He said, "No, no. I'm his grandson, that was my grandfather. My grandfather talked about you all the time. He went to college because of you and became a chemical engineer. He said you kept yelling at him because he didn't want to go to college after being discharged. You kept telling him, 'You have the GI bill, you have to go to college, otherwise you are a damn fool.' So when he got out of the Marine Corps he went to college and he joined a big company and he wound up being CEO of the company." According to his grandson, Ed would always say, "My whole life is changed because of Guy Molinari."

I said, "Is your grandfather alive?" He said, "No, he just died about five months ago on January 21 2009." Oh, my God, was I crestfallen to hear that I had an opportunity to talk to him, but called too late. I said, "Why didn't you guys call me?" He said, "Oh, we followed your career and it looked like you were way too busy."

I said, "You're never too busy for guys that you served in combat with, and he was very close to me." He said, "I know. All he did was talk about you and Korea."

The next day Ed's wife called me up and said, "It's so good to have heard from you. It's all Ed talked about was you and what an impact you had on his lifetime." So, I was pleased and down at the same time. Happy to hear that, but disappointed that I didn't get to talk to him before he died. But, that's the way it goes. Who would have known that somebody would have changed his whole life because of what I said to him in combat?

CHAPTER 6

Free to be a Lawyer

Like so many other Marines, when I returned home from Korea, I remember feeling that I was out of place. I was now a much different person than I was when I boarded the train for Parris Island. I had been hardened by the realities of war and I couldn't escape the unsettled feeling of anxiety which is so common for soldiers returning home to a "normal" life. I went through this period of assimilation and readjustment to civilian life like so many of my comrades in arms, and at times, I couldn't understand these feelings. My solace was in talking to fellow Marines and soldiers who had not only been there, but were exactly where I was. I learned that in order to really understand war, you had to be in one.

I was fortunate though, when I was honorably discharged from the service in 1953, I submitted a motion to be admitted to the practice of law in New York State. There was a special provision in the GI Bill stating that if you were drafted or enlisted in any of the military services and served at least a year and were discharged honorably, you wouldn't have to take the Bar exam. You would be automatically admitted to the Bar assuming you had finished the requirements of the law school; of which I had done before entering the service. On October 22nd, 1953, I was proudly admitted to practice as an Attorney and Counselor at Law in New York State. I had fulfilled my dream.

I wrestled for a miniscule amount of time with the concept of whether I wanted to work for my father's friend's large law firm in Manhattan or practice locally. The firm in the city had offered me a position, but I felt bound to Staten Island, so I turned them down and within a few months of returning home from service, I arrogantly hung out a shingle and said, "I'm a lawyer." Horowitz's Lawyer's Manual was the only book I had to help me. It had little chapters on each subject like "Buying and Selling a House." By using it as a guide, I learned the procedural and routine work involved in the general practice of law—in other words, the basics. I guess you could call Horowitz my mentor, and his book was the only one upon my shelf. That's how I did it. I started from scratch. The meat and potatoes of my practice involved real estate. Invariably, I was representing a seller or buyer of real estate.

In retrospect, it was an easy decision since my father had free office space in a building he owned in the New Dorp section of Staten Island. Being a principal in a startup law firm and not having to pay rent was a fantastic deal that I could not turn down. In addition, my father was a real estate broker, so I would get the closings from the sales that he made. My father was extremely proud to recommend his son to his clients, and as such, he was responsible for a significant number of my early clients who retained my services.

It worked out really well because when I started, there were a lot of Italian-American immigrants on Staten Island who couldn't speak English. I remember one of my first clients; a woman came to see me and started speaking in Italian. I said, "*Io non parlo l'italiano*," which meant, "I don't speak Italian." She got angry and wanted to leave and I said, "No, no, no stay." I told her daughter that I thought

I could make myself understood, and with perseverance she became my client.

My law office was located at 88 New Dorp Plaza. It was a three story building, but at that time, only the first and second floors had been completed. It needed a lot of work and my father didn't have much money, so work proceeded very slowly. On the plus side though, it did have one invaluable asset and that was plenty of parking. At that time, almost all the Staten Island lawyers located their offices in the St. George area near the ferries. The major problem with St. George was that there were no parking spots. It was so terrible that you could actually ride around for a half hour waiting to find a parking spot. Parking spot fights were a common occurrence in the St George business area.

Once word got out that I had opened up an office in New Dorp, the real estate brokers who didn't want to go to St. George because of the continuous parking fights would say, "Go to Molinari's office. There's plenty of parking." I was able to establish a thriving practice in very short order. I was getting plenty of work. One day I actually did four closings. So, before I knew it, I had too much work. I had to take a partner and then another partner. Eventually, I ended up taking on a fourth partner.

The only regret I may have regarding my private law practice is that I focused too strongly on the material benefits. I had a strong desire to do litigation as a new attorney, and I wanted to fight for what was right. At the time, as a new attorney, I had to make a choice: litigation or real estate, one or the other, not both. With litigation you could be on trial for weeks with no income. It was very difficult, if not impractical, for a solo practitioner in a startup law practice. The money, however, was in real estate, so I jumped where the money was for my private practice. Down the road, the litigation dream would essentially become realized when I was able to aggressively advocate for my constituents, since at times, extensive litigation would be the only means to achieve the goal.

My dream to establish a good law practice and to serve the people was coming true. It was fun and I liked being the "home town guy."

Although my practice centered on real estate, that is not to say I didn't dabble in other areas when the occasion arose, usually, as a personal favor to a friend. The practice of law can bring many challenges and quite a few of them are clearly comical when you look back on them years later. Such was the case with my dear friend Walter Marchese.

Every day I would go to the local diner and have a cup of coffee and a piece of pie to break up the day. I would interact with the local storeowners, and invariably I'd stop in to see Walter Marchese, who was a Marine like me. He had a TV repair shop up the block from my office.

One day, Walter called me up frantically screaming, "I've been arrested for bookmaking and I need your help!" "Okay, okay, relax," I told him. I immediately went to the stationhouse to see him and told the police I represented him. I told them he was a friend of mine. The reason why I knew he wasn't a bookmaker was because I was with him so much that I would have known if he was.

During the same time period, my uncle had been arrested and charged with bookmaking, yet he was not a bookmaker. I actually went to see John M. Braisted, the Richmond County District attorney at the time. I said, "What's going on here? It looks like the cops are trying to make arrests to show that they are working, but they are arresting innocent people."

So, as I'm talking to Walter Marchese at the station, Walter says, "Guy, do me a huge favor, I have my service pistol in my shop. If they get a hold of it, it's an automatic minimum of one year in jail because of the Sullivan gun law." He asked me, "The side window's open. Climb through it and get the gun. You can save me, please."

Here I am, an attorney, but of course being a Marine I said to myself, "He's my Marine buddy." As much as I didn't like the idea—because if I were caught with it, I would probably serve a year in jail for it instead of him—but a friend is a friend especially when we are fellow Marines.

So, foolishly but loyally, after I left him I immediately went over to his shop and I climbed in the window and found his pistol. As I went to climb out the same side window the police were entering through the front door to finish the search of his shop. I quickly slipped away without being seen and breathed a sigh of relief that I had succeeded in saving his ass. It was a close call.

Regarding the original arrest charges, he was eventually cleared. In the 1950s televisions were made up of numerous tubes and when one of them broke it had to be replaced. As a TV repair man he had all these tubes with numbers. He would mark those numbers down and the police thought it was a code for bets that he was taking. It was ridiculous. Fortunately, when it was professionally explained Walter was cleared.

So my practice was a totally hands-on practice. If you wanted to talk to me, I would be available twenty-four hours a day, seven days a week, three hundred sixty-five days a year. I learned that a key part of a successful law practice was having the ability to successfully interact with your clients, the community and business. So, I used to go to functions. It was mostly to try to get my name out there and maybe pick up some clients.

At that point in time, I also started going to political functions. Since my father was so active in local politics, it came natural for me to follow in his footsteps. I saw how much he enjoyed being involved in the political scene on Staten Island and once I started going to the functions I found that I loved interacting and being actively involved in local political issues as well. Many times I would attend the functions with my father. Democratic or Republican, it didn't matter. I enjoyed going to the events and it was also a great way to network and generate more business for my law practice.

I made many good friends such as Tony Gaeta and Nick LaPorte. Our personalities clicked naturally and we had many laughs together. Nick would wind up being the Democratic County Chairman and a City Council member and Tony would wind up being the Staten Island borough president. They were both hardline Democrats, but they liked me and it wasn't unusual for the three of us to go out together and make the rounds.

The people would wonder why a Republican and two Democrats were together like that. It was very special in those days to be able to have friends like that. We knew that we may be campaigning against each other at some point in the future, but we wouldn't do that unless we had to.

So I started becoming tuned in to the political scene and in some cases what I saw I didn't like. I kind of felt that we were electing people who forgot about us. It was my distinct impression at the time that Staten Island was being stepped on by the establishment. Staten Island was always the last one to be served and the elected officials that we had weren't strong enough or powerful enough to stop that. That's why we got things like the Freshkills Landfill, the Liquid Nitrogen Gas tanks, and so many other things that were wrong and bad. It was always the same story: "Send it to Staten Island. We don't want it, send it to Staten Island."

CHAPTER 7

The Blessing of Marriage, The Tragedy of Death, and The Miracle of Birth

It would not be unusual for me to prepare a contract for a client and hand deliver the contract to the real estate broker's office that made the sale. I never realized how such a simple hands-on action could change your life forever.

One day, as I was delivering a contract to the realtor at their office, I was taken aback by this beautiful lady seated behind one of the desks. She was very attractive, but looked quite young. I became a little tongue tied, so I dropped off the papers and left.

A few days later, one of my clients told me that he had stopped at the same real estate office, and Marguerite, a really pretty receptionist was asking questions about me. He says, "I think she may like you, you should call her." I said, "I don't know, she is beautiful, but she looks too young for me, if I have to guess she looks eighteen." At the time, I was twenty-eight, so the age difference stopped me in my tracks from asking her out on a date.

At this time, I worked every night till late. Afterward, I would meet my friends at the local bars, and we'd have a couple beers together, play pin ball machines, and horse around. I then would go home, get some sleep, and start all over again. Although, it was a wonderful time for me because I knew everybody in New Dorp, I had a nagging feeling that it was time to think about settling down.

A few weeks later, I received an impromptu phone call from Susan Wing, saying her daughter Marguerite wanted to say hello. Little did I know at the time that Susan would wind up being my mother-in-law, and a great one at that. I thought, "Uh oh, interesting. If the mother is making the call, the age difference must not matter." I got on the phone and I talked to Marguerite. She told me that she was babysitting that night for her relatives, so I suggested that I would stop by and meet her. I was thrilled when she agreed.

That night I went to Marguerite's cousin's house where she was babysitting and I asked her real age. She said she was eighteen. For a split second the age difference was a minor problem, but I fell in love with her so quickly that it became immaterial. I remember on our second date, Marguerite looked at me very fretfully and confided, "I have to tell you something." She then blurted out, "I'm part Chinese."

I looked into her eyes and having served in the Korean War I could understand her discomfort, yet I saw the woman that I could be with for the rest of my life and I said whole-heartedly, "So what? It's not going to change how I feel about you."

I could see that she was visibly relieved by my response and she then proceeded to tell me how her father was half Chinese and half Italian. He died suddenly when she was about nine years old. She cried as she recalled when her mother told her that he died of a heart attack. Marguerite was an only child. She showed me pictures of her father and I could see that he was a very good-looking man. She told me how he was well liked in the community because he always helped people in need. He was good with his hands. If somebody had something that broke, he would fix it.

When she was done she told me that her mother Susan was a full-blooded Italian and her personality complemented her father's so well. They loved each other deeply. When her father passed away Marguerite and her mother became inseparable. Her mother was the light of Marguerite's life. As time passed I was pleased to learn that Marguerite's mother had a terrific fun personality and as a result she was an extraordinarily easy person to get along with.

Once love called, we were off to the altar. I married my beautiful wife on Saturday, September 1st, 1956. We were two love birds without a clue what a roller coaster our life would be. She thought she was marrying a real estate attorney. Simple as that. Little did we know how things would change.

By the time I bought my first house, I had established myself as an expert in real estate transactions. I closed on the first house we bought in three days. It was located on Ridgecrest Avenue in the Great Kills section of Staten Island. The house's history had excellent karma for me, since I was a die-hard Yankee fan, and Karl Drews owned it. Karl Drews was a famous baseball pitcher who played for the Yankees, as well as other teams. Tragically, in 1963, he was killed at the young age of forty-three, by a drunk driver in Florida.

We lived there about a year until a close friend of mine, who happened to be a client, built a brand new house on Dalton Avenue in the New Dorp area of Staten Island. He could not sell the house. He said, "I'll sell it to you for cost. Why don't you buy it? It's a beautiful place." When Marguerite and I looked at the house we decided that it was an offer we could not refuse. So, we sold the house in Great Kills, and bought the Dalton Avenue house. When I came home at night and shone the car lights on the front lawn the view was beautiful. Many times the lawn would be loaded with rabbits, sometimes as many as thirty or forty.

At the time, I had a real estate business, and one day Vivian Lamby my partner in the business listed her house for sale. It was a beautiful house on Coventry Road in the Todt Hill area of Staten Island. When Marguerite and I went up to see the house we fell in love with it, and we bought it immediately. Of all of our houses this was our favorite.

I was really settling down in my life, between a lucrative real estate business, marriage; everything was on the right track. Then of course the sledge hammer fell. My father, the Fighting "Bob" Molinari, was dying.

For a few months my father had been ailing, but much like me today he just kept going and going and ignoring the issues. He had a constant cough that he attributed to something that would blow over. What we know about medicine today and in the 1950s is like night and day. No matter what we said he just brushed it off. He would only do what he wanted to do, not what we wanted him to do.

Finally, when he got seriously ill, a doctor who was a friend of my father, Dr. Mazolla did a series of tests and told us that he did not think it was cancer and if it was, it was not a typical cancer. He suggested he might know what it was and he was trying to find an antidote to save his life. It was all for naught since my father's condition deteriorated rapidly and he died on Friday May 31st, 1957 in St. Peter's Hospital Brooklyn. It was a devastating loss to my family and to me.

I was beside myself with grief. He was more than a father to me, he was my best friend, and my lifelong friend was no longer at my side. He was there for me through thick and thin. He was the person I could always count on.

I needed to know the true cause of death, as my dad was only 59 when he died. I ordered an autopsy and it did turn out to be lung cancer. The advances in medicine in the last fifty years have been extraordinary and maybe today he would have had a chance, but in 1957 it was a death sentence no matter how you looked at it.

The thing that pisses me off about his death is the fact that neither he nor my mother ever smoked a day in their lives. My father died from lung cancer and my mother died from lung disease, both at an early age. My family had talked about the causes of their diseases and we have all come to the conclusion that it had to do with the coal-burning furnaces that, in the first half of the century, were a fixture in many homes.

Growing up, my parents loaded the coal into the furnace. Asbestos sheets covered the ducts. In those days asbestos was not considered dangerous at all; it was the "Miracle Mineral." It was readily used for building materials of homes. Unfortunately, we now know that the inhalation of asbestos fibers resulted in serious and deadly diseases such as asbestosis, mesothelioma, or lung cancer, such as my father's.

During this depressing and emotional time period, the shining star in the dark clouds was the impending birth of our first child. On Thursday March 27th, 1958 my life would be changed forever by the most precious gift I could be given, my beautiful daughter Susan. Back in the 50s when people got married they generally espoused to have a family. Marguerite and I dreamed of a large family.

From the first moment I held my tiny newborn Susan in my arms, it was like the darkness of my father's death was lifted because I was holding in my hands part of our shared legacy. Susan was named after Marguerite's mother. There really are no words to explain the inner sense of peace and fulfillment Susan brought to me at that time. Marguerite and I were ecstatic and we both looked forward to many children. Once you hold your first child, the parenting instinct becomes unrelenting.

Unfortunately, within a few days after giving birth to Susan, my wife came down with a raging fever that almost killed her. Ultimately she was diagnosed with a very serious massive internal infection called peritonitis. So almost immediately the most joyful moment of my life was marred by the possibility that my beautiful young vibrant wife might die.

It was obvious that something terrible had happened during the delivery. So I immediately called the obstetrician who delivered Susan and asked him to come over to the house. He was so tired when he came over that we actually had to help him into the house. He had no answers about the cause but instinctively I knew it had to be a result of using a non-sterile instrument and that set off an infection. My wife was immediately hospitalized and they gave her all kinds of antibiotics to try to save her life. At one point it didn't look like they were going to be able to pull her through.

In the long run my wife survived the treacherous ordeal she was put through but it left lifelong scars. It set her on the road of taking too many drugs to control the residual effects of the massive systemic infection. I have always harbored resentment toward the doctor who delivered Susan because I felt he should have said, "I'm sorry, something happened during the birth." It wouldn't have made any difference with the treatment, but at least the person responsible would have acknowledged their mistake.

The most tragic consequence was the fact that my wife could not have any more children. So all our dreams, hopes and wishes for the future rested with our only child Susan. Looking back now, even though we had just one child, God was good to us because she is such a wonderful daughter. I spent as much time as I could with Susan when she was young and we are extraordinarily close to this day.

Since I was working and my wife was bedridden, my wonderful mother-in-law, Susan, spent most of her time staying over our house. She took wonderful care of Marguerite and my newborn. By the time my wife had recovered from the devastating illness her mother had become a large part of our household.

Her mother remarried a lawyer who was a bon vivant. He liked to hunt, fish, and live the good life, so he went his own way. Because of that, she had plenty of time to spend with her only daughter and she loved it. She also had unfettered access to her only grandchild, my daughter Susan. In the long run all three of them would become best friends. It took a lot of pressure off me. I was able to run my business without much interruption. To this day I thank God for the presence of Marguerite's mother during an extraordinarily difficult time period.

CHAPTER 8

A Fatal Car Accident

In 1968 things were going in the right direction. My law practice was flourishing and my personal life was extraordinarily fulfilling between family and friends. Some friends and I purchased a building in Mariners Harbor. We made it into a private men's clubhouse and called it HAVOL Men's Club. The HA stood for handball, and the VOL stood for volleyball. Ipso facto, HAVOL. I handled the legal work regarding the purchase of the building and other legalities. We fixed up the inside. It had indoor handball and volleyball courts, great food, and card games at the end of the night. Sometimes the card games went till four or five in the morning.

I have always enjoyed competitive sports throughout my life and I usually excelled. I enjoyed ping pong, racquet ball, tennis, handball, volleyball, hunting, running, etc. Many times during the hunting season with little notice my friends and I would go hunting. One of my clients was a really nice Norwegian fellow called Sven Knibestol. He was twenty-nine and an accomplished carpenter. He had only lived in America for a few years. One of the ways he embraced America was by learning how to play baseball and other sports that are popular here. He wanted to be Americanized, I guess. One day Sven heard us talk at our club HAVOL about our hunting trips and all the fun we had. He would constantly remark after that, that he would like to go hunting with us.

I told him, "Sven you're welcome to come, the only thing is we don't plan weeks in advance. Depends on how busy we are, when hunting season comes we check and see if enough guys want to go. We meet at my law office in the parking lot and we go. You don't get much notice when we call because it is a spur of the moment thing. When you get the call you have to be ready to roll."

On Thursday October 31, 1968 a group of us decided we would go hunting on the weekend. I called Sven and said, "The guys just called and we're going to leave tomorrow afternoon to go hunting. You constantly tell me that you want to join us, so this is your chance." Sven said, "Well, I don't know if I can do it…"

I said, "Well, if you want to go, you just be there, that's all." And, sure enough, he was the first one there the next day.

On Friday November 1st, 1968 after we had all finished working we parked our cars and eight guys piled into two cars and left for Rhinebeck, New York which was going to be the area that we were going to hunt. The drive itself is about two to three hours depending on traffic. We finally stopped at a motel that wasn't very far from where we intended to hunt. I didn't like the place, and some of them looked like they were going to rent a room there. I told them I wanted to go on further and see if we couldn't find something nicer. So we all piled back in the cars and headed out. It was a decision I will always regret.

As we left the place it was around 10:15 p.m. We merged back onto Route 308. Route 308 is a typical rural upstate two lane highway. Each lane goes in the opposite direction. It is a curvy road and the sides of each lane are lined with tall trees. In 1968 seatbelt laws were not in effect. As a matter of fact, many cars did not even have them in the back seat. It was not until 1984 that New York State

Senate passed the first law in the U.S. mandating the use of seat belts. I have always wondered whether what happened next may have been changed had we worn seat belts.

We were following the car driven by Freddy DiTommaso. Anthony Dacchille was driving our car and my friend Tony DiTommaso, Freddy's brother, was sitting next to him. I was sitting in the back seat next to Sven Knibestol. Suddenly we saw Freddy's car ahead of us and there was a woman driving a 1962 sports car speeding. When she came around a bend in the road, she must have hit dirt, sand or whatever and lost control of her car. She was headed right toward Freddy's car. She just missed his car but headed right into us. She hits us head on. The sound of crushing metal and the rolling of the cars was deafening and horrifying. I saw my life flash before my eyes.

Immediately after the accident, as the remnants of the two cars finally ceased their tumbling a gruesome sight was revealed. Both cars were demolished. The female driver's lower body was found in her car but she was decapitated. The driver of the car that hit us was identified as twenty-six year-old Reta Piez. In our car Sven was lying on top of me in the car and it was obvious to me that he was dying. Of the four people in my car one died and three of us were critically injured. It was a tragedy of epic proportions for everyone involved. The impact of the tragedy would never be forgotten by any of the survivors. We were all changed forever as a result of the devastating injuries we suffered.

The first thing I remember after the accident was Freddy yelling frantically, "The car may go on fire!! We have to get them out of there." He went to lift me and I screamed because my left leg was completely shattered. Even today the thought of that night forces me to revisit that sickening pain.

Every time they grabbed me to try and pull me out of the car I would pass out unconscious from the pain. Finally, somebody pulled out the backseat and when I woke up next, I was lying on the backseat of the car in the middle of the road on Route 308 on a frigid

November night. I lost complete track of time since I was passing in and out of consciousness.

My face and eyes had blown up from the impact of the crash. I couldn't see up at all, I could only see down. I noticed a State Trooper who was standing nearby but I couldn't see his face. I could only see his bottom because my eyes were almost swollen shut. Then I heard a voice, apparently a passerby who saw the crash and he asked the trooper, "Anybody die?" The trooper said, "Yeah the guy in the car is almost dead." Then he pointed to me and said, "And this guy ain't going to make it either."

I was shocked to hear that. There's somebody pointing a finger at me and saying that I was going to die. I said to myself, "What the fuck is he talking about? I am not going to die." I didn't feel like I was ready to go, I had so much left to accomplish in my life.

Sven and the woman were pronounced dead at the scene and all the critically injured were initially brought to a small community hospital called St. Francis Hospital. When we arrived at St. Francis, Freddy inquired whether they had surgeons there who were board certified. For some reason or another prior to our trip Freddy was told by a friend of his that if he was ever involved in an accident and he wasn't in the city, he should make sure that the doctors who took care of you were board certified.

When they said, "No, they are not board certified." Freddy said, "I won't let you take care of my brother, Tony, or Guy." They said that Anthony Dacchille couldn't be moved because he had a massive head injury and needed to be stabilized. Freddy told them, "Put Tony and Guy back in the ambulance and take them to a board certified hospital with board certified surgeons, and do everything you can to save Anthony." The ambulance took us to Vassar Brother's Hospital, located in Poughkeepsie. His forethought in a desperate situation eventually saved my leg.

I was extraordinarily fortunate to be treated by a highly experienced orthopedic surgeon named Michael Ettenson. Initially when he examined my injuries he told me that he might have to take my left leg off. He said the damage was so severe he wouldn't know until he performed surgery whether or not he could save the leg. That was the beginning of three surgeries.

After the surgery I was completely out of it for days. I had no idea what had happened, where I was, and the extent of my injuries. I was basically in a drug induced coma due to the medications they were giving me for the excruciating pain.

On about the fourth or fifth day, when my brother was sitting at my side, I woke up and said to him, "I'm not going to take the medication, I don't know what's happening in the world. I need to understand what's going on with me and around me." My brother warned me not to do that, but eventually supported my decision because he knew I would not back down.

So, when the nurse came to give me the pain meds I said, "I don't want them." She said, "Mr. Molinari, you better take them because if you don't take them and you start having a lot of pain, we are going to have to get the doctor to give a new prescription."

I said, "Ok, but I don't care I'm not taking them." I do recall screaming throughout the night because it hurt like hell, but I knew in my heart and soul that it was a better alternative for me than being out of my mind not knowing what was going on in the world.

They didn't tell me about Sven's passing right away. Once I came out of the drug induced stupor, I began asking about him incessantly. The last time I saw him I thought he was going to die on top of me, but I hoped that he had beaten the odds like me and survived. Unfortunately, he did not. I was devastated when they told me that he had died. He was a really nice friend and he was way too young to die.

At that time some local person came up to me and shouted excitedly, "Nixon won, Nixon won." I'm sure that they didn't know I was a political junkie, but at that point with all the excruciating pain, it really didn't mean very much to me at the time except for the fact that it was Election Day, Tuesday, November 5th 1968.

While I was there, Tony DiTommaso, Freddy's brother who was in the passenger seat of my car, was going crazy in the hospital. He had suffered a severe head injury. He would grab things, drink water incessantly, and he was trying to climb out of the bed constantly. Unfortunately, DiTomasso's personality would never be the same after the accident. Tony completely lost his sense of taste and smell. Food would never be the same to him.

I told the nurses that I wanted to move into his room. They said, "You have to get your doctor to approve that." I said, "I don't care what the doctor says, he's my friend. I want to help make sure he's ok. He's climbing out of the bed and stuff." So they had Dr. Ettenson come and see me. It was at that time that I learned how serious my injuries were.

Dr. Ettenson was begging me not to do it and said to me, "You can't do this Guy. You have no idea how bad shape you are in; your heart stopped beating during the surgery. You are having serious complications right now such as phlebitis, so it is a terrible idea. Your friend can be impulsive and combative; it's not a good situation. You can't let anything happen to your leg." Although he tried to talk me out of it he wasn't able to and I did ultimately move into Tony's room.

Immediately before I moved into Tony's room my wife was visiting me and I started coughing and hacking and I had a big pain in my chest. I spit up a big blob of blood. She was horrified and said, "Oh my God. What's that?" I said, "Shush don't say a word, I don't want this to stop the move to Tony's room."

And, as loving wives will do, she ignored me and she said, "We have to tell the doctor" as she walked out the room. She probably saved my life. So, not surprisingly, the doctor got nervous and put me on Heparin because they thought I might get a blood clot, which would cause a stroke, heart attack or pulmonary embolism, all of which could have killed me. So, because of the injuries and the medications I was getting, my whole body was colored black, blue, and green. When I looked at my disfigured body I did not recognize it, but the only thing I cared about was that I would be able to keep my leg. For the next several weeks Tony and I kept each other company. It was a good move in the long run.

One of my closest friends and law partner at the time, Al DiLillo asked Dr. Ettenson whether I would ever play handball or volleyball again. He responded emphatically, "No, he won't be able to. The injury to his leg is massive and he'll be lucky to walk, never mind play sports."

During my extensive hospitalization I developed a close friendship with Dr. Ettenson. I thought he was a brilliant doctor. He wouldn't let anyone visit me, yet he'd come in every night after he finished his rounds and we would talk. He knew I needed my rest but we really enjoyed talking to each other.

After many weeks at Vassar Brothers I was finally ready to come home. It didn't mean I could walk but I could be taken care of at home. I could only get safely home by ambulance. Before we started I heard a conversation with the driver of the ambulance and a hospital worker John. I liked John; he always treated me with compassion and was a really dedicated employee of the hospital. The driver said, "I can't take the ambulance on the expressway, so I have to take all the city streets, since I can't go on the expressway."

Little did I realize how this disastrous erroneous conclusion on part of the driver would make this the second most hellish vehicle ride of my entire life, the first being the accident itself. I screamed from the pain of the bumps and potholes in the road for almost the entire time. All I can say is it was a horrible, horrible, horrible trip.

By the time I got home and pulled up in front of the house my daughter looked at me and cried "Oh, Daddy." My wife was shocked at my appearance and said, "What happened?" All I could do was say, "Don't ask, please just get me inside." John helped me inside and I thanked him for everything. Regarding the ambulance driver if I could have kicked his ass I would have. Another step in this hellish ordeal was over. I was finally home.

When I came home from the hospital my family really came to my rescue. My daughter in particular was amazing. She was a beautiful nine year-old who threw herself into helping her father. When I had to go to the bathroom or to get out of bed, I needed someone to help me, but the pain was so intense that whoever did it had to be very careful. My wife was fairly good at it, but Susan was an expert. She learned to transfer me pain free quickly. So every time Susan was around I'd want her to help get me out of the hospital bed because she did it flawlessly and never caused me pain.

It's difficult to explain how important a safe and pain free transfer out of your bed to go to the bathroom could be in my situation. When I was in the hospital, there was one son of a bitch who was transferring me roughly out of bed. I screamed and yelled at the guy, and I wanted to hit him, because he had this look of pleasure on his face. I said to myself, 'This guy is a sadist. I should hit him on the fucking head.' I never did but to this day I wish I had.

So my family and friends rallied around my side. Regarding Susan, I asked her for nothing yet she gave me everything. It was a reversal of positions; my nine-year-old baby girl was taking care of her father instead of me taking care of her and with that she did a splendid job.

Then the word got around that I was home and my leg was in bad shape. At that point they told me I'd be out of work for a year and a half. I went back in less than three months, but in retrospect, on my part that was a mistake.

You live and learn. On the first day I went back to work, my two law partners were taking me up this flight of metal stairs and as we were in the middle, they went to put me down. My foot hit the step, and I screamed from the pain, and they almost dropped me. One guy dropped his side, the other guy jumped forward holding on to the wheel chair. I was in rough shape for the whole day. After that first experience going up the stairs. I wouldn't let them touch me anymore. I used to sit on the stairs and one by one I would go up on my butt, just pushing with my hands backward. If I had any pain, I had no one to blame but myself. I took my time and it worked.

In the ensuing months I actually had to learn how to walk all over again. Needless to say it was a tremendously difficult experience learning how to walk all over again by yourself. I would go on this little back porch area of our house and I would walk with the canes. I would use two canes, and just practice walking and walking. It was awkward, painful stuff. I had to learn how to walk on my own because back in those days no therapist came to the house.

Probably one of the dumbest things I did after the accident was not pay attention to the weather. It would not be unusual for me to go to the office on a Sunday to get caught up, especially since I was out sick for so long after the accident. Well on Sunday February 9th, 1969 I went to the office and although it was snowing a little bit, I continued to work. By that time, I was walking with crutches. I had heard no unusual weather reports before I left for the office in the morning.

When I left the office, I was stunned to see there was a great deal of snow on the ground. In fact, it was to be historically recorded as the "February 1969 Nor'easter." All I could think was, "Shit." I lived on Todt Hill at the time, which is the highest point on Staten Island. As I was going up the road to Todt Hill, cars were stuck all over the place because they couldn't get enough traction to get up the incline.

So the snowstorm was in full force, and my car got wedged into the side of the curb. I could not go forward and couldn't go back. I started thinking to myself, 'What am I going to do? It's ice, it's not just snow. Snow you could take a chance with, but this is ice.'

I kept on thinking about how I was warned repeatedly by Dr. Ettenson that, "The one thing that you can't do is fall. If you do you will lose your leg. I will not be able to save it. The amount of damage you have is incredible; you can't make a mistake." I became somewhat panicked at that point. It was cold as hell and if I got out of the car, I had to hobble on crutches the distance of a good ten blocks around winding curves. It would be very difficult if not impossible to hobble all that distance without falling.

I also knew I couldn't stay in the car or I would freeze to death. So I stepped out of the car and said to myself, 'I gotta try. I only have one choice really.' Even though it was an incline, I had to move since I'd gotten myself into this dumbass situation.

And then the magic occurred. It was like something out of a book. There was this heavy snowfall and then I heard a voice, which seemed like it was coming from another planet saying. "Guy, Guy is that you? Guy!" I couldn't see because the snow was so heavy, so I screamed, "Hello? It's Guy. Who is it?"

It happened to be a couple of my good friends who went out looking for me. They were worried that I would not be able to make it home. They had called my wife and she said I hadn't come home.

My friends answered and said, "Its Freddy, Freddy Loprimo and Nicky Lupari. Don't move. Stay where you are. We'll come to you. We'll get you home."

Oh boy. I felt like the Gods were finally shining on me from above. I could not believe my good fortune. I got back into the car, put the heat on and waited until they came. Somehow they were able to get me into their car and we eventually made it to my house. My hospital bed was still in the big family room. So we lit up the fireplace, poured a few drinks, and I rejoiced in my good fortune to have such good friends. If they didn't save my life that day, they certainly saved my leg.

By the time the nor'easter was over 42 New York City residents died and several hundred more were injured. Thankfully I was not one of them. It was a political nightmare for then Mayor John Lindsay for not dealing with the snow adequately. The city was completely blindsided by the impact of the storm. It became historically known as the "Lindsay Snowstorm." The city was crippled for almost a week after the storm. It truly is a miracle that I did not become the 43rd fatality of the nor'easter.

So during this difficult time period tremendous challenges were placed before me. I think that it gave me a better sense in the long run how to handle difficult situations. It was a long and arduous process but I got through it. To me it was almost similar to the Marine Corps in terms of learning about yourself, and meeting the challenges. As an example, even though Dr. Ettenson told my law partner I would never play handball again, I proved him wrong. I played handball with a steel rod in my left leg that weighed three pounds. And if I do say so myself considering the circumstance I was playing pretty well. Never say never to Guy Molinari.

After many months I had the third and final operation where they had to take three pounds of stainless steel rod out of my left leg. They told me there was a screw at the end of the rod and they would pull it out. The Doctor said it was supposed to be a simple operation an hour no more. Unfortunately, it lasted over four hours. When I awoke from surgery I was in terrible pain, worse than the second operation. When I saw the Dr. I said, "Mike what happened, you told me one hour and finished."

He said, "My friend you not only healed but you over healed, when we looked at it there was a layer of bone that shaped around the rod and we had to chip away at it to make it smooth so you won't have future problems. Also I had to cut through a lot of the sinew, since you played handball you have really strong tendons and ligaments. It's probably what helped to save your leg in the long run. It helped to absorb the shock of the whole accident. It is rare for me to see this."

Eventually, after the rod was taken out I started playing handball again on a regular basis and I must confess that I won a lot more games than I lost. I never did go hunting again after the accident though. It wasn't that I didn't want to, it was just by the time I recuperated, all the guys who would have originally gone hunting with me weren't hunting anymore. Time passes, and seasons change. It was just never in the cards for me again.

CHAPTER 9

The Dark Horse Candidate

My decision to formally enter politics occurred on a lark. I was at a political function in 1974 and Lucio Russo was present. Lucio Russo was an eleven term incumbent New York State Assemblyman representing the 60th District comprised of the south shore of Staten Island. He was initially elected in 1953 and had been an assemblyman for twenty-one years. That was a pretty impressive record for an assemblyman at the time.

Russo was a crusty character who would get irritated very easily. While at the function I saw a man ask Russo, "Do you know who I am?" Russo said, "Yeah, you look familiar." The guy said, "You're a liar, you never saw me before, this is the first time I have ever met you." Russo immediately started screaming at the man.

I went over to Russo and said, "Why are you screaming at him?" Russo said, "I don't like his attitude. What do you got to say about it?" I said, "You shouldn't yell at people like that, he just asked you a question." He said, "He can go to hell and so can you!"

Anyone who knows my personality knows that I speak my mind especially when I start getting hot under the collar. So I said, "Hey, slow down." He said, "Why do I have to slow down?" I said, "If you keep going on like that I might just think about running against you." He said, "It would be fun for me, just like the last guy, so be my guest." As you can imagine, the wheels started rolling in my head and so started another adventure.

I thought about it extensively. I had a lot of friends, so even though I didn't know everything about politics, I did have experience in running several campaigns. My first campaign experience came in the early 60s when I received a call from the Staten Island Republican leader, James Flood, asking me if I would help a candidate for public office named Bernard Berggren. I agreed because Berggren was an excellent candidate. Although he didn't win, I learned quite a bit about running campaigns.

Then in 1965, one of my closest high school friends, Anthony "Tony" J. Crecca Jr. ran on the Republican ticket to unseat Staten Island Democratic Council member Edward T. Curry. At the time Tony was a successful criminal defense attorney. I was his campaign manager. Unfortunately, he lost, but it did not discourage him from pursuing further positions in public office. Sometimes you have to lose to ultimately win in politics.

In 1971 I ran a successful campaign for Tony when he ran against Louis "Wally" Sangiorgio for the position of Staten Island Civil Court Judge. Wally was actually a friend of ours, so initially I did not want to run the campaign. Eventually several friends supported Wally so I felt that it was up to me to help out Tony since he was one of my closest friends. I ran an aggressive campaign and basically did all the campaigning. Tony was elected to the seat of the Judge.

Unfortunately, Tony hated the position immediately. Literally after spending only one day on the bench he called me up and said he wanted to quit. Tony said, "Boobie[5], I don't like this judgeship. I'm not going to stay!" I said, "Tony, you're only on the bench one day. You can't quit now, your reputation and career will be damaged for the rest of your life."

Tony said, "Well, what do I do?" I said, "You've got to serve at least a year. You can't walk away now." He said, "What's the difference?" I said, "You have to worry about your reputation, if you still don't like it after a year, even though it's not a great idea, you can resign then. Who knows? You might even change your mind. You have to at least try."

True to form, after serving two years he resigned from the bench. He returned to his private practice and continued to be one of the top criminal defense lawyers on Staten Island. Regarding Wally Sangiorgio, he was ultimately elected as a Civil Court Judge in 1978 and to the Supreme Court in 1981. He distinguished himself as a well-respected Jurist. So in the long run they both wound up doing what they loved and had distinguished careers.

So, after thinking about my experience in running campaigns both unsuccessful and successful, I finally decided in February 1974 that I was going to run against Russo. I felt that Russo had lost touch with the people. He had forgotten that it was the people that got him to where he was. At the time I was forty-six years old and a successful real estate attorney. I could have easily sat back and done nothing but Russo pissed me off. Also, always in the back of my mind was my father's sense of nationalism and pride in serving our country and I wanted to continue that honorable tradition. I had observed my father very carefully in my youth and was able to glean what to do and what not to do to be successful in a campaign.

The first thing I did was call up the Republican chairman for Staten Island, Philip Fitzpatrick. I knew that the first rule to running a successful campaign was to obtain the party's backing. I thought that that would be a ground ball for me since I had, at his request,

---

5 *Tony called me Boobie. I affectionately called Tony "Junie."*

recommended him when he applied to be admitted to the bar in 1962.

When I talked to Phil and told him that I had made a decision that I was going to run in the Republican primary against Russo he said, "You're making a big mistake. We tried to dump him two years ago because he was involved in corruption scandals but he ran an excellent primary. We ran a really good guy against him and Russo beat us 3-1. We've already made a decision that we're backing him. So if you're hell bent on running against him, you're going to lose 4-1, and unfortunately you're on your own." I said, "Well, you may be right, but I'm going to get it out of my system once and for all."

Of course I was extremely disappointed with Fitzpatrick's decision but since I had made my decision to run, I was moving forward with or without their endorsement. Once I set my mind to do something that I feel is important I am committed to the task at hand and I had the full support of my family.

So, there I was seemingly all by myself, missing the all-important Republican backing from the party. My campaign would be a grassroots venture because I did not have the support of the standing party. Money would obviously be tight and I knew my success depended upon my own dedication as well as the commitment of volunteers. In the long run I learned that I had something more important than the party endorsement at the time: loyal friends. You can never put a price on that. I went to all of my friends and asked for their help and support and they were there 110% for me.

Over the course of my legal career I had demonstrated to these individuals that I possessed the characteristics necessary to be an effective elected official. They believed in me and I believed in them. They knew I was a dedicated skilled negotiator who always fought aggressively for what was right. As such I would fight aggressively for the needs of the community I was seeking to represent. I was completely in touch with the needs of Staten Island, unlike Russo. I knew the issues that went to the soul of my community.

At the time, on a national level our country was in turmoil due to the devastating effects of the Vietnam War and the Resignation of Republican President Richard Nixon on August 9th 1974 due to the Watergate scandal. On a local level the city was on the verge of a fiscal crisis and crime was rising.

Additionally, fresh in everyone's memory was and always would be Feb. 10, 1973 when an empty liquefied natural gas (LNG) tank in Bloomfield Staten Island exploded. It occurred when an empty 600,000-barrel Liquefied Natural Gas tank owned by The Texas Eastern Transmission Corporation located on Staten Island's north-west shore in Bloomfield, exploded while the tank was being repaired. The explosion killed forty workers, all of them Staten Islanders. The incident, at the time, was the borough's worst industrial accident ever. Residents of Staten Island were afraid and the future was uncertain.

I knew that if I was elected as an assemblyman my job for my constituents would be to address local issues and help pass laws that directly affected their daily lives in a positive manner. So we organized a very targeted campaign strategy. I promised the voters of the 60th assembly district that I would be fighting for a safer Staten Island by securing and supporting legislation that would: ensure that no LNG tanks would ever be opened on Staten Island again; get rid of the garbage dump; decrease crime; help voters obtain affordable and acceptable senior housing; make mortgages attainable; upgrade the district sanitation and storm sewers; assure adequate transportation; preserve parks; and improve and maintain quality schools, just to mention a few.

We embarked on a determined grass roots campaign and hit the streets. We were tenaciously working seven days a week; there was no time for breaks. We had a mission to accomplish. I was out every day before breakfast pounding the pavement and didn't stop till late at night. I held my campaign meetings at the Shalimar, a huge catering hall located on Hylan Boulevard in the New Dorp neighborhood of Staten Island. I am proud to say that I had so many volunteers working on my campaign that we needed a lot of space and that is why we needed the Shalimar. We spent months non-stop campaigning and pounding the beat. Facial and name recognition was essential. Every hand I shook or voter I talked to could be the difference between winning and losing. There was no time for rest; that would come after we were victorious, for now it was all run, run, run.

In any campaign the period immediately before the vote everyone jumps into overdrive. The Republican primary was set for Tuesday September 10th 1974. I was able to make good use of the fact that Russo had one of the worst voting records in the Assembly. I promised the voters that if I was elected I would be there to vote. It was an essential part of the great responsibility I would be entrusted with.

On Tuesday September 10th 1974 the night of the Republican primary, we were gathered at the ballroom of El Sal Restaurant, which was located next to the Royal Flamingo Swim Club on Amboy Road. My wife and daughter who had steadfastly supported me through all the ups and downs of the campaign were at my side. It was extremely exciting yet gut wrenching since the race seemed like it was going to be neck and neck.

As the election returns finally started dribbling in, it became clear that I was going to win. I remember Tony Crecca went to the podium and shouted to the large crowd, "WE BEAT THE BASTARD!!"

Over 300 wildly cheering supporters were present. The crowd went wild and everyone was ecstatic that I had won. I stood at the podium with my family, so proud that I was close to ascending to the position that my father had held.

When I addressed the crowd, in addition to thanking them for their exhaustive unending support acknowledging that we earned every single vote, I then yelled over the roar of the crowd, "A lot of good Republican Committee people didn't work for Russo because they couldn't in good conscience. These are the people with guts, and I admire people with guts. We will tell the party to put up good candidates or we'll work against them."

I knew that I had to make it clear to the incumbent Staten Island Republican Party hierarchy that they made a major error in judgment in not supporting me initially. I was a force to be reckoned with and the party needed to recognize this immediately before the general election. There is nothing like your first major victory party. I was overwhelmed with joy at the goal we had achieved. We had one night to enjoy our victory and we had a wonderful time. The following day we would be right back at the campaign so that I would be successful in the general election.

The mood at Russo's storefront headquarters was starkly different where Republican County Chairman Fitzpatrick and State Senator John Marchi watched as the results started coming in. Basically it was stunned silence when it became evident that I had defeated Russo by a decisive margin. Par for the course, Russo refused to concede the victory to me on election night although he did admit that he was "dumbfounded" by the results. He blamed his loss on low voter turnout. He did acknowledge to the reporters that were present for the devastating defeat that he would probably have to proceed with only the Conservative Party endorsement.

I remember reading the *Staten Island Advance* the following morning and the headline said, "RUSSO IS TOPPLED BY MOLINARI." It was an awesome experience. A well-defined hard earned victory but the battle was not over. I had over 1500 votes compared to 1200 for Russo. A clear victory. Although I won the Republican primary, Russo was still on the Conservative Party line so he could still run in the general election. The paper quoted me as saying that, I am "not concerned with Russo's candidacy any longer. Mr. Russo is a dead duck, with the momentum we have now and the voters we'll pick up, we should win easily on November 5th."

There was no question that I had won the election but Russo defiantly refused to concede even days after the election. Russo accused me of arrogance and disloyalty to the standing Republican Party. He went as far as calling me a traitor to the Party. As for myself I went back to the campaign trail. The momentum that we had was tremendous. My campaign was on fire. The 60th assembly district applauded my victory and welcomed a man who had the guts to go outside the party lines. I had brought to the forefront in my first victorious election the fact that the Staten Island Republican Committee was also out of touch with the reality of the voter's conscience. It was time for a change, not stagnation. Staten Island needed leaders with a voice, and I was that man who brought the obvious to light. I reveled in the role, because I saw myself as being able to affect real change with such a dramatic victory for a first time "Dark Horse candidate."

To my delight, on September 13th, only four days after my victory, Lucio Russo finally recognized the finality of the situation and said he would drop out of the assembly race. He knew there was no going back; his political career was over.

Under the election law there was only one way that a candidate could legally drop out of the race: by being nominated for a state judicial office. The Republican and Conservative Party nominated Russo for a judgeship and the deed was done. Everyone knew at the time that he had absolutely no chance of winning a Supreme Court judgeship since he did not have a Democratic nomination. The Democratic Party supported all the judges elected in the past twenty years. It was a save face move for the public but in essence meant nothing. As expected, on Election Day Lucio Russo would lose his bid for the judgeship.

The moral of this story for any politician is that you always have to treat your constituents professionally and with respect. When you lose that perspective it is time to get out, because you lost focus on why you originally entered politics: "For the people." Someone like me comes along and will sense that you have lost your perspective and will blindside you, ending your political career.

The Republican Party was shaken up, but they realized that it was more important to keep the Republican seat in the general election so it was time to eat crow. The New York State GOP leadership was terrified of losing control of the assembly so Fitzpatrick had to make the right decision. No one wanted to be the person responsible for a shift in power. As a result, "The Right Guy," got the Republican endorsement. The Conservative Party then endorsed me and that was the difference in winning or losing. I was in, and Russo was out. Poetic justice. Now it was time to win the general election.

With Russo out of contention I would be running against John W. Russell, a Democrat and Kathleen Brandt, a Liberal. I was thrilled when I received the all-important endorsement of the *Staten Island Advance*. They wrote that I was not "a party-liner," that I was "energetic", and would "be an asset in Albany." Truly complementary things were being said about the "Dark Horse from Staten Island." Their endorsement further set my campaign on fire. There was nothing that would stop my volunteers and me from achieving my goals.

I continued to campaign vigorously and on Tuesday, November 5th, 1974 I formally won the election. Within two months I had snagged another major victory. The grassroots campaign I ran was the least expensive of any of Staten Island's legislative races. We spent less than $7,000 on my successful election.

The day after the general election the Staten Island Advance headline read "Island victors: Murphy, Marchi, Gaeta, Connelly, Molinari, DiVernieri, DeSalvio, " and "Only Marchi and Molinari survive Dem Tide." I had crushed the challengers in my race. I received 18,854 votes which was 55.3% of the turnout. Nothing less than an impressive victory. They called my campaign a Cinderella story and it was. It was a dream come true and I was ecstatic. I did it my way.

Unfortunately, the Republican Party in New York State suffered dramatic loses resulting in the loss of control of the New York State Assembly as a result of misguided election strategies. All, however, was not lost; the State Senate was still controlled by Republicans.

CHAPTER 10

A Homeless Assemblyman

Unlike the majority of the people in the Assembly, I was just starting out my political career at the age of forty-seven. I was not a career politician so now I would be the novice assemblyman. So here I was, a Republican member of the New York State Assembly. I had followed in my father's footsteps, but I vowed not to make the mistakes that he had made.

On Monday January 6th, 1975, Supreme Court Justice John A. Garbarino swore me in as assemblyman at Staten Island Borough Hall. It was a tremendously proud moment for my entire family. My world would now be consumed with traveling to Albany to fight for our boroughs' unique needs. At the time I never realized how effective I would ultimately be in fighting for my beloved Staten Island.

When I arrived in Albany that week for the start of the legislative session, there were only eight newly elected freshman Republican Assemblymen in our class. It would be the first of literally hundreds of three hundred fifty miles, six hours long round-trip car rides I would take to our state capitol. The car ride became thinking time while I charted my strategy for the sessions I was going to attend.

Unfortunately, in the 1974 state elections, the Republican assembly lost the majority and became the minority. The tables had turned to the detriment of my party. Unbeknownst to me at the time I was destined to be in the minority throughout my entire political career.

In 1975, the state was in the process of finishing the construction of the Empire State Plaza[6], a huge complex of several state government buildings in downtown Albany, started in 1959. At the north end of the complex is the original New York State Capitol building. When I arrived at the new Legislative Office Building (LOB) that housed the offices of the State Legislatures it was just being completed. The area had not even been landscaped. The main purpose of this building was to supply office space to members of the New York State Assembly and Senate.

Initially I was assigned an office in the LOB across the street from the capitol on the fourth floor. Surreptitiously that office was taken over by the Majority controlled Democratic Legislative leaders. Par for the course for the brand new Republican Assemblymen who were now in the minority, we received a heck of a welcome when we learned that there was not going to be enough office space for everyone. Being low man on the totem pole I was quickly evicted.

On Monday January 13th, myself and the seven other first-term Republicans were forced to draw lots for the available offices. Normally I would be excited about the prospect of my luck in gambling but somehow or another I got a bad feeling that I was going to be on the wrong end. In fact, I drew the very last pick for an office. I was number eight of eight. I couldn't pick any lower. My gut was right and I lost. I immediately became a homeless Republican assemblyman.

---

6 *The formal name is "Governor Nelson A. Rockefeller Empire State Plaza."*

Of course I was extremely disappointed because I recognized that your chances of being an effective increased dramatically when you were surrounded by your fellow assemblymen. It was common sense. I quickly thought about viable alternatives. First, I could rent an office a couple of blocks away in another building not associated with state government. The major downside would be that I would not be part of the process. It is essential to be where your fellow assemblymen are; you have to have access to each other, so this was a terrible alternative. I also knew that I had to get an office immediately, since I was being hampered from working effectively on my constituents' issues. I needed an office!

This was definitely not what I expected my first legislative battle to be about. I learned quickly that when one party loses control of one house, the backlash is never-ending for the losing side. Petty politics, the epitome of "payback is a bitch."

So, I brazenly decided that I would force the issue by setting up shop right in the Lobby of the LOB. I put a desk, with my nameplate "ASSEMBLYMAN MOLINARI" and several chairs right in the lobby of the building and basically said I am open for business. I was directly in the middle of everybody and obviously interfering with everything. I had my secretary sitting there and people would come by and say, "You can't do this, you're blocking everything!"

I said, "Well, I have nowhere to go. Get me an office. Otherwise I'm going to be working here for the next two years."

As a result, one of the senior Democrat Assemblymen from Nassau County Lewis Yevoli, who had actually evicted me, was gracious enough to share his office space with me until they found permanent space for me. He became a great friend throughout my political career.

Perry Duryea was the Assembly Minority leader and pursuant to the rules it was his responsibility to provide office space for all the Republican assemblymen. Jim Emery was the Assistant Assembly Minority Leader at the time and ultimately he gave me part of his office and that's where I finally set up shop. He converted a conference room in his office on the fifth floor to an office for me. So in less than a week's time, I was no longer homeless. I had a nice office on the fifth floor and when I looked out the window I was able to see the Capitol Building across the street.

In essence, as a skillful negotiator I had learned over the course of my legal career that if you don't complain about things that you are unhappy with, nobody is going to do anything to help you solve the problem. Many times you have to keep on bugging people until they listen to you and do what needs to be done. I am a firm believer in the saying that, "The squeaky wheel gets the oil." By the time I had retired from politics, I had emptied many barrels of oil, much to the chagrin of my opponents but for the benefits of my constituents.

Typically, I would drive to Albany on Sunday night and in the early part of the legislative session and I would stay till Wednesday or Thursday night. At the end of the legislative session, we would stay until everything was finished. Friday I would devote to my law practice in Staten Island. On Saturday I would see constituents in my law office. After they were finished talking to me about their particular problems, they would go on their way and then when they left, I would dictate into a machine correspondence, memorandums, or whatever. My secretary Lorraine Witzak would then type up the material. I would then come into my office on Sunday, pick up the outgoing mail, read it, sign it, make corrections where they were needed which were rare because I had such a great secretary. I would then drive back to Albany on Sunday night and I would leave the stack of signed material there and Lorraine would take care of the rest. As you could see the daily grind was tough on the family, but they were very supportive. At times I thought to myself, "You have to be crazy to do this job," and I would always say to myself, "There, I qualify."

In Albany, the Capitol Building is the hub of activity for an assemblyman. The Assembly Chamber is the largest room in the building. It is called the "Peoples' Chamber," and I always reminded myself that that was why I was there: for the people who elected me.

At the very front of the chamber is the podium where the Speaker of the Assembly presides over the proceedings. In the beginning of my term, the Speaker of the House was a Democrat named Stanley Steingut. He was a large man who appeared aged beyond his years and was publically considered a lackluster politician who hated the press. To his colleagues though he excelled in back room politics. Many, including myself, considered him cunning, street smart, and an extremely proficient leader in Democratic politics. Almost everyone got along with him and he was very easy to talk to and accessible which is an extremely important characteristic for a good leader. I found it easy to sit down with him and explain my constituent's problem and if he could help he would. He was an old school politician.

Prior to me being elected to the Assembly, an Assemblyperson would typically serve five months of the year on constituent issues. Essentially it was considered a part time job. That is not what happened in 1975 due the dramatic changes that were taking place in the world, our country, and New York State. Speaker Steingut decided to have the standing committees operate year round for the first time. So, in 1975 we wound up serving eleven months. An assemblyman was paid $23,500 per year. In the six years that I served in the New York State Assembly I never received a raise.

1975 was a hell of a year to start out in politics. One must remember that the year before newly elected New York City Mayor Abe Beame, a Democrat, had inherited a city immersed in the worst fiscal crisis imaginable from his predecessor, John Lindsay. Beame would be a one term mayor due to the incredible challenges he faced during his tenure. So much of my introduction into Albany was consumed with the fiscal crisis which engulfed New York City, and of which my legislative district was a part.

There were many compounding Liberal backed causes of the fiscal crisis, yet not one of them was the sole cause. This multifaceted effect resulted in a willingness of the prior city government to employ devastating deficit financing strategies, which nearly collapsed the

City of New York. In the late 60s and early 70s, New York City embraced a strong welfare state resulting in exorbitant welfare and Medicaid costs borne by the city in addition to subsidized public housing.

The New York City Democratic Party's policy was tilted toward complete subsistence of the disadvantaged to a quality of life that offered them no incentives to remove themselves from the social service system that served them so well. Yet at the same time this system was bankrupting the average working man or woman who subsidized the disadvantaged. A prime example of this was the fact that New York City was the only city in the country that offered free higher education to all under the municipal university system.

Nationally the catastrophic Vietnam War was unsuccessfully ending for our country when on April 23rd, 1974 President Ford announced to the world that America was declaring an end to the Vietnam War. Within one week Saigon fell into the hands of the North Vietnamese immediately after our Marines had evacuated U.S Embassy. Locally, by July, New York City was laying off essential employees and freezing wages, school teachers were going on strike, and police officers were picketing. And of course, who could forget, Jimmy Hoffa disappeared. To this day they are still looking for him. It truly was unprecedented times and issues.

As a result, the nation was not interested in digging New York City out of the mess that it had created for itself. The country's sentiment toward New York City's self-created fiscal disaster was vividly exposed on October 30th, 1975 when the New York Daily News ran a front page headline stating "FORD TO CITY: DROP DEAD." The headline came immediately after President Ford defiantly said he would, "Veto any federal bailout of New York City to prevent a default." As Abe Beame would be a one-term mayor, Gerald Ford would be a one-term president.

When I went to Albany immediately my attention was focused on Staten Island and my constituents. I quickly publicized my legislative goals for the 60th assembly district many of which encompassed the entire Borough of Staten Island. Instantly I distinguished myself as a politician who was not defined by strict borders. I was willing to extend my political goals for the benefit of the entire island.

I had many goals, the first of which was stopping LNG tanks from being re-opened after the disastrous explosion in 1973. If empty tanks could kill forty people could you imagine how many people could be killed with filled tanks? Additionally, improving the quality of life of the residents by improving all community services and carefully monitoring development of Staten Island. Of course always in the back of my mind was the fact that I wanted to rid our borough of the dump. It was a lifelong goal that I would pursue. It would be an impossible task at the time since I was in the minority and the other boroughs were ecstatic that the garbage dump wasn't in their borough. I vowed to keep up my campaign promises. I would be a politician who you could trust to keep his word.

CHAPTER 11

Early Political Rollercoasters & Life in the Minority

During my earliest days in Albany, I became involved in a major political controversy that would rear its ugly head for several years. A disastrous "theme" park was being proposed on a one-hundred-acre tract within Staten Island's Bloomfield Industrial Park. Lobbyists in Albany supported this idea, but none of them were from Staten Island. Just like when dealing with the garbage dump, non-Staten Islanders always thought they knew what was best for Staten Island. It was a mindset that I was determined to eradicate, so from the get go I strongly opposed the amusement park. The addition of the park would have been a traffic nightmare of epic proportions for the entire borough.

I became aware of the proposal in early March of 1975 when Senator Marchi called my office in Albany and asked me if I was busy. I said, "Not really." He said, "Can you come over now? I'd like you to meet former Assembly Speaker Joseph Carlino." I said, "Sure."

I knew that Carlino was the former leader of the Republican assembly from 1959 to 1964 and was now a powerful, well known, and successful lobbyist in Albany.

When I arrived at Senator Marchi's office we talked about social stuff and the beauty of his ornate office. Then Carlino asked Marchi, "John, I have a client of mine who wants to invest a lot of money in a piece of property on Staten Island. He is going to build an amusement park. Do you believe that it would be a booming success?" Senator Marchi said, "I think that Guy can give you a better answer than I can."

So, Carlino said, "Guy, you want to help us out?" I looked at Carlino and said, "Look. This is not only a bad deal for Staten Island, but I think trying to go through with this is a mistake on your part as well. I don't think you're going to get away with it, and I'm going to be leading the charge against it. If you're still going to consider it, well I guess I'll meet you at the bridge and we'll do battle." With that, Carlino said, "Well, then I'm going to tell my client not to put any money in it even though I think you're missing the boat. Staten Island is going to lose it." I said, "so be it, it would be a fight till the end, because as I told you, the residents of Staten Island will be strongly opposed to the idea. I know it is a terrible idea."

Personally I was thrilled that he had asked my opinion because I thought that Senator Marchi and I had killed the bloody thing before it even got started. That was what I was aiming for when I decided to enter into politics: I was hoping that my reputation would carry me and I wouldn't have to actually do battle. Common sense and the best interests of Staten Island would rule. The fact that Guy Molinari was opposed to a bad project or idea hopefully would be enough to kill it.

On that day we all left on good terms. Shortly after the meeting I saw an article in the *Staten Island Advance* stating that they were going ahead with the amusement park plans. I felt the anger rising from my gut. I thought we had an agreement that he wasn't going to do it. With that, the unwanted battle began.

Carlino denied to the newspapers that he said to me that he represented the interest of the sponsors of the Amusement Park at the meeting. That was in stark contradiction to my statement when I told the *Advance* that Carlino clearly said he represented the interests of the sponsors at the meeting. Carlino said he had nothing to do with the Amusement Park and that we were engaged in only "casual" conversation. I knew there was nothing "casual" about the conversation. Carlino was looking for a green light when he brought it up with Marchi and me. Instead he hit a brick wall. He was trying to backpedal out of a difficult position for himself.

I believe that he knew based on my initial response that it was going to be a long, expensive legal battle which he would ultimately lose since he did not have the support of the residents or the politicians of Staten Island. So, as a lobbyist, his best option was to distance himself from a losing proposition, even though it could have been a highly profitable situation.

I was thrilled to learn that when the reporters asked Senator Marchi about his recollection of the meeting, he supported my recollection of the conversation. Here I am, a brand new assemblyman, and Senator John Marchi backed me up. He said, "If Guy says this is what happened, I believe Guy." He supported me even though Carlino was his longtime friend and political ally. It was a wonderful testament to my reputation.

To the best of my recollection this is the only time in history that Marchi was on my side concerning a Republican political issue. He was Alpha Italia, and I was forced to be a street fighting Marine. We came from two different worlds. Our differences notwithstanding, it was a big plus for me starting out that "The Senator" backed my recitation of what really happened. I scored a lot of political points, catapulting my political effectiveness to a new level. In my opinion your word is everything in politics and Senator Marchi had stood by my side against the interest of his longtime political ally Joseph Carlino. As a result, people started to take notice of me and

I enjoyed it because I was proving to myself that I could be effective and my reputation was beginning to speak for itself.

The theme park proposition would rise from the ashes over the course of the next few years, but ultimately it would die the slow death it deserved. Outsiders would select different locations on the Island such as Charleston and push their agenda. As promised, I would be fighting them at the bridge along with nearly every other elected Staten Island politician regardless of party lines. I let them know that it would only be over my dead body that a theme park be erected on Staten Island. We didn't need it and we didn't want it. As long as I was in office I would adamantly oppose any talk of it. I would fight every battle possible to ensure that it never became a reality in Staten Island. To this day it has never come to fruition. But I have learned as a seasoned politician that there is no such thing as a totally dead issue. That's why you always have to be ready to jump up and be heard as soon as you hear rumblings of a resurrection.

Regarding Senator John Marchi, I admired him before I was elected. Initially I hoped if he mentored me, I could be a highly effective assemblyman, despite being in the minority—especially since Marchi was the chairman of the Senate Finance Committee. The chairmanship of the finance committee carries with it a great deal of power. There are those who say the post ranks in influence right behind the Governor, the Senate majority leader, and the Speaker of the Assembly. You don't get much more powerful than that in New York politics. Marchi was there a long time and he was held in very high esteem.

Unfortunately, a great friendship was something that would always elude us. It would be one of my disappointments on my entry into politics. I assumed, being a fellow Republican that he would be working with me. I was sadly mistaken when I found that he started working with Betty Connelly, a Democrat, instead of working with me.

I remember Assembly Minority Leader, Perry Duryea speaking to us immediately after the election when the Republicans lost the majority in the assembly. Duryea said, "The good members on the Senate side will still work with the minority guys. The others will work with the Democrats." As he had predicted Senator Marchi began pandering to the Democrats and so ended my relationship with him.

In retrospect it may all relate to my initial election into the assembly against Marchi's longtime friend and colleague Lucio Russo. So, throughout my tenure in the legislature, we were on opposite sides supporting different Republican nominees. Although we saw eye to eye on many of the issues germane to Staten Island, the Republican leadership in Staten Island was another story.

In the long run from my standpoint I found that Marchi was a man unto himself. Although he was held in high regard because he served the longest legislative seat in the history of the country, over fifty years, and he was seen as a statesman by others, I kind of got the feeling that he was indeed a lonely man and was either intimidated by me, or outright disliked me. When I say lonely, a more accurate term might be 'solitary.' When Senator Marchi went over to the watering hole to grab a bite, you would see him more often than not partaking in a meal and eating all by himself. In fact he rarely ate out and nearly always ate by himself in his office unlike the rest of us. He wasn't a bad guy, but for me John Marchi was John Marchi: A man unto himself who really didn't do much to assist me in my political agenda. I remember at the time Senator Marchi was the only legislator in the 210-member legislature (150 assemblymen and 60 senators) who brought his spouse to the six month legislative session. We were all on our own.

By early September of 1975, Republican County Chairman Philip Fitzpatrick, a Marchi protégé, and I were at war again. From the minute that I won the primary election and abruptly ended Russo's political career, Fitzpatrick perceived me as a threat. Fitzpatrick knew that I had beaten the Republican machine against all odds by running a great grassroots campaign comprised of Molinari Republican loyalists. Most embarrassing to Fitzpatrick was the fact that I did it without the S.I. Republican Party endorsement. As a result, Fitzpatrick perceived me as the troublemaking outsider Republican who wouldn't back down and wanted to shake up the party. I was a threat to his reign and it was clear from the election results that I had an incredibly loyal following.

My goal was not to start out like that, but that is just how it worked out. I wanted to have a good working relationship with the old guard. Initially I never wanted to have anything to do with control of the Party. I never wanted to pick my person although I eventually did because I was forced to correct an off course Republican strategy. Since Fitzpatrick saw me as a threat to him I would never be given the luxury of being a peaceful assemblyman, simply addressing constituent and party issues in a calm manner. At the onset, that's all I wanted. I wanted to do work and be left alone because there were enough issues there to keep you going. But that was not in the cards that were dealt to me.

Looking back, I wonder how things might have been different if Fitzpatrick had originally endorsed me when I asked for the Republican Party endorsement. I was really surprised when he refused, especially since I had sponsored him for his admission to the New York State Bar in 1962. I expected him to offer some support, but that never happened. He felt his flank was exposed and he felt threatened by that. It was a terrible mistake on his part and it thrust me into the world of politics fighting from the get go. I'm sure in hindsight he wished that he had endorsed me.

I realized early on that in order to do my job, I couldn't do it with the leadership that was there. Fitzpatrick wouldn't take anybody in tow if they weren't subservient to him. He surrounded himself with a bunch of young inexperienced kids. He would scream at them and they would kiss his ass. He knew he wasn't going to be able to talk to me that way. No one wanted an all-out war but it wound up being one anyway, and it got pretty nasty at times.

George Hart, another attorney, was running against Fitzpatrick for the Staten Island Republican County Chairman spot. George

Hart had tried to work with Fitzpatrick over the course of the years but Fitzpatrick rebuffed him outright. That fueled the fire in George Hart's bid to run against Fitzpatrick.

Fitzpatrick thought that I made George Hart run and that he was my pawn. Fitzpatrick publically stated that George Hart was only a "Front Man" for Guy Molinari. Fitzpatrick fully believed it was me, not Hart, that was going after the party—even though it was Hart's name up for nomination.

The reason I supported Hart at the time was that I felt it was time for new leadership, since the Staten Island Republican Party seemed to be slipping down the mountain. Fitzpatrick was spending too much time on his own issues and not on running well thought out election campaigns. He should have been targeting patronage-rich political offices such as the Staten Island District Attorney's office. I knew if you organized a good campaign strategy and were aggressive you could win these elected positions. As such the Republican Party was blowing good opportunities to expand the power of the Republican Party in Staten Island.

Fitzpatrick proclaimed that the "insurgent's" campaign was being run out of my law office located at 88 New Dorp Plaza. I laughed. He was right in giving me due credit for the fundraising, mailings, and strategy of Hart's campaign. I supported Hart, and when I support someone I do so whole-heartedly. I gladly became the heart and soul of the campaign to accomplish what I believed was best for Staten Island and the Republican Party—in this case the removal of Fitzpatrick. I would not back down because I knew that the party needed new blood with fresh ideas.

On September 27th the Staten Island Republican County Committee held its bi-annual convention. The election meeting itself was a rambunctious night filled with catcalling from both sides from start to finish. There were hundreds of interested parties present from both sides and the process lasted almost five hours.

The committee members who I supported were considered the "insurgents." It is a title that I would wear proudly throughout my political career. As long as I have the fight in me, I will always stand up and be heard.

Calls of "Point of order," "Sit down and shut up," and of course various colorful expletives bellowed through the air from both sides. Senator Marchi supported Fitzpatrick and I supported George Hart. When I walked down the aisle to get the microphone to nominate Hart the Fitzpatrick supporters on both sides of the aisle were screaming, "You prick, you son-of-a-bitch."

It was a tough position to be in because even though I had recruited quite a few County Committee candidates, I knew we didn't have the votes. So, sadly, I was pretty sure we were going to lose. But the "insurgents" would be unwavering till the end.

George Hart himself could stoke up the fire. George was six-foot four, and a big six-four at that. Between him and myself, who was never one to walk away from a challenge, you had the ingredients of a good, interesting convention. The problem was we had mostly older people on our side. If a physical altercation broke out, we were probably not suited for the task. Back in the day you had to be prepared to fight. I can recall convention after convention or meeting after meeting where I would be the most vocal candidate or speaker in the audience. When I'd get up and speak at one of those forums the veins in my neck looked like they were ready to burst. The flip side is that due to my energy, enthusiasm, and commitment, the people were ready to follow me. As a result we were very successful.

As I predicted by the end of the night Fitzpatrick was reelected chairman of the Republican County Committee. The residual effects of that hard fought, animosity filled battle though would haunt Fitzpatrick because we, "the insurgents," made it clear that we would not back down. Fitzpatrick knew that he had a hard ass on his back named Guy V. Molinari.

As a result of the 'Great Insurgency,' albeit an unsuccessful one, Fitzpatrick had to offer an olive branch to save his political career. Shortly after the elections Fitzpatrick called George Hart and myself and asked for a meeting to see if we could work out an amicable working relationship. For several months we negotiated back and forth regarding the goals and expectations of both sides. There were rumors of the "insurgents" putting up a candidate to run against Marchi, so everyone within Fitzpatrick's circle was jumpy.

By January of 1976, we reached an accord to cease the internal disharmony so that each side would be satisfied with the outcome. A major component of the agreement was that when key committee positions opened up they would be filled with "insurgents." The agreement was for two years, until Fitzpatrick ran again. We all honored the agreement for the time period. During those two years I steadfastly built up my strength and the support that I had.

During this insurgency time period, I was also doing my best to become an effective freshman New York State Assembly member. I was addressing many important issues that directly affected my constituents. I wound up developing my leadership style as an assemblyman. I was being recognized as a skilled, dedicated, and hardworking assemblyman without borders who was able to negotiate exceptional outcomes for the residents of Staten Island. I would not ignore an important issue just because it did not fall within my assembly district's boundaries. If it was important to Staten Island, regardless of which part, it was important to me.

For example, I opposed the power plant in Travis, an area known as "cancer alley" because the area had the highest rate of deaths from lung cancer in the city. The Travis plant would use coal as its primary fuel, but would also be capable of burning up to 2,100 tons of garbage a day. This was three-and-a-half times the amount of garbage that Staten Island produced. I saw it as an impending disaster for Staten Island. Again I would scream the war cry that, "It was always fine with the other boroughs to increase the pollution in Staten Island."

I was very lucky that I was a lawyer and fully familiar with legal battle strategies in court. I was more than willing to resort to looking to the courts for a satisfactory legal remedy especially if I felt Staten Islanders were being taken advantage of.

I, along with other politicians, was able to successfully negotiate the killing of the auto use tax increase in the proposed bailout. I sued the TBTA regarding excessive tolls being collected on the Verrazano Bridge. Under the law, the Verrazano Bridge was not allowed to make a profit unlike all other surrounding bridges. Additionally, I fought the unreasonable bridge toll hikes that adversely effected Staten islanders. These would have negatively affected Staten islanders in their daily commute.

Of course the assembly was also working on the bail-out plan for the City due to the fiscal crisis. I fought the absolutely unbelievable audacious Con Edison, which requested additional exorbitant rate hikes when the average New Yorker was struggling to make ends meet. I helped construct legislation on bills for issues important to constituents such as proper notice when their property was on a street scheduled to be widened.

When you serve in the Assembly, you have to establish a home away from home. I became good friends with fellow Assemblyman Armand D'Amato, who was Alphonso's brother, and John Zagame. Initially I wondered if they were going to accept a guy from Staten Island and luckily they did when the group asked me to become a housemate. I accepted immediately. It is one of my happiest, pleasant and fun memories during my years in public service.

I would drive up to Albany on Sunday night, get settled and have a drink with the guys. We would talk about legislation that was coming up. If we didn't like a bill, we would organize to try to defeat it. We planned debates and stuff of that nature.

The time with my housemates, Armand D'Amato and John Zagame, in Colonie, an Albany suburb, was very relaxing because we all got along great and over time we all became great friends. I would always joke that "They do the cooking and I take out the garbage. It's the same job I have when I'm on Staten Island: my wife cooks and I take out the garbage."

Looking back, I had real fun sometimes being in the minority. I learned that New York City Republicans were part of what they called "F Troop" because they had a commonality. In the assembly it was always upstate versus downstate. The name developed due to the fact that as a Republican you're not going to get anything from the majority of the Assembly, so your group tends to become renegades.

For example, we were locked into the chamber one night and we were pissed off. We went to our leader, Perry Duryea, and said, "This is bullshit. They locked the door and we're locked in here. What are we, a bunch of kids?" He said, "What do you want me to do? Do you want to knock the door down?" We all said, "Yeah," so he said, "Okay, let's go."

I thought he was joking, but the doors were broken down. Of course this made the Albany papers when they wrote about a bunch of hooligans that were out of control.

When someone is not treating you fairly sometimes the only thing you can do is pursue guerilla tactics. As an example, when sitting in the assembly chambers at our desk we would sneak our microphone under our desk so that no one could see. At the appropriate time we would rub a comb over the microphone creating a terrible ear shattering sound that echoed through the assembly chambers as well as the legislative offices. It was extraordinarily annoying to say the least and fortunately we were never caught. Yes, if you treat me well I'll leave you alone, but if you don't, we go to war.

Many of the Democrats were pretty decent guys. I got along well with them and I think they respected me. Of course there were times that you had to fight the enemy and I have always relished a good fight. That's what politics is all about. When you're fighting your job is to learn how to win the fights. The first part of the strategy is to learn what to do and determine where the conflict is. Draw the battle line. Then analyze how you can win the fight. Generally, what I would do was organize. I would seek out experienced people who knew that issue better than the rest. I would follow the same method when I went to the United States Congress.

As you can see, I had a full plate and it would have been easy to ignore the political infighting but I was a Republican at heart and that was not part of my moral fiber. A technically part-time job became full-time. I reveled in the challenges and was very proud I was able to effectuate positive change for my district and Staten Island as a whole.

CHAPTER 12

Mid-70s Mayhem

By December 11th, 1975 the fiscal crisis' tentacles had wrapped themselves around the soul of Staten Island and the Staten Island Rapid Transit System (S.I.R.T). As a result, the employees were forced to go on strike. From the beginning I became an active participant in trying to resolve the strike for the benefit of Staten Islanders as a whole. I felt it was my responsibility as an elected official to do whatever was necessary to improve the lives of my constituents and neighbors.

I had a Democratic counterpart named Elizabeth "Betty" Connolly who was elected mid-year in 1973 for the 61st assembly district when Edward Amann left the assembly after he was appointed a Judge to the Court of Claims. Initially I had a wonderful relationship with Betty. During my freshman year, she a senior assemblywoman helped me learn the ropes and treated me like a colleague because we were both from Staten Island. Her assistance definitely made life a little easier for me.

Unfortunately, things began to sour quickly in my second year when Betty Connelly turned a blind eye to the strike issue. It wasn't until the media began extensively reporting my efforts to help resolve the strike that she became interested. Apparently the publicity generated concerning my efforts negatively affected her reputation and drew attention to her inaction on an important issue to Staten Islanders. To mitigate the damage, she had a private meeting with Democratic Governor Carey along with fellow Democrat Assemblyman Louis DeSalvio in January 1975 to discuss the S.I.R.T. strike, specifically excluding myself and Senator Marchi, their Republican counterparts.

I was livid that Republicans were not invited to this meeting to discuss an issue I was already aggressively trying to resolve. Unlike others, I did not shy away from a sticky situation. I confronted it head on and tried to resolve it. I felt that political lines should not be drawn, and that the resolution should be worked on as a bipartisan issue. In this situation, Governor Carey had publicly refused to become involved in the strike and yet now he was meeting with Democratic elected officials while deliberately excluding Republicans.

Regarding my overall relationship with Carey, we did not get along. Although he was a clever politician, he was a staunch and inflexible Democrat. As a result of his rigidity, I had neither a personal nor professional relationship with him. In retrospect, I clearly didn't need one. I stood on my own two feet as a proud Republican. My record of accomplishments as a minority freshman assemblyman was extraordinarily respectable due to my diligence and perseverance. To me, the very essence of a democracy is to have a legitimate two-party system, and Carey and I represented that dichotomy perfectly.

As a result of the lack of cooperation concerning the strike, I readily fed information that I had heard from reliable sources to the *Staten Island Advance*. When working with the media I always maintained the confidentially of my sources and that is why people trusted me. They knew the information given to me would be professionally and cautiously revealed in order to reach an appropriate resolution. With this approach I was able to ruffle the feathers of people who were trying to do things behind the back of my constituents. It rooted out some semblance of the truth.

One of the most important transit issues being rumored about was the fact that non-Staten Islanders wanted the S.I.R.T. system disbanded. They felt that we only needed a bus system and that they could supplement our mass transit with additional busses and eradicate the railway system completely. I was adamantly opposed to this. Our borough needed the S.I.R.T. just as much as Brooklyn or the Bronx needed their railways. It was another example of the other boroughs in the city robbing Staten Island to help themselves. Ultimately my efforts were effective after a long drawn out process in resolving the strike for the benefit of Staten Island and the S.I.R.T. employees.

During this time period in early February I was distressed to learn from my constituents that a pornography shop had opened up in Grant City, located at 2189 Hylan Boulevard. The residents from the area were outraged that a porno shop was allowed to open up near five schools and several churches that were located within a few blocks of the store. I was immediately inundated with letters and phone calls from residents, church officials and school personnel in the area who were adamantly opposed to this porno shop.

When I heard about the situation I immediately went down to take a look at what it was all about. The neighbors were going crazy. We walked into the shop and there was a wise guy in the place. He said, “Can I help you?” I said, “Yeah, you can help me get the boxes out, start packing and close up shop.”

He said, “We're not moving anyplace. We just moved in.”

I said, “Let me tell you something: the people outside are gonna burn this place down. The only question that remains is whether you're gonna be in this place when it burns down or not.” He said, “What are you talking about? Are you threatening me?”

I said, “I'm not threatening you, I'm just telling you what's gonna happen. But I do know of similar situations where people did get hurt. You guys are crazy opening up a shop like this with all the churches and schools here. You know that you're not going to be able to stay open."

He then said, "Who the fuck do you think you are?"

I said, "I'm Assemblyman Molinari and I don't want to be mean or nasty; I just want to make sure no one gets hurt."

He said, "I don't give a shit if you are an assemblyman, we have a constitutional right to stay open and that's what we are going to do."

We kept going back and forth and I finally left. His absolute disregard toward the concerns of my constituents left a bad taste in my mouth.

It was clear to me that this guy was not going to listen to reason. He was there to make a profit regardless of how offensive his business was to the surrounding community. So I got a few people together, concentrating on community residents, and we all went down to the porno shop with cameras in tow. No one knew that the cameras didn't have film. We took "blank" pictures of anybody that went into the store. Once someone started to walk in the store, we let them know that we had their picture and were going to publish it. With that knowledge they would run away.

The word went out quickly that community residents were armed with cameras and were taking pictures of customers entering the porno shop. No one wanted their picture published in the paper entering a porno shop; within three days, the store was profitless. Nobody would go in. The store was not making a nickel. At that point the porno store owner got the message, when it hit their pocket, so they counted their losses and left. That was a "Battle without a Shot."

My final straw with Elizabeth Connelly came in March of 1976 when she literally stole my property bill. During my first year, I spent many months extensively researching, consulting, and meticulously drafting a bill that would grant a tax break to property owners whose land would be directly affected by proposed street widening. It was a major piece of legislation; the proposed street widening projects affected almost half of all real estate parcels in Staten Island. I introduced this bill in 1975 and unfortunately the bill died on July 11th when the 1975 legislative session closed.

On Wednesday March 10th, 1976 Connelly introduced a bill under her name that was nearly identical to my bill that had died in session the prior year, with insignificant changes. When I saw her bill I turned around to the Republicans near me and said, "I just can't understand it. Betty and I had a great relationship last year, and now she's stealing my bills." One of the Republicans said. "You jerk; you have to understand that this is an election year. In an election year, people steal your bills, especially if it's a good bill." I was not going to let that happen.

So, when the one of my bills came to the floor I motioned to the speaker that I wished to address Mrs. Connolly and to debate her. I was granted the time and so I started my tirade in telling her that she plagiarized my bill and submitted it as her own. I had no problem confronting her to her face with this accusation since it was true. I wanted everyone in the audience to know that this was my bill and not hers. Let credit go where it belongs.

I said, "Mrs. Connolly, I'm a little puzzled by your prior bill regarding street widening." She said, "I'm sorry that you're puzzled by the bill."

I responded, "What puzzles me is that your bill is almost identical to my bill that I introduced last year but died in session. Betty, last year you were so generous with me but now with the plagiarizing of my bill I guess the rules of engagement are somewhat different now."

She said, "I never even saw your bill, I was asked to sponsor this bill by the Ways and Means Committee whose staff members drafted it." Again I reiterated how it was my bill but it was clear she didn't give a damn. So I said, "Well, I guess we're going to have a different relationship now, because this is *my bill* that you're going to get credit for!"

Some of the Republican scallywags in the galley were hooting and hollering yet Betty seemed bewildered over the exchanges that took place. She kind of waved off the apparent conflict by blaming it on the Ways and Means Committee people. As a new assemblyman I was dismayed to learn that this practice of stealing another party's bills was not uncommon. A key difference was that typically credit or acknowledgment would be given to the original drafter; such would not be the case in this scenario.

It was a total downer in a sense because it took a lot of time-consuming work to produce bills that would have a positive impact on your constituents. In this situation when I introduced bills as a Republican minority, they intentionally did not pass it. The Democratic majority under Connelly then reintroduced my bills with her name on it and it passed as a Democratic bill. The only word that came to mind was "thief." I find it despicable when the majority party gets credit for passing a significant bill they had no part in creating. Inherently unfair, yet this was the learning curve regarding partisan politics.

After this incident, our relationship completely changed. It became more partisan and it was too bad because I enjoyed the working relationship that we had during my first year. She worked hard and deserved a lot of credit for the things that she did. But, this is what they call learning the hard way. Thereafter we would butt heads on and off.

In April of 1976 as with the LNG tanks and the garbage dump, more bad news was headed for our Island. The state revealed their intent to convert the Arthur Kill Rehabilitation Center used for drug treatment into a medium security state prison. Again this was just another example of the state, specifically Carey, dumping on Staten Island.

On April 20th Senator Marchi held a hearing regarding the prison at the St. John's University Grymes Hill campus. I led the delegation of elected officials who came to oppose the prospective takeover. We were livid that we were never notified by the governor of his intent to place the prison on Staten Island. It boggled my mind that in a vast state such as New York with massive empty space, the governor would insert a prison in a congested residential area to house 950 state prison inmates. It made no sense. It was another travesty thrust upon our borough.

This was a battle that we would not win because of the times. On September 9, 1971, the Attica prison riots occurred when the prison inmate population seized control of the prison, taking forty-two staff hostage. When the riots were over, forty-three people were dead, ten being correctional officers or employees, and thirty-three being prison inmates. Overcrowding was a major cause of the riots. So the time was ripe to slip a jail facility in Staten Island due to public pressure from state residents and full support of the prison facilities statewide, their employees and most importantly Governor Carey. The doors of The Arthur Kill Correctional facility opened shortly thereafter.

A key victory came for me in my second year when I played a pivotal role in the fight against a bill to authorize the city to enter into contracts for private waste disposal plants. In the beginning of the proposed bill in 1975 there were no safeguards put in to protect the interests of Staten Islanders. Basically we would continue to be a major dumping ground for everyone else's garbage. We needed to have an absolute limitation on the amount of garbage that could be dumped on Staten Island in the future and that's what I ensured.

Approval of the Garbage Plant bill only came about after it was tailored to address the objections that I raised. The key issue was finally addressed when the bill was amended to limiting the amount of garbage that may be disposed of in any one borough to three times the volume of garbage that is actually generated within the borough.

At 5:30 in the morning of August 30th, 1976 after months of extensive negotiation, and five previous rejections, due to my efforts the bill was finally passed on the sixth time with an "absolute tonnage" limit on the amount of garbage that could be disposed of on Staten Island as well as "locking in" eighteen proposed plant sites of which only one would be on Staten Island. The purpose of these provisions was to prevent Staten Island from becoming a major dumping ground for the entire city as it had been in the past.

Passing something like the "Garbage Plant Bill" so early in my career was a major victory and established me as a mover and shaker in the world of Albany politics. I was steadfast in my drive to obtain positive benefits for my constituents and I identified myself as a skilled negotiator to my legislative colleagues. It was considered a monumental coup for a minority freshman.

In 1976 I was up for reelection for the first time and my main opponent was Mary Codd, who held a seat on the New York City Council at the time. She ran against me on the Democratic/Liberal line. Every campaign has a memorable moment and one of my favorites in this campaign was right before the November primary on October 27th when we were asked about the state power authority's proposed coal-burning power plant in Travis.

Mary Codd stated, "I would favor the plant if it did not add substantially to existing air pollution problems." It was a ridiculous statement for her to make and I found her position to be both mystifying and contradictory. My campaign for reelection was given a huge 11th hour boost when my immediate response, which hit the hearts of every Staten Islander was, "That is like saying I would favor the LNG tanks if I thought they would not blow up."

When I said this, I knew that every Staten Islander would never forget the 1973 LNG explosion. This blast will always have a lasting legacy on Staten Island. It ultimately brought to a halt the construction of two larger LNG tanks in the Rossville section of Staten Island. Experts predicted had the tanks been full it would have blown up over half of Staten Island as such half our island population would have been wiped out.

After months of campaigning, I felt comfortable that I would succeed in re-election, but I never let down my guard during the entire process. No matter how popular you may think you are you have to run an active, driven, and nonstop campaign. Once you get cocky that's when your world crumbles in politics.

The election night returns were a daunting experience. We were at the GOP headquarters' in Great Kills when the results started rolling in and it was not a good time for Republicans in the country or state wide. Carter replaced Ford and the Democrats continued to retain control of the New York State assembly.

At GOP headquarters it was a happy yet sad night for me. It was difficult to be happy when I looked at what happened to the members of the team who worked so hard to be elected. Ken Grossberger who ran for Congress, Joseph Maltese, and Robert Minogue who ran for the assembly against unbelievable odds and all made respectable showings but they ultimately lost to their Democratic rivals. Basically the only survivors of the Republican slaughter in Staten Island were Senator Marchi and me.

In May of 1977 I became totally frustrated by what I perceived as a typical Tammany Hall run-around regarding a bill that I had drafted. I was introducing the bill for the second year in a row. It would protect new property buyers from getting stuck with the unpaid city taxes of the seller in specific circumstances. I had submitted my bill on May 11th to the legislature print shop. On the same date, thirty other legislators had submitted their bills. As of May 25th mine was the only one of the batch that had not been sent to the Speaker's desk for debate.

Stanley Fink was the speaker at the time and Louis F. DeSalvio was the acting speaker. DeSalvio was appointed the acting speaker because he was the longest serving assemblyman. His district covered lower Manhattan and part of Staten Island. All tolled DeSalvio would serve for thirty-eight continuous years in the Assembly. Normally DeSalvio would conduct the proceedings and Stanley Fink would be seated in the majority member's chair that was on the floor itself. Stanley could take over the proceeding whenever he wanted since he was the actual speaker.

Every day when the legislature was in session, I'd get up and say, "Mr. Speaker!" DiSalvio would bellow "What, Molinari?"

"Mr. Speaker, the next bill is my bill. Can you tell me if it was ready for debate?" I knew it wasn't because it didn't have a number on it. "No, it's not ready for debate; it hasn't come back from the printer."

I thought to myself, "How come it didn't come back from the printer? I can't let him beat me at this thing." Everybody's amendment was being passed except mine. My bill was not coming back. Why? Because the city and the Democratic majority controlled assembly did not want it. I believed that the Democratic strategy was to delay the printing until the end of the session and then let the bill die on the final agenda. It all boiled down to me allowing them to kill the bill, or take action.

I then thought of a novel approach to how I might be able to beat the Democratic majority controlled assembly. There is always a way you just have to figure it out. You just have to outsmart them and outwork them. And that was what I set out to do in this situation. I decided that I would print the bill myself. This idea could actually expedite the legislative process in my situation.

I asked Perry Perez, my handball partner who was a printer as well, "Can you print a bill for me?"

"Sure. I can print anything."

So just like that I got the bill printed at my own expense. He printed 150 copies of my bill.

On May 31st I had the printed bill wrapped in a brown envelope and I brought it with me to the Assembly. What I had to do was to get Speaker Fink to bite. He was a tough son-of-a-bitch, so I offered the amendment, "Mr. Speaker, I'm offering this amendment." This is probably the seventh or eighth week that we were going through this exercise and Fink was on the floor in the rear talking to some guy who was on the aisle and he wasn't paying attention to me as I was carrying on and on.

Finally, Fink bellows, "Mr. Molinari, what are you doing? What's going on here? Are you having a friendly conversation here or are we doing legislative business? What is going on?"

I responded, "Well, Mr. Speaker, I checked: the day my bill was submitted, there were thirty-one bills submitted that day and thirty of them have been moved upon, some of them twice and others more. They were all acted on except one: my bill. Am I not entitled to the same courtesy as everybody else in this place? I'm not saying the obvious, but I'm demanding my bill be taken up."

Fink says, "Look. If we had the bill here today, we'd hand it out to the pages, they would give it out, and three days later it would be live in debate."

I said, "You don't mean that." Fink said, "What do you mean? Are you attacking my integrity?"

"Wait a second," I responded "Of course I am not attacking your integrity, Mr. Speaker," as I reached underneath my seat and retrieved the brown envelop, ripped it open, and called the pages, "Here Hand these out!"

The assembly members present at the time dropped their jaws and the place went bananas. They were shocked that I had the fore-thought and tenacity to come up with such a novel idea.

Meanwhile Fink was trying to figure out how he could stop me legislatively. In the ensuing uproar Fink argued that it was illegal to take-up a privately printed bill. It all came to a civil end when a big Irish assemblyman, John Flanagan, a Republican from Suffolk County, got up and said "Mr. Speaker. I've never seen anything like this before. Why don't you be a mensch and let him have his bill already?" He basically chided Fink by saying "Let's face it, Stanley, you've been had."

Fink acquiesced. He immediately came up to me afterwards and said, "If I give you my word that your bill will be the first one acted upon, will you pull back the bill? It violates the contract with the printers' union." Of course I agreed with his request since I had his personal assurance that it would be acted upon. This is when you have to know when to back down.

I said, "Absolutely, I'll take your word anytime."

I pulled the bill back and on Tuesday June 7th the bill was passed by a vote 110 to 16. Of course Fink was one of the 16 who voted against the bill. In the long run I was able to do something that actually expedited the legislative process.

In May of 1977, I supported and actively worked on the campaign of Anthony Giacobbe who was seeking the position of Council Member at Large, for the New York City Council. As in the past, Fitzpatrick did not support Giacobbe's campaign and threw the Republican Party's support to Ruggiero. Again I saw Fitzpatrick miss the mark in a key election campaign, and saw this as another betrayal.

Regarding the leadership under Fitzpatrick I vehemently and publically stated in a letter written to members of the Republican County Committee on May 3rd as follows:

> Republican enrollment is down, that the party has not been overly successful at the polls and that it has been suggested that the "Grand Old Party way is on the way out. I disagree with this I believe we can reverse the trend. We need to present our most qualified candidates to the voting public, candidates who can speak for us and make Republican common sense visible in our community.

My candidate Giacobbe was the right candidate and the most qualified.

Again I said to hell with Fitzpatrick's lack of endorsement: I would do it my way, because I believed it was the right way. With my letter, the battle lines were drawn again. I had honored my two-year agreement with Fitzpatrick, but now the insurgents were back and my goal was to have highly qualified individuals take control of the Republican County Committee to further the interests of Staten Islanders.

This time I would be successful because for two years I had generated a tremendous amount of support within the committee.

My time was not spent idly; I was working behind the scenes focused and determined so now would be the time to see if my strategy had paid off.

During this time period, while I was involved in Giacobbe's campaign, the summer of '77 was turning out to be an extremely distressing time for New York City. The "Son of Sam" killer had been terrorizing the city for over a year. By July he had killed six victims and maimed seven other with a .44 caliber handgun.

Then on July 14th, 1977, during an oppressive heat wave, the Great Black Out occurred and New York City went dark. Looting and vandalism were widespread, hitting thirty-one neighborhoods, including most poor neighborhoods in the city. Arson was rampant with some twenty-five fires still burning the next morning. Brooklyn and the Bronx were hit the hardest. When the lights came on and the dust settled, 550 police officers were injured in the mayhem, 4,500 looters were arrested, and property damage was estimated to be $300 million, which was an incredible sum at the time.

On August 10th, 1977, the "Son of Sam" killer was finally arrested and identified as David Berkowitz. The city's young population could finally breathe a sigh of relief and walk freely in the streets without fear of becoming a victim of the elusive killer who had terrorized the city.

Less than a week later the entire country mourned on August 16th when one of the most significant cultural icons of the twentieth century, "the King of Rock and Roll," or simply, "the King," Elvis Presley died of a drug overdose.

So the summer of '77 was filled with turmoil, and one of my jobs as an assemblyman at times would be to offer hope to my constituents. They needed to know that they were safe and that the future held promise. I did my best to instill that hope by continually concentrating on the Republican ideals that I believed in that would promote the safety and welfare of Staten Island. I would continue to fight to strengthen the Republican threshold on the Island and thereby improve the Island. So I continued to work tirelessly on securing supporters within the Republican Party as well as working aggressively on Giacobbe campaign.

By September 1977 things had heated up in the Staten Island GOP. On September 8th the primary election was held and fortunately my candidate won. We emerged as the Molinari–Giacobbe faction. I was completely dissatisfied with Fitzpatrick's running of the party and was determined to ensure that we would replace Fitzpatrick with new leadership. Under the election law, the Republican County Committee had to convene within 30 days of the primary to elect new leaders. The talk was that whoever the Molinari-Giacobbe faction supported as a candidate would be the front runner in the race for GOP Chairman of the party. Obviously I liked what I was hearing.

On September 15th Fitzpatrick smartly announced that he would not run for reelections. He cited the typical "business and personal reasons." The Chairmanship was now ripe for the picking. Everyone recognized that over the past two years I had generated tremendous support within the existing party, which was a complete reversal of fortune from two years ago when I did not have the numbers to win.

After an intensive vetting process by the Molinari-Giacobbe faction we convened an ad hoc steering committee of approximately 35 members at my law office to conduct a secret ballot regarding the two most highly qualified candidates, Arnold R. Thompson and Elliot Zemek. Arnold R Thompson, a member of my original insurgency in 1975, won the secret ballot.

On Wednesday October 5th at our convention at Susan Wagner High School I nominated Thompson for leader and my nomination was seconded by Giacobbe and then joined in by the party's three district leaders, Ralph Molinari, Robert E. Jackson, and Ferdinand C. Marchi and in a gesture of party unity, by Fitzpatrick himself. Thompson was then elected chairman of the Republican County Committee without opposition. The party was starting to come together and think outside the box.

Right after the election we had to relocate our storefront located at 1576 Richmond Road in Dongan Hills to a smaller office located at 77 Manor Road. We found out the organization was $3,000 in debt and behind on the rent. Thompson correctly surmised that we didn't need a political clubhouse but rather a place to strategize Republican ideas, fund raising and campaign events. Quickly the finances were in the black and moving in the right direction for resurrecting the Republican Party Committee on Staten Island.

CHAPTER 13

Upward Mobility in the Republican Political Hierarchy

ON JANUARY 10TH, 1978, REPUBLICAN ASSEMBLYMAN JAMES EMERY OF Genesee County, the Chairman of the Republican Assembly Campaign Committee asked me to take over his position. The goal of the Chairman of the Committee was to elect qualified Republicans to the assembly so that Republicans would become the majority. With a Republican majority assembly, we would be able to promote the principles of the Republican Party. I agreed, but it was on the condition that I would get a co-chair to handle upstate. Emery said no, so I told him to get someone else. I refused because I knew it would take me out of my home district too much and I would not be able to adequately represent my constituents.

Although I was very flattered, I found it crazy when after only one term in the assembly the Republican Party would come to me and ask me to take over all of the assembly races in New York State. It was especially unusual because I was a New York City boy and there were very few Republicans from "The City." I was shocked that they wouldn't offer the position to somebody with more terms under their belt or from the upstate area.

I was told that the reason why they wanted me was because everyone was impressed by my success in unseating Russo, a popular twenty-two year incumbent, in the primary. Subsequent to that I successfully ousted Fitzpatrick and replaced him with my Republican "Insurgents." They told me they needed someone to shake up the party regarding election strategy and apparently they saw me as that man.

Emery came back to me a week later and said they would give me the co-chair. I knew the co-chair was necessary because New York is such a big state. Emery came up with a great guy who had agreed to co-chair with me, Clarence Rappleyea. When they told me who it was I immediately agreed to do it. Like myself, Rappleyea, who we called Rap, went to Wagner College and he understood my role.

Rap came to me and said, "Look, I'll run interference for you. You know better than I do what the politics of this is all about: You run that show, and whenever you need me to do something, I'll do it." What more could I ask?

On Wednesday February 1st, 1978 Perry Duryea formally named me as the Co-Chairman of the Republican Campaign in the Assembly with Clarence Rappleyea as my co-chair. This appointment catapulted me into the state's Republican Party hierarchy. During my tenure as the co-chairman I created an excellent campaign model. I had watched my father closely when I was younger and observed how he ran his campaigns. In essence I had learned from his mistakes.

One of the major aspects of a successful campaign is the recruiting concept. Recruiting is something that should always be done but seldom is. It's the duty of the current leaders to come up with the best candidates; those who have the best chance of winning will continue your party's success. Rap and I gave lectures on recruiting, how to run campaigns, how to master television interviews, basically how to win. We shared our successful campaign tactics with fellow Republicans.

We had training camps in Albany for prospective promising Republican candidates that lasted about four days. We brought assembly members in who were experts in different areas and had them lecture the candidates. They instructed them on the current relevant political issues that were likely to come up. This way the candidates knew how to react when their campaign actually started. It was hands-on learning from experienced politicians and that information was invaluable to a new candidate. After the intensive training we would see a tremendous positive change in the candidate. We sent them out better informed with a greater chance of success. This is what needed to be done in order to resurrect the Republican Party in New York State. Additionally, we would check with the campaign directors all over the state to see if they needed any assistance. The first year we beat five incumbent Democrats with almost no money. So the results Duryea and Emery were looking for happened under my leadership.

We had about $750,000 allocated for the entire state. With our meager budget, I wanted to be sure that it was well spent. I remember there was a campaign manager in Queens who was a crusty old man. We would go and talk to the campaign managers and try to figure out the best way for them to spend the money we would give them. This guy didn't want that, he wanted the money without telling us how he would spend it. We told him that we didn't give out money directly. He said, "Go fuck yourselves." Enough said. We are on our way out and as we are leaving I said, "You know, you're making a mistake, with an attitude like that you're bound to lose." His client lost by a slim margin. Had he listened to us, he would have won. Instead of winning five seats we might have won six. That does make a big difference in politics. Sometime people are too thick to see that the end doesn't justify the means and this was one of those situations.

Unfortunately, when I left the assembly they did away with my model almost immediately because it was time consuming. There can be a lot of frustration when you work on a really good model and your successors don't take the time to follow through with it. To this day I believe that if they had pursued the model that I created, they might have eventually been able to get back in the majority.

Since early 1977 I was adamantly fighting against the proposed 6.1 million dollar Travis Power Plant that would generate 700,000 kilowatts of power in the confines of the Arthur Kill and Fresh Kills Creek. Many times I felt like I was all alone in my efforts but I continually plugged along for the benefit of Staten Islanders. The hearings would occupy a lot of time, but it was time well spent. Like the lottery, you have to be in it to win it.

I had agreed to coordinate the opposition since I knew this would be a complete ecological and health disaster for every Staten Island resident. I knew that in order to win I would have to research, and obtain expert testimony from professional environmentalists and engineers concerning the environmental and health impacts on the Staten Island community. I knew that the average citizen complaining about "dirty air" would have limited value. You have to do it right to win. You can't take a shortcut or just pray. If you prepare properly you have a good chance of winning.

By February of 1978 it was clear that Governor Carey was hell bent on putting a power plant on Staten Island. I vowed to myself that I would fight this till I had nothing left in me. I would be a bulldog. His staff argued the plant would have no adverse health impact whatsoever wherever it was built. The environmentalist research did not agree. A study conducted by the National Academy of Sciences in 1975 concluded that there definitely would be adverse effects from the proposed power plant, such as extensive air pollution, premature deaths, and respiratory diseases affecting adults and children alike. I found it repulsive. The study also found that these effects would be dramatically reduced if they placed the plant in a less populated area, such as upstate New York.

In April of that year, I was livid when Harold Fisher, the chairman of the MTA and Gov. Carey's former campaign manager asked for a formal criminal investigation to be conducted by District Attorney Thomas Sullivan regarding my efforts to settle another S.I.R.T. strike that had occurred spontaneously on Monday April 3rd. He stated that I, as a "public official," conspired with illegal picketers to violate a lawful court injunction enacted in February of 1976 when Brooklyn Supreme Court Judge Thomas Jones issued a permanent injunction banning strikes by S.I.R.T. employees.

I readily and proudly acknowledged that I did go to the St. George Ferry terminal on Monday April 3rd at 1:30 in the morning when I was informed that the workers were going on strike and there might be some issues. I wanted to calm things down and get the men to agree to go back to work. I felt it was my duty as a public official to help resolve the situation if at all possible.

I did have sympathy for the workers, because I believed and it ultimately came to pass that the S.I.R.T. workers deserved parity with their fellow Transit Authority employees. They both did the same work but the Staten Island guys were paid significantly less. Both the Transit Authority and the S.I.R.T. were members of the Metropolitan Transportation Authority.

I publicly stated that, "If my presence at St. George in trying to calm down the workers is construed by Mr. Fisher as being involved in picket line activity, then I think the man is sick and should quit." I was never one to mince words and of course I charged him with malfeasance in office. One thing about politics, and it continues to this day, you will always have someone looking to take you down.

Within a week I wrote my own letter to D.A. Sullivan asking him to clear my name and also to investigate if the MTA did all it could to avert a strike. Sullivan smartly refused to enter the controversy on behalf of the MTA or myself. Clearly it wasn't a criminal matter and Fischer should never have followed that path.

My fellow legislative colleagues were shocked at Fishers' actions as well, so fellow Republican Dominic DiCarlo made a formal request by "Unanimous Statement of Consent," which is a motion that required informal clearance from the other members present on the floor of the Assembly. That day he asked Gov. Carey to investigate Fischer for misconduct. If this could happen to me in exercising my duties it could happen to any other assemblyperson. In other words, it was just plain "wrong."

In sum I was really the only elected official to take a personal interest in the tangled labor situation that constantly threatened to disrupt service on the S.I.R.T. line. As a result, I was maligned and condemned by those in power but I generated tremendous respect from the men in the trenches that were serving our island.

Regarding the garbage dump, Ed Koch, the newly elected Mayor, was a fanatical supporter of the Staten Island Dump. It would be one of the key areas that I would be adamantly opposed to him during the course of our relationship. I personally liked Koch a lot. Koch was a guy that you could talk to. He was somewhat opinionated, yet most politicians are, including myself. Also he wasn't shy about stating his positions. Again, similar to myself.

In May I blasted Koch over his decision to ship garbage from the Bronx to Staten Island when Koch decided to keep the Ferry Point landfill in the Bronx closed. Staten Island would be getting over 50% of the entire city's garbage. These actions drove me nuts.

During this time period I was co-founder of United Activities Unlimited. It became a highly praised volunteer organization which provided educational, recreational, counseling and social programs for children and young adults. I started this program as the result of a community initiative by concerned citizens who responded to the challenge of providing positive alternatives to young people in the wake of the financial crisis of New York City that forced the closing of many of the Board of Education afternoon and evening centers. By 1978 the program received the highest evaluation of any youth program in New York City. The program also produced a dramatic decrease in vandalism in the participating schools and surrounding communities.

In August, I jumped at the opportunity to ridicule Harold Fischer, my nemesis, when he appointed Francis Gabreski, an outstanding World War II fighter pilot, to head the Long Island Rail Road. Gabreski, although a phenomenal and well respected pilot, had absolutely no rail road experience.

Subsequently, I jokingly requested a Kamikaze pilot to run the Staten Island buses since the bus drivers felt they were on a suicide mission every time they drove a bus due to unsafe conditions the MTA repeatedly failed to address. The MTA concentrated their money and efforts on the L.I.R.R. and ignored Staten Island. My statements generated the attention I needed in order to refocus the MTA on Staten Island and address the woeful conditions of the Staten Island bus fleet.

On Tuesday September 12th, 1978 I won a primary election by a margin of 4 to 1 against my challenger, Frank Wall. Wall was a Fitzpatrick protégé and the results of the election were seen as a repudiation of Fitzpatrick. He was basically through in the Republican Party. Overall we did extraordinary well in the races and it marked the first time the GOP organization committee candidates fared well in a primary election. I remember saying, "I don't think the Republican Party has been stronger on Staten Island. Our efforts are definitely paying off."

By this time Gov. Carey had publically stated that the Travis Power Plant would not be built on Staten Island. I did not believe any of them. I saw this as an election year trick and if Gov. Carey was successful on his reelection he would resurrect the Travis Power plant issue on Staten Island. He would blame it on the economy, and renege on his word as he had done many times in the past. In order to address the issue head on I needed court intervention to secure a definitive promise. A novel approach but something a lawyer was good at manipulating. So, on October 18th I petitioned the court to move up the Travis Power Plant hearing prior to the elections scheduled for November 7th.

By the time November elections were coming up I was known as the Republican Activist on Staten Island. People considered me an ombudsman of Staten Island. They knew that I had assumed the role of the watchdog and I would not allow non-Staten islanders to dump their shit on my borough. On November 7th I was reelected for my third time by a two to one margin. That election was my most impressive victory so far.

On December 16th as a show of bipartisanship, James Emery and I met with Mayor Koch at his invitation to discuss the city's problems and priorities in the upcoming session. At the time Emery informed Koch that I would be appointed the ranking Republican on the Assembly Real Property Taxation Committee since I was so knowledgeable in real estate issues. Koch, being the "Social Mayor," also informed us that he would be inviting the entire Republican assembly delegation on February 22nd, 1979 for a tour of the city and to discuss the city's issues. Koch was extending a hand in order to help his constituents and that is why I liked him.

There was a bill that I carried during this time period and it concerned the garbage dump. This was a major piece of legislation. I had an agreement with the Democrats that they would not put up my bill if I was outside the chambers.

One evening we were working late and I was talking to Peter Harrigan, a smart young reporter for the *Staten Island Advance* in the rear of the chamber. Peter was looking toward the chamber floor and I was facing outwards. Peter suddenly says, "Hey, isn't that your bill they're talking about now?" I turned around and listened, and sure enough when my back was turned they pulled the bill. I was furious. The Democrats reneged on the agreement.

I ran back in and grabbed a microphone and screamed for attention. I yelled, "You guys have violated ethics, broke your word, and dishonored yourselves by bringing this up behind my back." Eventually, after reaming them all out good and proper, I got back to the bill.

Previously I had gotten verbal commitments from six Democrats that they would support my bill. During a session with a full galley you would typically need 76 votes to pass a bill that you sponsored. The vast majority of votes taken in the state legislature at that time were done via a "fast roll call" which simply required those opposed to a bill to raise their hands. In this situation the initial vote was against my bill.

There was a technicality called a "slow roll call." On a slow roll call, every single vote is recorded verbally. A slow roll call is rarely used but since I was blindsided I called for a slow roll call.

Now of course my immediate concern was whether those six Democrats would keep their word and vote with me. A couple of them were in leadership positions so I thought it doubtful that I could hold all six. The vote finally started and the fate of my bill would be determined shortly. Any time a Democrat voted with me, the Democrat leadership would run over to that person and try to get them to change their vote. I was worried. I only had six promises and I needed every one of them to be successful.

I looked at George Miller, a Democrat from Harlem, who was part of the Black Caucus, and my heart leaped when he cast his vote for my bill. There were a couple of the six who I would have bet a million dollars that they wouldn't keep their promise but they did. As the clerk tallied the votes, I sat in hushed silence praying. It then became clear that my bill had passed. I won by one vote. It was a tremendous achievement. God bless each and every one of those six Democrats who honored their commitment to me. I won even though I was in the Republican minority. This was a big victory for me as an assemblyman. Everyone respected me for beating the odds.

In the 70s, newspapers were a pivotal part of a successful campaign and a resource to let your constituents know what you were doing for them. We did not have Twitter, Facebook, cell phones, or the internet. Television, papers, and radio spread the news. I have had an on and off relationship with the most important local newspaper in Staten Island, the *Staten Island Advance* for the majority of my political career, particularly when Les Trautmann was the editor. Fortunately, in the beginning of my political career that relationship was on.

After the vote I drove back home to Staten Island. The first thing I did when I got home was to drive down to the local newsstand to buy the *Advance*. At the time they had editions where you could buy the early edition of the Sunday paper on Saturday night. This was going to be my first big legislative bill victory. My heart dropped when I saw the headline, "MOLINARI LOSES." I said, "Oh, My God, they got it wrong."

I ran home, called the *Advance* and remember saying, "There's a mistake on the front page. You guys got it wrong!" They got Peter Harrigan who was a great reporter and he was new like I was. He wasn't totally familiar with the legislative process.

When I spoke to Peter he said, "I was there. I was in the chamber with you and you lost." I said, "Yeah that's the way it looked initially but I won on a slow roll call." Peter checked, and sure enough, I was right. So, Peter had to correct the story for the Sunday morning edition. I recall the Sunday Final edition was put out with "MOLINARI WINS."

It reminded me of the headline on the front page of the November 3rd, 1948 *Chicago Tribune* when they famously, and incorrectly, reported: "DEWEY DEFEATS TRUMAN."

CHAPTER 14

"Let's Play Hardball"

After four years as a seasoned veteran of the legislature, it was easier to get things accomplished, or at least figure out a good strategy on how to come out ahead instead of behind. I had surrounded myself with extraordinarily talented and dedicated staff members. Lorraine Witzak was my executive secretary and she ran the office flawlessly. My cousin, Ralph Molinari was an administrative assistant and counsel. It irked many Republicans when I hired Democrats such as Robert Dizard Jr. as my Chief of Staff and Harold J. Otterbeck, my law partner at the time, as my administrative aide on Staten Island. I responded to the negative comments by adamantly stating that "I am happy with my choices and I just don't want to appoint people because they are loyal party members. I based their hiring on their unique qualifications."

I wanted smart, bold individuals who were able to think outside of the box. That was the only way that I would continue to be successful in accomplishing things in the minority. As a testament to my choices, Robert Dizard would become the Deputy Librarian of

Congress.

I was settled into a really good routine at the time and was enjoying myself. In 1976 my daughter Susan graduated from St. Joseph Hill Academy in Staten Island and began her freshman year at the University of Albany. I was able to see her frequently and I really enjoyed the fact that I was so close to her. We would go for morning runs and out for dinners and, of course, if she was short on cash as many college students are, Daddy was right there. As an added benefit, Susan was also getting a good introduction to politics at the time as well. She made me proud.

In the late 70s, bold colors, wide ties, and polyester suits were the style. It was a style which could be considered the complete opposite of conservativism. At the time we thought we looked sharp. Looking back at the pictures the style brings out a robust chuckle. Typically, I would be seen puffing a cigar during my leisure time. It was a habit I enjoyed immensely at the time, a drink and a cigar. Today many people consider a cigar smoker persona non grata unless they are in a cigar bar.

As a legislator you can be wined and dined every night you are in Albany. The bars near the capitol were always crowded with legislators and their staff until the wee hours of the morning. As for myself I preferred to engage in competitive sports in my leisure time.

In spite of the awful car accident in 1968 I was able to rehabilitate myself back into a formidable athlete. I worked hard to overcome the pain and for many years I was successful with my rigorous exercise regimen. When I would go home to Staten Island I would play handball and volleyball at my club the HAVOL.

I was an avid tennis player while in Albany. My doubles partner was my friend Lewis Yevoli, a Democrat from Nassau County. I reveled in a good game. I particularly loved playing against my Democratic colleagues. They may have been able to beat me on the assembly floor since they were in the majority, but on the courts I ruled. It was my chance to win. I loved to play against the Chairman of the Ways and Means Committee Arthur J. Kremer, another

Democrat from Nassau. Kremer blocked any of the bills that I, or other GOP assemblymen, put forth from getting out of committee. Many times during these aggressive matches I would chide Kremer about blocking my bills and immediately the match would get brutally fun. An athletic victory would have to satisfy my hunger for winning. So I played tennis hard and only to win.

Regarding Staten Island issues, I continued to push bills through the legislature. I really enjoyed reading the papers when I pushed through many bills and they would refer to the day as "Staten Island Day." I wanted relief for landowners whose property rested partially on areas mapped for future street widening. Transportation issues from the Ferry to the S.I.R.T continuously emerged. Pollution, garbage, and LNG were never far out of sight.

In June I blasted Betty Connelly on the assembly floor regarding a bill restricting Atlantic Menhaden fishing also known as bunker fishing. It is the predominant bait fish in Staten Island waters. Betty again copied my bill and was again going to get credit for it. Even though it "happened all the time," I would still voice my displeasure about a practice that was inherently wrong. It was a violation of the assembly rules. This was another example of the minority GOP bills dying and then being reintroduced by a majority Democrat who would get the credit.

When the legislative session was ending I was slapped in the face again when my transit bill asking for parity for the S.I.R.T. employees with their counterparts on the L.I.R.R. and TA was not acted on. My displeasure would not go without notice. I was able to garner support from eighteen colleagues and we debated legislation sought by Mayor Koch regarding the creation of twenty resource recovery sites in the five boroughs. Speaker Stanley Fink withdrew the legislation since it was clear that a prolonged filibuster was going to block all other bills at that time and the session would end on a bad note. Koch was livid. I had warned him that it would be costly if he refused to support the S.I.R.T. employees and I followed through with my threat. If anything, I was always a man of my word. If they played hardball with me I was more than willing to play hardball with the city.

On October 10th I found out that industrial wastes were discovered in storage tanks and at least one thousand fifty-five-gallon barrels in the Travis section of Staten Island. Apparently the poisonous and explosive chemicals were indiscriminately dumped onto wetlands. Several arrests were made, but the residents were terrified. No one knew the long term health effects of such illegal dumping.

On November 11th, 1979 I announced that I would run as a national convention delegate committed to former California Governor Ronald Reagan. I started putting together a full slate to represent the 17th Congressional District, made up of Staten Island and Manhattan for the GOP convention to be held the next summer in Detroit, Michigan. From the start I said the slate would be an all Staten Island ticket since all Republicans basically came from Staten Island in the district and that Manhattan was blatantly Democratic.

The state GOP under Dr. Bernard Kilbourn had adopted a strategy of neutrality in the upcoming elections but for me it did not make sense. I was a local politician and I had to follow my instinct of what I thought was best for Staten Island. I believed that Reagan had the most professional and promising presidential campaign of all the candidates at the time I wanted to be on his bandwagon. I flatly told everyone I was a local legislator and my major concern was what would work best for Staten Island. Fortunately, I was able to convince everyone else to join me as well and we got a full ticket together of Staten Islanders in support of Ronald Reagan.

Within two days I was with Conservative County Chairman James Molinaro at the Hilton Hotel in Manhattan where Reagan formally announced his candidacy for President of the United States of America. It was an exciting moment and it was my formal introduction to presidential election politics.

The year ended with a bang when I appeared at the resumed Travis Power Plant hearings at the World Trade Center in Manhattan on November 27th. Every freaking day, I was the only politician from

Staten Island there in opposition to the Power Plant. Anybody could go, any elected official, but nobody showed up. Of course that placed greater pressure on my shoulders because I was the only one, other than the city, that was fighting the project.

The hearings themselves were well attended by Staten Island residents, especially in light of the recent chemical dumping in the Travis area. Many of the Staten Islanders wore black bands around their heads and cards around their necks that read, "We are the **UNGRATEFUL** dead of Staten Island." It was an impressive sight.

Judge William C. Levy conducted the hearing. As soon as the proceeding started the audience began booing, jeering and chanting their displeasure with the proposal. The judge was chided for not having a microphone so that the attendees could appropriately hear the proceeding. When I rose to address the judge, the room went ballistic and the crowd gave me a standing ovation as they yelled, "Tell the judge like it is. Tell him all about the pollution on Staten Island."

Although I was embarrassed, internally I was proud of my constituents. They believed in me as their leader in the fight to get rid of the Plant proposal. My message had been heard.

I started to tell the judge how his rulings were biased against my community and that's when Judge Levy ordered me to sit down, saying, "You, Mr. Molinari, are out of order." As I continued to speak my voice was drowned out by the crowd as they began to chant, "Stop PASNY or die with Dyson." John Dyson was Chairman of the Power Authority State of New York (hereinafter "PASNY").

Judge Levy then left the room abruptly as he called for a recess. When he came back he stated to me, "You will cooperate so that the proceedings can proceed." and then he said, as if he was talking to a little child, "I hope you can behave yourself."

Although the city was opposed to the project, it was a kind of lip-service type of opposition, and essentially they were doing a terrible job. Their lawyers didn't know what they were doing. One of the city's expert witnesses was rejected as a qualified expert. That could've been the end of our ability to stop the project. Without having an expert witness involving sewers, we could not win.

I quickly started asking the city to find an expert. There was one guy who worked in the sewer department who I thought would qualify. So on this fateful day I tried to resurrect a sewer expert for the city because it was a critical element of defense. I called him as a witness and I asked him questions to assert his qualifications.

I was shocked when the judge interrupted me and said, "Alright, Mr. Molinari. You've been up on your feet long enough, I've heard enough. I want you to sit down and stop your questioning."

I tried to convince the judge to allow me to proceed by saying, "Your Honor, I don't understand what you're saying to me. I'm here trying to protect my community and I view this power plant as a very serious threat. You know, we're both lawyers, and you know what it is to try to qualify an expert witness and this is key to the whole case."

He said, "Mr. Molinari, you're not listening to me. I told you time and again shut up and sit down I don't want to hear anymore."

I said, "Your Honor, I'm trying to bring up a point that is critical to this matter—whether the permits are going to be issued or not, and I demand the opportunity to represent my people, and I'm trying to create a record here for a possible appeal. This issue goes to the heart of the case."

Levy said, "Well, I'm telling you for the last time: shut up and sit down."

I thought I'd lose this case if that happens, so I folded my arms, looked at Judge Levy eyeball to eyeball and said, "*Make me.*"

Judge Levy said, "What did you say?"

At this point I lost my temper somewhat and said obviously angry, "You heard me, *make me* sit down. I'm here fighting for my community, and I'm not going to sit down just because you're telling me to sit down."

The judge was completely taken aback and so he slammed the gavel down and yelled, "We're in recess," and then mumbled "We'll reconvene in fifteen minutes."

During the recess some of the people in the room were telling me Levy was going to find me in contempt of court. I said, "Well I guess he's going to have to carry me out. I'm not backing down."

After fifteen minutes Judge Levy comes back from his chambers and enters the court room and calmly says, "Mr. Molinari, you may continue." I don't know who he called to this day, but whomever he called said that he had better listen. Obviously he thought it would not be a good idea to hold me in contempt of court.

The following day when I looked at the *Advance* to see how they reported my interaction with Judge Levy the paper showed a picture of the Assemblywoman Betty Connelly. I called up the *Advance* and said, "Hey, what's going on here? Betty Connelly wasn't even there." The woman who wrote the story wasn't in the office. She called me up later and said that Connelly was there, but she was there during the recess for lunch. That really irked me and I thought, "Great. Connelly shows up for lunch and gets her picture in the paper? I have a fight with a judge and get nothing?" I was annoyed because as a politician I did want my constituents to know that I was fighting for them.

I plodded along representing my district in the Assembly. In March I was able to secure a fantastic expert witness, Dr. Joseph L. Melnick, the Dean of Graduate Science at Baylor College of Medicine in Houston to testify at the Travis Power Plant hearing. He had impeccable credentials and was internationally known. He was just what Staten Island needed to defend their position. I was proud that I was able to produce him as our expert witness. It was the true turning point for the Travis Power Plant odyssey: His testimony would ultimately turn out to be devastating to the position of both Governor Carey and the Power Authority. My expert testified that up to 1.3 million people over a wide geographic area would inhale virus-coated droplets from the Travis Power Plant's 400-foot cooling tower.

That was all I needed. Of course the other side was not going to buckle easily but when the public heard my experts' testimony they were livid and scared. I particularly loved it when Melnick said that the cooling tower operation would be equivalent to, "A test system of biological warfare." I considered him to be our ace in the hole.

So that was a fight, and we eventually won and ultimately stopped that bloody plant from being built. The power authority tried to jam it down Staten Island's throat but we spit it right back at them. That was my first serious legal battle. It went on for a period of time and kind of trained me for what was to follow. During my tenure it was one serious problem after another and I must admit that as difficult as it was, it's also kind of fun to be David fighting Goliath. You know, the little guy fighting the establishment.

CHAPTER 15

1980 Congressional Run

1980 STARTED OFF WITH A BANG WHEN THE TRAVIS Power Plant hearings resumed at the Twin Towers on January 8th before Judge Levy. The hearings would go on for months. The most memorable event for me was my show down with the Judge.

At about the same time, Assembly Minority Leader, James Emery named me to the Power Plant Task Force in the Assembly. The purpose of the Task Force was to develop legislation to correct serious deficiencies in the existing state power plant laws. In 1980 the laws were definitely tipped in favor of the authority and against the legitimate concerns of the communities such as Staten Island, which were essentially forced to accept PASNY's proposed plants.

By February the Island was filled with rumors that Congressman John Murphy was involved in "The Biggest Criminal Investigation since Watergate." It concerned a bribery probe and became known worldwide as ABSCAM. ABSCAM was a fabricated justice department "sting" operation in which agents of the FBI posed as Arab business men offering bribes to various public officials. As a result of Murphy's implication in the sting operation there was a long line of Democrats frothing at the mouth waiting to run against him. As always, the sweet smell of a scandal opened up prospects for people to run with a fair chance of winning against an incumbent. Albany itself was abuzz with the disastrous impact the alleged corruption scandal had on the reputations of politicians.

In late March rumors started that I was going to throw my hat into the ring running against Murphy. My response at the time was that I had no interest in it. But the political pressure from top Republican leaders was starting. One of the key reasons I did not want to run was that if I won, I would remain a minority member of Congress just as I have been a minority member of the Assembly. Obviously your goals are much harder to attain when you are in the minority. I kept on asking myself if I could make it work. If the answer was "yes" then I should do it. If the answer was "no" then I shouldn't.

At the same time, I was spearheading the support of New York politicians for Ronald Reagan's Presidential bid. I knew that a Republican President would definitely improve the lives of Staten Island's residents. The primary for Reagan delegates resulted in a landslide on Staten Island. Overall the national enthusiasm for Reagan was swooping throughout the country. The country was ready for a new leader. I was thrilled to be a delegate for a national campaign. Staten Island was totally behind Ronald Reagan and I hoped that when Reagan was elected he would return the favor.

In early April I received a call from Dr. Bernard Kilbourn, who was the Republican State Chairman headquartered in Albany. It was a strange call because normally if the State Chairman asked you to meet with him, you'd go to his office. When he called he said, "I want to see you. I'll come to your office."

When Kilbourn walked into my office he had a big book under his arm. He told me it was a poll. He said, "I'd like to talk to you about running for Congress." I said, "I'm sorry, Bernie, it's not my cup of tea."

Bernie said, "Well, we did a poll and the poll shows that everybody else would lose badly, but you have the best chance at beating Murphy." I reiterated, "No, I'm not going to stay in Albany forever. I'm going to leave Albany soon and will be back to my law practice. I thoroughly enjoyed my practice and I made money. There is no money in politics for me. So why would I want to continue this business?" my response was firm.

When Kilbourn walked out he intentionally left the book on my desk. I went over, picked it up, and it was the poll. The poll found that I was the only one out of several names that the State Republican Party polled who could win. I was shocked and flattered at the same time. I guess my message was being heard loud and clear by the people. The poll was conducted by Arthur J. Finkelstein and Associates on March 25th, 1980 for the Republican Congressional Campaign Committee at a cost of $8,000 and was referred to as the "Finkelstein Poll." At the time I never had a desire to be a congressman. If anything, my first choice would have been to succeed State Senator John Marchi.

Regarding my thoughts on Murphy, in 1970 I had actually campaigned for him even though he was a Democrat. I respected Murphy during his early years as a congressman. He stood out as a consummate politician, an extraordinarily good-looking guy, and very articulate. He was a graduate of West Point with a distinguished military record. In addition, he was a Korean War hero who received the Distinguished Service Cross and the Bronze Star. He was known as a "Hero of West Point." They called him "Blackjack Murphy" because his beard was so heavy. Under the right circumstance he might have been able to run for President of the United States

I remember in 1970 it looked like Murphy would not be reelected. In 1966 and 1968 Murphy lost Staten Island but overwhelmingly won Manhattan which was and is heavily Democratic. Unfortunately for Murphy, in 1970, reapportionment took place and Manhattan was going to be replaced with Brooklyn. Historically

Brooklyn was an area where Murphy would lose. So it was clear at that time he was headed for defeat.

Some of my clients at the time had received very good treatment from his office and I thought that Murphy was a good congressman. Even though I was a Republican, I liked the man so I worked aggressively on his 1970 campaign. I believed it was the right thing to do. I headed up an outfit called "The Republicans for Murphy." Murphy provided ample funds for us to set up a headquarters for him. As predicted he lost Brooklyn, but he had a decisive win in Staten Island. Our work had ensured that Staten Island voters offset the losses in Brooklyn. As a result, he was reelected to Congress. "The Republicans for Murphy" basically saved the day for him.

In fact, Murphy was so grateful for my support that in 1971 I received a phone call from his office saying, "The Congressman would like to invite you as his guest tomorrow. He is going to spend the day in Manhattan with the Speaker of the House as well as a number of others. Afterwards you will be his guest at the Joe Frazier and Muhammad Ali fight at Madison Square Garden." I was thrilled with the invitation, especially since tickets for the fight were impossible to get.

Needless to say, it was an incredibly interesting day. We went to an exclusive private restaurant for lunch and I remember one of the attendees saying, "Can we speak confidentially here?" They were looking at me because they didn't know who I was. Murphy said, "Of course, he's okay. You don't have to worry about him, everything will be kept confidential." Afterwards we all went to the fight. We were seated in about the sixth or seventh row, arguably some of the best seats in the house.

Personally, I didn't like Mohammed Ali, or Cassius Clay, as he was known back then. In 1967, three years after winning the heavyweight title, Ali refused to be conscripted into the U.S. military, citing his religious beliefs and opposition to American involvement in the Vietnam War. As a result of his refusal, he was stripped of his title. I felt that he was getting the best of everything our country had to offer and yet he did not want to serve our country. That never sat well with me, and a lot of other people. Everyone with us on fight night was rooting for his defeat. People wanted to see Ali get his ass beaten. But, we all recognized that he was a great fighter and excelled in the sport of boxing.

It was an extraordinary fight. Being so close to the ring I was shocked at the sounds made as the fighters hit each other's bodies; kind of like bombs going off. I'm looking at this and saying to myself, "These guys are going to suffer some permanent physical damage. You can't take that kind of punishment without getting hurt somehow." Subsequently, I was not surprised to find that this fight was referred to as the "Fight of the Century." They were both warriors. We were all thrilled when Frazier was declared the victor and retained the title with a unanimous decision. Frazier dealt Ali his first professional loss.

So, politically and personally, it would be a very difficult decision for me to decide to jump into the ring with Murphy. Yet the Republican vetting process was not over. The Republican hierarchy still firmly believed based on the poll that I could pull an upset in a heavily Democratic district especially if there was a three-way race in November. They asked me to go to Washington and meet the Republicans from New York State. Within this group were two people that I served with in the Assembly: Representative Gary Lee of Ithaca and Gerald Solomon of Glenn Falls. Before I made a final decision, I had breakfast with the New York guys, and they explained how the political system worked in Washington.

The two Congressmen wanted to convince me that I could be "effective" in Congress and get things done for Staten Island. The whole prospect was becoming interesting if not intriguing. I started to think, "Well, I've already decided that I'm not going to stay in the assembly for my entire life. Maybe it was a good time to move into the national theater." The only question was would I be able to do things at the congressional level for Staten Island that I couldn't get accomplished in Albany? Could I make it work for the benefit of Staten Island?

At the same time, hungry Republican candidates started formally announcing that they were seeking Murphy's congressional seat. The most infamous in my book was Louis Wien, a businessman who ran an unsuccessful campaign for mayor in 1977. He would be a pain in my ass for many years. During this campaign he was continually bumped by the board of elections for not having the appropriate numbers of petition signatures. Subsequently he would hurl ridiculous allegations in order to smear my name, none of which would have a factual basis. As a result, I had to expend an inordinate amount of time and money responding to his useless allegations. Additionally, he filed a formal complaint against me regarding an absurd conflict of interest with the New York State Assembly which they had to investigate. All of which was a waste of time and tax-payer's money. Wien was a Harold Stassen-like character, always running for public office but never having the following to make a serious race. He became an irritant to the legitimate contenders such as myself.

Campaigns are always difficult since it is a 24/7 proposition from the minute you ultimately announce. It takes a tremendous toll on your family. I would not run if I did not have the full support of my family. I knew the toll it would take and we all had to willingly go down the path together. Fortunately, in my situation my family was extremely supportive as they had been in the past. They believed that I would be the best congressman for Staten Island and they wholeheartedly supported me.

By this time, I felt that the John Murphy of 1970 was much different than the John Murphy of 1980. In 1980 I felt that my little State Legislative office in Albany had done significantly more for Staten Island than John Murphy's big congressional office had done during my last six years as a legislature. So with the support of my family, and based on the information I was given from the National Republican Committee, I decided to jump into the race and run. I knew it was going to be an extremely tough campaign. At the time Murphy hadn't been indicted, and when I made my decision it looked like he wasn't going to be indicted.

The first order of business was to get a campaign manager. There was only one person I would consider, Mike Petrides. He was my lifelong friend, and I believed he was the smartest strategist in Staten Island politics. He was one of the few guys who knew politics, and wasn't a phony. He would just do it quietly in the background. He immediately agreed to be my campaign manager. Now it was a done deal. So by early May I had decided to run for Congress but was not ready to make a formal announcement. Before I announced there was work to do.

In my opinion nobody had a clearer vision of what to do in a political campaign than Mike. Mike was an academic strategist and his thought process was crucial to my successful campaign. Additionally, Jimmy Molinaro, the Conservative Party Chairman agreed to work on my campaign. Jimmy was a guy who didn't go to college, but he had political common sense, loyalty, and was street smart. In essence, they were the yin and the yang whose contrasts ultimately made it work.

While considering our campaign strategy for the congressional run we reached out to Emil Micha, a graphic design artist who worked for the *New York Times*. I asked if he was interested in working on my campaign. I said, "I'm thinking of running for Congress and I'd like you to come over to my house, meet my team, and talk with me about possibly helping design my campaign."

The following day Mike Petrides, Jim Molinaro, and I were sitting in my living room when Emil came in. I had never met him and I was surprised at his size. He was tall. In fact, he was six foot four.

I asked Emil, "What do you think your role will be in my campaign, and most importantly, what you can do for me to help get me elected?"

Emil responded, "I confess that I am not a political expert by any means. But I could make you look professional and I could do something for you that would stay with the reader, not something that they would crumple up and throw away. Assemblyman Molinari, you have a strong message and a strong personality. If I can convey this to the voters, I can help you get elected."

I said, "All right, how's that going to work?"

Emil said, "We will do a campaign that has substance because Mr. Molinari you have substance. The campaign will reflect the man. Your opponent is under a cloud of suspicion. ABSCAM permeates the air. Guy, you represent someone who is going to rescue Staten Island from the clutches of somebody who was taking money for God knows what, that is the heart of it."

Finally, Emil said, "I believe a major key to a successful campaign is good images, good photographs of the candidate. I work with a consummate photographer, David Chalk. David is a documentary photographer not a posed picture photographer. That is what your campaign needs. Something different."

Mike said, "Jesus, how much is that going to cost?"

Emil put a figure on the chair and said, "I don't know at least $1,500.00."

Today this figure would be laughable and a drop in the bucket but back then Petrides nearly fell off the chair and jumped up saying, "Hell no, we don't need that. We can't afford that. I have a friend, a fireman, who takes pictures. He can do the same job."

Emil said, "I don't know about that. A professional photographer is a professional photographer. A fireman is a fireman. Apples and oranges."

Jimmy Molinaro seemed to get the picture right away. Mike didn't. But then again Mike knew that we were cash strapped and as always a grassroots campaign runs with minimal funding. We ended the meeting with Mike saying, "No way will we pay that!"

Everyone left. I had a lot to think about if I really wanted to win. I thought about the campaign all night. In the morning I called Micha and said, "Pay no attention to those guys, you're hired and so is your photographer." And that is how the advertising campaign for my run for Congress got started.

On Thursday May 16th, I formally announced my decision to run for Congress against Jack Murphy. I entered the race not because of any probe of Murphy but because the Republican National Committee asked me to and convinced me not only that I could win, but also that I could better serve my constituents in Congress.

On Tuesday June 10th I got the nod from the Staten Island Republican County Committee to become their candidate for the Congress. I was nominated by Councilman Anthony Giacobbe who said, "Staten Island is not represented in Congress and Guy Molinari is 'Accepted as a Fighter,' and we need someone to fight for Staten Island's interests. Molinari is the only Republican who can defeat the Democrat in the 17th Congressional district." When the night was over, I was the Republican candidate fully endorsed by the Staten Island Republican County Committee.

A week later, I received the Conservative County Committee nod and was selected as their candidate for the 17th Congressional district. Both these endorsements are essential to a successful campaign. It is always better to have your name on multiple lines on the ballot.

The next day the shoe dropped for John Murphy. He was formally indicted on five counts of bribery/conspiracy by a Brooklyn Grand Jury on charges of taking a $50,000 bribe during the FBI's sting operation.

Murphy had Bill Corley, a dynamite Democratic political organizer, managing his campaign. Corley had also run the campaigns for Robert F. Kennedy's presidential run, and New York City Mayor Abraham Beame's mayoral race. So he was a formidable candidate. Corley knew how to get the troops together.

Fortunately, I had Mike Petrides. In order to be successful I hustled with my team from the minute I announced my run until the minute the polls closed on November 3rd. We knew that the *Staten Island Advance* coverage was crucial at that time. Everybody in the borough read the *Advance*. We flooded the papers with our campaign slogan.

Little did I know when I was a teenager that the name Gaetano would make such nice campaign slogans, some of my favorites being: "Stand-up GUY;" "Send the right GUY to Washington;" "A Good GUY." I did find it amusing when Mary Codd's Democratic campaign committee stated that, "Even Mr. Molinari's campaign slogan, 'Send the right GUY to Washington' is sexist and demeaning to women."

We were in the *Advance* with ad after ad: Nice GUY; Tough GUY; Smart GUY. We played on my name and it caught on.

The ads we ran in *Advance* were brilliant because they were fairly small, but the headlines were big. Simple pictures, simple headlines. People got it. For example, when I went out campaigning in Bay Ridge Brooklyn, people knew me from the advertisements and mailing. Simple puns helped me get elected.

We had constant meetings. Emil and his crew of Dewey Evan and David Chalk spent lots of time on graphics, following me around Staten Island. We went everywhere. Veteran Halls, senior centers, schools, LNG tanks, prisons, and of course the infamous dump. Always taking pictures. I did what many politicians didn't do in those days: I became part of the community. Most politicians would sit for a picture, put it up on the telephone pole, and remotely say, "Vote for me." Not me. I hustled and was visible throughout Staten Island and Brooklyn day-in and day-out.

Soon, the mailings started getting a response. Now "Send the right GUY to Washington" became an active discussion among people. It was a slogan that generated attention. We saturated the radio with Ads Vote for "Elect the right GUY, Guy Molinari." Mike Petrides was the genius. Always thinking, sometimes too much. My wife would get so mad at him because he would call up every night after eleven and he would have me on the phone for a good hour.

One of the funniest mailings we did concerned a garbage bag. Everything we did was controversial. People would say you couldn't do that. You couldn't put out a mailing on a piece of brown paper.

At the time I wanted to talk about all the issues and I wanted to do a very extensive mailing piece with detailed descriptions of what I was going to do with education, the economy, veterans, heath, safety, and other policies.

So the team is working on this mailing and Emil starts realizing it has to be a big piece of paper to contain all the text. Emil didn't have a piece of white paper he had a piece of wrapping paper. So Emil did the layout on the brown wrapping paper. When it was all done Emil looked at it and said it looks pretty good, it's rough. He thought it reflected my personality. He presented the mailing on brown paper to a room full of campaign staffers. There were kids Emil shows everyone his work and nobody liked it. Petrides flat out said, "It looks like a garbage bag, its crap." Someone else said, "I would be embarrassed to show that to anybody."

Jimmy Molinaro speaks up and said, "Wait a second I like it, it's different." I finally told everyone that I would make the final decision. Finally, I said, "Yeah I like it too. Let's do it." Emil and Dewey Evan were ecstatic since they put a lot of work into it. So we printed it on brown craft paper and it went out. As predicted voters looked at it and actually read it because it did not look like anything else. And that's what I liked, I always liked to have something different, not the same old crap that everyone else did. The mailing made a difference in the campaign because it got a response. People talked about it. You could always gauge what worked and what didn't. If you did something and no one was talking about it then it wasn't successful. In this case it was a total success because everyone talked about it.

I remember thinking when I was preparing to debate Murphy that I couldn't forget the guy was a war hero. He was on very powerful committees in Congress and he won nine elections in a row. He was not going to be a pushover. The trial for ABSCAM wasn't going to happen till after the election, and Murphy maintained his innocence throughout his campaign. He was a popular congressman. So it was easy to question my chances of winning in the beginning. But as the campaign progressed people started talking, and the campaign gained momentum.

Throughout the campaign I had to keep reminding myself that the most important thing I could do was to be myself. Never try to be somebody else because it doesn't work. Everybody has their own personality, and if you let your own personality through, it'll work. You'll be more comfortable and you'll be a better candidate. Unfortunately, that doesn't happen very often; candidates always want to be somebody else. They always want to put up some kind of front. My campaign revealed the man I was. People saw my ability, skills and dedication.

On Tuesday September 10th, Murphy squeaked out a win in the Democratic primary when his two Democratic contenders split the ticket. Everyone knew he was in grave trouble at that time because if the ticket was not split it was clear he would have lost.

By this time, I had the full support of the Republican National Committee. They saw our campaign strategy and agreed to back me. They saw me as a promising candidate who could capture a Democratic seat. They committed the "maximum resources available" to help me beat Murphy. On October 2nd Congressman Jack Kemp from Buffalo hosted a fundraising event for me. Jack was one of the most sought after speakers in the country at that time based on his work on the Kemp-Roth tax bill which was the cornerstone of the GOP economic plank.

On October 3rd, I got the endorsement of former President Gerald Ford. It was a great boost to the campaign. We were coming down to the last minutes and every bit of press I could muster was free publicity and helped sway uncommitted voters to my side.

I felt at this time I had the support of Staten Islander voters so I campaigned very hard in Brooklyn to try to secure the district. During these walking tours I encountered tremendous anti-Murphy sentiment. It wasn't just about ABSCAM, it was about Murphy's special interest campaign contributions, involvement with controversial leaders such as the Shah of Iran, ousted Nicaraguan President

Anastascio Somoza, and most importantly the fact that Murphy hadn't actually lived in his district for the last several years.

As I had set up a campaign in 1970 in support for Murphy, the former Democratic County Vice Chairman Jerome M. Neuberger set up "Democrats for Molinari." It was amazing the support I was being given from all sides. My constituents rallied behind me. They knew I was in the trenches with them fighting for the good of Staten Island. I stood up to be counted when others just watched silently.

Murphy's central theme was "There is no time for a freshman." Yet he was wrong. People wanted change and they wanted a fighting freshman. By this time many voters believed Murphy was a cocky congressman who seemed to think he was a cut above the people he represented. It reminded me of my first campaign where I trounced Russo. Another politician was out of touch with their constituents. It always turns out to be a fatal flaw in a hotly contested battle.

For the first time, I ran in an election in which the *Staten Island Advance* declined to endorse any candidate. It was a good thing for me since I was endorsed by them each time I ran for the Assembly. It was a very bad sign for Murphy since the *Advance* had endorsed him in his ten previous runs. Now he did not have their endorsement. In essence the *Advance's* failure to endorse Murphy was a vote against Murphy.

The fury of a campaign is nonstop until the closing of the polls on election night. It is not for the weary. You have to have boundless energy and be able to work with no sleep. We worked endlessly. Finally, Tuesday November 3rd, 1980 had arrived. The fight for my political career was at its peak. On the day of voting I took out my final ad in the *Staten Island Advance* expressing a heartfelt thank you to my constituents. In it I stated:

Thank you Staten Island.

Thank you for moving us into the lead in today's very

close Congressional election.

And thank you for your trust in my integrity: for carefully examining—and rejecting—groundless charges by John Murphy, his desperate attempt to hold on to the office he has dishonored.

Thank you for opening your homes to me, your churches and schools—even your picnics and parties—as I walked through our Island neighborhoods these past few months, talking to people about decisions that must be faced. Thank you for telling me, as candidly as you have, exactly what's on your minds—and hearts. And thank you for your unfailing courtesy in listening to what I had to say, even when we didn't agree. Now the campaign is over, and it's all up to you, if you haven't done so already, I urge you—please get out and vote your conscience. The polls will be open till 9 tonight. Tomorrow we will begin the real campaign—translating all the talk into ACTION in Washington.

Thank you,

Guy Molinari

By the end of the night I would know whether I had been successful or would have to suffer the agony of defeat after such a hard fought race. Again I was the political underdog but I came in with high powered guns backed by the Republican National Campaign Committee.

At our campaign headquarters located at 1720 Hylan Boulevard, Mike Petrides and my cousin Ralph Molinari along with dozens of loyal campaign workers tabulated the election returns as they came in. Ultimately Ralph screamed at Mike, "Guy slaughtered Murphy!"

I knew from the conversations I was having over the phone with them that the atmosphere in the headquarters was electric, since I had been there many times in the past. On this night I stayed at home with my family until a final result was called. When it was clear that we had won I left with my family and Jim Molinaro, the Conservative Party leader. Our first stop was the victorious campaign headquarters. When we entered an ecstatic staff and a well-earned champagne toast greeted us. Champagne was poured into Dixie cups and I toasted my amazingly hard working campaign staff. The glory of victory was always so fulfilling.

At ten o'clock that evening, I arrived at the Shalimar in New Dorp. There was a huge crowd outside the catering hall. The atmosphere was euphoric. I had secured a resounding victory against the Democratic kingpin, Congressman Murphy. It is difficult to describe the emotions that you feel after months of campaigning and ultimate success. I remember pulling up and seeing Mike Petrides lifting Emil shouting, "We won! We won!" It was a sight to see since Emil was tall and Mike was short.

When I entered the Shalimar, everyone sang, "For He's a Jolly Good Fellow," and gave us a standing ovation.

Mike Petrides started off by saying, "It was an absolute blowout. We won and we won big." My joy and relief was obviously more amplified with the presence of my wife and daughter at my side during my monumental victory. When I gave my heartfelt victory speech their eyes wept with happiness.

Unlike typical politicians I vowed to work from day one. There would be no vacation. I would spend the next few days going back to the districts and people who supported me to reassure them that I would keep my campaign promises. I was not a person of mere words; I was a person of action. The drive I brought to the assembly would be the same drive I will bring to congress. At the age of fifty-one I felt I was in my prime. I was reinvigorated and I knew that I had made the right decision. I would not let the people of Staten Island down.

The next day the *Advance* headlines stated, "Molinari routs Murphy for Congress." My campaign had smothered Murphy in Staten Island. It was a tremendous testament to my following. It was a political landmark in Staten Island politics. In addition, Ronald Reagan and Alphonse D'Amato had secured landslide victories. The resurgence of the Republican Party was at hand.

CHAPTER 16

Off to Washington

Traditionally, when a New York State Assemblyman vacates their seat, their fellow assemblymen give them the chair that they sat in with a nice plaque on it. In my case, my fellow assemblymen came to me and said, "We're going to give you a garbage pail with your name on it instead of your chair since you never shut up about the garbage dump on the Island." I laughed at them and said, "I love the thought, but I love my chair, so I want the chair."

As much as I loved Staten Island I did not want a garbage pail to be my parting gift when I left. I felt the chair was much more appropriate. But, it was a true testament to my dedication to ridding Staten Island of the garbage dump. Everyone in the New York State Assembly clearly understood where I was coming from. I could only hope the same would happen in Washington.

It was exciting to know that I would be going from managing two legislative offices and a meager staff on $20,000 a year as an assemblyman to being a Republican congressman working with a Republican President, a Republican Senate, and a staff greatly enhanced by a budget of roughly $350,000 a year. My sense of victory in this situation was very similar to my first win as an assemblyman beating Lucio Russo the twenty-two-year incumbent. Both were awesome victories and this one would have decisive positive effects on my future political career as a congressman. I had a fire burning inside of me again, and I knew that I was privileged to be elected a congressman. The only disappointing issue was the fact that Congressman Murphy had never personally reached out to me. On election night he never conceded or called me. More importantly, post-election I was anxious to ensure a smooth transition of the office and thought he would too. I knew the campaign got heated at times, but good politicians put things aside after the campaign is over. The people had spoken. I did consider him enough of a man to give me the guidance and support I am sure he knew I could use. This was a crucial olive branch that the losing incumbent typically offered to their successor. Unfortunately, in this situation, the olive branch was never offered by the incumbent.

Within days of becoming the Congressman-elect one of the first things I did was to formally write a letter to President-elect Reagan regarding stopping the Travis Power Plant on Staten Island. As I had promised to my constituents, I followed through on what I considered my number one priority: preventing the construction of the Power Plant. I would use everything in my arsenal. In the letter I congratulated Reagan on his "smashing victory," and then recognizing that Reagan favored increased reliance on coal, I stated that "I am confident that you recognize the importance of the responsible siting of these new plants and the environmental implications of coal conversions." In essence, Staten Island was not the place for the Travis Power Plant.

Next I had to set up a transition team to work with Murphy's staff. This was extraordinarily crucial since I had no personal contact with Murphy. I did this relatively quickly. I tapped into my great friend Mike Petrides to recommend candidates to serve on my permanent staff in Washington and Staten Island. Unfortunately, Mike was not interested in a permanent job, since he was thoroughly satisfied as the Assistant Dean at the College of Staten Island. His heart was always in education. I was also able to hire Thomas K. Murphy as my interim Chief of Staff for my transition team. Thomas, no relation to defeated Congressman Murphy, held key Republican positions within the New York State GOP. I had worked with him in the past, and really liked his work ethic and political style. They had conversations with Murphy's Chief of Staff, Eric Vitaliano who assured them that there would be a smooth transition.

I owed my family a vacation after all the sacrifices they made in order to help me get elected. So, prior to the intensive training I would be receiving in Washington and Boston, I took my family on a well-deserved vacation to Aruba. It was a beautiful time to just relax with my wife and daughter in the beauty of the Caribbean. We all knew that when I returned home it would be non-stop work, so we relished every moment as a family together. It was amazing how quickly my daughter had grown. She was still in the University of Albany graduate school and had matured so much.

On Monday, December 1st, I went to Washington along with all the other newly elected members of the Senate and Congress to participate in the Republican Caucus for the 97th Congress. It was an incredibly proud moment for me. I knew my father's heart was glowing with pride in heaven at my accomplishment. His father, an immigrant from Amantea, Italy, almost eighty years before had a son who was father to a New York State Congressman. It was more than my grandfather could have ever imagined when he stepped upon the shores of New York.

When I arrived in Washington I participated in the biennial office lottery for freshman Congressmen. At least this time, I did better than my introduction into the Assembly. I wound up with Room 501 in the Cannon Building. The Cannon Building was the oldest of the three House Structures. My office was right next to an elevator and relatively close to the Capitol. Location was important because as a congressman you could be making as many as a half-dozen trips to other offices buildings and the Capitol on a routine day. All told each trip was about a half-mile. At the same time, I was reviewing over 600 resumes to fill my permanent Congressional staff. Needless to say there was never an idle moment.

For the next three weeks, I attended intensive orientation seminars. As new Congressmen, we learned the mechanics of parliamentary procedures, the bell and buzzer codes that signal floor activity, the intricacies of the congressional computer system, the rules governing travel, the customs and traditions of the Senate and Congress and overall Congressional Ethics. It was a jam-packed three weeks. During this time period we were also expected to maneuver ourselves into the specific committee that we wanted to serve on.

Although I would still be in the minority in Congress, the Republicans held a Senate majority for the first time in twenty-six years. It was a good time to be a Republican. I was hoping that the win by President-elect Reagan and a Republican Senate would help offset my lack of seniority in the Congress. I would be tapping into every hook I could possibility think of to achieve my campaign promises for my constituents.

Within days of arriving in Washington, on December 3rd, my predecessor John Murphy, was found guilty on three counts, one being conspiracy and two lesser charges, by a Brooklyn Federal Court Jury. It was an extremely sad day in the halls of Congress. I felt bad for the man, but he was his own worst enemy in this situation.

After a month of almost no post-election contact from Murphy, on Thursday, December 11th, after numerous unanswered calls to Murphy's office seeking a sit down to ensure a smooth transition in the handling of routine district affairs for the upcoming session, as a last ditch effort, I decided to stop by his office in the Rayburn Building. At that time, although Murphy was in his office, his aide told me that he had a, "full schedule and was unavailable." That was it for me! There were some reporters present at the time and I told them, "If you ask me if I'll try again, the answer is *no*. I clearly understand that Congressman Murphy would have been very happy if I did not stop by. I got the message loud and clear." Needless to say I was surprised and disappointed. I thought that he had more character than that, especially since I had helped him get reelected years before, but that's just the way things go sometimes.

On December 15th, all forty-five newly elected members of Congress were given the privilege of going to Harvard University in Boston. We attended more seminars specifically designed for newly elected Congressmen. These courses have been given every two years since 1972. The program consisted of a week of intensive seminars on subjects ranging from the nation's military budget to how to run a congressional office. It was intended as a necessary overview that newly elected representatives needed. In my situation, since Murphy was incommunicado with me since his defeat, I needed it drastically.

I loved the whole experience and always thrived in the learning environment. I was like a sponge soaking up every piece of useful information I could get regarding how I could help my Staten Island constituents. I was a true believer in doing my homework on key issues in order to achieve the best outcome and that is why I thrust myself into the seminars. For me it provided thought provoking moments and a lot of concrete information that would definitely be hard to come by elsewhere.

Another thing I had to do was establish a home away from home during the week when I would be in Washington. Since I had a great relationship with Assemblyman Armand D'Amato, as well as being excellent roommates, his brother seemed a natural choice. Alfonse was just elected senator and we would both be learning the ropes together in Washington. So we became roommates and rented a place together in Crystal City, a thicket of high-rise buildings adjacent to National Airport, just across the Potomac River from Washington. After a while another friend would join us later, Dominic DiCarlo. Dom DiCarlo was a brilliant guy who was a New York State assemblyman from 1965 to 1981. Based on my recommendation to President Reagan in 1981, Dominic was nominated and confirmed by the Senate to be the Assistant Secretary of State for

International Narcotics Matters. He held this position from 1981 to 1984.

On Sunday, December 28th, at the holiday victory celebration given by the Staten Island Republican County Committee in the Richmond Town Courthouse, Senator Al D'Amato publicly vowed to stand by me in my support of the Public Health Service Hospital and to fight the Travis Power Plant. I earned this crucial support by being among the first assembly members to endorse Alfonse D'Amato in the Senate race. Staten Island was the only one of the five boroughs in New York City that was clearly for D'Amato. D'Amato won Staten Island by two to one in the general election. He was indebted to my borough and I would use that for Staten Island's benefits. It is always better to stand with others in solidarity on an issue than by yourself. I had done enough of that in the past. Now was the time to cash in the chips and start using them.

By this time, I had managed to secure my permanent Congressional Staff. I was fortunate to lure twenty-nine year-old Skylar Baab to head my Washington office. Baab was much coveted by members of both Houses. He worked on the National Republican Congressional Committee. Baab turned down several more lucrative job offers saying he was impressed with my energy and believed that I could be a force to be reckoned with in the House even though I was in the minority. After five years of flying over 200,000 miles a year, Skylar decided it was time for him to settle down and he ultimately agreed to work for me for $42,000 a year. Conservative County Chairman James P. Molinaro would head my Staten Island office. Additionally, I hired as my press secretary Brian Sweeney, a young twenty-three year-old NYU graduate who came from Madison, Wisconsin.

On Saturday, January 3rd, 1981, several days before the formal swearing in on the floor of the Capitol in Washington D.C., I along with over 200 friends, relatives and supporters rode the Staten Island ferry to Liberty Island for an informal swearing in. My longtime friend and colleague, Federal Judge Mark Costantino, swore me in on Liberty Island at the foot of the Statue of Liberty.

When I saw Judge Costantino I couldn't help but chuckle. He was hobbling around with a cast on his right foot, which was apropos for our relationship, seeing as how when I first met him years ago it was after the fatal automobile accident where I almost lost my leg. So at the time I had a cast on my leg. Injuries of past and present aside, the ceremony was beautiful.

I thought it was a wonderful idea since Liberty Island was midway between the two portions of my district, lower Manhattan and Staten Island. It was a beautiful ceremony, the likes of which were never done before, and in hindsight I see why. The weather was brutally cold. This would come back to bite me in the ass. Still, with the symbolic significance of Lady Liberty, if I were given the chance to do it again, I certainly would.

As luck would have it, I wound up contracting pneumonia because it was freezing when I went to the Statute of Liberty. So, when I was driven down to Washington on January 6th, 1981, for the swearing in with my childhood friend Tony Dacchille and his wife they were throwing blankets on me to keep me warm. My wife Marguerite had the flu so she had to stay home in Staten Island.

I remember thinking on the way down that this is not how my formal introduction to Congress should go. When we got to the Capitol, Tony took me to the House physician, Freeman Casey. Tony said, "We just want Guy to get sworn in and then I will take him to the hospital."

Dr. Casey said, "Nope, he's in bad shape. Take him now. I don't care what you say; he will not be waiting around." Dr. Casey refused to allow me to be sworn in. He said the pneumonia was very serious and I had to get to Bethesda Naval Hospital immediately. He called an ambulance and that was that.

Needless to say it was extraordinarily disappointing for me, but even more so for the three busloads of friends, relatives, and supporters who had made the trip from Staten Island to celebrate my first official day as a U.S. Representative. My daughter was on one of the buses. As always, she loved being in the thick of things. In actuality she was the only healthy person in the family at the time. I thought, "Oh to be young and twenty-two again."

When I was at the hospital I heard that Thomas "Tip" O'Neill, the Speaker of the House was in the hospital at the same time. I sent him a message and asked him if he could swear me in at the hospital. We had a very big class and if he was able to swear me in I would have had seniority over everybody else that was being sworn in two days later. Unfortunately, being the smart Democrat that he was, he refused to do it.

On Friday, January 9th, after five days of hospitalization, I was finally discharged and immediately went over to Congress to be formally sworn in on the house floor by Speaker Tip O'Neill. It was not the way I wanted it to go, but at least now I was a full-fledged congressman.

As a freshman congressman, I quickly learned that you have to develop special relationships with Democrats and vice-versa. So the initial induction process, especially concerning committee assignments, built the relationships that would serve me for the rest of my professional career. I had hoped to get on the Energy and Commerce committee as my first choice, but that was just wishful thinking.

On January 28th, I learned that I had secured a spot on the Committee on Public Works and Transportation. It was considered a very prestigious committee. This committee controlled legislation on issues ranging from port development to mass transit. Although it was my second choice, considering I was a brand new congressman, I had secured a spot on a respected committee and I was lucky. I knew that I would be able to help find solutions for the city's deteriorating subway and bus systems.

I had also hoped to get on a minority committee as well, but the Democrats were insisting on holding a disproportionate share of seats on the Houses' four top panels. The Democrats freely acknowledged that they had to keep majorities on the key committees or risk losing control over the legislative process in the House. Although the Democrats had suffered sweeping losses during the election, they were going to ensure through Tip O'Neil that they maintained control of the Congress.

So, by the end of January, my introduction to congressional life was done with and it was time to get down to brass tacks and do the job of congressman for the 17th congressional district.

CHAPTER 17

An Independent Republican Congressman

BY THE END OF JANUARY 1981, I HAD ALREADY made a formal decision to appeal what I knew would be a negative decision by the siting board regarding the Travis Power Plant. The decision was expected on February 6th, and everything indicated that it would clearly be in favor of the PASNY. Within thirty days of the decision a petition would have to be filed documenting the reasons for the basis of the appeal. So my anticipatory decision was a crucial legal strategy that had to be followed to the tee in order to be successful on the appeal.

Councilman Anthony Giacobbe, Assemblyman Robert Straniere, and I began recruiting experienced attorneys as well as law school students who were willing to work on the petition pro bono. Our recruitment efforts paid off handsomely. If we had to pay for the legal services it would have cost our constituents well over $100,000. Twenty thousand pages of testimony from the hearings had to be weeded through as well as volumes of documents submitted during the prior proceedings. Therefore, the sooner we started preparing the appeal, the better our chances. It was estimated that PASNY had already spent over $25 million to support the plant. This was becoming a real case of David versus Goliath.

On February 2th, 1981, Frank D. Paulo, the Surrogate of Richmond County since 1961, suddenly died of a heart attack. The judicial position of Surrogate on Staten Island was, and is, a highly coveted position. At the time, you were elected for life and made $68,000 year. Essentially, you were set for life and the position itself offered political patronage. Basically it was every politician's dream, except mine of course.

Many of my Staten Island political colleagues had jokingly suggested that I run for the position of surrogate. In typical Molinari style, my imagination went off the chart and I decided to push the envelope in trying to get rid of the Travis Power Plant by any means necessary. I came up with what I considered a smart ploy.

Since I did more to help Ronald Reagan than any other newly elected congressman in our forty-five-member group, I knew politically I was there. They couldn't take that away from me. I found myself in a position where I was a player already before I even got started. The Republicans were in power. The last thing that they would want to do is lose a Republican seat in Congress.

By early March rumors were rampant that I was thinking of resigning to run as the Republican candidate for Surrogate of Staten Island. I knew the Republicans in the White House would fear that my withdrawal could pave the way for Democrats to recapture the seat. At that time, I went to the Republican leadership and said, "I've been asked to run for the position of Staten Island Surrogate. As you know, it's a great job; everybody wants it because you hold it for life. It's hard for me to turn it down, but I would if I knew that the administration is fully behind me in ensuring that Travis Power Plant is permanently killed." I said, "It's up to you guys to help me kill it."

They called my bluff and basically said that they didn't have a direct way of killing it so they could not make that promise. At the time, though we all knew that if the President of the United States came out against the Travis Power Plant that would be the kiss of death, even though technically the President did not have the legal authority to intervene. If the administration really wanted to go out on a limb for me, indirectly they could have killed it by calling in votes.

On Friday, March 13th, President Reagan came to New York via Air Force One and I was one of the lucky politicians asked to be his guest. This was to be the first of several rides on the historic Air Force One. I must confess whenever I rode on the plane I would steal everything that wasn't glued down. I would stuff my pockets in front of the president. It was considered a rite of passage. Mementos from a historic ride were something that you proudly shared with family, friends and constituents. I took so many matchbooks that sometimes I thought I would catch fire.

I remember President Regan push his face against the glass of the windows of the car as we drove to Manhattan after landing at the airport, trying to give people the chance to see him.

President Reagan turned toward me and said, "Isn't it a shame that I can't be up on top of this limo so that people can see their president? It's a terrible thing." As we drove along though, people still got very excited just seeing him through the glass.

The President had a very busy schedule, but he wanted to thank the Italian-American voters for their support in the election. So, Senator D'Amato and I had arranged for a lunch with the President in Little Italy. The support and greeting that Reagan received was tremendous from New Yorkers. Supporters lined the street to get a glimpse of him. The day itself was frigid, but the crowds were there. Ronald Reagan had captured the hearts of New Yorkers on that day.

We arranged a quintessential Italian lunch at Angelo's, an iconic Italian restaurant established in 1902, in the heart of Little Italy, on Mulberry Street. A platform was set up in front of the restaurant and

Senator D'Amato addressed the crowd. I then spoke and squashed any rumors about me leaving Congress. I was totally committed to the job of congressman. My ploy had failed, but the fact that I even attempted such a novel approach was hysterical. Afterward, President Reagan spoke and then we went into the restaurant and sat down for a relaxing typical Italian meal of antipasto, homemade fettuccine, veal marsala, and of course white wine.

On March 30th, 1981, after less than three months in office, an earthshattering event happened when psychotic gunman John Hinckley shot President Reagan when he was leaving the Hilton Hotel in Washington D.C. after addressing an AFL-CIO conference. The six shots that Hinckley got off left a path of destruction from which some of the victims would never fully recover.

When we got word of the assassination attempt I immediately thought of his first trip to New York less than two weeks before and thought, "My God this is why they wouldn't let him stand up and wave to the crowds on the limousine ride. There are so many psychos out there that wanted to kill the president." It was a horrible reality that had come to pass regardless of all the precautions the Secret Service took.

Hinckley seriously wounded Reagan when a bullet ricocheted off the presidential limousine and hit Reagan in the chest. Reagan's Press Secretary James Brady was shot in the right side of his head and was paralyzed for life on the left side of his body. Police Officer Thomas Delahanty and Secret Service Agent Timothy McCarthy were struck as well but not as seriously.

At the time of the assassination attempt Reagan thought he broke a rib when Secret Service Agents tackled him to the ground. He underwent emergency surgery to remove the bullet and repair a damaged lung. Reagan maintained a sense of humor throughout the life-threatening ordeal. When his wife Nancy arrived to see him, the first thing he said was, "Honey, I forgot to duck." He also told a doctor, "I hope you're a Republican," to which the doctor replied, "Today, Mr. President, we're all Republicans."

At the age of seventy, Reagan's handling of the entire incident was remarkable. Reagan was the first serving U.S. President to survive being shot in an assassination attempt. In the aftermath of the shooting any concerns about his age faded since he was a survivor. His reputation for toughness, humility, and strength blossomed. The nation was in shock but extraordinarily grateful that he had survived. It reminded everyone of how quickly life can change. One minute you're on top of the world, the next minute you're fighting for your life because of a psychotic lunatic.

As Reagan recovered, Washington politics continued. On March 29th, I was livid when I learned that the Interior Secretary under Reagan, James G. Watts, was floating a plan for New Jersey and New York City to assume responsibility for Gateway National Recreational Parks $8.4 million annual budget and also to assume responsibility for a $300 million twenty-year development plan that was approved by the Federal government in 1978 for a sprawling recreational area. I knew this was ridiculous. This plan was totally unaffordable for New York City. It was the Federal government's responsibility, not the local governments.

The Gateway National Recreational Area encompasses over 26,000 acres from Queens, Brooklyn, Staten Island and Monmouth County New Jersey. The land was given over to the Federal government in 1972 in order to protect and preserve the unique and natural area encompassed by a sprawling urban environment. The land is managed by the National Park Service and oversees the beaches, preservation of birds, boating, hiking and camping for United States residents. Today over ten million people visit the area annually.

I saw this as an absolute disaster. There would be no way to maintain the parks with local resources especially since we were trying to recover from the fiscal crisis. I thought that all the hard work of the last twenty to thirty years would be undone and wiped out. The response from all politicians in the local area was extremely negative and everyone vowed strong opposition for any further thought of such a ridiculous idea.

Regarding local politics, Democratic Mayor Koch was up for re-election and he was pushing to be the first "fusion candidate" in the history of New York City Mayoral Politics. Electoral Fusion is basically when two or more political parties on a ballot list the same candidate. So, after much hankering back and forth, the Staten Island Republican Party was revamped again over this issue. George Hart replaced Arnold Thompson. I was behind the revamping again, because you always have to be on top of your game in order to have a successful Republican Party, especially in Staten Island.

Overall, Koch reached his objective as Mayor since he was able to turn around the city from a dire financial situation to glimmers of hope for prosperity. The fiscal crisis seemed hopeless, but he was the cheerleader for the city saying, "It's going to be okay, everybody's okay." He convinced businesses that we were going to survive the fiscal crisis. He deserves a lot of credit for that. So one of the best things he ever did was being the "morale keeper" at a time when everybody else was dragging their heels.

Staten Islanders warmly received him. I would say probably in the last fifty years, it's easy to say that he was one of the most popular mayors. When he came to Staten Island he was animated. On St. Patrick's Day he wore a beautiful, woolen Irish sweater and carried a shillelagh in his hand. He loved being an extrovert and enjoyed all the press that he would get because of it.

Koch was a guy that you could talk to. Yet although he was a friend, he had to be watched, because if it came to Manhattan versus Staten Island, you knew where he was going to be. But I respected him because I at least knew where he was coming from. It just made sense at that point in time to give credit where it was due regardless of party line. So, Koch as a Democratic Mayor received the Republican nod from Staten Island for another term which virtually ensured his re-election.

Immediately before the summer recess I wrote a letter to the editors of the *New York Times* regarding the nightmarish Travis Power Plant. They published my letter on August 1st, 1981:

To the Editor:

It is unfortunate that the editorial board of the Times, *a group of individuals who are usually very sensitive to the many environmental concerns of the region and country, have decided to continue to support Governor Carey and the Power Authority's proposal to build a coal-and garbage-fueled power plant on Staten Island.*

Your editorial of July 23 applauded Governor Carey's veto of a piece of legislation that simply would have required the Power Authority to adhere to the New York City air-pollution standards, something every other business, including Con Ed, must do.

It was implied in the editorial that the opponents of the plant used "slick legislative maneuvering" to pass the bill. What the editorial did not point out was that the vote was an overwhelming 132 to 7 in the assembly, and 42 to 5 in the senate, a vote that exhibited strong concern, from legislators throughout the state, to preserve the environment of New York City [.]

During this time period, new Congressmen would be assigned floor duty. What this entailed was sitting at a desk and explaining to the members present what the vote was all about when they came in for a vote. For example, you would tell them, "This is a Republican vote; it's a safe vote for everybody." Well, I would sit there and I would get bored just doing that, so I would watch the debate and I would jump in sometimes and get involved. I thought it was fun. I was never one for idle hands.

There were several White House representatives that would come around from time to time to see you and ask for your support on issues. Sometimes, as it happened in my case quite a lot, we wound up fighting. Unlike most of the other representatives, I was an independent Republican. I couldn't stand and I still can't stand Republicans who, no matter how they felt on an issue, would vote with the administration. To me I perceived them as little bobble-head dolls saying, "Yes, sir. No, sir. Whatever you want, sir." That's not the way our country should be operating. The members should independently think about the merits of a particular piece of legislation and vote not with their party necessarily, but with their conscience.

I rarely attended conferences. I preferred getting a workout in the gym and playing paddleball instead. I hated the idea that you would go to a conference and the party leaders would try to twist your arm so that you would vote the way they wanted you to. So, the Republican hierarchy quickly learned that Guy Molinari was not an automatic vote. I had a miserable streak of independence and they couldn't control me no matter how many times they tried to. There were times that worked to my disadvantage, but the majority of the time it was to my constituent's advantage. That was what mattered most.

My staff and I worked long hours. At the end of the night around 9:00 p.m. or so, we would go over to the Capitol Hill Club, which is right across the street from the Capitol on First Street, to have a soda and maybe a hamburger or a cocktail or two. The club was a Republican "members only" club or by invitation. There was a pub downstairs and when they saw me coming downstairs to the pub I would be greeted with a chorus, "Here comes Molinari. Get out your dollars! We're going to play liar's poker!"[7] Many times we would wind up having as many as twenty people playing one game of liar's poker.

7 *A gambling game, usually played with $1 bills. Players pick from a pile of face down, mixed up bills, and use the serial number on the face of the bill (kept private) to shape their playing strategy. It is a consecutive bidding game where players "bet" the total # of occurrences of digits on all bills involved in the hand. The winner of each hand is decided when players call somebody's bid. If the person makes the bid he wins everybody's dollar, if he loses the bid he pays everybody a dollar.*

One night I was playing liar's poker and a grey haired guy at the bar was watching us play. He said, "Congressman! I'd like to challenge you to a game." I said, "Okay, what do you want to play for?" He said, "I'll tell you what: let's go for broke. Let's play for $50."

I didn't know the guy, so I agreed to it. I reached in my pocket, took out a $50 bill, threw it on the bar, and he threw his out. We picked up our bills, and I lost the game. I started questioning the guy, because I thought he was setting me up. You could not have four of the same numbers on an individual bill. It was extraordinarily rare, if not impossible.

So, the next week he came back and asked to play another game. I said to myself, "Let me see what happens." I said, "Okay, I'll play another game." I put my $50 bill on the bar, he goes to throw down his $50 bill and I grabbed his hand, and I yelled, "No, no. Take a different bill." He said, "No, I want to play with this bill."

I continue yelling, "No, you're not going to play with that bill. If we're going to play, we're going to play with another bill." Now everybody is listening because we're yelling at each other. He finally agreed and we played the game. He had to use a different $50 bill, and now on even footing, I won.

When the game was over, I said to him, "Don't you ever pull that on me again. I can't stand cheaters." I went back to my booth and sat down.

As I'm sitting at the table the grey haired guy comes by as he's on his way out and he says, "You treated me harshly there, and next time you're going to regret it."

He walked out of the room to take the elevator and I ran after him, grabbed him, and threw him against the wall. I said, "You son of a bitch, after what you pulled on me with the $50 bill? Put up your dukes. There's nobody around."

He said, "I'm not going to fight you." I said, "C'mon. I want to fight you, but I'm not going to hit you unless you put up your dukes." I'm screaming at him at the top of my lungs, and I screamed,

"If I see you here again I'm going to walk right over to you and punch you out. That's it. You're barred."

We could do that. We had the right to say who comes and who doesn't. Little did I know that there was a chess game going on in another room. The door was closed, but the people playing the game of chess heard every word; the screaming, cursing, shouting, and everything else. I was so embarrassed.

The guy didn't come back for a long, long time. When he did come back, he came over to me and asked permission to stay.

So, as with everything in life, even though you can be involved in really important issues 24/7/365, you are only human and can get upset over unimportant issues that make your skin boil. Even still, I always have, and always will, hate a cheater.

CHAPTER 18

Welcome to America, Lukasz

THE CONGRESSIONAL SUMMER RECESS STARTED ON AUGUST 5TH, 1981. For me a portion of my summer recess would be spent in Israel as a guest of a Jewish organization based in Staten Island that had set up a meeting for me to meet political and military leaders in Israel.

Several days before I was getting ready to leave for the trip to Israel with other members of Congress, I received a phone call from the *New York Post*. They told me that there was a sick baby, Lukasz Pniewski, who lived in Warsaw Poland, and he was scheduled to have brain surgery done in Poland. The paper called me because the Pniewski family had a relative who lived on Staten Island.

At the time, Poland was behind the Iron Curtain and the country was in chaos. This chaos resulted from a severe economic crisis which led to the rationing of most products and materials, including basic food. A tragic consequence of the floundering economy was a large exodus of the educated Polish workforce in the 1980s. Highly trained professionals such as doctors, engineers, and architects fled to other countries for a better life. As a result, there was a brain drain occurring in Poland. In essence, the experienced doctors and resources necessary to conduct the lifesaving brain surgery that Lukasz needed were nowhere to be found.

Lukasz was diagnosed with hydrocephalus, essentially water on the brain. If left untreated he would die due to the gradual buildup of pressure on the brain. According to pediatric neurosurgeons at New York University Medical Center the child would probably die or suffer severe complications if he had the surgery in Poland because of the lack of resources. As a result, the Pniewski family was terrified that he would die, become mentally disabled, or blind if he had surgery in Poland. They were convinced, as I was, that in order to save Lukasz' life he had to be brought to New York so that his brain surgery could be performed by our world renowned surgeons. The *New York Post* asked me if I'd be interested in helping bring that baby back. Of course, I said, "Yes." So, in addition to going to Israel, I embarked on a humanitarian mission to help Lukasz Pniewski.

While in Israel I spoke to the State Department every day. It was an arduous and time consuming process, since we didn't have the cellphone technology we have today. My staff in Washington was trying to coordinate bringing the baby to the United States. Every night, I would call the State Department representative and say, "What do you have? Do you have any good news?" She would always say the same thing, "It looks good. It looks good."

Finally, when it came time to leave Israel, I realized that nothing was happening; they were stroking me. So, I threatened the State Department by saying, "If you don't have permission for me to bring the baby back by the time I leave Israel, I'm not going to go back home." The woman said, "What are you going to do?"

I said, "I'll go to Poland." She said, "You obviously have a passport, but do you have a visa?" When I responded in the negative, she said, "Well you won't be able to get into the country without a visa." So, I simply said, "Then get me a visa."

When she said, "We don't issue visas, but we can get you one. It does, however, take a long time," I was livid. I said, "Why didn't you tell me that a couple of days ago?"

We had a heated conversation and I hung up on her. On Tuesday evening as I'm preparing to leave Israel, I made one last call to the woman from the State Department. I asked, "Do you have my visa?" She said, "No." I said, "Okay, at six a.m. tomorrow I'm going to hop on a flight to Poland."

She said, "You got to be kidding." I said, "No, I'm not kidding at all."

As promised, at six in the morning, Wednesday August 19th, I was at the Tel Aviv airport ready to take a plane to Vienna, Austria, as the stop over point for Poland. The State Department woman, who never personally met me, came over and started talking to me. She said, "You really are going try to go there without a visa?"

I said, "Absolutely, I'm gonna go there without anything and I'm going to bring the baby back to the United States."

She looked at me and said, "You know, you're bullheaded."

I said, "Okay, but that's what I'm doing."

I hopped on the plane to Vienna and when I arrived in the Vienna Airport I waited for the connecting flight to Warsaw, Poland. I was at the airport bar having a beer and a gentleman started calling out, "Molinari, Congressman Molinari." I waved at him. He came over and I said, "I'm Molinari. Are you from the State Department?" He says, "Yeah."

I said, "Good, I'm happy to see you. You want a beer?" He says, "Yeah."

He sat down and we were talking for a while. He suddenly says, "I got to get back to work."

I was stunned and said, "Don't you have the visa for me?"

He said, "Visa? You don't have a visa?" I said, "No, I thought you were bringing me one."

He said, "They're going to throw you in jail." I was pissed and said, "Yeah, I'd been told that before." He said, "No, you don't understand what they do there: You'll be thrown in jail." I told him, "Well, then you guys are going to have to get me out. It's as simple as that."

He left without offering help, or providing me with a visa, even after I bought him a beer!

I boarded the LOT Airlines flight to Warsaw, Poland. When the flight landed and I got to the front of the line to enter the country, a Polish guard working there said, "Give me your passport." So I gave him the passport. He stamps the passport and hands it back to me. He puts his hand out and said, "Visa? Where's your visa?"

I pointed to the passport. "There." He said, "No, no. Passport. This passport! Visa!"

I point my finger. "This passport is my visa." I tried a little game of bluffing at this point. My years of playing liars' poker were coming in handy.

"Passport, visa. No! No! No!" He couldn't speak very much English and he started yelling. Another guard heard him yelling and came running over.

I ask, "Can you speak English?" He said, "A little bit."

"Tell this man that I'm a Member of Congress from New York and I've got a combination passport visa. He doesn't understand that." So he said, "Let me see." He took my passport, looked inside, and said, "There's no visa here. No visa." So he calls more security people and they're getting ready to escort me to a holding area.

Suddenly a government official appeared out of nowhere and yelled, "Congressman Molinari!" The official came running toward me, waving a piece of paper with all kinds of colorful ribbons.

I said. "What's that?"

He said, "It's a visa, a twenty-four-hour visa."

I was ecstatic since, now I had legal entry into Warsaw.

When I got out of the airport the first thing I did was head to the American embassy to see our Ambassador, Francis J. Meehan. He was a very distinguished man. He said, "Congressman, I think I know why you're here." I said, "Mr. Ambassador, I'm trying to save a life. A baby's life."

He said, "But you know that this place is ready to go up in smoke. Right now, the relationship between our countries is not very good at all and I'm doing my best to put down any confrontations. Please understand that I appreciate what you're doing and commend you for doing it, but the timing is just not right."

I knew prior to committing to help Lukasz that the Polish government implemented another food price hike, so Lech Walesa led a strike at the Lenin Shipyard in Gdansk. This strike was televised around the world and gave rise to a wave of strikes over much of the country. Solidarity, which was the first independent mass political movement in the eastern Soviet Bloc, of which Lech Walesa formed, quickly grew to over ten million Polish members. This was over a quarter of Poland's population. Lech Walesa quickly became an international hero.

By the summer of 1981, which was the time I was there, Poland was in its worst economic crisis since the Second World War. Virtually all food products were being rationed. In Warsaw, the public transit authority buses had no spare tires. The company announced that only main routes would be kept open and said that the public just had to get used to the situation. As a result, the Polish population started widespread "Hunger Demonstrations." I remember seeing a solidarity poster in Warsaw that depicted a black skull with a crossed knife and fork under, symbolizing the Hunger demonstrations.

I said to Ambassador Meehan, "I can appreciate all of that, but I promised I would help this child and that's what I am going to do." He didn't say anything so I added, "By the way, Lech Walesa is my hero. I keep watching and reading about him. I'd love to meet him if that's possible." He shrugged and said, "I suggest that you go to room 206 and I'll see if I can get somebody to help you."

While I sat in room 206 the phone started ringing. After it rang for a while I said to myself, "Do I dare to pick up the phone when it's probably not for me?" I finally said, "The hell with it," and answered the phone.

A person said, "Hello. Congressman Molinari?"

"Yes?"

"What the hell do you think you're doing?" the voice said.

I said, "Sorry?"

He reiterates frantically, "What the hell are you doing, causing all this freaking trouble here? Do you know what the hell you're doing? Poland is like a time bomb and you're here with all this bullshit about a kid. You Congressmen are all the same."

I said, "What did you say? Do you know who you're talking to?"

He says, "Yeah, you're a big deal. You're a congressman. Yeah, I know who I'm talking to." He said, "I'm coming over there. What room are you in?"

I said, "206." He spurts out, "I'll be right there."

I had no idea who he it was. I hadn't slept in days and I've got this son of a bitch screaming at me. This big burly guy enters the office. He tells me right off the bat that his cousin is Teddy Kollek from Israel. He was the Mayor of Jerusalem so we're talking about a big name. I'm thinking that I am definitely missing something in the conversation.

Then he immediately starts this cursing rant, "Hey, big deal Congressman. Do you know what the fuck you're doing here?"

"Yeah, I know what I'm doing here," I said. "I'm trying to save the life of a baby, and I would hope that the embassy would be working with me to help save that child." He said, "You've got this whole thing mixed up. There are thousands of babies being killed in countries around the world, not just one, but there could be a lot more if a confrontation takes place. If you knew what the fuck you were doing, you wouldn't be doing this shit just to get your name in the paper."

So I start yelling back, and he motions to me that people were listening. "You don't know what you're doing!" He keeps going on like that. He finally starts walking to the door and silently motions for me to follow. I follow him and after several minutes we get outside of the embassy and after several blocks he finally says, "That fucking place is all wired for sound. There isn't a room in that place that's not bugged. That's what that yelling was all about. I got to make it look like we are pissed at you. The fucking commies have eyes and ears on us everywhere in that building."

Poland was still part of the Communist Bloc and everything was watched and recorded. It was just the way the Polish people lived, constantly paranoid that the government was spying.

When we got outside to a safe area there was a 180-degree turn in the conversation. He became my best friend in Poland. He says, "You really want to go see Lech Walesa?"

I said, "I'd love to." He said, "I've got the duty to go there tonight. So, I'll pick you up later with my wife. I've got a Volkswagen, not a lot of room."

So, a little while later, in this tiny little Volkswagen, this big burly guy, his wife, who was a short tiny lady, and I head off to the see Lech Walesa.

As we were driving in the car I was surprised to see a long line of people waiting in front of a bicycle shop. It sounded stupid but I said, "All these people are buying bicycles?" And the guy laughed and said, "No." I said, "What are they buying?"

His response shocked me when he said, "They don't know what they are buying. It may be food. The people just don't know. They're hoping it might be food. They have no way of knowing, so, they just get on line hoping to get something, anything." Then I understood why the Polish people had started their hunger demonstrations. The magnitude of the crisis in Poland was evident and it just confirmed my conviction to get the baby out of this country so that he had a chance at a good life.

When we arrived at an old school house there was a Solidarity meeting in a progress. We walked up five flights of well-worn wooden stairs that had grooves from years and years of wear. When we reached the top we looked over the balcony. The entire complex was packed to the rafters. You couldn't even move. Looking down into the room there was a big table and even though I couldn't speak Polish I could tell the meeting was in full progress by the serious tone of their voices.

Suddenly, my escort says to me, "Don't move." I couldn't move if I wanted to, I was jammed in. He said, "In a couple of seconds, I'm going to give you a signal and at that point we're going to run outta here. When I say run, I mean run."

I said, "What's going on?"

He said, "There's a press conference going on, and they just said, "We're pleased to have Congressman Guy Molinari with us."

I was stunned, and shouted over the noise "How the hell did they know I'm here?"

They then said, "And we want him to join in with us. Mr. Congressman, come join us."

My escort knew, as well as I did, what a terrible idea this was, since, we did not want to create an international incident, especially when I was on a humanitarian mission. At the time Ronald Reagan was exerting tremendous pressure on Russia to allow democracy to flourish in Europe. The Soviet Bloc was a tinder box and all it would take is one mistake on my part and diplomatic relations would disintegrate. As much as I wanted to meet Lech Walesa, I could not jeopardize the foreign policy agenda that Ronald Reagan had instituted. So my escort said, "Follow me and run." The big burly guy, his little wife and I run down five flights of stairs and quickly exit the building and got into the Volkswagen. Off we went and we head back to the embassy. I was grateful that an international incident was avoided.

The next day I came back to the embassy and I had a couple hours to kill. I thought to myself, "I'm probably never going to be seeing Warsaw again, so I'll take a walk". I became lost in the historical significance of the walk I was taking and lost my sense of direction. It was getting time for me to meet the Ambassador and I suddenly realized that I was lost. I thought "What a schmuck I am, as if I didn't have enough problems in Poland I had to go and get lost."

I approached a couple of people, but they didn't speak English. I started to explain to an old man "Guy Molinari, I'm from New York." He nodded his head. "I'm looking to go to the U.S. Embassy. Embassy. Embassy?" I'm trying all kinds of pronunciations, and he motions, "Follow me." And we walk, and walk, and walk and I guess after maybe an hour, we walked up in front of this building and he pointed at it. I looked at it, and it's not the building, the embassy. I said, "That's not the embassy." He's shocked.

I said, "The *strasse*, *strasse*, the Germans came in. The street, big, wide street?"

He motions again, "Follow me." We do another long walk, at least as long as the other one, and we finally walked up the stairs to the embassy. The embassy employee says, "My God! We have the entire Marine Corps looking all over Warsaw for you. We thought you were kidnapped."

I thought, "Holy shit." I really felt bad because I'm causing them an awful lot of problems.

Then I learned much to my chagrin that they were not going to allow me to take the baby to the United States. The twenty-four hour visa I had was now expired. The ambassador tried his best to have me leave.

And I said, "Mr. Ambassador, I'm not leaving this place. I don't care who says it, I've stated my position when I started and I'm taking that same position now. I don't care whether they arrest me and throw me in jail for the rest of my life. That doesn't bother me. There's a baby's life to be saved and to me that's a tremendous responsibility."

And he said to me, "Mr. Molinari, what do you want us to do? There's nothing more we can do." So I said, "Well then you know what I'm gonna do? I'm going to leave this place and start walking and keep asking people and maybe find somebody who can help me; I'm just not going to give up."

I went back to my room and got all my stuff and as I was walking down the stairs to exit and I got a call that the Ambassador wanted to see me. So I ran back to the Embassy to see the Ambassador. He said, "Good news. We have another twenty-four-hour visa."

"Great," I said.

At that time, I was told that the parents of Lukasz, Michal and Violetta Pniewski, one was an architect, one was an engineer, whom I had never met wanted to treat me to supper, but the powers that be would not permit it.

The following day, Friday, I was told that the Polish government finally agreed to let Lukasz go to America. When I went to the airport to take off I thought it might be an easy process to take off with the child in tow, but a lot of strange things happened that triggered my internal Marine Corps radar. The government wanted me to take the first flight out and said that the Pniewski family would follow on the next flight since there were not enough seats.

While I'm waiting there the Pniewski family arrived and it was the first time I had ever seen them. It was clear that they were packed and ready to leave Poland with me. I was told that the Polish government took the position that they were never going to come back once they left, and that's why they didn't want to let them leave. I said, "Give me the baby and let one of the parents come." In effect, they could keep the other parent here to guarantee that the other spouse would come back home. They didn't buy into that.

So again I had to take a stance and I refused to go on a separate plane. I was livid about the amount of games that were played when a child's life was a stake. That's all this amounted to, playing games. Finally, they said, "Okay, you can leave together." Now I'm ready to get on the plane, and they are telling me to go on the plane first so I get a good seat. I said, "No. I'm not getting on that plane without the baby in my arms."

By this time, I knew what they would've done: they would have had me get on the plane, and then they would've closed the door. The plane would have taken off and that would've been the end of that. No, I'm a Marine and I'm not letting that happen, so they deciphered what was taking place and my position, and they finally said okay.

The parents gave me their child and then we all got on the plane together. The baby was fifteen months old at the time. When we landed in New York on Friday, August 21st, 1981, the news had spread that Lukasz was coming to America. When we arrived at Kennedy airport as we exited the plane the parents insisted I carry the baby and everybody was applauding. I said, “Lukasz, say hello to the United States of America. This is where everybody wants to live.”

The miracle of the whole story was that Lukasz was completely misdiagnosed in Poland. The doctors at New York University Medical Center determined that the best treatment for Lucas was not to have any surgery done. NYU doctors said that he would outgrow his medical condition and that is exactly what happened. He grew up to be a beautiful healthy man. The water was actually outside of the skull and not on the brain. It was a confirmation of the aggressive action taken on Lukasz' behalf that it was worth the battle. As the Polish government predicted, the Pniewski family did not return to Poland. They became proud American citizens.

Four months after I left Poland with Lukasz, on December 13th, 1981, the communist government of Poland instituted Martial Law in an attempt to crush the political opposition of the Solidarity Movement. Thousands of Solidarity activists were incarcerated without charge; Lech Walesa was one of them. He was jailed for eleven months. Fortunately, due to the international publicity generated from his battles on December 9th, 1990, he became the first democratically elected President of Poland. This would eventually lead to the fall of communism throughout Europe ending an era known as the Iron Curtain.

CHAPTER 19

The Freshman Congressman Beats Tip O'Neill

IN EARLY OCTOBER OF 1981, WORD CAME DOWN FROM the Reagan Administration that the Staten Island Public Health Service Hospital (hereinafter Staten Island Hospital) located at Bay Street and Vanderbilt Avenue, overlooking the Narrows, along with eight other Public Health Service Hospitals throughout the country, were being ordered to close their doors to the public forever in an effort to decrease federal spending. Staten Island Hospital was the largest of the Public Health Service Hospitals in the country, and it was an integral part of the community. It was a 407 patient bed facility that had been in existence for over 150 years and had evolved into an essential part of Staten Island's infrastructure. Yet, the administration's stance was firm: they did not want to pay for it any more. They had to cut dollars out of the budget by any means necessary.

The borough's three private hospitals—St. Vincent's, Staten Island, and Richmond Memorial—said they would be financially drained and physically overwhelmed if they were forced to care for the patients no longer treated at the Staten Island Hospital. The hospital was ordered by the Reagan Administration to stop admitting patients and to close by October 31st. This order created a "state of chaos" on Staten Island regarding health care for its residents.

Again, my blood boiled. As a freshman congressman my duty to Staten Island was to be a staunch defender of the Staten Island Hospital since it served our community so well. I would never meekly submit to a plan to phase out such a valuable service without a fight. I got the fact that the nation had to recover from a federal economy that was on the verge of collapse when Reagan took office, but it did not have to always be to the detriment of Staten Island and her population.

In Staten Island's case, St. Vincent's Hospital had offered to take over the Staten Island Hospital only if the federal government provided the funds to renovate the facility. Staten Island Hospital was actually in excellent condition but needed to be updated to comply with state and local guidelines if it was to be taken over privately. Under federal operation, hospital compliance with state and local guidelines was exempt. When the hospital was first built the practice was to house patients in large, open wards. Much of the renovations would be to change the wards into semi-private rooms. The 407 patient facility would essentially become a 204 patient community hospital under the proposed plans. St. Vincent's, in order to become part of the formula, needed to know that the hospital would continue to remain open until the actual conversion was completed.

Unfortunately, I learned that when we were getting ready to go on a recess there would definitely not be enough money in the budget for the Staten Island facility to stay open. I was totally depressed and could not stop thinking about how we were going to be able to care for the patients who would normally be cared for there. I knew it was going to be a colossal mess when I got home.

As a member of Congress you were able to watch the debates from your office as well as the gallery. In mid-October, I was sitting in my office because I was not feeling well. I was physically and emotionally drained, so I watched the debate on closed-circuit TV about the Continuing Resolution that was presently on the floor.

A Continuing Resolution is one of three types of appropriations bills. An appropriations bill is a bill that sets aside money to specific government departments, agencies and programs. The money provides funding for operations, personnel, equipment, and activities. Traditionally, regular appropriations bills are passed annually, with the funding they provide covering one fiscal year. The fiscal year or accounting period of the Federal government ran from October 1st, 1981, to September 30th, 1982. At the end of the fiscal year, if Congress has not enacted the regular appropriations bills, it can pass a continuing resolution, which continues the pre-existing appropriations at the same levels as the previous fiscal year (or with minor modifications) for a set amount of time. If a continuing resolution bill is not passed, a government shutdown for essential services can occur. [8]

I closed the door to my office, which I rarely did, and as I was sitting there watching the debate something moved me to go over to the House Chamber. To this day I don't know why, but I got up, and it was almost like a religious experience as I felt like I was being drawn to go to the debate even though I felt terrible and was not up to it. As I walked through my office and passed my Chief of Staff he said, "Where are you going?" I said, "I don't know. I'm going to the floor, I guess, I don't know." He said, "You don't look well." I said, "I know, I'm not feeling well."

I walked over to the House floor and Tip O'Neill was sitting in the Speaker's chair. Congressman Silvio Conte was the Republican in charge of the Republicans' debating time. Silvio was Tip's best friend even though he was a Republican congressman and Tip was a Democrat, they were both from Massachusetts. They commuted

---

8 "Continuing Resolution." Wikipedia, The Free Encyclopedia. Wikimedia Foundation, Inc. 22 July 204. Web. 14 April 2015.

back and forth from Washington together. As I got there the debate was getting ready to close down so there was not much time left. I felt that I had to try to do something even though I did not plan on speaking,

I spontaneously went over to Silvio Conte and said, "Silvio, I need a couple of minutes. Can you spare them?" I'm thinking to myself, "Tip O'Neill has one of these hospitals in his district. I'm going to embarrass the son-of-a-bitch." This was one of the rare occasions that Tip was actually sitting in the Speaker's chair. Silvio was a gruff, tough Italian-American, and he said, "Hey pal, where the heck have you been? I only have five minutes left and I have eight people who want to talk. I can't do it."

I guess he felt bad since he came down heavy on me, because a few minutes later he leaned back and said, "Hey, Molinari. I'll give you one minute of my five minutes." I said, "I can't do it in one minute, I need two minutes."

Conte started cursing and said, "Ah-ha, there you go. I find one minute for you, now you want two. What am I gonna tell these other guys?" However, he somehow managed to do it and I was allotted two minutes speaking time.

With that, when my turn came, I stood up and I addressed the House, but more importantly, I addressed my remarks to Tip O'Neil and I remember saying, "Mr. Speaker, would the Speaker yield to a question?"

He looked puzzled and I could see that he's trying to figure out why I would be asking him a question. Especially, since I was a brand new freshman congressman. He says, "Of course, please do."

"Mr. Speaker, we're leaving today and we're going to sign this Continuing Resolution, and the Public Health Service Hospitals are going to close before we come back because there is going to be no money allocated for them to continue to operate. Mr. Speaker I'm only here a short time, but in that time I have been listening to you and others on your side of the aisle talk about the Democrats being the party for the weak, the poor, and the sick. Well, Mr. Speaker, I don't believe it anymore. You can't prove it, because Mr. Speaker, you have a Public Health Service Hospital in your district that is going to close and so do I. As a matter of fact, I have the biggest one in the system in my district. There are over 400 beds in the facility on Staten Island. How do the citizens pick up that slack? Patients are going to be thrown out of the hospitals while we are on recess. At home, it will be awful news for the poor and sick people in the hospitals. What do I tell the people? What do I tell the sick patients? What do you tell the people, what do you tell the sick patients?"

So the Speaker turned very silent and asked somebody to take his place in the chair so that he could be involved in debate. He asked me, "Would the gentleman from New York yield to a question?" I said, "Of course, I would be happy to yield to the Speaker."

He said, "Why didn't you offer an amendment providing money for it? I know you're a freshman, but you have to learn the rules here." He was trying to make me look bad. I said, "I did." He said, "So what happened?"

I said, "Mr. Speaker I did want to offer an amendment and I went to the Parliamentarian and asked him. The Parliamentarian said that I couldn't do it. He said it was out of order and it wasn't germane, so we couldn't do it." Now I'm starting to get the momentum on my side.

At this point, Tip stopped the entire proceeding, had someone take the gavel and he was down in the well talking to three or four people and consulting with the Parliamentarian. The Parliamentarian and Tip were poring over the books. During their discussion the phone rang in the little office right off the chamber and I was called off the floor to receive the call.

When I answered the phone it was the United States Secretary of Health and Human Services, Richard "Dick" Schweiker, on the other end. He said, "O'Neill's going to give you the amendment and I'm going to tell you what to do. With your amendment put in 65 million dollars for the operation and conversion of the facilities. Of that, 26 million will go for your facility; 26 million for Seattle; 10

million for Baltimore and 3 million for Boston." I said, "It sounds great to me."

I didn't know what the hell was going on, but you can bet I was ecstatic when I heard his words. I could not believe that I had received a commitment from the Federal Department of Health and Human Services. The hospital was actually going to be saved. Even to this day it is a big blur, since I was so sick. Again it was like a religious experience where somebody was pulling my hands and putting words into my mouth. Had I stayed in my office the hospitals would have closed immediately.

Of the four federal hospitals included under the amendment, all had already found local sponsors who were willing to merge with the hospital after they had been updated in order to conform to state and local health and building codes. That is what the federal money was to be used for, to update the hospitals so that their operations could be merged into the private sector hospitals.

Finally, O'Neill turned around and said, "Okay, I talked to the Parliamentarian and we looked it over and decided that it is germane and it can be offered. Do you have an amendment?" I said, "It's being prepared as we speak, Mr. Speaker. I should have it any second now."

So the amendment was typed up and circulated. Tip read it and asked me if I would yield again. I said, "Of course."

O'Neill gets up, now everybody watching, whether they're in their offices or whatnot, this is the Speaker, now involved in a debate with a guy in the minority on a Continuing Resolution. It's a partisan thing; people are trying to figure out what the hell I'm doing. Again everyone knew I was in the minority; it was a given that he, O'Neill, controlled the votes because he was in the majority. He says, "Alright, my friends. Here's what we are going to do. To all those on the Democratic side of the aisle that are watching in their offices or whatever, I'm asking you to vote 'No' to the Molinari amendment. When that's voted down, I will offer the same amendment with my name on it and you can vote 'Yes' for that one, since it is a partisan issue." Tip did this because it was unheard of to have the Speaker of the House have a Continuing Resolution won by someone in the minority.

Even though they were best friends, Silvio Conte jumped up and in his basking Italian accent yelled, "Oh, no, no, Mr. Speaker. No, no, no. You can't do it because you need unanimous consent to do that and I'm telling you guys that I am going to object. So you're not going to get past it. If you guys want to save the hospitals in your district, you're going to have to vote for the Molinari amendment, this is the only time you're going to have a chance to vote on it. Therefore, it is your only chance to save those facilities. So if you got people from your districts that go to these facilities, you better vote 'Yes' on the Molinari amendment, or they're going to be closed, and you're going to take the blame for it."

Silvio was able to separate friendship from what was best for his constituents and that is what made him a great congressman. He knew that regardless of the outcome, he and Tip would be out later that night and have a few drinks together. They both understood the rules of the game. Silvio was doing his job and so was Tip. Regardless of what happened in the chamber, they were the best of friends when they walked out.

So, there we are, the Continuing Resolution, the Speaker himself involved in the debate and a partisan vote. I'm still a relatively new member. They called for the vote, and I'm looking around. I'm looking at the board and I'm wondering, "Wow, can you imagine if I win this thing? To beat Tip O'Neill, one of the most powerful Speakers in the history of Congress, what a thing that would be for me." Even though I didn't know what the hell I was doing, somehow I was beginning to think I pulled a rabbit out of the hat as I'm watching the board as the vote is taking place. I see a couple of Democrats voting for me. The number showed up 15/15 and I looked up again to see 30/30, looked up again and the vote continued within one or two votes of each other and finally the final vote for the lot. I won by three votes, obviously a very tight vote. Out of a total of 435 members all it took was a margin of three votes for David to topple Goliath.

It was a fantastic way to end the session, and a completely solid victory for my constituents in Staten Island. Instead of going home to a mess, I was going home to a grateful community who still had their hospital. Within a short period of time, The Staten Island Hospital would become renamed Bayley Seton Hospital when it was merged into St. Vincent's Hospital.

The following day it was reported in the papers that the Reagan Administration approved an agreement that would avert the closing of the federal Staten Island Hospital. In my opinion, it was a win-win for both sides. The federal government would ultimately be relieved of the burden of carrying the hospital and the Staten Island community would be able to have the hospital continue serving the community, but under private control.

When the federal government's rescue mission was publicized, residents of Harlem were in an uproar. They felt that the government should have bailed out Sydenham hospital in Harlem a year before. Sydenham was the first hospital to have a fully desegregated interracial policy with six African-American trustees, and twenty African-Americans on staff. It was New York City's first full-service hospital to hire African-American doctors, and later became known for hiring African-American doctors and nurses when other nearby hospitals would not. Historically it was a racially groundbreaking municipal hospital.

Unfortunately, after Mayor Koch took office in 1977 while dealing with the fiscal crisis, he announced an additional 10% reduction in funding for municipal hospitals and two hospitals in East Harlem, Metropolitan and Sydenham, were slated for closure. There was intense community outrage when word of the closings leaked. In the long run, Metropolitan Hospital survived the purge, but Sydenham did not. Koch said that the city was in terrible financial straits, and his budget director recommended the closing of Sydenham since it was a higher cost per patient than any of the city's other hospitals, and reports showed the Sydenham was not rendering good medical care to the community. So to Koch it just did not make sense to keep it open.

In essence though, regarding the relationship to the Staten Island Hospitals, it was apples and oranges. Sydenham Hospital was not a federally funded hospital it was a municipal hospital and the decision to close it was Mayor Koch's and not the federal government. The liberal media portrayed the deal I had obtained as one standard of health care being applied to Harlem and another to Staten Island. In fact, that was not true. It was a question of a federally funded hospital as opposed to a municipality funded hospital. New York City had dug itself into an economic crisis of massive proportions, while the federal government, although in bad shape when Reagan took office, was nowhere near as bleak. Looking back, I know that I did the right thing by Staten Island. I fought hard and I was able to get the funds for the hospital. I was doing my job that I was elected to do.

In November of 1981, President Reagan presented the Soviet Union with a so-called zero option in which all Soviet and U.S. intermediate-range nuclear missiles would be removed from Europe. In his speech, the President called for cancelling deployment of 572 intermediate range Pershing II and cruise missiles if the Soviets in turn would dismantle its approximately six hundred SS-20, SS-4 and SS-5 missiles. The President was scheduled to meet with the Russian leader Leonid Brezhnev, who was the chairman of the Presidium of the Supreme Soviet, in Geneva, on Monday November 30th to begin talks at controlling medium-range weapons in Geneva.

When President Reagan made that speech calling for the removal of missiles I wrote a letter to Soviet Ambassador Anatoly F. Dobryin. In the letter I wrote, "I implore you to stress to the Supreme Soviet leader the urgent need for immediate discussion of the issue. It would without a doubt lead to a permanent resolution of what could very well be a question of world survival."

Needless to say, I was quite surprised when I was informed by a staff member that around lunchtime on Wednesday November 25th, the day before Thanksgiving, two rather large Russian gentlemen came knocking on my office doors in Washington. The office was closed and I had a skeleton staff working. My legislative assistant, Russell J. Schriefer, was the only one there. When Russell opened the door, Nikolai Smirnov, the second secretary of the Russian Embassy, was standing there with his body guard. Mr. Smirnov stated he was there on behalf of Anatoly Dobrynin, the Soviet Ambassador to the United States. He told Russell that Mr. Dobrynin wanted to meet with me at my earliest convenience.

Needless to say, when Russell told me about the impromptu visit my first reaction was what the hell do the Russians want from me? Should I set it up? I immediately contacted the State Department who sent the FBI to come and see me. I was directed to keep the appointment and that they would debrief me afterwards. I then set up a meeting the following week.

At the time, there was an Englishman named Bill Aylward working in my office. He was about my age and very sharp. Bill asked, "Can I come with you to the meeting with the Russian Ambassador?" I said, "Yeah, sure."

When we went and had the meeting with Ambassador Dobryin it was just the three of us. I started by asking Dobryin, "What do you want to see me for?"

Mr. Dobryin said, "Because you are important. You're one of the five freshmen Congressmen who is supposed to be a leading star."

I said, "Yeah, sure, and the tooth fairy was here." I then said, "I'm a freshman congressman, I'm not important."

He said, "No, no, no. You're more than a freshman. I know what I'm doing; I've been doing this a long time. We know that you're going to be a player and we want to make an introduction."

Right after this, Bill and the Ambassador started getting into a war of words. They had a fierce argument about our system of government and their system of government. It was fun to watch, but we had to be careful because this guy was from Russia and I didn't trust the sons of bitches way back then. Come to think of it, I don't trust them now either.

At the time, Russia was still a communist country and evoked mistrust in the eyes of America for good reason and was not looked upon with favor by Americans. The whole time I was in his office I couldn't figure out what they really wanted, but it was clear they were looking for somebody to make a subversive deal.

After the meeting, when I contacted the State Department for the debriefing, I asked them who the man really was. They told me that he was in charge of the KGB in the United States. I asked them, "Why don't you get rid of him?"

They said, "He's a very bright man, but we know his MO. If they send someone else we would not know his MO. So we prefer to have people like you call us so that we can keep an eye on him." In retrospect their rationale made sense.

So, the world of being a congressman always brought surprises your way. Working in Washington meant addressing global issues as well as local issues. You had to continually be able to bounce yourself from one direction to another without making mistakes. You had to think on your feet. You had to pay attention and always keep your guard up, as with the Russians. Trust was hard to gain once you lost it in the international community and as a politician you always had to remember that.

CHAPTER 20

Denise Attilio's Brave Battle

I REMEMBER ONE DAY I WAS READING THE *STATEN Island Advance* in my office and I was deeply affected by a beautiful picture of a young woman that appeared in the paper. As I read the extraordinarily sad story I learned that twenty-two year-old Denise Attilio was dying of a progressive liver disease. Her family could not afford to pay for a liver transplant. In the early 1980s, the cost of a liver transplant was about $100,000. Tragically, neither federal nor state governments would provide any medical coverage for liver transplants.

I found out that Denise lived with her parents in the Castleton Corners section of Staten Island. In 1959, three months after she was born, she was diagnosed with chronic biliary atresia. If this disease was left untreated it was always fatal. The disease itself occurs when a child's common bile duct is blocked or damaged by scar tissue. As such, it is impossible for bile to flow out of the liver. With the progression of the disease it would ultimately result in cirrhosis of the liver and death. In Denise's case, her body was slowly being poisoned. It was predicted that if she did not get a liver transplant within six months she would die a horrible death, since everything would start failing inside her body, one organ after another.

That beautiful photo of Denise touched me, yet at the same time haunted me. I felt compelled to tackle her problem head on and try to help her get a liver transplant. After talking to Denise and her mother Louisa, I learned that they and the Children's Liver Foundation had previously applied for New York State and Federal Medicaid funding but their requests were repeatedly denied because liver transplant surgery was considered "experimental" at the time and as such were not approved for federal or state funding anywhere in the country.

They told me about their efforts to raise money to pay for Denise's liver transplant. I was initially toying with the idea of getting involved with the fund raising efforts but then I thought, "Why not as a public official, try to get state and federal funding for the liver transplant?" It was readily apparent to me that the family would not be able to raise the $100,000 in time for the lifesaving transplant surgery for Denise. It was after this odd realization that I decided the best option was to get the government to pay for the surgery so that it could be done quickly.

Subsequently, I contacted Dr. Thomas Starzl who was the Chief of Transplantation Services at Presbyterian University Hospital in Pittsburgh. He oversaw the largest and busiest transplant program in the world. He was a pioneer in performing liver transplants. He performed the world's first human liver transplant in 1963. As a result of his expertise he has often been referred to as the "father of modern transplantation." He had performed over 200 liver transplants and 1000 kidney transplants. In addition, he was instrumental in the development of the class of anti-rejection drugs such as Cyclosporine A that would help a body accept a new liver. It was these developments that allowed liver transplants to progress from the "experimental" phase to a viable acceptable treatment for irreversible liver disease funded by Medicaid, such as Denise's.

As busy as Dr. Starzl was saving lives, we had numerous telephone conversations about his personal successes at performing liver transplants surgery as well as Denise's battle. Based upon his expertise and success rate, I became convinced that liver transplants should be approved for medical coverage. Dr. Starzl was emphatic that the State and Federal governments were wrong about their conclusion that liver transplants were "experimental." He provided plenty of data on the success rate of liver transplants at the time. In fact, even back then, his success rate at the hospital was almost 75%.

So, the first thing I did was call New York State Lieutenant Governor Mario Cuomo. Since I had extensive conversations with Dr. Starzl I knew that the Federal and State Governments' conclusions were flawed because they were based on incorrect and outdated information. I said, "Mario, I think that we are all making a big mistake in denying state funding for liver transplants. New York State should be a leader in groundbreaking legislation to provide for state funding for this life saving procedure. Dr. Starzl has documented proof that 75% of the liver transplants are successful. How much more proof does the state need to embrace this highly successful procedure?"

Lieutenant Governor Cuomo listened intently and then referred me to the Health Commissioner, Dr. David Axelrod. I had many conversations with Dr. Axelrod trying to convince him that the thing to do now was to approve state funding for liver transplants since Dr. Starzl had ample documentation about the success rate of liver transplants.

Immediately before Christmas 1981, I was informed by Dr. Axelrod that the State of New York had reconsidered its earlier position and certified Presbyterian University Hospital, in Pittsburgh, for Medicaid reimbursement for liver transplants. It was an extraordinary accomplishment! New York became the first state in the nation that approved Medicaid funding for a liver transplant.

When I informed Denise of the state's decision I remember her saying, "This is the best Christmas present I've ever had, and I know that this decision will help others in the same position as me." We still had a lot of work to do, but everything was finally moving in the right direction for Denise.

Unfortunately, the battle for Denise Attilio's successful liver transplant was only half finished. Now I had to fight to get the second part of the formula: I needed the federal government to cover their half of the liver transplant. I had previously contacted the Department of Health and Human Services and they had told me, just like New York State initially determined, that they were denying coverage because the procedure was considered "experimental." They stated the reason why liver transplants were considered experimental was due to the extremely low success rate for liver transplant surgery. As such, Medicare law prohibited payment for experimental and investigational procedures. Since New York had already reversed their original decision I was hoping that this would be an easier battle.

I then vigorously pursued discussions with the Secretary of Health and Human Services, Richard Schweiker. Fortunately, the *Staten Island Advance* continued to report on Denise's situation bringing her plight to the nation's attention. Finally, a former schoolmate and friend of Denise's, Patricia Mezzacappa, sent a letter to President Reagan begging for his assistance. Then the New Year's miracle occurred. On Wednesday January 6th, 1982, Denise received a call from Secretary Schweiker who said, "President Ronald Reagan wanted to make sure that you are all right and I personally guarantee that the Health and Human Services will fund the surgery." Denise told me it was like a belated Christmas present and the happiest day of her life.

On January 18th, 1982, she received the formal letter from Secretary Richard Schweiker which stated as follows:[9]

> Ms. Patricia Mezzacappa has written to the President concerning your need for financial assistance in

9 *Letter to be reproduced in book.*

> obtaining a liver transplant. President Reagan asked that we try to be of help. Congressman Molinari also was in touch on your behalf.
>
> I am pleased to report that the State of New York has extended Medicaid coverage to liver transplants; we have also been informed that you have been found eligible for Medicaid assistance and the New York State Department of Health will approve Medicaid coverage of the transplant. The U.S. Department of Health and Human Services will share with New York State the cost of your liver transplant operation. You should be receiving notice of this favorable decision from New York in the near future.

As soon as these decisions were made, Denise flew to Pittsburg with her mother and was admitted to Presbyterian University Hospital to await a potential donor for the liver transplant. On Thursday, January 21st, 1982, Dr. Starzl performed a twelve-hour surgical procedure and transplanted a new liver in Denise. Three days later one of the first things Denise's mother did was to give her daughter a mirror so that Denise could see her reflection in the mirror. For most of Denise's teen years, due to her malfunctioning liver, her skin and eyes were always tinted yellow. On this day her skin color was a beautiful normal color giving justice to her stunning face. When her mother told me this I was no longer haunted by her ordeal. We had performed a small miracle for a magnificent woman.

After Denise's liver transplant became a reality, I wrote to the Governors and Health Commissioners of every state in the union to tell them what we did in New York. I urged them to adopt the same position. Of course, not all states followed New York's lead, but many did. This decision has resulted in the saving of thousands and thousands of lives. Today the United States performs approximately 6,000 liver transplants annually. Thank God for Dr. Starzl's dedication and extraordinary background as well as Denise's perseverance. Without them I seriously doubt that 6,000 lives would be saved every year due to liver transplants.

On an unexpectedly sad note, Denise died on November 17th, 1982, ten months after the lifesaving surgery. Although she did well after the initial transplant several months later she became bloated and jaundiced. The Doctors felt that she was rejecting the liver and preformed a second liver transplant in November of 1982. She passed away six days after the second transplant because her body did reject the liver.

I received an inspiring letter from Denise's sister, Gail twenty years after Denise's groundbreaking surgery. She believes, as did her family, that of all my years in public service this had to be my greatest achievement. To this day her family is so proud, and I share in that pride, that Denise Attilio was the first person in our country to obtain state and federal Medicaid funding for liver transplants. Thousands of other liver transplant patients have benefited from Denise Attilio's legacy.

This battle reinforces the fact that you can succeed with extraordinarily difficult issues such as this only if you are willing to take on the challenge. These challenges require commitment, research, devotion and extraordinary amounts of time. In so many different areas during my political career I have taken a course of action that I should never have been able to win. Yet, amazingly, I wound up winning the majority of them. It's almost like an addiction: The more victories you have on these difficult issues, the more you want to take on.

CHAPTER 21

The Death of the Travis Power Plant

The fight to stop the Travis Power plant dragged on. On March 2nd, 1982, a federal environmental agency gave a final air-quality permit for the Travis Power Plant. John Dyson, the Chairman of PASNY, was hot on his feet to get the project completed. I let him know that I would appeal the decision within a stipulated thirty-day period to get a review by the E.P.A. Administrator, Anne M. Gorsuch. If she refused, I would appeal to the Federal Court within sixty-days. I would exhaust every legal remedy available to prevent this plant.

On March 23rd, the Appellate Division of 2nd Department told the New York State Board on Electric Generation Siting and the Environment to reopen its hearings to reconsider whether the city's air pollution laws were "unreasonably restrictive." Findings that the city's air pollution laws were unreasonably restrictive removed the major hurdle to building the plant since, as designed, the plant would supposedly comply with federal and state guidelines yet would exceed New York City's tougher air quality requirements for airborne pollutants. The court held that the board, in finding the city's pollution laws restrictive, had placed the burden of proof on the city. The court ruled that it should have been placed on the authority. It was a massive game changing decision in Staten Island's favor toward crushing the building of the Travis Power Plant.

I would have loved to be a fly on the wall of Dyson's office when he heard about the decision. I can only imagine that he went ballistic. When the decision came out I again reiterated my position that I would go the highest state and federal courts if necessary to block the plant. It was one of the few times where I welcomed the phrase, "The wheels of justice grind slowly." If it took a thousand years to fight the battle I would be there. As long as the proposed plant would never spew any filthy pollutants on my beloved Staten Island, it was worth the battle.

As a congressman you are reelected every two years so during this time period I was also working on my reelection campaign. Redistricting had taken place and now my Congressional District was the 14th District and included the Bay Ridge section of Brooklyn and Staten Island, as opposed to lower Manhattan, which remained the 17th. I was pitted against Leo C. Zeferetti, a four term-Brooklyn Democrat congressman who currently held the 14th district seat. I had established myself as an independent Republican who was not afraid to say "No" to the president. This was crucial especially when the country was getting frustrated about the decrease in social programs and the continued increase in military spending.

One of the highlights of my campaign occurred on Monday, October 11th, when Vice President George Bush came to Staten Island for, in his words, "A pure unadulterated political visit on behalf of the campaign to reelect my friend Guy V. Molinari." It was a tremendously successful event held at the Shalimar in New Dorp. 750 people paid $50 a head to hear Bush speak and 50 people paid

$500 for a private reception with the V.P. At the time, that was a remarkable fundraiser generating over $60,000 for my campaign in a few hours. On Tuesday, November 2nd, I handily beat four-time incumbent Democratic Congressman Leo Zeferetti. I received 57% of the vote compared to his 42%.

The outcome did not work out for many of the Republicans whom the public saw as "Reagan Robots." The public wanted Congressmen who showed some independence from the Whitehouse, such as myself. Reaganomics was not going over well and the country began leaning in a more Democratic direction.

On December 10th, I voted with Democrats at a committee meeting, 28 to 11, to cite Anne Gorsuch, head of the EPA, for contempt of Congress for withholding subpoenaed documents, concerning the toxic waste cleanup program, on President Reagan's orders. The vote followed party lines with only one exception: me. Of course by many Republicans this was considered heresy, but I was following the conscience of Staten Island and I had to be ethical in my decisions. I would do whatever I could to prevent the building of the Travis Power plant. The administration was playing games and I was not going to be their pawn. I would not be a puppet in their charade. The vote came after Gorsuch, acting on Reagan's orders, invoked executive privilege in withholding documents dealing with the EPA's toxic waste cleanup program.

Hallelujah! When Mario Cuomo was elected Governor I was thrilled even though I was a Republican. One of the main reasons for my exuberance became clear when he announced that as Governor-elect he would live up to a campaign promise, to halt the longstanding plans for the Travis Plant. Finally: redemption for Staten Island. For me the plant was like the "cat with nine lives."

I was thrilled to hear that the Governor-elect said, "They don't believe you when you make campaign promises. I think there is an expectation that all the things you said during a campaign should be reconsidered immediately after the election. I'm serious. I'm against it. You should be able to take campaign statements seriously."[10]

It was a great way for me to go on Christmas recess. A total victory for Staten Island against insurmountable odds. I had fought this battle for over seven years, and I finally saw light at the end of the tunnel. No words could express my relief that the battle was finally over. I did not foresee any resurrection of the battle. Everyone that would reconsider this issue would know that I would be battling against it at every opportunity. I would be tireless and so it would be a fruitless proposition. My perseverance had finally paid off and I know that the benefit to my community and constituents was incalculable.

I knew it was a done deal when Governor-elect Cuomo wrote a letter to the New York Times on December 30th, 1982, and stated as follows:

> In a Dec. 29 editorial you charged me with "unworthy opportunism" in acting to keep my campaign promise to stop the proposed Arthur Kill power plant on Staten Island. I'm surprised at your cynicism and your failure to make a factual presentation.
>
> My opposition to the plant dates from 1977. I have argued against it repeatedly since then, at times when no election campaign was imminent or in progress. I have consistently based my opposition on environmental grounds – and have been joined in the opposition by Mayor Koch, Representative Guy Molinari, Assemblywoman Elizabeth Connelly and other public officials [.][11]

---

10 *New York Times Dec 22, 1982 Michael Oreskess "Cuomo says He will Cancel Plans to Build Arthur Kill Power Plant" A1 &B13*

11 *New York Times Dec 30, 1982 Mario M. Cuomo Governor-Elect "Why Cuomo is Against the Arthur Kill Plant" A18 Letter to the editor*

This was clearly one of times that I could say that a completely nonpartisan issue fully benefited Staten Island. Party lines were crossed for the greater good of a community. That is really what politics is all about doing the right thing regardless of party lines.

CHAPTER 22

The Poisoned Texas Water at Air Force Plant 4

In early 1983 I was on a trip to Dallas, Texas, concerning a Congressional hearing. I was sitting by myself in my motel room at night since I was the only Republican there. My room was on the ground floor and the door was open. Next door to my room was a room full of Democrats. They were having a very loud discussion and I couldn't help but overhear the conversation since their door was open as well. What they were talking about was completely unrelated to the reason why I was in Texas.

They were discussing a hearing regarding some sort of application that they were interested in. From the bits of conversation that I caught, they were talking about toxic chemicals and poisons that existed in a facility in Texas that made airplanes. I was able to glean from the conversation that the manufacturing facility was a huge source of income for Texas' economy. Before too long it became very clear to me that they were talking about a dangerous environmental issue that involved the possible contamination of the local water supply. It sounded like they were brainstorming how to make the problem disappear without informing the public. It seemed like a classic cover-up. I obviously did not like what I heard. I couldn't sleep that night, since it sounded like they wanted to completely ignore the negative impact on the health of the residents in the area.

The next day I went to get some coffee. Again, as the sole Republican I was by myself. To help pass the time, I started reading one of the local papers. I read a story about some lucrative manufacturing project that was being done at Carswell Air Force base located in Fort Worth, Texas. The base was located in the Speaker of the House Jim Wright's 12th Congressional District. General Dynamics was a multi-billion-dollar aircraft manufacturing company and manufactured aircraft at the facility. This was an immense source of revenue for the local citizens and The State of Texas.

The paper described how the facility had massive open pits on site for disposal of chemicals. General Dynamics claimed that there was no risk to the public because the residue of the toxic chemicals called leachate, which drained into a creek bed, was safe. They claimed that the creek that the leachate drained into had an impermeable bed so it was impossible for toxic chemicals to enter the underground water supply via the creek bed. General Dynamics and their ally Jim Wright took the firm position that it would never gravitate to the public drinking water supply.

Putting two and two together I immediately realized that the conversation I heard the night before was about the same General Dynamics Facility in Fort Worth Texas. I knew that it was a complete fluke that I had stumbled upon a very important toxic environmental issue. That was not the reason why I was in Texas. I immediately thought to myself, "If General Dynamics is wrong, especially after what I overheard, the citizens of Texas could be in for an environmental disaster, if I was right, clearly a huge portion of the area's population was at risk."

I also knew that Jim Wright was very close with the parties involved. In fact, General Dynamics always made substantial contributions to his political campaigns. It was obvious that their relationship was extremely cozy and I believed that Jim Wright would do whatever he could to protect that relationship.

My moral fiber could not ignore the issue; so as I learned in law school due diligence required relevant research in order to determine if my instincts were right. What I eventually found out was that the government owned the facility called Air Force Plant 4, located immediately adjacent to Carswell Air Force Base in Tarrant County just outside of Fort Worth Texas. The government contracted out to the private company, General Dynamics, who manufactured military aircraft since 1953 at the site. The military aircraft they produced at Plant 4 included production of iconic airplanes such as the B-36, B-58, Mach-2-capable B-58, F-111, F-16, and others.

Through my research, I learned that in the fall of 1982, a hunter passed a discharge pipe from the General Dynamics facility that entered a creek bed adjacent to the plant. The hunter observed a suspicious thick liquid being discharged from the pipe. The hunter notified General Dynamics and the company found that leachate from a disposal pit was infiltrating the storm drain and entering the creek bed area. The creek entered Lake Worth, which was the drinking water source for Fort Worth and neighboring communities.

At the facility, each open containment pit was designated for disposal of different toxic chemicals such as fuels, excess oil, paints, etc. General Dynamics would just dump the toxic chemicals into these pits. When informed of the infiltration problem by the hunter in early November 1982, General Dynamics installed a French drain to intercept the leachate which was entering the storm water discharge system via the creek.

Geographically the surrounding area of the plant was highly populated. Six schools were within a two-mile radius of the plant. Lake Worth bordered the plant and supplied municipal water to the City of Fort Worth Texas, and was a recharge source to the underlying Paluxy Aquifer[12]. The City of White Settlement, Texas received their municipal water supply from the wells completed in the lower Paluxy aquifer. To my understanding no formal studies had been done on the actual soil and groundwater for concerning possible contamination that may affect the surrounding community.

With this knowledge in hand, I then personally contacted the federal investigative agency called the National Enforcement Investigators Center, (hereinafter NEIC) located in Denver, Colorado. NEIC operated under the EPA. The director was Thomas Gallagher. NEIC knew me from the Congressional work that Elliot Levitas and I were doing concerning EPA violations as members of the Investigation and Oversight subcommittee. These EPA employees, many of whom were scientists, understood the magnitude of the deadly impact of toxic issues if left unchecked. They were not politicians: They knew their job could be the difference between life and death for citizens in environmentally affected areas and they took their job very seriously.

I told them that I didn't like what I heard and found regarding a potential contaminated water supply. It sounded like the public was being unknowingly exposed to toxic chemicals. I asked the NEIC to send a crew over to the facility to take samples of the drinking water supply at the creek and surrounding area.

When NEIC compiled the results of the tests they conducted, the results were extremely frightening: NEIC determined that there was a potentially serious ground water pollution problem attributable to as many as ten waste disposal pits at the General Dynamics facility.

NEIC found as many as thirty-nine priority pollutants on site, of which over seven were deadly carcinogens such as trichloroeth-

---

12 *Paluxy Aquifer is the name of the geological aquifer supplying most of the water to the highly populated area just west of Fort Worth. Geographically, it comprises the upper layer of the Trinity Aquifer from the Red River south to the Texas Hill Country. It is one of nine major and 21 minor aquifers that supply about 60% of the state's water supply. In the Paluxy aquifer the water flows slowly through honeycomb formations of limestone, sand and silt.*

ylene, chloroform, 1,2-dichloroethane, benzene, arsenic, and cadmium to name a few. Additionally, their testing revealed that the surrounding soil and upper-level ground water were apparently already grossly contaminated with a variety of toxic chemicals. Finally, they determined that there was a high potential for human health hazard if the underground water in the city wells became contaminated.

Clearly, General Dynamics and Jim Wright were completely wrong. It appeared to be a critical mistake that totally jeopardized the residents in the surrounding Air Force Plant 4 area. The fact of the matter was that the creek was not impermeable: Not only was it at least semi-permeable, it could turn into an epic environmental disaster in two short years. Lives could definitely be lost, and there could be countless health issues to deal with because of their error.

In essence what everyone learned from the quiet investigation that I initiated through the NEIC experts was: THE BAD NEWS, the above ground water supply was contaminated; THE GOOD NEWS was that the toxic chemicals had not permeated the underground drinking water supply yet.

However, their findings indicated that within two years if things kept on progressing the way they were, the toxic chemicals would reach the underground water supply. What would have happened next was that people would start dying from the toxic chemicals. The poison levels of these chemicals were off the charts.

In my correspondence with the EPA regarding the initial investigation they told me that they had made five repeated requests to the Air Force and General Dynamics officials for data concerning the site, the most recent which was on April 23rd, 1983. The Air Force and General Dynamics completely ignored those requests. I knew that time was of the essence to address the imminent toxic environmental disaster that I believed could be prevented, but immediate action was necessary. It was clear to me that General Dynamics and the Air Force were blatantly disregarding the EPA findings based on not responding to the EPA's requests.

Now I had the fact specific information that the public was clearly at risk since the facility was dragging their feet in correcting the public hazard. Since General Dynamics manufacturing facility was in Jim Wright's 12th Congressional district in Texas I had to figure out how to make the public aware in a politically smart manner. I knew from experience that Jim Wright was probably one of the toughest Democratic Speakers of the House that Congress ever had. He was considered a very difficult man to deal with if you were on opposite sides of the podium.

So instinctually I consulted with Elliot Levitas, my trusted bipartisan counterpart. I said, "Elliott, look at what I found. I talked to NEIC because they know us from our great investigative work. They did a great job at my request. The long and short of it is that the creek is not impermeable. The toxic results to the community are off the chart: People could die if they drink that water. We can't just sit on this information!"

Elliot said, "Oh, my God, this is terrible. I hope that you are going to take it up with Jim Wright?" I said, "No, I'm not."

Elliot said, "You have to. He'll go crazy. He's a tough guy." I said, "Well, I'm afraid if I tell him first he will definitely try to squash it. Sometimes you just have to follow your gut. I know that he'll try to use any tactic that he can, to stop me from coming out publically with the information. He can be a real son-of-a- bitch. Wright will scream, shout, rant, and rave. We both know that's what he would do. So I'd rather take the hits from him, but let unfold what's happening in Texas so that we can take care of the public health hazard that's confronting the residents. There's no second way of handling an issue like this. The public's gotta know about this. I'm going to tell him after the fact. This is too important."

Elliot said, "Yeah you're probably right, but please do me a favor: Don't tell him that you and I had this conversation."

I said, "Don't worry, Elliott, I have no intention of doing that. He will never know about this conversation." We both knew that it would drive Jim Wright crazy to know that his Democratic counterpart was in cahoots with a Republican regarding a major negative environmental issue in his Congressional District. Yet I knew that I was the only congressman who had the knowledge of what was happening in Fort Worth Texas and the guts to go public with the information. Sometimes the path to righteousness is the hard one, and that is the one I chose, because it was the right one for the public good.

On April 28th, 1983 I put out a Press release titled "AIRFORCE AND GENERAL DYNAMICS DELAY IN CLEANING UP HAZARDOUS WASTE DAMAGE." As expected the proverbial shit hit the fan and the whole sky fell down around Jim Wright's world. The press attention was enormous. In the press release I stated, blatantly aware of the adverse negative attention I was thrusting on Jim Wright through his own inaction:

> I neither wish to alarm the people of the Fort Worth area, nor make charges that the areas drinking water supply is unhealthy or dangerous. However, I have information that raises concern and there are several questions that need to be answered. I am particularly disturbed about the repeated failures of both the Air Force and General Dynamics to provide the data on toxics at the site.[13]

Jim Wright called me immediately. He started off by saying, "What the fuck are you doing, Man? Texas doesn't need New York guys telling us how to run things in our state, you've got to put out something saying it was wrong, or whatever." Knowing that he was a total son-of- a-bitch I said, "Well, Jim, I'm here to tell you what they are doing is wrong and it's not a good picture you are painting. Regardless of party lines, understand that I am an American first and

---

13 Congressman Guy Molinari Press Release 28 April 1983, "AIRFORCE AND GENERAL DYNAMICS DELAY IN CLEANING UP HAZARDOUS WASTE DAMAGE"

foremost. Understand that I'm not out to get you, but this is dangerous and the public has to be protected. "

Wright then used every possible trick in the book to try to soften me up. He tried the nice guy approach. "We can work together, you know," he said. "I'm the speaker; I can help you out. You're a minority, I can help you with some of the bills you're putting in just drop this thing, we gotta work together and not against each other."

He soon realized that I had been around too long to take any of his bullshit.

When that didn't work he threatened me. He said, "You better back off this issue, it will not be good for your political career." At the time it was an extraordinarily difficult thing to do because I knew that he could hurt me politically. I had bills that he could have killed. Yet I had no choice, I had to do it. As a decent person, I had to do it.

So I told him, "Jim I'm not going to buckle to your threats, that's not why I came to Washington. I am going to hold my ground. I came to Congress to try to protect the people, not to hide things." Wright was furious but at least the story was out.

It was ironic that he blatantly lied to the media when they asked him for a response to my press release. They asked him, "Did you contact Congressman Molinari to discuss what he stated?" Jim Wright said, "No, I didn't. Why should I call him? Texas has nothing to do with him."

Fortunately, in the long run it was agreed politically and ethically that it was necessary to clean up the site on a federal level. By October of 1984 the General Dynamics facility was included on the National Priorities List (NPL) of the most hazardous toxic waste sites across the country. At the time after much insistence the Department of Defense (DOD) finally agreed to cooperate with the EPA. This cooperation lead to an unprecedented agreement between the DOD and EPA to share information and act cooperatively in addressing hazardous waste problems at DOD facilities across the country not just addressing the Texas facility.

Ultimately the Comprehensive Environmental Response, Compensation and Liability Act of 1980 (CERCLA) or "Superfund" as it is widely known was utilized to clean up the site. Under the Superfund, crews came from the NEIC and they proceeded to formulate and execute a clear, timely efficient cleanup effort so that nobody was ever poisoned from the toxic chemicals in the Fort Worth Texas area. Since the initiation of this incident, periodic meetings have been held to keep the local authorities and community informed of environmental activities at Plant 4.

This was one of those situations where I look back on my Congressional career and know I did a good job, and that I saved a lot of lives and stopped a lot of people from getting sick against all odds. It was ultimately a case of being in the right place, at the right time and making the difficult right decision. In Congress it may be easier to ignore issues that don't concern your district, but the right path is to address the issue for the greater good of our country.

CHAPTER 23

The Death of the LNG Tanks

In 1979 Public Service Electric and Gas (PSE&G) found itself still holding title to an empty set of tanks in the Rossville section of Staten Island. So PSE&G applied to the Federal Energy Regulatory Commission (hereinafter FERC) for permission to store domestic pipeline gas for use during heating fuel shortages that might occur during the coldest winter weeks in the two remaining tanks.

A great deal of credit has to go to Eugene and Edwina Cosgriff in successfully stopping the LNG tanks to be utilized for gas storage. They were the husband and wife team that for years, even before the original explosions, carried on the local fight to stop the tanks. They inherently knew that such facilities should not be in populated residential areas. It was stupidity of the highest fashion. The Cosgriffs founded the organization "Bring Legal Action to Stop the Tanks" (hereinafter BLAST) to prevent the threat of transporting and storing liquefied natural gas in Rossville. I became very close with them over the years.

After doing substantial research, I was also extremely concerned about the safety of the residents living near the LNG tanks. Extraordinarily similar issues to my opposition to my successful Travis Power Plant fight. For the record, it was the third LNG tank that blew up on February 10th, 1973, and killed 40 workers. They were repairing the tank at the time. So, now in 1979, Staten islanders were again faced with the prospect of impending disaster. A leak in the two remaining tanks could ignite the LNG gas product itself. When released from its base, it would turn into a gas form and could be ignited from any source whatsoever. We were advised at the time that if the tanks blew up it would kill over half the residents of Staten Island.

When the legal venue changed to Washington and the hearing were ready to begin before the Federal Energy Regulatory Commission (FERC) the Cosgriffs were thrilled to learn that I agreed to battle PSE&G personally in Washington. When I attended the first hearing I asked for permission to be an intervener. The Judge granted my request. As a result, I was granted the right to cross-examine witnesses, and even call my own witnesses. It was an incredibly stressful situation since I was a full-time congressman as the hearing proceeded. I would later learn that it was the first time a sitting member of congress tried a case before FERC.

Obviously, wearing two hats at the same time, without any backing from the City of New York, was a very serious issue. So, I called up Mayor Koch. I said, "Ed we need lawyers down here in Washington. As you know, it's a very complex case. The city's opposed to it, so please send down some lawyers from the corporation counsel to pick up the slack and back me up."

He said he would get back to me. During the trial I had a driver outside the courthouse waiting and every time the buzzer went off in Congress indicating that a vote was taking place in the Capitol, I would jump into the car and race down to the Capitol which was almost a fifteen-minute drive. In Congress, when voting occurs you only have fifteen minutes to get your vote registered. I would jump out of the car, vote and then I raced back to court. I was lucky that I had a very patient and excellent judge presiding over the case. He gave me enough slack to carry on the battle.

I kept calling Koch saying, "Come on, Ed. We gotta have someone here from the corporate counsel. You got a lot of bright guys there; I'm doing my best, but every time they call a vote in Congress, I have to leave, vote and shoot back to the hearing." Also, I told him, "I'm at a disadvantage, because, I really don't understand a lot of the issues because it is highly technical. I need lawyers to do the research so that we can win this thing." Thank God, halfway through the proceedings, Mayor Koch did send two attorneys to help.

FERC concluded hearings in 1982. The agency withheld its decision until PSE&G could satisfy objections raised by the Federal Department of Transportation on the company's safety plans. When they released their decision I was shocked we had won. The battle we carried on was written up glowingly in a periodical called "Inside FERC."

By the end of 1984, just weeks after a chemical leak in Bhopal, India killed more than 2,000 people, PSE&G decided it was futile to continue with a legal battle and finally abandoned the project. As a natural consequence of the Bhopal gas tragedy in India, United States utility companies are not allowed to build the tanks in highly populated areas anymore. Anyplace near a residential community is verboten

A couple of years later, I was waiting at the airport to catch a plane to Washington, when this tall gentleman came over to me and said, "Congressman Molinari. How are you doing?"

I looked up and recognized him as one of the attorneys from PSE&G. He said, "I just came back from getting records on the LNG facilities."

I said, "Oh my, don't tell me we'll be facing another battle?" He said, "No, no, no. If we got turned down, nobody else would ever have a chance being able to utilize those facilities for LNG, so that's over." I breathed a sigh of relief and thanked him. During the hearings we had rancorous confrontations throughout the hearings, but that's the way a legal battle goes. So, I thought he was a gentleman to come over and talk to me as he did.

So, that huge threat was finally over. Over the years as I passed those tanks time and again, I would think about all the battles that took place here in Staten Island. It is so important to be able to get the public to support you and to join in. Without support things do not get done. Everyone has to work together for the common good of the community. I was fortunate to have many constituents who would always do the right thing by standing up and being heard.

CHAPTER 24

Stealing the Naval Homeport

IN 1983, MY STATEN ISLAND DISTRICT OFFICE WAS LOCATED at Fort Wadsworth. I wound up there because Congressman Jack Murphy, against Congressional protocol and etiquette, refused to allow me to take over his Staten Island office, located at the Castleton Corners Post Office after I defeated him in 1980. Fort Wadsworth was an Army facility. Fortuitously, in the long run, it worked out much better than Murphy's original office. Sited on the facility was the worldwide Navy Resale Offices. This was the headquarters for all of the Navy PX's (Post Exchange) around the world. When my constituents came to my office there was never a problem parking and the area was beautiful.

Eventually, I became quite friendly with the Admiral in charge. Over the course of time he invited me to his house for dinner and to meet some high level Naval personnel. At his house I met the Assistant Secretary of the Navy (Manpower and Reserve Affairs), Chapman Cox, and other high-ranking officers. As a Marine I was in my element and we all took an immediate liking to each other. In my life the camaraderie of military service has always opened up many opportunities that I never could have envisioned since I was drafted into the Marine Corps over thirty years ago.

In January of 1983, Mr. Sidney Frigand, the Public Affairs Director of the Port Authority of New York and New Jersey, received a call from Chapman Cox. The Navy was looking for a base in the northeast region of our country that would support the battleship Iowa and six other combat ships. The site qualities that the Navy was looking for was maneuverability and berthing for the ships, housing, utilities, ship services, base and personnel support on land, quality of life for the Navy personnel, and operational consideration and costs.

Cox asked Sidney to submit a formal proposal on behalf of New York and New Jersey for the basing of the fleet. He wanted the Port Authority to oversee the submission of technical and site information. Of course, Mr. Frigand agreed since it would be an economic boom for the New York/New Jersey Area. The only other area that was a major contender in site selection would be Boston Harbor, and of course from the beginning, Tip O'Neill insisted that the only logical site would be Boston Harbor. After all, he was the Speaker of the House, and everyone knew that when the Speaker roars the masses typically follow. He expected nothing less from the Navy.

The Port Authority, mindful of the political nature of such a deal, reached out to local politicians for support. Well, they hit the jackpot when they contacted me. When I got wind of the proposed Naval Base I went full steam ahead in trying to secure it for Staten Island. After all, the lucky winner would increase their local economy by an estimated five hundred million dollars a year as well as adding 9,000 jobs to the local economy. It was something that Staten Island drastically needed.

The only feasible location that was a possibility on Staten Island was the waterfront piece of property midway between Borough Hall and the Verrazano Bridge. It was relatively narrow so some of the experts told me that it wouldn't work.

Regardless, without further ado, I called up my friend Chapman Cox. I was extremely fortunate to have a good relationship with him. I knew him as a friend that I could trust. I said, "Chap, I want to get involved in this thing. Can you help me?" He said, "Absolutely, I'll tell you everything you're going to need to be a formidable contender."

So he started feeding me crucial information that would be essential to gaining the approval for the base to be located on Staten Island. Nobody knew about our relationship, so I had a heads up on what I needed to do. I knew instinctively that I had to do it very quietly. At the same time, I was running all over the place trying to put all the critical pieces together.

In March, The Port Authority of New York and New Jersey, after meeting with a delegation of interested politicians, myself included, from both New York and New Jersey, put in a proposal for three potential contenders for a Naval base. They were located at Stapleton, Staten Island; the Brooklyn Army Terminal; and Bayonne, New Jersey. By June the Navy had eliminated Brooklyn and Bayonne and asked for a new proposal from Staten Island. So at this point, the choice had been narrowed down to Staten Island or Boston.

When the two other sites were eliminated, I got a phone call from the Commanding Officer of the Army base at Fort Hamilton, and he said, "Congressman, you will never get this done with what you put in, but I'll tell you what you can do to get it done. Why don't you incorporate Fort Wadsworth, the army base on Staten Island, into your proposal? You're not going to be able to get the Homeport with just the Stapleton site. It's too small and too narrow. With Fort Wadsworth you've got functional buildings already there that the Navy can use tomorrow. They're already built, they are in use, and that coupled with what you have in the Stapleton area would be more than adequate."

One of the key issues with the initial proposals was inadequate readily available housing. When George Sawyer, the assistant Secretary of the Navy, working under the United States Secretary of the Navy John Lehman, heard that there were 400 to 500 readily available housing units at Fort Wadsworth, his head spun. This was the key to snagging the deal.

Obviously, I was very grateful to the Commanding Officer and did what he suggested. I quickly recognized the value of the unused facilities available in the Fort Wadsworth site. So, we immediately changed the proposal and incorporated the Fort Wadsworth facility and resubmitted the proposal. This was the game changer that the other contenders, particularly Tip O'Neill, did not know about.

The most amusing part about the whole thing was that after the proposal was resubmitted I had a private conversation with the Secretary of the Navy John Lehman, a very well-known and aggressive figure. He would ultimately be making the final decision on the location of the Homeport in the Northeast. I explained to him what I was doing and why. I told him of my relationship with the critical Navy people that helped me and worked directly underneath him. Most importantly, I emphasized to Secretary Lehman that when it came to support for the military, New York was almost always there; Massachusetts could rarely be counted upon. In the military, loyal support is crucial to any successful mission. I used everything within my arsenal to get the homeport.

In the political arena, in order to be successful for your constituents, you have to know how to negotiate intelligently, pay attention, listen to others, be flexible and use your resources: political, military, and social. During the course of the entire vetting process, I got the distinct impression many times that Boston was initially their number one choice. But at the end of the game, by following my well thought out strategy, I felt like I was changing the direction of the top echelon Naval hierarchy's final choice for their Naval base site selection. Staten Island had become a strong contender.

Now the battle for the Homeport was turning to Washington. As Boston was the only feasible strong rival for the northeast area, the Speaker of the House, Tip O'Neill, was going public with the fact that he expected the Navy base to be located in his Congressional District in Boston Harbor. As I have said before, Tip O'Neill was probably the most powerful Speaker in the history of the United States government, but I would not tip my hand to Tip O'Neill. No pun intended.

At the end of July, before the formal announcement of the Navy decision of the choice for the Naval port location, I had another promising conversation with John Lehman. Secretary Lehman said to me, "Congressman, I'll tell you what we'll do: if I select your facility we'll have a code. I'll have somebody from my office call your office and say, 'Is the Congressman coming to my breakfast tomorrow?' That will be the signal that the port's coming to Staten Island." I said, "Okay great."

I started getting excited because I felt like I was in the game. If somebody called and said that to my office it meant that we were getting the Homeport. My only mistake is that I never told my staff about the agreement.

So one day, I was at committee hearings and meetings all day. I was dragging myself back to the office. When I entered the office I remember my Chief of Staff Bob Dizard and some of my other staff looked at me oddly. Bob said, "We got the craziest phone call in the world." I said, "What are you talking about?"

He said, "The Secretary of the Navy's office called and they wanted to know whether you were going to his breakfast tomorrow morning?"

I said, "What did you tell them?" He responded, "I said no, you had prior commitments."

I said, "What the hell did you tell them that for!"

They all chimed in and said, "Well we didn't know anything. What is it all about? It's not on your schedule."

I said, "No it's a code that means the Navy is coming to Staten Island. We got the Homeport!"

Oh God, what excitement filled the office that day! Everyone was jumping up and down and clapping. We had pulled off a major victory against all odds. Of course, all the excitement had to remain in-house for the time being, since I couldn't say anything officially without the permission of Lehman. Tip O'Neill had no idea about the selection and he continued to tell everybody that it was coming to Boston Harbor. We had every reason in the world to lose the fight to get the Navy here, and here I am beating Tip O'Neill again when the Democrats are in the majority.

I immediately thought, based on how things were going in Congress, "I know, I did all the work but when it comes out, D'Amato will get all the publicity because he's a senator."

Anticipating this, I called up John Lehman and I said, "John, look, can I go public with this? Otherwise, I will end up with no credit."

He said, "Yeah, but I don't want you guys bantering this all over the place. I want this low level and whatnot, because Tip O'Neill is going to scream."

We both knew when he said it that in politics there is no such thing as low level. Once the word was out the wheels started turning. But, the key thing was, I had his permission. That was all I needed.

When I hung up I said to myself, "Okay, I know D'Amato well. Al and I were roommates, so I know what he's doing and what he isn't doing." Regarding the Homeport, he did virtually nothing to get it. I was feeding him information all the time telling him what I was doing, hoping he would jump on the bandwagon to get the Homeport for Staten Island. It was strange because I could just not get him interested in the Homeport issue. He was usually a tiger with projects. I thought maybe he was preoccupied with other matters and he just did not have the time.

So, I started calling the media up before I spoke to D'Amato. I knew I didn't have much time, because once they talked to me, they would then call D'Amato. Once D'Amato got involved, forget it: I'd be cut out. That's just the way things work in Washington. So, I started making phone calls and then of course D'Amato got involved and did his thing.

As anticipated, as soon as Tip O'Neill got wind of the decision, he bellowed as only Tip could do. He screamed bloody murder. He hollered, "I want an investigation, I want hearings, I want…"

My God, he directed his anger directly at the Secretary of the Navy. He publically stated that the decision to put the Homeport in New York would "come back to haunt Lehman." I do believe that Tip failed to recognize that Lehman didn't care. The Navy was going to do what was good for the Navy and that was that. Lehman knew that Staten Island was right choice in the long run.

On Friday, July 29th, the Secretary of the Navy formally announced the decision to place the Homeport on Staten Island. He did the announcement from the deck of the Intrepid, a retired aircraft carrier berthed at Manhattan on Pier 86. It was a tremendous victory for me and I was proud that the announcement was made from the flight deck of the Intrepid before a large American flag billowing in the Hudson River breeze. It was a great day and a fantastic accomplishment. A short period of time later, the United States Navy came to our shores. That was a heck of a win for me and a very proud day for Staten Island and New York City.

Unfortunately, when the liberal David Dinkins along with his cohort at the time, Elizabeth Holtzman, came into power they would effectively destroy this major win. It would be one of the saddest things for me to witness. Losing the Navy base after we had fought such a tremendous battle to bring the Navy to Staten Island. Obviously, I will further elaborate at the appropriate time.

After winning the homeport an interesting thing happened to one of my friends, Marine Corps Commandant General Paul Xavier Kelley, known throughout the Corps as "P.X. Kelley." This incident reinforced to me that the military always has to be careful when dealing with the press because certain members of the press will always be on the lookout for anything that they can spin into an embarrassing situation.

On Wednesday September 21st, 1983 Secretary of State George Schultz and General P.X. Kelley testified at a hearing before the House Foreign Affairs Committee regarding continuing the presence of Marines in Lebanon for another 18 months. During the hearing General Kelley had inadvertently described American forces in Lebanon as the Marines who went into "Vietnam." General Kelley immediately corrected himself and said "Lebanon." An innocent mistake, easily corrected and the hearing proceeded.

Well the following day the *New York Times* plastered a front page picture of Secretary of State George Schultz with his head buried in his hands as he was sitting next to General Kelley. The caption below the photo clearly implied that Secretary of State Schutz was reacting to the misstatement of General Kelley by cringing and hiding his face from the hearing panel. In essence it looked like Secretary of State Schultz was saying, "Oh my God. I can't believe General Kelley said that."

If in fact Secretary of State Schultz was doing exactly that, it was a total embarrassment to the Marine Corps and reflected extremely poorly on General Kelley. The photo was publicized in many papers as well as extensively covered by the television networks.

When my Chief of Staff Bob Dizard came to work that morning he heard me cursing. He said, "What's the matter?"

I said, "Take a look at papers. They are trying to bury the man!"

At that point Bob took a look at the papers with the photo and said, "Wait a second I saw that hearing last night on CSPAN and all Schultz was doing was rubbing his eyes because he was tired. Schultz's actions had absolutely nothing to do with what Kelley said. Its total crap!"

I said, "Bob, are you sure about that?" Bob thought for a moment and after a short pause Bob said, "Guy, I am positive."

Knowing Bob as I did, I knew what he was saying was accurate. As such I had to do something to help my friend General Kelley. Being a Marine myself I knew what the negative ramifications of a misinterpreted devastating picture could do to your reputation in the Corps and his military career.

Things can snowball quickly from a fallacy, so I grabbed the papers and ran out of my office and ran over to the house chamber. It was a ballsy decision on my part since I just going by Bob's word, but I knew that time was of the essence while the story was running full tilt.

When I entered the house chamber, as luck would have it, they were doing one minute statements. Every day before the session started any congressperson who wanted to speak could speak for one minute, no more. You could get up and talk about a bill you were introducing, a hero coming home, etc. As a member of congress you had broad latitude to speak on any issue.

I asked for one minute and then got up in front of the house, raised the papers and I said, "You see these newspapers? Great picture isn't it? Wonderful picture. The only problem with it is - it's false. It's dead wrong." I went into a harangue. I blasted the photo and the papers and the media who falsely report the story.

As a direct result of my actions the following day the *New York Times* stated that the photos carried a "Misleading" caption. As we all know this is a rare admission from the media. The media stated that there was actually a seven second lapse from General Kelley's statement and Secretary of State Schultz's actions. The two events were separate and distinct actions that had absolutely no relationship to each other. As a result, the misleading story was put to death quickly and General Kelley's reputation remained pristine.

I was thrilled to help him salvage his reputation because the Corps loved him. I would always smile when Marines talked about the military prowess of P.X. Kelley. Within the rank and file they would tell the stories of how when P.X. Kelley arrived on a battlefield like a true Marine, he would put on his helmet, flak jacket, and head straight to the front line to see what was going on.

This story always makes me think of how the press can distort a situation. So the saying that a picture is worth a thousand words is not always true. Sometimes it depends on the interpretation. General Kelley called me up afterwards and I remember him saying, "My God, you saved my life. I was a dead duck." He continued in his position until his retirement in 1987.

Under P.X. Kelley and John Lehman the country's military strength flourished with Congressional and Senate approval. Many times P.X. Kelley would remark how without Congressional support spearheaded by myself, our military might not be as strong. I never embraced accolades but I must say it always felt good when I heard him make these remarks since it reaffirmed I was on the right political path toward improving our country's military strength. Since we both had an extensive military background we recognized the importance of having the finest equipment available for our men and women in combat.

As our military is there to protect our nation, in my role as congressman, I tried to ensure they had the best military equipment necessary to achieve that goal.

I remember when P.X. Kelly retired from the Marine Corps on June 30th 1987 he told me that as he was standing on a tank in Camp Lejeune, he reflected that a majority of the military weapons used in 1987 had something to do with John Lehman, P.X. Kelley, and their friend in congress – Guy V. Molinari. During our professional relationship, we worked unflaggingly on military modernization because it needed to be completely revamped due to the cutbacks. P.X. Kelley felt that we were instrumental in the vital rebuilding of our nations armed forces military equipment. As a result we helped ensure that the United States of America was the strongest 20th Century military organization in the world. To this day P.X. Kelley and I remain good friends.

CHAPTER 25

Martin Luther King Federal Holiday Controversy

During this time period I had to make an extraordinarily difficult decision regarding a racially sensitive issue. On Friday, July 29th, 1983 H.R. 3706 was introduced with significant bipartisan support titled "A Bill to Amend Title 5, United States Code, To Make the Birthday Of Martin Luther King, Jr., A Legal Public Holiday." The bill passed Congress with over 75% of the congressional members voting "Yea" in a strong show of bipartisan support. The bill was ultimately enacted into law when President Reagan signed it on Wednesday, November 2nd, 1983. Since that day, the third Monday of January has been celebrated as a federal holiday. A federal holiday is actually a fully paid day off for government employees. Most states, private companies, and certain businesses generally observe paid federal holidays. In the long run it is a massive expense.

I was not a member of the "Yea" group. I voted "Nay" based upon sound economic reasons as well as being sensitive to our overall national population diversity. Unfortunately, many people interpreted my vote as an act of outright prejudice against the African-American community. Hardly the truth! Yet sadly, over the course of my political career members of the African-American community, and other ethnic groups would cite this particular vote, when they were at odds with my political decisions. By interpreting my vote incorrectly, they would try to paint me as a racially biased and prejudiced politician.

There were several reasons why at the time and to this day I didn't agree with the proposal: First, although I personally believed that Martin Luther King deserved the holiday, I felt it could be legally observed on a Sunday avoiding a substantial economic impact on government as well as private business. I believed that it could have been declared a day of national observance by presidential proclamation. U. S. law provides for the declaration of selected public observances by days, weeks or months by the President of the United States as designated by Congress or by the President himself. The great aspect about this is that with minimal exceptions there is no requirement that government or businesses close on these days yet we still reap the benefit of a "national observance." As a national observance the country gets the privilege to honor a public issue, social cause, ethnic group, historic event, or famous individual with minimal financial impact on the federal government and private businesses.

Today, especially with the national debt at an astronomical level and many businesses suffering financially, I still firmly believe I cast the right vote. It was a bad precedent to set since we are a global economy. We are competing with all nations of the world. So how do you do that to our business community? How many times can you create holidays? It makes it more and more difficult for the business communities to survive and thrive.

Secondly, I believed that we were setting a precedent that would be difficult to follow and could ultimately offend many other ethnic groups. For example: the Latino community—which in the future may be the majority population community in the country.

I believed at the time that the same thing would happen when the Latino community came forth with a historically significant Latino and said, "Now it's our turn!" I said to my congressional colleagues before the vote, "What are you going to do, say no to them?"

My predictions did come true when in 2008 a strong campaign by the Latino community was promulgated to promote the backing for a "Cesar Chavez" national paid federal holiday. At the time it was supported by then Senator Barack Obama. The bill did not pass as a paid federal holiday in 2008, but on March 28th 2014 President Obama proclaimed March 31st as the national Cesar Chavez day. It was a "Presidential Proclamation" not a paid federal holiday like Martin Luther King. In the long run one must ask what makes one ethnic group more deserving than the other.

So it was a difficult decision for me to vote "Nay" but I followed my conscience. I handled the backlash since I believed that you really have to have to demonstrate strong moral fiber to cast what may be interpreted as an unpopular vote. You have to be able to live with your vote and defend it. To this day, regardless of my vote, I've enjoyed a very good working relationship with the majority of the African-American community in my home district as well as nationally throughout my political career.

Yet, it is interesting to see this issue resurrect itself even today because it is an issue that can easily be misinterpreted; I believe it is best to set the record straight once and for all. I stand by my original vote for the above mentioned reasons. Finally, at the time I said that most of the nation would be spending the day at barbecues and/or working for time-and-a-half instead of taking their time out to express their feelings toward Martin Luther King. In essence it would just be another holiday. That is exactly what has happened.

So looking back, I believe that a "national day of observance," specifically on a Sunday, would have been a much better choice since there would not be a serious financial impact on our country. Additionally, it would have been better suited to Reverend King's intense spirituality to have the day of observance on a Sunday, and it could not be interpreted as offensive to the other nationalities that have attempted to pass similar legislation for their iconic leaders without success.

CHAPTER 26

1983 Marine Barracks Bombing – Beirut, Lebanon

AT APPROXIMATELY 6:00 A.M. ON SUNDAY, OCTOBER 23RD, 1983, a shocking event happened to the United States Marine Corp unit stationed in Beirut, Lebanon. A suicide bomber drove a 19-ton Mercedes Benz truck carrying 2000 pounds of explosives to the Beirut International airport where the 24th Marine Amphibious Unit (MAU) was stationed. The MAU was part of the Multinational force (MNF) in Lebanon. The MAU was there at the request of the United Nations to act as an international peace keeping force during the Lebanese Civil War. The peacekeeping force had been stationed in Lebanon since the withdrawal of the Palestinian Liberation Organization (PLO) following the Israeli invasion of Lebanon in 1982.

The suicide bomber detonated the massive bomb right next to the building serving as a barracks for the 1st Battalion 8th Marines. The death toll was 241 American Servicemen: 220 Marines, eighteen sailors, and three soldiers. Another 128 Americans were wounded in the blast, thirteen of which would subsequently die of their injuries. It was the deadliest single-day death toll of Marines for the United States since the battle of Iwo Jima.

Several minutes after the bombing of the Marine barracks a second suicide bomber drove a vehicle to the French barracks and detonated a bomb at the nine-story 'Drakkar' building in West Beirut. The military death toll for the French would be fifty-five paratroopers from the 1st Parachute Chasseur Regiment, three paratroopers of the 9th Parachute Chasseur Regiment, as well as fifteen injured.

A Hezbollah lunatic named Imad Mughniyeh, a mentor for the infamous Osama Bin Laden, masterminded the bombing. Bin Laden would use the Beirut massacre as the jihadist template for his murderous reign of terror to come. These acts of international terrorism would forever be remembered as a wakeup call to our military, especially the Marine Corps.

When I heard the devastating news of the deadly explosion, I immediately called up the Vice-President of the United States, George H.W. Bush, and I said, "I hear there's a plane taking members of Congress to Lebanon on a fact finding mission and I would really like to be on that plane. I feel it's my obligation as a Marine to be there for them."

Vice President Bush said, "Actually Guy, it's not a plane under my jurisdiction: The members going are being picked through the committees in Congress and I have no jurisdiction over that. I'll do what I can, but it is in the committees' hands. In the meantime, see if you can get in touch with the committee members. You know if I had anything to do with it you would be the first one on the plane."

Following up on his advice, I found the committee that was organizing the trip. Not being a member of the committee, I could not request or demand that I be on the plane. Yet, it was reasonable to let everyone know that I really wanted to be a part of the fact finding team. I felt I owed it to the Marines.

The night before the plane was going to leave for Lebanon, I received a call from Congressman David Martin from upstate New York who was on the committee. Something urgent came up and he could not make the trip. David said if I got to the airport at six o'clock the next morning, I could take his seat, and that's exactly what I did.

Prior to arriving in Beirut we visited some of the wounded servicemen who had been airlifted to Germany. We offered consolation to the survivors who had been through a horrible incident. We promised them that we would bring justice for their fellow Marines who had died. The strength and resolve of the injured Marines was heart breaking: Marines whose bodies were badly disfigured were not concerned about themselves, but about their missing comrades. That was and always will be the battlefield spirit of a United States Marine.

The following day, on October 29th, our Congressional delegation toured the MAU compound in Beirut. The sights were surreal. We were provided with the current security situation and the immediate steps taken to reduce future car bomb vulnerability. Retired Congressman General "Sonny" Montgomery, a personal friend of Vice-President Bush, and a very popular guy, led the group. The other members of the delegation consisted of nine representatives, four Republicans and five Democrats. Our job was to try find out how this could have happened and if something could have been done to prevent it. Everybody involved, regardless of party, was a dedicated, pro-military congressman. We all worked together. Unfortunately, you don't see very much of that today in Congress.

The military personnel warned us about going into a very large tent, because the odors and the sights were very rough to take in. Well, having been in combat, I knew that it was something I could handle, but it was never something you really wanted to see. But, in order to understand the whole situation, it was something that had to be done. Most of the Congressmen in the delegation went in.

I'll always remember what I saw: I saw these wonderful Army men and women who would take a detached finger that they found on the ground and inject the finger with water so they could make fingerprints. They were devoted to the task at hand because the victims were their fellow comrades. They would expect nothing less than if it was they themselves who had died in the terrorist attack. So, to see them all working like they were, in such a sad environment, was pretty tough. There was no way you could walk away from such tragedy without the deepest of respect for the individuals that were trying to identify the deceased personnel.

While I was at the MAU, a young man from Staten Island approached me. His name was John "Chip" Chipura. He was a twenty-one-year-old radio operator with the 24th MAU. He asked me, "Congressman Molinari could you do me a favor and call my mother up and tell her that I survived and I am alive? I have not been able to contact her yet, and I don't want her to continue to worry that I have been killed."

I said, "Of course, it would be a privilege and an honor." I called Chips' mother and told her that her son was fine. She was overcome by emotion because she feared the worst and was thrilled to hear that her son had survived. I also told her how he had saved another Marine's life during the bombing. At the time, John took pictures and sent them to *The Advance*. The paper ran the picture of him standing next to me dressed in combat fatigues. I learned later that he proudly displayed that picture in his living room, framed for all his guests to see. That was the last time I saw John.

Although I never saw John again, that was not the last time that he entered into my life. One day when I was at the Staten Island garbage dump at the request of then Mayor Giuliani, since he could not meet some V.I.P.'s who were coming to examine where the remains of the victims of the 9/11 Twin Towers attack were being processed. While I was there I saw a guy standing all by himself. It was a hot summer day and after I said my goodbye's to the V.I.P.'s this fellow came over to me and said, "Borough President Molinari, can I talk to you?"

I said, "Sure."

He asked me, “Do you remember making the trip to Lebanon when the Marine barracks were blown up by terrorists?”

I said, “Of course. How could anyone forget something like that?”

He asked, “Do you remember taking a picture with a guy from Staten Island?” I said, “Oh, yeah, I do. He sent it to *The Advance*. I think they published it.”

He said, “Yeah.” Then, lightheartedly, “He’s my best friend.” I said, “Oh, really?”

He said, “Yeah, would you like a copy of that picture?” I responded, “Yeah, I would love it.”

He said, “I’ll get a copy for you.”

I said, “Wonderful.” So, I said, “How’s he doing? What did he do after that stint?” His friend then proceeded to fill in the gaps of John’s life post Lebanon.

The story began with, “Well, John came back from the service, and he joined the NYPD and then after twelve years of highly decorated service he joined the FDNY to become a firefighter.”

When I heard “Firefighter,” I thought, “Uh, oh.” Sure enough, he came out and told me that John was killed. He told me how on September 11th, 2001, John responded to the WTC with Ladder 105 from Brooklyn immediately after the planes overtaken by terrorists were flown into the Twin Towers. Unfortunately, Chip was killed while he was evacuating people from Tower 2.

The first thing that hit me was that they missed him in Lebanon, but the bastards got him on 9/11. It was all so terribly sad and totally bizarre. His friend told me that on November 28th, 2000, on the 225th anniversary of the USMC, Chipura had written these amazing words: “We Marines are truly blessed. We get to enjoy the sweet taste of freedom because we know its price.” In the end, that price was his life. The specter of terrorism chased him around the globe.

On a final thought about Chip, he was a man whose presence is always felt when anyone thinks of him. I remember one day being visited by Detective Mike DiBenedetto who was a detective on the

Staten Island D.A.'s staff. Mike sat in my office talking to me, and he looked at the picture of Chipura and me.

Mike said, "Is that Chip Chipura?"

I said, "Yes." At that exact moment the identification sign at the bottom of the picture jumped off the picture, hit the table and kept bouncing and bouncing off things before it hit the floor.

I looked at DiBenedetto, and he looked at me and said, "Did you see that?"

I said, "Yeah…I saw it. How do you figure?"

I bent down, picked it up and re-attached it. We both felt like Chip was actually in the room listening to us and sent us a message that he was okay.

Going back to the fact finding mission, it was a situation where American military personnel lost their lives trying to protect others. It was a tough thing to witness and criticize. Yet, as with all things, we must learn from our mistakes. Everyone was amazed by the fact that the area the Marines had set up their command post on was so vulnerable. Essentially, it violated everything a Marine is taught. We all felt that the Marines never should have gotten themselves in that position. I daresay they probably never will again because they learned from that incident.

For example, when I first got to Korea back in 1952, our command post was in what they would call a "Defilade Position." In other words, if the enemy is out there and sent missiles against us, we were on the side of a mountain where they couldn't possibly hit us.

That's basic stuff that was not observed in Lebanon, and I guess the question is what happened? Why didn't they do that in Lebanon? Who is responsible? For me, as a Marine, it was absolutely shocking that this could have occurred. Somebody slipped up.

Ultimately, everyone came to agree that senior military officials were responsible for major security lapses and misjudgments that were made by the military site selection committee. I would have thought that mistakes like these would not have been made in the 1980s after all the wars that we have been in and all of the terrorist attacks that were taking place around the world. We should have been on notice to better protect our servicemen on duty abroad.

The investigations suggested that there might have been many fewer deaths if the barracks guards had carried loaded weapons. Additionally, they found that a barrier more substantial than barbed wire certainly would have prevented the bomber from driving into the facility. Today concrete barriers protect these types of compounds.

In fairness and deference to the military commanders, they indicated that for political reasons the Marine Commander had not been allowed to maintain a completely secure perimeter before the attack due to the categorization as a peace keeping mission. In essence foreign policy political correctness tied the Marine Commander's hands.

I must admit, I was not pleased with the reaction of President Reagan. I thought he came off as being weak and we did not have a solid foreign policy aimed at Lebanon. Serious questions arose over the lack of security in the American sector of war torn Beirut. I felt that the other nations of the world looked at him as a weak leader at the time and it did not give our country confidence about protecting our shores. In President Reagan's national address, immediately after the bombing, he vowed to keep the Marines in Lebanon, yet just four months later he announced the end of the American role in the peacekeeping force. On February 26th, 1984, the main force of Marines left Lebanon leaving just a small contingent to guard the U.S. embassy in Beirut.

The only justice to this tragedy was that on the night of February 12th, 2008, Mughniyeh was assassinated in Damascus, Syria. A car bomb was detonated while Mughniyeh walked by the car. As he did to others was done to him. The attack was attributed to Israeli intelligence by the foreign media. I can only vividly picture his body being incinerated by a car bomb as true justice for all the terrorist acts he committed throughout his hideous life. And as a final thought, I pray that his soul rots in hell, suffering for eternity.

CHAPTER 27

The Holy Spirit Envelops Pope John Paul II

In November of 1983, I was asked to go to Rome as part of a delegation to represent Congress before the twenty second session of the Food and Agricultural Organization (hereinafter FAO) of the United Nations. The head of our fourteen-person delegation from the United States was John R. Block, the Secretary of Agriculture under the Reagan Administration. In 1983, the United States donated over 50% of all the world's donated food to the countries in need. Historically the United States has always been an extremely generous country to foreign countries in need. Almost every country in the world sent representatives to the conferences.

At the conference, my role was to ensure that everything was being done properly in accordance with congressional guidelines regarding our donations and that they were being used for the right reasons. It was a wonderful trip, since I was able to bring my wife and daughter along when I went to Rome. During the day, I would attend FAO meetings while my wife and daughter took trips to historic sites in Rome, restaurants, and shops. At night we would all go out together for an authentic Italian dinner.

One day, our delegation was scheduled to go to the Vatican to have an "audience with the Pope," as they called it back then. Unfortunately, at the time in Italy, the unionized workers were notorious for calling wildcats' strikes. They would strike the airline industry, garbage collectors, mail delivery, telephone operators, teachers, train and bus drivers, anything. It was anyone's guess who would go on strike and when.

Well, on this date, the transportation industry went on strike, making it extraordinarily difficult to get around in Rome. Fortunately for myself, I had a driver and car assigned to me. I was excited about the opportunity to meet the Pope. These are once in a lifetime opportunities and I did not want to pass it up.

When I entered St. Peter's Square and stood before St. Peter's Basilica in Vatican City, I knew I was on my own in my quest to get an audience with the Pope; the other members of our delegation couldn't make it through the city due to the traffic as a result of the strike. At the same time, I was so proud to be standing in Vatican City as a congressman for the United States of America. I was in the country my grandparents were born in. I was standing in Vatican City, the center of the Roman Catholic Church, and within a baseball's throw of seeing Pope John Paul II personally.

There was a doorway on the right hand side of the steps to St. Peter's Basilica. I walked up to an exquisite old door and knocked on it. It finally opened and standing at the ready was a Pontifical Swiss Guard. The Pontifical Swiss Guards have served as the Vatican Military force since 1506. The job is to protect the Pope and Vatican City. The Swiss Guard had on the traditional three colored dress uniform and helmet whose style originated in the Renaissance era. It was an intimidating presence, to say the least.

"What are you doing here?" the guard shouted. I was lucky that he could speak English.

I said, “I am Congressman Molinari and I am in Rome with a delegation for the FAO. The group was supposed to meet for an audience with the Pope today. Because of the strike, apparently I am the only one able to make the meeting.”

He then said, “You shouldn’t be ringing the door. Why are you using this door?” I said, “I don’t know what door I am supposed to use or not use.” I was getting frustrated and was beginning to think that I had missed my opportunity to see the Pope in person. Then a voice in the background said, “What’s going on?”

Luckily he was the head Swiss Guard. When he saw me he said, “Come on inside, come in.” We hit it off immediately. We talked for a while about what I was doing, what he did and Vatican City in general. He then asked me, “Would you like an audience with the Pope?”

My heart leaped and I said, “I would love an audience with the Pope!”

He then instructed me to, “Go upstairs to this room and you will see an old gray haired guy called Giuseppe. Giuseppe will put you on the aisle so that you will see the Pope first hand.” When I was leaving he said, “By the way, I kind of like you. If you have any friends coming over from the United States, just tell them to call me and I will arrange for them to have an audience.” It was a tremendously kind gesture on his part. I did have people call him up over the years and true to his word he followed through.

So, I then went to the room and I sat down where I was directed by Giuseppe. While sitting there, a few minutes later, I heard a knock on the door at the rear of the room. The door opened and his Holiness Pope John Paul II walked out. It was a mind blowing experience, because there was a white aura surrounding the Pope when he walked into the room. It took my breath away and I said to myself, “*Wow!* What is that?”

There was a young lady sitting next to me and I asked her, “Do you see that?” She said, “Yes I see that.” I said, “What is it?” She responded, “That’s the Holy Spirit.”

The young lady seemed to be on top of papal knowledge and she wasn't surprised at all by what she saw. I was nearly speechless but I was able to say, "Really?" She said, "Yes, don't you know that?" I said, "No, I didn't know that and I have never heard of this before."

Pope John Paul II then proceeded up the aisle. By the time Pope John Paul II got to me, the glow of the Holy Spirit had disappeared. When he walked by my section, the Pope reached across to me and shook my hand. I kissed his Papal ring as was customary since the early days of the Catholic Church. Needless to say, I was totally blown away by the whole experience. Pope John Paul II was a marvelous Pope. That experience has stayed in the back of my mind ever since.

As I grow older, this is an experience that I often look back upon. As a practicing Catholic, it reinforces my firm belief that there is life after death. To this day, I believe that I witnessed the Holy Spirit enveloping Pope John Paul II while I was in the same room with him. I have never been able to explain the event that I witnessed fully, but I do believe it was a unique religious experience that I was given the opportunity to witness. It was a divine feeling seeing that white aura envelop the Pope. What it was all about I have no idea, you don't question things like that. If I did not see it myself, I probably would not believe someone else telling me this story.

Guy V. Molinari
The King Of Midland Beach

Election night victory speech at the shalimar with my wife

Me and President Reagan at the White House

Hard to believe I was able to play racquetball smoking a cigar

Susan, Bush "41" & myself

Columbus Day October 9th 1989
Our Paths crossed – but we did not know each other Lieutenant Patricia Feerick overseeing parade while I campaign with Mayoral hopeful Rudy Giuliani

Early 90's Demonstration against Mayor Dinkins' proposal to decrease Staten Island Ferry service

Eugene and Edwina Cosgriffs founders of BLAST at
the LNG Tanks site after the battle ended in 1982

October 2nd 1999
Mayor Rudy Giuliani endorses George W. Bush for President

Wednesday Night Concert in the Park at Great Kills Park - 1996
I sang "Hey Jude" dressed up as Bruce Springsteen

September 30th 2004
Me and my daughter

Meeting Pope John Paul II at the Vatican November 1983

January 9th 1981
Speaker of the House Tip O'Neil swearing me in as
the freshman New York State Congressman

Mayor Ed Koch supporting the military on Staten Island

CHAPTER 28

A Crisis in the Skies & The Evil Newt Gingrich

In early August of 1981, the Professional Air Traffic Controllers Organization (hereinafter "PATCO") declared a strike. The controllers walked out after the government refused to meet their demands for better working conditions, increased pay, and a thirty-two-hour workweek. President Reagan immediately declared the strike illegal and a "peril to national safety." He ordered the controllers back to work pursuant to the Taft-Hartley Act of 1947, which prohibited strikes by government workers.

President Reagan gave the strikers an ultimatum: return to work within forty-eight hours, or be fired. Only 1,300 returned to work before the deadline. True to his word, on August 5th, Reagan fired 11,345 controllers who continued to strike. Additionally, President

Reagan banned the fired workers from federal service for life.[14] Due to the nature of PATCO's illegal strike, the Federal Labor Relations Authority discredited the union from its right to represent workers on October 22, 1981. At the time, I supported President Reagan's decision to fire the controllers under the Taft-Hartley Act. I felt it was definitely the right thing to do because you couldn't have unions working for government agencies randomly walking off the job. Too much was at stake.

The President's actions in firing the strikers were seen as a big boon for employers. He had struck at the heart of not only the air traffic controllers union, but also labor unions nationwide. In essence, he sent a message to the private sector that unions need not be feared anymore. It was a huge domestic policy initiative that was embraced by the private sector employers. It was seen as a bold defining moment of his presidency.

In the long run, approximately 6,300 controllers and 3,300 supervisors were left to handle the national air-traffic control system. In the wake of the mass firings, the FAA was faced with the task of hiring and training enough controllers to replace those that had been fired. Under normal conditions, it would take three years to train a new controller. In the following months, the FAA augmented the work force with some military controllers and other FAA personnel who passed controller certification tests. Still, the agency was forced to cut back scheduled flights by one-fourth in some places.

Over time, the firings of thousands of experienced air traffic controllers led to intense apprehension about airline safety associated with the dangers of inadequate staffing, over stressed and demoralized controllers, and dangerous working conditions. Following the strike, the FAA had assured the public that it would rebuild the air traffic controller system within two and a half years. Such was not the case. In actuality, it would take closer to ten years before the

---

14 *President Reagan lifted the ban prohibiting service in all other areas in December of 1981 but still prohibited the fired air traffic controllers from being air traffic controllers for life.*

overall staffing levels returned to normal. During this time period the reports of near mid-air collisions increased dramatically.

As luck would have it, when I was elected to Congress, I became really good friends with Congressman Elliott Levitas, a Democrat from Georgia, since we both sat on the Committee on Public Works and Transportation. Elliot was a smart man, a Rhodes Scholar, and I admired him deeply. Regardless of our different party lines, our work ethics and common goals just clicked. It is something rarely seen in the halls of Congress today. We were able to cross party lines and work together extraordinarily well to achieve goals that benefited the citizens of our country. Elliott was in the controlling majority in the house. As a result of our relationship we were able to accomplish some great achievements, particularly in regards to aviation and environmental issues.

In 1983, after I was reelected to Congress, I looked at a coveted sub-committee called the Investigation and Oversight Committee that fell under the Committee of Public Works and Transportation. In examining the members of the Public Works and Transportation Committee I realized that although there were four members that were senior to me, I might have a shot at being appointed the Ranking Republican member of the sub-committee. The sub-committee itself had a tremendous history of doing great investigative work, something which I loved. Still, I knew that I did not want to assume the responsibilities and duties of the ranking member and work my butt off for two years just to get bumped by somebody who was senior to me. There was a tremendous amount of background work that had to be done on this sub-committee and I wanted to make sure that I would be able to stay on more than one term before taking on all that responsibility.

I asked each of the senior Republican members—Bud Shuster, Pennsylvania; Arlan Stangeland, Minnesota; and William F. Clinger Jr., Pennsylvania—if they had any interest in being appointed the Ranking Republican on the sub-committee, but they all turned it down.

Newt Gingrich from Georgia was the final person I had to ask. I can vehemently say during my congressional career the most disheartening memories were my interactions with Newt Gingrich. When I first met Newt I got a bad feeling. Call it instinct. I knew in my gut, for whatever reason, that I just couldn't trust the guy. In politics trust is everything. Your word is your bond.

Unfortunately, Newt sat on the subcommittee and he had two years' seniority over me. Obviously, he was the only person that I didn't trust in the group. Newt had a reputation of being a turbulent person, as such, many people including myself of course, could not and would not trust him. The other Congressmen I had spoken to were nice guys. I knew their word was written in stone and I could always count on their support if I needed it. Newt was a different story.

So, I finally went to Gingrich and said, "Newt, I would like to be the Ranking Republican on Investigations and Oversight subcommittee. I've already talked to all the other committee members that are senior to me, and they've all agreed to allow me to take that spot. They all said they would not knock me off by seniority in the future. I am calling on you to see if you are interested in being the Ranking Republican on the subcommittee."

Newt said, "No, no. I don't want it. It's much too much work for what I want to do in the future. I am on the Aviation, Surface, and Transportation subcommittees. So, Guy, you can go ahead and take it. I definitely don't want to be the Ranking Republican on the Investigation and Oversight Subcommittee."

I didn't quite trust Gingrich so I asked, "Newt since this is a lot of hard work and a real commitment on my part do you mind if we put this agreement in writing?"

I was pleased when he said, "No problem, you write it up and send it over to me and I'll sign it."

So I swiftly wrote a brief agreement memorializing our discussion to wit: Gingrich acknowledged that he had no desire to serve as the Ranking Republican on the Investigation and Oversight sub-committee and agreed to my assignment as the Ranking Republican. Newt signed it and sent it back.

With that done, on February 2nd, 1983, I was appointed as the ranking Minority Member of the Public Works and Transportation subcommittee on Investigations and Oversight. It marked the first time in ten years that a second term member had been elevated to an influential position on such a prestigious sub-committee.

Elliott Levitas was the Chairman of the sub-committee. Most of the members of the sub-committee would come to the meeting, check in for their roll call, and then disappear. Such was not the case with Elliott and me. Behind our backs we were labeled the "Working Fools." It was a title we proudly wore. In Congress most of your work is done on committee level. What I found after a short period of time was that the staffers, Democrats and Republicans alike, were excited about their input, but their members didn't want to do the exhaustive work required to achieve the results. So, the staffers would funnel their memorandums and stuff to me hoping that I would pick it up and run with it; and, in most cases, I did.

As you can surmise, the Investigation & Oversight sub-committee was a tremendously difficult committee because it required an awful lot of work on a daily basis. Many times we worked until the wee hours of the morning. As the Ranking Republican on the subcommittee, over the course of the next two years, I developed a reputation of being a thorough, dedicated, and tireless investigator and legislator.

I remember one day in early 1984 when Elliot told me, "We're going to do a hearing tomorrow on aviation safety." I said, "What are you talking about? We haven't done any other hearings on airline safety and I'm knee deep in this EPA stuff. I don't want to stretch myself too thin. Can't we get someone else to pick up the slack?"

Elliot said, "Nope if it's going to be done right, it's me and you."

He knew that once he called me and gave me his spiel, I was going to do the aviation thing regardless of other commitments because it was the right thing to do.

When all things were said and done, Elliot would often reflect back and say, "I'll always remember when I told Guy Molinari that we were going to be doing a hearing on air traffic safety the next day. He looked at me with a scowl on his face, like it wasn't something that he wanted to do. But, in a short period of time he was the expert in the halls of Congress."

And yes that was true, through hard work and perseverance I became the Congressional expert on what was often referred to as the "Crisis in the Skies," concerning aviation matters. At the time, I did not realize that this was a battle that I would continue with for over four years, many times angering the Reagan Administration.

Regarding my relationship with the air traffic controllers, once I got my teeth into the issue I began meeting controllers secretly during the nighttime in their basements, or wherever they chose as secure location all over the country. They trusted me, based upon my reputation, to maintain their confidentiality and to *never disclose their names*. The controllers were afraid of being labeled whistle blowers, and facing the possible loss of their jobs for being truthful and candid about the dangers to the public flying. They knew that based on past firings by President Reagan that they would be foolish to talk freely in front of the supervisors at the public hearings.

The controllers told me how they were forced to continually work six days a week, mandatory overtime, and were barred from taking a vacation in an incredibly high tension job. Yet, everyone in the business, especially supervisors, knew they needed to be well rested and mentally prepared to perform their duties. As a result, the controllers were always doing crazy things to keep their adrenaline going and to stay awake. So, I got scads of relevant information that nobody else was getting, because they knew that I wouldn't expose them.

I had one controller who called me all the time. I remember the day he called me up on the phone and his voice was shaking. He was crying hysterically. He sounded like he was ready to fall apart. I asked him, "What is the matter? You sound terrible!"

The controller said, "Believe it or not, I almost caused a collision between two planes. Here I am telling you about others who do these things, and today I was almost the cause of the loss of hundreds of lives."

After this call, I decided that I needed to go see firsthand how the tower was operating. After all the conversations with the controllers, I inherently knew that the only way to really understand what was going on was to watch them at work. The intensity in the air traffic tower was amazing; their legs were shaking; their hands were trembling. It was so surreal; I had to convince myself that these issues were not isolated instances, so over a long period of time I went to many facilities.

Typically, before I went to a tower facility, I would almost always attend a secret meeting the night before with the actual controllers, minus the supervisors. That's when the guys could open up to me. The following day I would watch the controllers as they worked in the towers. It was exactly what I needed to see in order to put everything in perspective.

As a result of these secret meetings and the visits to the towers, during the formal hearings, I was fully prepared to address the serious safety issues that I had investigated. At the hearings the FAA would have all their so-called experts present and I would hear the official FAA version first. Immediately after their presentation, I was able to address the real issue because of the inside information I had obtained. I was able to call out the FAA supervisors on safety issues that they chose to ignore. The administrators of the FAA would be pissed. They kept trying to figure out how the hell I got all the information that clearly revealed dangerous safety issues in the air traffic control towers throughout the country. Of course, this was an incredibly time consuming task but that is how I became the expert. By the end of my investigation I knew the issues better than just about anybody on the Hill, including the Federal Aviation Administration officials themselves.

I learned that in order to be an effective minority member of the house, especially when at the time **seniority** meant everything, you had to know what you were talking about and attack the heart of the issue head on. Consequently, I found that the key to being successful in congressional or committee hearings was PREPARATION.

Throughout all of the investigations I conducted during my extensive political career, I developed a particular method of operation regarding my involvement in hearings, be they sub-committee or committee hearings. First and foremost, I always fastidiously studied and investigated the subject matter of the hearing beforehand. By the time the hearing came around I was the most prepared participant.

I found that most elected officials would not put the time in that was necessary to fully learn the issue at hand, due to the tedium it required. Over and over I saw politicians testify at hearings by reading verbatim the drivel that their staff had prepared for them. When they finished they simply walked out. Although they may have appeared to be well versed on the issue, in reality they knew nothing about what they just read. If they were asked a specific question about the issue they would invariably be blindsided by a person like me who was well prepared. So, after observing that, I decided that I was not going to be a "yo-yo;" I vowed to myself that whenever I was involved in a hearing I would know the issue inside out and would not have to read a prepared statement. The only time I read verbatim was when I thought the statement itself was so important and imperative to have it "on the record," but after I read the statement I was fully prepared to address any questions that were thrown my way.

Typically, before every hearing, the majority and minority congressional staff members would prepare a briefing memo. Sometimes they were as thick as a book. Although I would read the briefing memo, I never relied entirely upon it. If it was relevant to my responsibilities as a congressman I would study the issue myself. At the hearings I would listen intently to those who testified before me. Since the lineup went by seniority, by involuntary circumstances I was invariably at the tail end of the lineup. I used what may seem like misfortune to my benefit: I paid attention! When it was my time to participate in the hearing I was able to intelligently put forth a good argument to support my position, and also point out the flaws in the opposition's position.

Interestingly, once I had clearly established myself as a skillful and effective independent Republican Congressional voice during hearings I found that the opposition's Democratic staff, anonymously of course on many occasions, actually fed me their questions ahead of time so that I would address the concerns during the hearing on the record. The reason why they would slip me a question was that they were doing their homework; they did not want to do such tedious research and have it considered inconsequential or detrimental to the party's stance. To them it only made sense to address their issue during the hearing and I was the man to do it. Everyone knew that they were not supposed to give the information to me and they would probably be fired if it got out. Yet they all knew that my word was solid as stone, I was a Marine and would never snitch.

Finally, I also found that the media was a very useful tool to get information to the public prior to and during the hearings. Sometimes I would feed the media relevant information with the agreement that I would not be named as their informant, ensuring I protected my source and myself. This was very effective especially when it came to aviation safety since it was covered heavily on shows like "Face the Nation," "Nightline," and "Meet the Press." This maneuver ensured that the issue at hand would not be swept under the rug.

Additionally, since I was so well versed on the issues, the opposition knew that I was not afraid to go on television and talk about this issue. Regardless of the issue, I was effective in my efforts due to the research I conducted. By this time everyone knew that I had a unique ability to reel in a person and basically set up a witness. I would not go to the punch line right away; I would wait until it was the perfect time for the witness to sink their own boat. I loved going back and forth with a combative witness: just like a fisherman, I toyed with my prey and knew when it was time to strike the final blow.

During the course of our investigation, Elliot and I set a record for the amount of subcommittee hearings in Washington, as well as outside of the capital, regarding aviation safety. Now, I don't know if it still stands, or ever really did stand, because I never looked it up, but regardless of the actual numbers I know anyone who wants to beat our record is going to have to work damn hard. We did a lot of good work for our country on very important issues. Our hearings ensured that passengers would fly safely and not be at risk due to the inefficiencies and lack of staffing in the air traffic towers. The attention we were bringing to the lapses in safety was generating intense public interest which in turn resulted in safety reforms.

At the very end of 1984, it was time to select the committee and sub-committee assignments for the next term. To my chagrin I started hearing rumors from the staff, such as, "Congressman Molinari, we hear rumors that Mr. Gingrich is going to bump you on that committee. I hope that is not true."

They clearly didn't want to see me go. I would respond, "No, that's just rumors." I didn't tell them that I had a written agreement with Gingrich in which he explicitly agreed not to do that. In my mind he would be crazy to bump me after he had given his word that he would not do it on paper.

Well, on the very last day that we had to select our assignments, I received a disgraceful call from Newt Gingrich. Consistent with rumors that have been flying around, Gingrich informed me, "Guy, I'm sorry to tell you this, but I've decided that I want to take over the subcommittee you have. I'm going to block your reassignment as the ranking member of the sub-committee based on my seniority and take the spot for myself."

I flipped out and said, "Newt, you can't do that!" He said, "Yes I can, I'm senior to you."

I said, "Yeah, you're senior by two years, but we have an agreement. We have a written agreement that you wouldn't do this, that you wouldn't bump me." Newt said, "No, we have no such agreement of that kind."

I screamed, "Newt! We have an agreement, and it's in writing. I have a copy of it. I'll get a copy out and I'll send it right over to you." He then said, "No, no, no. It wouldn't make any difference. Written agreement or not it's too bad; I'm still going to bump you."

I knew exactly what was happening. Gingrich came from Atlanta, Georgia, and the hub of Delta Air Lines corporate headquarters was located at the Hartsfield-Jackson Atlanta International Airport. I was giving Delta Airlines, as well as other major airlines, a very hard time over aviation safety, but Delta's board were Gingrich supporters, and they wanted to get rid of me. So, I learned that day that my initial instincts on Gingrich were right. He could not be trusted. He was and is a man who didn't care about a written agreement with a colleague.

Well, needless to say, I was absolutely furious. In Congress, it was unheard of that you could not trust someone's written word, especially when they are from the same side of the aisle. So, I had two of my friends on the subcommittee, Republicans Clay Shaw from Florida and Nancy Johnson from Connecticut, fight the bumping on the subcommittee level. I then spoke to Ranking Republican Gene Snyder of the Public Works and Transportation committee. I told him what was happening, and Gene said, "Look Guy, if it was on the basis of personality, you would win big because the sub-committee just doesn't like him and they like you. But, on the Republican side it's not personality, its seniority. It's sacrosanct and that's what runs the show. So, I can tell you now, no matter what you do, you're gonna lose that fight."

I said to him, "That's okay. I don't mind losing the fight, but I want to fight nevertheless. I have to let everybody know what this man is all about." I thought to myself, "I want to expose him for who he is. I cannot sit by quietly and let him get away with this, this is all about character and the man has none."

So, we had this raucous hearing, and like Snyder predicted, the vote went Gingrich's way. Even though I lost something that was very near and dear to me, I was glad that I did not go down without a fight. To make matters worse, Elliot Levitas, my Democratic friend, lost his election that year in 1984. I would sorely miss him since we did such great work together. So, 1985 started out as a real downer concerning my Congressional service. It was probably the most infuriating experience for me as a congressman because everything goes by seniority and I had to start over, which is what I did.

I picked the only subcommittee that was left, Public Buildings and Grounds. This was a committee that had to take a look at every lease or agreement to buy property for the Federal government. The burning issue for my new subcommittee was that a decision had to be made as to whether they should buy a facility or lease a facility. Since I was an expert in real-estate issues, I understood this field. Nobody had really looked at these issues for a long, long time.

The Chairman, Fofó Losefa Fiti Sunia, was the first non-voting delegate from American Samoa to the United States House of Representatives. In 1988, he was indicted on federal charges of running a payroll padding scheme, pled guilty, and went to jail. So, during the course of my tenure, I kind of ran the entire committee. I saved the taxpayers an awful lot of money, but it was a non-descript assignment, totally boring, and it really didn't do much for anyone's Congressional career. Nevertheless, I zealously performed my duties, just as I had in Investigations and Oversight. While I exceled there, I knew in my heart that it was not "my dream job."

In 2011, when Gingrich announced he would be running for the 2012 GOP presidential nomination, I again reminded everyone about what he did to me. I thought it was a disgrace that he could think that after his divisive political rhetoric that he had any chance of becoming President of the United States. I was horrified. I reiterate to everyone today that, "I have nothing but distaste for Gingrich. I believe him to be a very dangerous man and I do truly think he is a little psycho." I believe, to this day, that his hate mongering rhetoric over the course of his political career is most responsible for the breakdown of bipartisan relationships between Republicans and Democrats. His ideology took an axe through the House that forever separated Democrats and Republicans and it has never been repaired to this day. That is Newt Gingrich's legacy: tearing down trust and destroying bipartisanship within the hallowed halls of Congress.

CHAPTER 29

Never Change Your Vote

On Friday, March 15th, 1985, I was unable to make a tri-monthly luncheon held in New York because I was sick. It was always well attended by political and social friends, including Senator Al D'Amato, Assistant Secretary of State for International Narcotics Matters Dom DiCarlo, Assemblyman Al DelliBovi, and at least twelve other individuals. In the privacy of the backroom of a restaurant, we would eat, drink, and talk about personal matters, as well as current political issues. On this particular occasion the dinner was at Senator D'Amato's favorite restaurant, Angelo of Mulberry Street, in New York City's Little Italy. A main topic of the conversation was the Homeport; everyone was still talking about it since we had let the cat out of the bag.

I was pissed that health issues would not permit me to make the luncheon, so, I decided to invoke my presence via the telephone and play a joke on D'Amato. I have always had a knack for playing telephone jokes on unsuspecting good friends. I would call up good friends and pretend I was someone else. I was and still am able to disguise my voice quite well. I felt that Al needed to be pranked due to the tremendous amount of positive publicity he received because of my behind the scenes political maneuvering in securing the Naval port. It was one of the instances where D'Amato took credit for something for which he had done basically nothing. But again, I had to accept that was the way of Washington. He was in the Senate, and he had control. Yet, it would have been nice if he gave credit where credit was due. You learn a lot about yourself and your colleagues during these situations.

So, I gladly made the prank phone call to the restaurant where the luncheon was being held. D'Amato's press secretary, a sharp lady, answered the phone. "Hello, Senator D'Amato's line. Who is this?"

I said, "Is Senator D'Amato there, my name is Lieutenant Such-And-Such. I am calling on behalf of Naval Secretary John Lehman. Secretary Lehman would like to talk to the Senator."

His press secretary says, "Oh, hold on." She goes in the back room and says to D'Amato, "Senator, the Secretary of the Navy wants to talk to you."

My friend, Dom DiCarlo, who was always wise to my antics, said to the others immediately after D'Amato leaves the room, "That's probably Guy." They said, "Yeah, it's probably Molinari. He's well known for these kinds of pranks."

D'Amato got on the phone and he said, "Hello?" I say, "Hold on Sir, Secretary Lehman is getting on the phone."

When Senator D'Amato thought Lehman was on the phone he says, "Johnny! Johnny! How are you?"

I said, "Not too happy, Al! I thought we had an agreement that you guys weren't going to go crazy with this thing?" D'Amato said, "That wasn't me, that was Molinari."

I said to myself, "Oh, that son of a bitch, he gives me up right away."

True to form, he was willing to take all the credit for getting the Homeport but none of the negativity from ruffling feathers. So, I said, "Well, it's unfortunate because Speaker O'Neill is going crazy now and I was trying to avoid that. I thought we had an agreement with you guys and you're not living up to it." Again D'Amato says, "It was Molinari."

I finally revealed myself to Senator D'Amato and said, "You no good son of a bitch, you give me up that easily!" D'Amato says, "You got me." And of course we both laughed and I said, "Yes Al, I got you, alright."

Senator D'Amato rejoined the others at the dinner table and shortly thereafter, his press secretary told him that he had a phone call from President Reagan. Unbeknownst to D'Amato, the President was actually personally calling senators to line up support for an upcoming vote on the MX missile, a cornerstone of the Administration's defense buildup. President Reagan knew that the outcome could very likely be decided by a single vote.

When D'Amato received the call from the President, he was positive it was me on the phone and not the President of the United States. He answered the phone by barking loudly to President Reagan, "Molinari, you creep, cut this bullshit out."

Then, D'Amato heard a confused voice on the other side of the line, "Senator D'Amato?"

Quickly, D'Amato realizes that this *really* was President Reagan. He had to back paddle his ass out of an exceedingly awkward situation. Senator D'Amato then had to listen intently to Reagan's pitch for the MX missile. So a previous practical joke turned into the crème de la crème of practical jokes.

When the press contacted me about D'Amato's interaction with the President, I said with a touch of pride, "I guess I have gotten a little proficient with my imitations, but I'd be very careful about doing the President." You could say that D'Amato was quite miffed at me because of the embarrassment he had suffered during the conversation with the President.

The MX missile policy was an extremely controversial issue. President Reagan got annoyed at me because I did not robotically support him without equivocation on his Strategic Defense Initiative concerning the MX missile (often times referred to as the "Peacekeeper Missile). I never understood the proposed rationale concerning the "Dense Pack Strategy." His Secretary of Defense, Casper Weinberger, held multiple meetings with the members of Congress and explained the President's plan for the MX missiles "Dense Pack Strategy."

As described by Weinberger, the plan called for a series of ten to twelve hardened missile silos to be grouped closely together in a line and buried under some kind of impermeable substances. As such, it was called the "Dense Pack Strategy."

My military training taught me that the "Dense Pack Strategy" was absolutely contrary to basic military strategy. You should disperse your military weapons, not cluster them all together. Lumping them closely together makes it incredibly easy for the enemy to blow them all up in one shot. The administration's policy did not make any sense at all to me, or to many of my congressional colleagues. Both Democratic and Republican Senators and members of Congress found the "Dense Pack" so controversial that behind the Reagan Administration's back they referred to it as the "dunce pack."

So, after Weinberger's presentation, we met with the President in groups of ten. Reagan made his presentation as Weinberger was sitting at his side. After President Reagan made his presentation and he was leaving the room he said, "I want to thank all ten of you who are here today. I have to now speak to another group that won't be as friendly. So, thank you for listening to me."

Based on his statement I was certain that President Reagan thought all ten members of Congress present could be counted on as votes for him. So, I spoke up as he was leaving the room and I said, "Mr. President, I don't want you to leave the room thinking that I'm going to vote for this, because I'm not. I don't agree with the 'Dense Pack Strategy.'" President Reagan looked very surprised and shocked. I said, "Cap Weinberger gave a similar presentation today and it did nothing to convince me that it is the right move. The theory just goes completely against my military training. So I'm not going to be voting for your proposal."

President Reagan didn't say a word. He was clearly annoyed and he promptly left the room. Casper Weinberger was right behind him. I could see that he was annoyed as well.

It always reminds me of one of the first lessons I learned in congress: *never* change your vote even if it's the wrong vote. You don't change it. If you change for the administration you're nothing more than a lap dog and they will always see you as a pushover.

I learned this lesson from a fellow Republican, Hank Brown of Colorado. We started in Congress together and were in the same class. Hank was an extraordinarily bright, super athletic guy. One night a few of us were sitting around in the gym after playing ball. We started commiserating about life in Congress. Hank talked about a bill that came up and President Reagan needed thirty additional votes to get it passed. Hank changed his vote solely because the President asked him to. Hank regretted it from the moment he did it.

Hank said, "I learned my lesson. I will never change a vote. It's bad because it shows, number one: that you don't really know what you are doing; and number two: all it takes is a phone call from the President and your idea of why you voted for the bill doesn't count anymore. You have to understand that the people back home put you here, not the President."

I will always remember his words. I stood by them throughout my career. That is why I had a strong reputation as an independent Republican. The only way I would ever change my vote was if somebody legitimately convinced me that my vote was completely wrong and irrational. That rarely happened because I always based my vote on carefully evaluating the issue and researching any legitimate questions I felt needed to be answered. My votes reflected the best interests of my constituents because they were who elected me to Congress, not the President.

These days, elected officials change their vote all the time. Once they arrive in Washington they forget about the people back home who elected them and vote the way their party dictates. Hank learned his lesson the hard way and I learned not to make his mistake. I always followed my principles and voted my conscience.

While I strove to work within my party, I was also willing to disagree with the party and party leadership when I knew that it was the right thing to do since I was following the will of my constituents. You have to follow the will of the people who elected you even though at times it may be to the detriment of the party. But it is this detriment that changes political visions and that is a good thing.

Another prime example occurred when I had to butt heads with President Reagan. He wanted Republican support for a Democratic sponsored revamping of the federal tax code in December of 1985. I was adamantly against it since I felt that the bill would definitely hurt our economy and it could never be reshaped in the Senate to reflect the President's goals. I felt that our alternative bill was definitely better. During the week prior to the vote, in the late Fall of 1985, President Reagan met with recalcitrant congressmen, such as me, at Camp David trying to sell us on the tax reform bill.

I had never been to Camp David, and in retrospect, I would have been happy if I never went there. I met with President Reagan, a man who I have always admired personally. There was a nine-hole golf course within the Camp David compound and we proceeded to walk the golf course while he lectured me on why I should change my vote. He relentlessly tried to sell me on voting for the Democratic Tax reform Bill which at the time in President Reagan's opinion would ultimately reflect Republican Tax reform when it was amended in the Senate.

I told him, "With all due respect, Mr. President, I cannot vote for the bill and you will not be able to change my mind." I also told his White House representatives who were present that they would be much better off bringing other congressmen who could be persuaded to change their position instead of wasting time with me. It was all to no avail. After we walked the whole course and it was time for me to leave, I told President Reagan, "Mr. President, you know I admire you greatly, and I am sorry but I totally disagree with you. I think you're wrong on this issue. I would like to do what you want, but I can't. In good conscience, I cannot do it." I could see that he was pissed, but I stood my ground based upon my principles.

Several days later on a frigid windy Sunday, December 15th, 1985 I received a call at my residence in Staten Island. I was watching the Chicago Bears versus New York Jets football game with my wife and family. The phone rang and my wife answered it. Marguerite said, "Guy, it's the President of the United States."

I took the phone from her hand and said, "Mr. President. Good afternoon."

I remember President Reagan said in a very friendly manner, "Guy, what are you doing right now?" I said, "I'm watching the Jets' game right now."

President Reagan said, "Hey is that refrigerator guy playing?" He was referring to William Perry, who was hand-picked in the first round draft of the NFL in 1985. At that point in the conversation "The Refrigerator" was not playing so I told the president, "Nope he's not involved in the game right now." And immediately the President went into his pitch in trying to convert me to support his position regarding the Tax reform Bill being sponsored by the Democrats.

When he was done I respectfully said, "Mr. President, I'm sorry but I am dead set against it. There is really nothing you can say that can change my mind." I could sense that he was obviously angry with me again regarding my response. I said, "Mr. President you sound like you are upset with my response."

I remember President Reagan said, "Yes, Guy. Obviously I am. I am totally frustrated with your response. I wish there was a way I could change your mind."

I said, "With all due respect, Mr. President, I told your guys that I am not going to change my mind. You are not being served well by the people around you. They should have listened to me and not wasted your valuable time on someone like myself. I freely and honestly told them that you should spend your time on people where you can have a chance at changing their vote. Unfortunately for you I am not that person."

Again I stood my ground. Ultimately the President was able to get the bill passed, yet I proudly continued my reputation of being an independent Republican. At times like this it was a difficult path to follow.

Regarding my knack for practical jokes, I was not one to save them for fellow politicians. Anyone and everyone was fair game (except for the President). I remember, in 1985, I hired a new Press Secretary, Eddie Burke. Before I hired him he was working in the community relations section of a hospital. He had heard through word-of-mouth that I was looking for a press secretary. He came in for an interview, and when we finished, Eddie felt that he had to fully disclose a current medical condition. As Eddie was walking out of my office, he turned around and said, "Congressman Molinari I think you need to know that I recently had thyroid cancer surgery and I have to do a course of radiation treatment. I will have to be off for the month of October for the radiation treatment."

Eddie believed that any future employer should know his medical condition, because it might impact his ability to do the job he was hired for. At the time, he believed that there was a high probability that any prospective employer would actually say, "Well, I really can't accept you, because we need someone here full time."

Instead, when he told me about his medical condition, with a twinkle in my eye, as if to reinforce our connection, I said, "Don't worry about it. Do what you have to do to get better, you are hired."

After he was hired, Eddie would reflect back about our first interaction and say, "I'll never forget your expression, in that moment, during our interview when I mentioned I was undergoing treatment for cancer. You looked at me, eye to eye, as if we were lifelong friends. It was a purely human moment. A person's challenges become your challenges and that is what I love about you. I chuckle remembering I was afraid we would disagree about the issues of the day. Silly. It's the issues of the heart that matter."

So, knowing that I had an employee that could use a good chuckle, after Eddie was on the job for about three weeks, I decided to prank call him at home. When I called his house I said, "Hi, I'm Producer So-and-So from Channel 9. I have to say I am really pissed." Burke, said, "Why are you pissed?"

I then proceed to yell at him, "You had a press conference today on aviation safety and everyone was invited except for our channel. Why weren't we invited? Do you have a problem with Channel 9, or does Molinari?"

Burke said, "Gee, I'm really sorry: we invited everybody. Let me take your name and I'll call you back and try to determine what went wrong." I then said, "Aren't you his press secretary?" Burke said, "Yes."

I said, "Do you consider yourself a good press secretary?" The line goes silent when Burke hears my wife Marguerite in the background saying, "Guy, leave him alone." At this point, I was busted. Burke was hysterical laughing that a respected congressman would play such a practical joke. That incident solidified our relationship. Eddie was an excellent press secretary and good friend during my days in Congress and remains one of my close friends to this day.

I found that in order to break up the stress of the job, it was good to add some humor into our daily lives. It worked like a charm. I had a fun, energetic staff that was upbeat and dedicated to the task at hand.

CHAPTER 30

Like Father, Like Daughter

Obviously, the biggest joy of my life has been my daughter, Susan. Since Marguerite and I only had one child, all our dreams and hopes for the future rested with her, and she delivered big time. As she was growing up I attempted to teach her whatever I could, as my parents did with me. The majority of the time I was challenging her and she always persevered through the challenges. In her younger years, before I entered politics, I used to leave the office where I conducted my real estate law business as early as I could so I could play with her and have some precious moments at home. I saw first-hand through my father's eyes the sacrifices a family goes through by having a politician in the household. So, I did not run for elective office until Susan was in high school. When Susan was in high school I encouraged her to pursue forensics. Initially it was never a dream of mine that Susan would become a Molinari political heir. We just wanted her to be happy and pursue a successful career.

Once I entered politics things changed dramatically. I believe that one of the most difficult things for anybody holding public office is the relationship that they have with their family. In particular, serving in Congress is a very time consuming proposition that detracts from family. You're in Washington more than half a week each week and when you're home you go to event, after event, after event.

My first term in Congress I actually tracked my appearance obligations and on one weekend I attended thirty events from the time I arrived in Staten Island to the time I hopped on a plane to go back to Washington. Obviously, the quality time spent at home was limited.

When I was in Albany as an assemblyman, I would see Susan occasionally since she was a student at Albany University. I remember one day when I was sitting in my office in Albany and I heard a loud explosion outside my office window. I found out that it was my daughter's car engine that blew up as she was driving through Albany with the old car that I had given her. Fortunately, she did not get hurt.

In college, Susan became her own person. She was more and more involved with her friends and with campus life. My wife missed her dearly, since they were so close, but she had to accept that was the path to our daughter's development as a young adult. At times, there would be periods where my daughter and wife were fighting with each other over what I consider inconsequential issues. For me it was always the age-old question, "Do I agree with my wife or my daughter?" As a husband, you almost always come to the conclusion that you kind of have to back your wife regardless of whether she is right or wrong. That's just the way marriage goes. Your daughter might leave the nest one day, but your wife will always be there.

Regardless, Susan loved the daily challenges of college. It was there that she learned to make positive things happen on her own. Surprisingly to me, she also became somewhat attracted to the political scene. During this time period, my daughter broadened her political knowledge when she served as an intern for State Senator, Christopher Mega. When she graduated from SUNY Albany, she earned a B.A. in communications graduating *cum laude*, with an M.A. in political communications. Needless to say, as parents we were both very proud of her academic achievement.

A year or so after Susan graduated from Albany she asked her congressman father to help find her a job. I was unsuccessful. Yet, one day she walked into my Washington office with a sarcastic smile on her face and said, "Congratulate me, I have a job." I said, "Really, what is it?" She said, "The National Republican Governor's Committee as a financial assistant!"

I immediately thought to myself, "Ha! Go figure. A Republican entity hired her and yet her daddy couldn't help her get a job." I never really lived that down.

So, when she got this job, Susan approached me and said, "Dad, we can rent a place together. Would you be willing to move in with me?"

I readily jumped at the opportunity.

This arrangement wound up being bliss for me. For the next two years, Susan agreed to see to it that we had a good home-cooked meal, and it helped solidify the life long bond between my daughter and myself. The whole arrangement was great because I got to see my daughter often. Now, my home away from home on the outskirts of Washington, located in Virginia, was more like a home than just a cold, cold apartment. We would run together in the early morning hours, have late night dinners, and share political ideologies. It was my favorite time in Washington.

In 1984, during the time period when Susan was living with me, my wife went to see a condominium in the Bay Terrace area. Marguerite came to Washington a few times in my first term, but after that she didn't want to go anymore. It was one of those things where she supported me in what I was doing, but she preferred to stay in Staten Island. Whatever she wanted to do was fine by me as long as she was happy.

After seeing the condominium, Marguerite called me up and said, "Guy, I love this place and I really want to live here. I know we both love the Todt Hill house, but with Susan out of the house, it's just too big. You wouldn't have to worry about shoveling snow, cutting the grass, or any of that stuff." To me it didn't matter, since I didn't do any of the things she mentioned. We simply hired people. However, since I was in Congress and we spent many days apart, I quickly realized that if she was going to be happy with the condominium, I would be too. The saying "A happy wife makes a happy life" rang in my ears. I recognized that I was rarely home at the time due to political commitments, campaigns, and all the jobs that came with being a congressman. As it happened, the condominium that Marguerite chose is the place I call home today.

After a while Susan was starting to tire of the Washington scene and she started looking at other job opportunities. She actually applied to the Peace Corps, yet at the same time as her application was pending, she got a call from the Staten Island Republican County Chairman and he said, "Susan there's a City Council seat that's opening up and we'd like you to run." She never told me about the call.

So, one day in early 1985, when I was in my office, my daughter visited me. She said, "Dad, I'm going to run for public office." I was shocked because she had never given me any inclination that she was interested in holding office. Now suddenly she was telling me she is going to run for public office.

I asked her, "What office are you talking about?" She said, "City Council. I will be running for the seat that is held by Frank Fossella."

I said, "Susan, Frank is a good friend of mine. You can't run against him." She said, "Dad, you and I disagree. I'm able to make my own decisions and I made a decision that I'm going to run."

So, once it seemed that Susan was serious and that I could not talk her out of it, I said, "Okay, God bless you. Let's go. Of course you have my support."

We embarked on the campaign knowing it was going to be a difficult race. To this day, my relationship with the Fossellas is not the same. There were a lot of hard feelings, but again, that is the world of politics. It was my daughter's decision to run, not mine. As a father, I would always stand by my daughter.

On February 12th, 1985, my daughter was ready to formally announce that she would be running for the City Council seat. I remember immediately before Susan went to the podium she told me she felt nervous and nauseous. As she went up to the podium she had to pass my cousin, her uncle, Ralph Molinari. He grabbed her by the arm as she was proceeding to the stage. He said, "Susan come over here."

She said, "Ralphie, please, not now, they're waiting for me." Ralphie said, "No, this is important. You know the family is very upset with you and your position on abortion."

Susan said, "Ralphie. I'm sorry, but that's my position and you're not going to change me!"

Ralph kept on ranting about other issues. Susan was furious, understandably so. When I heard about it I was furious as well. Fortunately, Susan did a wonderful job when she announced her intentions to enter the race for the City Council seat.

When I think back to that day, I'm amazed how she has now matured to a point where she can go on television anytime, any-place, and discuss every issue without any nervousness whatsoever. Abortion has always been a big moral issue, and the differing stances that Susan and I held separated the family into two different groups, some in one corner, some in the other.

When the press asked me how I felt about my daughter's running, I said, "I'm more excited today than any time I ran." It was the absolute truth. My daughter was entering politics and it was something that I never foresaw. Once the announcement was made, Susan moved back to New York to campaign for the position. Although I missed her dearly in Washington, I was so proud of her work ethic and determination to succeed in the election.

It became evident that she had learned many important lessons during her life surrounded by politics. I was so proud that she paid attention. I had to laugh because there were so many times during our life together that I thought that she was ignoring what was going on. As a parent, you get annoyed when you think your children are overlooking the significance of an important event. Yet, over time, it became clear that she was paying attention to everything.

From the moment she announced that she was running for the City Council position, many people incorrectly thought that I asked Susan to run. That was never the case. My dear friend, Mike Petrides, was coaching her and helping her make a difficult decision. Mike was very close to Susan, almost like a step-father. She looked to him for guidance, and he played a very active role in her campaign. Mike wanted a Republican in the City Council, since there had been no Republicans sitting on the Council for the past three years. Mike knew that if she won she would be the minority leader, since she would be the only Republican. So, to set the record straight, while I had nothing to do with her decision to run, I am extremely proud of her independent decision to run. It was an extremely honorable decision.

At the time, a lot of people were saying, "Her only qualifications for public office is that her father is a politician," and things of that nature. It annoyed the hell out of me, since they knew nothing about my daughter. Fortunately, Susan's skin was tough, and she knew that I was always there for her.

The race itself was an extremely tough race because Frank Fossella was very active in the Democratic Party and he ran a strong campaign. He had a very large following in the Democratic community. This campaign was fought the old-fashioned way: on the streets, in the mailboxes, and in actual debates before neighborhood groups. Both sides spent their money on leaflets and mailings, not radio or television. It was a matter of getting your face in front of the public and getting recognized for who you were. Susan fought till the end and was indefatigable in her stamina.

On Tuesday, November 12th, the most important day of my daughter's life was upon her. The final vote proved the race to be an extraordinarily tight one. Susan won by a slim margin of approximately 132 votes on that night. Talk about hanging on by the skin of your teeth. We were ecstatic to see that Susan won. Susan was now the only Republican currently serving on the City Council, and, in fact, the first Republican to serve in the past three years. Since the vote was so close, the final results were not officially announced until three days later on November 15th, when the absentee votes were tallied. In the long run, my daughter held a lead of approximately 248 votes over Fossella. When you look at the numbers you can clearly see where the saying "every vote counts" comes from!

How proud can I say I was? *EXTRORDINARILY.* Standing beside her, it blew my mind to think that my father, who came from Italy, was elected to New York State Assembly. I then followed him in his footsteps and was ultimately elected to Congress. Now my daughter was a New York City Council member. She had achieved that position against all odds. Three generations of Molinari's serving the public.

At the age of twenty-seven, my only child was the youngest-ever council member, as well as the youngest City Council minority leader. In essence, she was a leader of one: herself. Susan was the sole Republican to sit on the thirty-six-member council. As the minority leader, she was entitled to sit on all committees.

It didn't get any better than that. I was a proud daddy. Yet, I was always proud of Susan as I watched her adjust to new situations in life. The Molinari's were not society people; we were just good family people surrounded by a legion of friends who helped us achieve our goals as well as theirs.

After she was elected, she was able to make clever quips at press conferences that made everyone laugh such as, "I can say with assurances that I will nominate myself to be the Minority Leader and I will second my nomination. Then, I will vote for myself, and when I graciously accept the position, I will thank the Republican minority for the unanimous vote of confidence." Additionally, as an in-your-face moment to the Democratic majority, Susan said, "I pledge that while the Democrats might bicker, the minority will always be united."

The media seemed to take an immediate liking to her since she was not the typical politician. She was also welcomed by her Democratic colleagues and formed some very close alliances.

With this position came many political perks, such as a $20,000 tax-payer-financed stipend. This was in addition to her $47,500 salary, plus thousands more for office expenses, a chauffeured car, an executive secretary, legal counsel, and an office in City Hall. Initially she wanted to turn down the perks that went along with the minority leadership position. When I heard that she was considering that, I told her, "Susan you really have to accept the fringe benefits even though you are the only Republican. If you turn them down, you would be setting a bad precedent for the party in the future. You have to preserve these kinds of things if you want to try to elect Republicans to the City Council in the future."

Oh, it was a big controversy, but she made the right decision once she understood the magnitude of the future impact on the Republican Party in the City Council.

Upon Susan's entry into politics it was readily apparent that her biggest joy was the mere fact that she was serving the public. We both saw this as a privilege and an honor. It was nothing that we took for granted. Because of my daughter's wonderful personality, over a short period of time, she became very popular with the constituents she served. She did a great job in the City Council, she was well-liked, and well-respected. As testament to this statement, when she ran for reelection, she won with 75% of the vote.

I was delighted that throughout the rest of my Congressional career, Susan and I would be working together on issues that affected our constituents. Since we were both Republicans and Staten Islanders at heart, we used our unique political relationship to put forth political ideologies that addressed the issues that concerned our constituents as well as we could.

CHAPTER 31

Dr. Lawrence Burton: Visionary, or Medical Quack?

I FIRST LEARNED OF THE BURTON CLINIC THROUGH ELAINE Boies, a reporter for the *Staten Island Advance*, whose husband, Jack was stricken with terminal prostate cancer. In the winter of 1984, Jack had gotten to the point where he could no longer stand on his own and was told by his doctors that he only had a few months left to live. When Elaine heard about Dr. Lawrence Burton's Immuno-Augmentative Therapy (IAT) clinic in Freeport, Grand Bahamas, she immediately took her husband and children so that Jack could get this treatment that was not available in the U.S. By that time, Elaine's husband was so sick that he needed to be on a stretcher for the entire flight.

When Jack got to Dr. Burton's clinic he immediately began receiving the IAT treatment. Elaine wrote a series of eloquent and heart-rending articles in the *Advance* chronicling the entire family's experience while Jack was being treated in the Bahamas.

Within a matter of days of receiving the treatment, Jack was able to stand again. In short order, he was swimming in the crystal clear waters of the Bahamas with his wife and kids. It was amazing to witness the progress that Jack made as an apparent result of Dr. Burton's clinic and the specialized treatment they offered.

Unfortunately, there did come a point where Dr. Burton told Jack that it was time for him to go home because there was nothing more Dr. Burton could do for him. Jack came home and he died within a short period of time. Yet the time he spent in the Bahamas was priceless to Jack and his family. He was gifted with a quality of life that he would never had experienced if his wife did not pursue alternative medicine for her terminally ill husband. These were truly admirable and selfless pursuits for the entire family.

Shortly thereafter, on July 17th, 1985, the Bahamian government closed Dr. Burton's IAT clinic amid a swirl of unsubstantiated allegations that its operation posed a serious health hazard. At the time of the closing of the IAT Clinic, Dr. Burton had treated over 2,500 patients. Immediately, after the impromptu closing of the clinic, I was told that a busload of his patients was coming to Washington to plead with their respective Congressional representatives to help reopen the clinic. They adamantly felt that Dr. Burton's clinic was their only chance to survive terminal cancer.

I jumped at the opportunity to become actively involved in the plight of my constituents who had pursued alternative medicine for the treatment of hopeless cancers for either themselves or family members, but not before exercising diligence on my own. I had my office do extensive research on Dr. Burton's treatment and background. I had heard that the "cancer community" had labeled him a quack. By the time we were done researching his efforts in finding alternative treatments for cancer, I became somewhat of a believer. Although the medical community in the U.S. may have labeled him a quack, I believed in my heart and mind that he was definitely on the cusp of developing relevant medical alternative treatments, as opposed to the standard cancer treatments approved by our government.

I learned that Dr. Burton received his PhD. from New York University in 1955 in experimental zoology with a background in etiology, which is the study of disease causation. Upon graduating from NYU, he became a research associate at St. Vincent's Hospital in New York working with mice. He discovered a natural substance in the blood, "an inhibitor," which was found to slow the growth of tumors. Upon this discovery, he received research grants from the U.S. Public Health Service and other cancer centers to pursue his research.

During this time period he butted heads with Memorial Sloan Kettering's cancer scientists. The Sloan-Kettering scientists became enraged that an unknown scientist, Dr. Burton from St. Vincent's, was receiving accolades from the scientific community concerning his research. During this time period, Dr. Burton became the Senior Investigator and Senior Oncologist at St. Vincent's Hospital Manhattan.

Dr. Burton believed that the Sloan Kettering scientists considered themselves "The World Famous Cancer Research Hospital." As such, Sloan-Kettering considered it ludicrous that any significant cancer research could come from an unknown doctor called Burton who practiced at St. Vincent's. Yet, Dr. Burton's reputation continued to grow with his research. During this time period, he would publish sixty-five articles in peer review journals and was asked to be the keynote speaker at many scientific conferences.

In 1966, at the American Cancer Society's Annual Science Writers' Seminar in Phoenix, Arizona, and in 1967, at the New York Academy of Medicine meeting, Dr. Burton demonstrated his IAT serum by injecting it into mice with large cancerous tumors in front of hundreds of journalists and scientists. Less than two hours after the injections the tumors lost their hardness and shrunk to half their former size.

Despite the many eyewitnesses at the demonstrations and simultaneous newspaper articles proclaiming a "Cancer Cure," the American Cancer Society representatives refused to believe that a little-known researcher had discovered a possible cancer treatment. They could not fathom scientists endowed with huge grants working in the largest, best-equipped laboratories at nationally known cancer institutes had failed. So, Dr. Burton's demonstration was completely ignored by the medical community and labeled a hoax.

Ultimately, the long and short of it was that St Vincent's Hospital was threatened with the loss of millions in grant money by the local cancer establishment if Dr. Burton continued with his cancer treatments since they were not "officially" approved by the government. The local cancer establishment, in Dr. Burton's case, was Sloan-Kettering, National Institute of Cancer (NIC), and the American Cancer Society.

So, in 1973, Dr. Burton left St. Vincent's and opened the Immunology Research Foundation (IRF) in Great Neck, New York. He began treating cancer patients with IAT therapy at the clinic, and obtained U.S. patents on the four proteins they used in the therapy as follows: a deblocking protein (DP), a tumor antibody 1 (TA1), a tumor antibody 2 (TA2), and tumor complement (TC). Based on his research, Dr. Burton claimed that when these substances were used in the right combination, they could restore normal immune function in cancer patients. During this time period, he also applied to the FDA for an Investigational New Drug permit.

After several years it became obvious he would never be able to satisfy the FDA's seemingly endless harassing requests for additional information and clinical studies. Even though he was able to achieve remarkable results in treating cancer patients as compared to the national averages, and treated many patients referred from physicians around the country, he was politically and economically forced to close the New York research facility. The harassment from the FDA and the cancer research establishment was relentless. He could not monetarily afford to continue his work in the U.S.

Committed to continuing his alternative cancer treatment, Dr. Burton quit his battle against the local cancer establishment bureaucracy in the United States and in 1977 he received approval for the opening of the Immunology Research Center (IRC) and relocated to the Bahamas. It was fully sanctioned by the Bahamas Ministry of Health. It was there that he was free to treat terminally ill cancer patients with his Immuno-Augmentative Therapy until its abrupt closing. At the time of the closing, Dr. Burton's Clinic was actively treating approximately 500 terminally ill cancer patients.

So, when hundreds of Dr. Burton's American cancer patients believed that their last hope for fighting their terminal disease had been yanked away from them, they picked up their battle axes and started fighting the cancer establishment. Dr. Burton's patients brought the fight to Washington. I was one of the Congressmen who heard their battle cry and greeted dozens of them on the steps of the Capitol. Their plight intrigued me, and at the same time, broke my heart. I listened to his patients and I promised them that I would visit the clinic to see whether the conditions responsible for its closing could be rectified.

I told them, "I am not a scientist, or medical doctor, I am a humanitarian congressman who believes that if a patient is terminally ill from cancer, and their doctor tells them there is nothing more that can be done for them, then I believe they should be allowed to pursue that last hope, whether the treatment works or not. It should be their option and choice." I still believe that patients should be given the opportunity for alternative therapy if they are given a death sentence. Why not? Sometimes it appeared to be successful. If it was me, I would take the chance as well.

Once I became involved in the cause, I spoke to Dr. Lawrence Burton often. He was a good old Brooklynite who was totally committed to treating terminally ill cancer patients and finding a cure, if possible, along the way. During my conversations, he freely admitted that his treatment was not a "cure" for cancer, but rather that in many cases it seemed to "control" the growth of cancer.

After meeting his forsaken patients, I immediately contacted the State Department and they arranged for me to meet and hold a public hearing with the Minister of Health for the Bahamas and tour

Burton's clinic. I wanted to discuss the reasons for the closing of the facility and whether or not it could be reopened.

Within a week, after meeting Dr. Burton's patients on the steps of the Capitol, I arrived in the Bahamas. When the plane landed the Deputy Ambassador to the Bahamas met me and confirmed the visit to the clinic, but he informed me that the Ministry of Health had changed its mind and refused to have any meaningful discussions or a public hearing concerning the clinic. I was pissed, to say the least, that the meeting and public hearing were cancelled.

This visit was sanctioned by our State Department and now it was cancelled. Once I learned that I would not be meeting with the Ministry of Health, or having a public hearing, the main purpose of my trip to the Bahamas was ruined.

The only good thing that came out of this trip was the fact that I did go and visit Dr. Burton's clinic and I was impressed. Although it was closed, I was able to talk to many of the experienced doctors who worked at the clinic, the majority of whom came from the United Kingdom. I felt it was my humanitarian obligation as a congressman to visit the facility that had given hope to so many terminal cancer patients. Again, this was clearly an international issue and not merely a local issue. People from all over our country, and the world traveled to Dr. Burton's clinic. When I returned to Washington, I decided the best strategy to quickly address this issue was to conduct an investigational hearing. I went the investigative hearing route, even though I would have preferred that the hearing be conducted by one of the appropriate Congressional committees or subcommittees having direct jurisdiction over the matter. That normal route would have required many months of preparation for the hearing, but the time table would not work because many of Dr. Burton's patients who wished to testify were terminally ill. I decided, after I conducted the investigational hearing, I would provide copies of the transcripts to the committees having jurisdiction over the matter.

By the time the hearing date had arrived, over thirty other Congressmen had contacted my office on behalf of their constituents regarding Dr. Burton's clinic. Can you imagine: thirty other congressmen were interested, but I was the only congressman stupid enough to take the extra step.

In the interest of conducting a fair and balanced hearing, on December 26th, 1985, I wrote to Dr. Otis Brown, Secretary of the Department of Health and Human Services and offered as follows:

> ...I feel it is imperative that an open forum be conducted to flush the fabrications from the facts regarding this issue. I am not a scientist or medical authority and therefore cannot offer a substantive opinion or assessment of the IAT treatment formula. Nor can I offer a medical explanation for what some patients are referring to as "successful results" with the treatment. I bear no particular allegiance to Lawrence Burton, Ph.D., the researcher and founder behind the IAT clinic, but feel it is beholden to us, for the sake of the many patients who do have faith in Burton and his treatment, to at least grant a gesture of concern for their plight and proceed with an informational investigation...
>
> ...Burton and his staff, as well as several patients with particularly dramatic recoveries to report, will be providing testimony at the hearing. It is essential in conducting a balanced, constructive hearing on this issue to include representation from the United States Health and Human Services Department, in particular qualified representatives from NCI, CDC and FDA. I am determined that the hearing allows all voices on this issue to be heard – those of Burton's proponents and critics alike. I do not wish the hearing to favor any one individual or point of view, but I do believe the absence of our top cancer-related

> agencies at this event may only serve to fuel the fire of the clinic's supporters on the matter of mainstream uncooperativeness [.]

As promised on, January 15th, 1986, I conducted an investigative hearing on the "Immuno-Augmentative Therapy of Dr. Lawrence Burton," at 26 Federal Plaza in Manhattan. Representatives that I invited to testify at the hearing declined the invitation, to wit: The American Cancer Society, The National Cancer Institute, Centers for Disease Control, and even the Secretary of the Department of Health and Human Services himself. It spoke volumes to me that the "cancer establishment" refused to testify at this hearing. Their refusal to testify only fueled my passion for exposing the truth. When someone shuts the door in my face it does not silence me, in fact, it angers and energizes me.

The hearing itself lasted over nine hours. The result of the hearing generated a nationwide surge in constituents' letters and phone calls advocating support on behalf of the clinic.

On March 7th, 1986, I was proud to announce that the Burton Cancer Clinic in Freeport, Grand Bahama Island reopened after an eight-month shutdown. I told the public that, "apparently all the confusions and controversies surrounding the cause for the clinic's closure last year have been cleared up to the satisfaction of the Government of the Bahamas." Of course I also recognized the fact that the Bahamian government was losing a tremendous amount of money with the closure of the Clinic.

My main concern has always been for the patients of IAT, who I thought should not have their last hope for effective control of their disease yanked away from them. These are terminally ill cancer patients and from a humanitarian standpoint, they should be allowed to receive this therapy, if they so choose, so long as it does them no harm. In my heart, I knew that the positive publicity concerning the support of Dr. Burton's alternative cancer treatment therapies was a major motivating factor in the Bahamians Government's decision.

On August 5th, 1986, I received a very heartwarming letter from Dr. Burton. In it, he stated as follows:

> I have been told that it is a virtual certainty that the OAT evaluation will take place. A fair evaluation of the therapy is something that I no longer dared hope for. Certainly that would never have become a possibility if not for your determined efforts. I hope that it will be the first and most significant step which will ultimately lead to sweeping changes in the way cancer research and treatment is done in the U.S. If that comes to pass, all cancer patients and their families, indeed all Americans, will owe you and your staff more than words can convey....[15]

Dr. Burton passed away in 1993. I will always remember him as a man who stood up to the establishment. In my opinion, he never looked for financial gains such as the "quacks" sought. He was not a medical quack, but a cancer research genius. I did my research and I stand by my opinion. He had the balls to say, "Screw them all. I'm going to the Bahamas and continuing my treatment of terminally ill cancer patients." In Dr. Burton's situation, the mainstream medical establishment was labeling him as a quack. Why? Because they were not making any money off his discoveries. Shame on them, and kudos to Dr. Burton.

His clinic in the Bahamas continues to draw patients from around the world diagnosed with terminal cancer. They go to his clinic for the hopes of an alternative medicine treatment that they cannot be afforded in their own country due to inflexibility at the hands of the self-proclaimed private industry and government spon-

---

15 OAT is the Office of Technology Assessment

sored "cancer establishment." Dr. Burton changed many families' lives and offered hope when one felt hopeless. A terrific legacy for a man that I consider to be a dedicated physician who thought outside the box.

CHAPTER 32

One-way Toll

In the mid-1980s well over 150,000 vehicles traveled in either direction on the Verrazano Bridge. The bridge is the only link between Staten Island and Brooklyn. During the morning rush hour, traffic routinely backed up across the island to the Jersey bridges because commuters were waiting in exceedingly long lines to pay the Verrazano tolls. It was an abominable situation and the subsequent morning commute was awful for the drivers.

The inevitable result of this traffic congestion was deadly pollution from car emissions on the arterial highways leading to the bridge. Since the toll booths were all on the Staten Island end of the bridge, eastbound traffic would back up on the expressway, and the cars would spew exhaust fumes over nearby neighborhoods. If the westbound traffic backed up on the bridge, the car exhaust would dissipate over the water. It was yet another issue where my constituent's health was negatively affected. The Staten Island Expressway's air pollution needed to be curtailed, and based upon my research the one-way toll was part of the solution.

Previously, Governor Mario Cuomo had vetoed a one-way toll proposal on the state level. After serving in Congress for over five years, I learned the system and became innovative on how to resolve issues. I did some research and came up with a clever and unique approach on how I could legislatively make the Verrazano Bridge change to a one-way toll on the federal level.

On September 12th, 1985, I aggressively argued on the floor of Congress for the passage of the one-way toll. I had attached an amendment for the appropriation bill of the United States Department of Transportation which stipulated that if the tolls on Brooklyn-bound traffic were not removed by March 20, New York State would lose 1% of its federal transportation aid. If approved, under the congressionally mandated experiment, motorists crossing the Verrazano Bridge to Brooklyn would pay no tolls, while those driving from Brooklyn to Staten Island must pay a double toll of $3.50. As a result, everyone's morning commute to Brooklyn would be infinitely better with less pollution.

During the course of the debate, Congressman Steve Solarz, from Brooklyn, was the lead debater against me. We went at it for an hour which is a long period of time for a debate between two individuals in Congress. Solarz was very cocky about the whole thing, since he was in the majority. He incorrectly felt that it was a ground ball win for him.

The debate itself got very nasty. I appealed to the audience, arguing that there was no better test than actually implementing the one-way toll on an experimental basis and then evaluating the results in a fair and impartial way. We needed to make it real for the residents of Staten Island. If it failed, it failed, but at least we would have tried. A major issue that bothered my Congressional colleagues was: why should Congress be allowed to tell a local authority how to collect tolls when a bridge begins and ends within the same state? I was able to easily overcome the issue by explaining that the Verrazano Bridge was part of Interstate Route 278. As such, being an Interstate Route, federal intervention was completely appropriate.

The most fortuitous thing that happened during the debate was when Solarz made a huge mistake. He didn't know what side of the bridge the tolls were being collected from. So, I embarrassed the hell out of him on his ignorance of the issue. When the debate was over I called for the vote. When all was said and done, the legislation passed. That shocked the heck out of Solarz who was standing next to me. He looked over to the board and said, "I don't understand this." He was looking for an answer and he couldn't understand why he did not carry the Democratic side.

I thought to myself, "You made an epic blunder. When you argue an issue before Congress you have to be prepared and know the issue inside and out." I was able to convince the voting members, Democrats and Republicans alike, that my position was right. On the flip side, the voting members were not convinced by Solarz' argument because he was clearly unprepared. Solarz's blunder allowed me to pull off a legislative coup and created the one-way toll payment system on the Verrazano Bridge.

The bill that passed was a very fair piece of legislation because it provided that after six months, the Governor of New York could petition to do away with the one-way toll collection if one of two things occurred: first, if there was an unsafe condition such as excessive traffic congestion and or pollution during the course of the toll collection; or second, if there was a substantial loss of revenue.

Koch was livid when he learned that my legislation had passed. He vowed to do whatever he could in his power to overturn the legislation. It was one of those areas where Koch stood firm on the side of Manhattan and against Staten Island. Manhattan representatives were falsely claiming that the institution of a one-way toll would increase congestion in Manhattan and Brooklyn. I knew that whenever an issue was between Manhattan and Staten Island, Mayor Koch would always side with Manhattan because that was where his Mayoral heart was. So even though I won the battle, the war was not yet over.

On Thursday, March 20th, 1986, the one-way toll officially went into effect on the Verrazano Bridge. It was to be a six-month experiment. Throughout this time period, the Triborough Bridge and Tunnel Authority (TBTA), which oversees the bridge, and the Metropolitan Transportation Authority (MTA), the TBTA's parent agency, strenuously objected to the one-way toll. They did acknowledge though that they had to follow the Congressional mandate. It did not stop individual entities from going into state and federal courts and suing over the issue.

During the trial process the experiment was attacked with negative publicity from individuals outside of Staten Island. This opposition came primarily from Mayor Koch who I felt was completely irrational about this issue. In essence, he was a loose cannon and completely out of control. In order to spark the controversy, I publically stated, "A gutless wonder leads the City of New York." Koch saw me as a crusader squarely on the side of Staten Island fighting the anti-Staten Island establishment led by him. Koch protected SoHo. I protected Staten Island.

Mayor Koch, as promised, sought an immediate repeal of the one-way toll in Washington. He wasn't content to allow the six-month trial period to run, which most experts agreed was the minimum amount of time needed to calculate the data necessary to evaluate the merits of the one-way toll.

Koch, knowing that the democrats were in the majority, recruited a well-respected congressman, Robert Mrazek, from Nassau County, to put in an amendment onto the Transportation Appropriations bill which would allow the MTA to abandon the one-way toll if traffic congestion and revenues losses were incurred. Missing in Mrazek provision was the word "substantial" which is a much higher threshold to meet.

I tried to override his amendment with my own amendment which would have required the city and state to petition the Secretary of Transportation, not the MTA, for the change, while also requiring local officials to prove that the new system caused "substantial" revenue or traffic problems.

On July 30th, 1986, the Democratically controlled House paved the way for scrapping my one-way toll on the Verrazano and returning to a two-way-fare system in September. With the amount of negative publicity being thrown about, I knew that I wouldn't be able to carry the bill against Mrazek since he was very popular. As predicted, not one New York City or New Jersey representative voted to keep the one-way toll. Due to Koch's effort and the MTA at this time, I was completely outnumbered.

The residents of Staten Island were thrilled with the initial results of the one-way toll. This would be a major step backward if the experiment was unable to proceed. Traffic congestion and air pollution in the surrounding areas were significantly decreased with the introduction of the one-way toll.

As tenacious as Koch could be, I could match him when it involved Staten Island. If he thought I would roll over, he was dead wrong. I may have been beaten in the House because I was in the minority, but in the Senate I had a powerful friend in the majority, Senator Al D'Amato who sat on the Senate Appropriations Committee. He totally supported the one-way toll. He stopped the legislation in the Senate. In fact, the Senate then voted to leave the original law intact with federal control. Koch was again livid.

So, the one-way toll continued. Governor Cuomo was silent on whether or not he would support the one-way toll until the MTA completed environmental studies which were supposed to be done by the end of the year. Seeing how aggressive the opposition was, I knew that I had to muster the troops in Staten Island and let the people's voice be heard loud and clear. I knew that in order to be successful, I needed Staten Island "people power" to back my plan up. I helped form a private citizens' committee called, "Committee to Preserve the One-way toll." It was run under the leadership of Monica Romero, a Staten Island mother of a young five year-old, who lived right off I-278. She did a wonderful job.

On Saturday, September 20th, six months into the initiation of the trial run, we held a rally at Willowbrook Park. It was attended by hundreds of Staten Islanders hell bent on keeping the one-way toll. Staten Islanders knew the results of the one-way toll were an outstanding success. The one-way toll had dissolved the almost daily tie-ups that once backed up traffic for four miles on the Staten Island Expressway. I let everyone know at the rally that it was 'People Power' that was ultimately going to keep the one-way toll. We would not lose if we were united and allowed our voices to be heard. Everyone in the crowd was completely motivated and revved up for the battle of the one-way-tall. They had signs "Keep the one-way toll," and "I want to breathe." It was truly another one of those grassroots movements that would be successful because they were dedicated. I made it clear that one way or the other we would win the battle. We had taken the fight into the public political arena.

I played my cards right and went easy on Governor Mario Cuomo. I felt that with the intense media pressure he would realize that voting against the one-way toll would draw the wrath of Staten Island residents. After all, he was up for re-election and you would not want to piss off an entire borough by voting against something that was close to their hearts.

The same could not be said of Mayor Koch. The committee members hung an effigy of Mayor Koch on the back of a flatbed truck. Koch was clearly on the wrong end of the stick in this situation. They would have burned the effigy but they were unable to get the appropriate permit.

Immediately after the rally, we proceeded to have a massive car caravan, well over a mile long, on the Staten Island expressway drive over the Verrazano Bridge in support of the one-way toll. It was an incredible show of solidarity on a Saturday morning. The cars had signs plastered on them in support of the one-way toll. They were decorated with streamers and balloons and as the cars proceeded along the expressway they honked their horns in support of the one-way toll.

Of course part of the caravan was the effigy of Mayor Koch being hung on the back of a flatbed truck being carted over the bridge. Needless to say, this was a huge statement to the Mayor from his Staten Island voters. The sound of blaring horns carried the demonstrator's message loud and clear across the bridge. It was done in a civilized organized matter with the full cooperation of the police. It generated a tremendous amount of publicity, and I cannot tell you how proud I was of my Staten Island constituents.

It's very hard to get Manhattan media to cover a story on Staten Island. Such was not the case on this day. Every media outlet was covering the story. CBS, NBC, FOX, ABC, and Channels 9 and 11 all came out to see what all the fuss was about. By the end of the night, the entire city, state, and country learned that Staten Islanders loved the one-way toll and they were committed to keeping it.

During this time period, I spoke to Robert Kiley who was the Chairman and CEO of the MTA. I asked him, "How is it going with the environmental studies because we are in the six-month period?"

Kiley said, "What are you worried about?" I said, "What do you mean?" He said, "There is no danger whatsoever. All those things that we thought might happen have not happened, and there is no loss of revenue so you're in good shape."

Needless to say, I was happy to hear that all the critics did not know what they were talking about. It was just speculation. That is why it was good that the experiment went forward. As time went on, I was thrilled when the American Automobile Association came out and fully supported the one-way toll, as well as shadow traffic and other traffic experts. Immediately before the rally I was delighted to learn that the Automobile Club of New York conducted a survey at their own expense and found that the one-way toll was an outstanding success. Robert McGowan, the President of the Automobile Club of New York, sent a letter to Governor Cuomo urging him to keep the one-way toll.

Since the one-way toll was my legislation, it had to be renewed on a year-to-year basis. So, each and every year, I would fight the fight. We would hand out flyers at the toll booths encouraging everyone to continue to preserve the one-way toll. After I left congress and my daughter Susan became a congresswoman, she continued with the cause. After a while she realized that it was stupid and we should just make the one-way toll permanent. Fortunately, she was in the majority in 1995, so she had the legislation made permanent under the National Highway System Designation Act. It no longer had to be extended on an annual basis.

This whole issue demonstrates that sometimes an answer to a complex problem can come from the people themselves. Many times, as in this case, the agencies vested with the responsibility do not have the expertise that we think they have. On February 2nd 2012 the unused toll booths were dismantled.

On a final note on the Verrazano Bridge, through my years as a congressman and borough president, I was repeatedly involved in battles for a fair reduced toll for my Staten Island residents. I held numerous public hearings, as well as debates, regarding a reduced toll for Staten Islanders. I would invariably let the other elected officials go first. I would watch them thunder as they shouted, "We will not stand for these toll hikes, if you think that you're gonna put this over on the community you have another thing coming!" as they fulminated from the top of their voices.

Having seen these dynamic politicians on stage, I would then watch the politicians leave the podium. When they left the stage, you knew it was all political rhetoric. It was clear they only came to be seen. They said their piece to the audience and then they did nothing more. There was no energy or commitment to the real issue. It was as if they evaporated into thin air, since they never did anything relevant to get the reduced tolls. As soon as they were done speaking, they would immediately leave. They were too busy to stay for the entire proceeding.

I did not follow the other politicians' lead. I did something profoundly different. I would stay and listen to what the public had to say. When dealing with the reduced toll I resurrected the slogan

"People Power." My voice, as well as the voice of affected Staten Island residents, needed to be heard in order to get results. After the public was done, I would then get up and address the issue at the public hearing.

Regarding the toll hike protests, I remember one time there was a group of protesters from the North Shore of the Island that organized a protest. I went to the bridge to show support for the organizers. Only a handful of people showed up. It was a disappointment to the organizers. The following week they planned the event better, and a Sunday rally attracted over 1000 people.

The protest got a little out of hand because the protesters wanted to close down the bridge. I did not agree with that strategy because you just can't stop traffic completely. If you closed the bridge completely it could endanger public safety. As such, serious consequences may result from closing the bridge. Emergency vehicles had to be able to get to their destination, the sick needed to get to the hospital.

I attempted to open the flow of traffic so that emergency vehicles and things like that could get through. I actually wound up fighting with the protesters. At the same time, the head of the Triborough Bridge and Tunnel Authority Police ended up getting into a fight with me.

He said, "You are going to be arrested for blocking traffic and for inciting a riot." I was furious and I told him, "I'm here trying to make peace and trying to call off this protest, and you are accusing me of inciting a riot? I'm trying to get them to stop blocking the toll booths. You don't know what the fuck you are talking about." I was so pissed, I told him, "If you arrest me, I will drag your ass before a hearing in Congress, and you can explain why you mishandled this whole thing."

It was a tough time, but the people were out there in big numbers and wanted to demonstrate the unfairness of the toll hike system. The continually increasing tolls were killing the average working person. The problem with this protest was that they had professional protesters participating. In essence, agitators. It was a difficult protest to attend since I wanted to support them, but not if they were out of control.

After the sixth toll hike, I had finally reached my boiling point. It was one toll hike too many. We spent three weeks rallying up Staten Islanders telling them they had to fight or the tolls would never stop. We rented a bus to get people to the rally. We got bull horns and spread the message. We went to the toll plaza handing out cards that said, "Stop the Toll Increases." It was a huge amount of work, but it was well organized and the execution paid off.

On the night of the rally, Hylan Boulevard, a major throughway on Staten Island, was swamped with throngs of people who wanted to fight the increased toll. During the course of the night almost ten thousand people jammed into New Dorp High School.

That's unheard of then and now – it has never been duplicated. The auditorium only seated 900 people. So we had to have rotations. I had to repeatedly say, "Folks, we got room after room with lots of other people who want to come in. We are going to ask you to cooperate with us and after a couple of speeches here, to move on and let the others come in. I want to give everybody a chance to show their support and hear what they have to say."

It was an unbelievable show of force that resulted in a cause and effect: a discounted toll for Staten Island residents as a direct result of "People Power."

CHAPTER 33

A Democratic Nicaragua?

As early as 1981, President Reagan condemned the Nicaraguan Sandinista Government for joining with Cuba in supporting Marxist revolutionary movements in other Latin Countries such as El Salvador. It was an issue that would resurrect itself throughout his Presidency, but Reagan would be firm in his initial position: The Contras were right in trying to eradicate communism in Nicaragua, and the oppressive Sandinista government had to go.

When Reagan heard that the Sandinistas and their sympathizers referred to the Contras disparagingly as counterrevolutionaries, Reagan responded, "God bless the Contras for being that way. If being opposed to communism makes the rebels Contras, it makes me a Contra, too." Reagan was fully committed to eradicating communism throughout Central America as well as the world. That fight would be one of his major presidential legacies and one that I personally admired.

It was interesting since the country of Nicaragua seemed inconsequential to lives of the average American citizen. But, in fact, to a Republican congressman representing Staten Island, Nicaragua's struggle represented the essence of a democratic existence for the world. This is exactly where the role of congressman came into play. I was in Washington for national, as well as local politics. The two go hand in hand.

When we talk about Nicaragua, I will always remember the story about a conversation between former Secretary of State Kissinger and the then current Secretary of State Shultz. Kissinger told Schultz, "You know, when I was Secretary of State, I never paid fifteen minutes of attention to Central America." Secretary of State Schultz responded by saying, "Yeah and now look at the mess we have."

That being said, I was more than happy to involve myself in promoting what I considered the correct resolution to international affairs. I agreed with President Reagan's position on the tumultuous situation in Central America. We both felt that something had to be done to promote democracy and eradicate communism.

By way of history, prior to the Sandinistas coming into power, Nicaragua was under the rule of Anastasio Somoza. On Saturday, December 29th, 1972, a devastating earthquake leveled much of Nicaragua's capital, Managua. In its wake there were widespread casualties. Almost 6,000 people were killed, 20,000 injured, and over 250,000 were left homeless.

In the aftermath of the devastating earthquake, and the subsequent pouring in of monetary support from all over the world, it was revealed by the international media that Somoza's government was replete with corruption. Somoza and his cronies had plundered much of the foreign aid in order to enrich themselves, to the detriment of the people.

This blatant corruption sparked the Nicaraguan Revolution, resulting in the communist Sandinista government gaining control of Nicaragua when Somoza was overthrown in 1979. In hindsight, the communist Sandinista government was no better than the Somoza government, as they were both oppressive and corrupt regimes.

Regarding the Sandinista Regime, when Reagan first came into office, El Salvador, Honduras, and Guatemala were all under military dictatorships. Yet, within five years, they had all become democratic societies. It was a fabulous movement in the direction of democracy in Central America. Also, under President Reagan, there was never a military coup against a democratically elected President in Central America. That in and of itself said a lot.

The problem-country in Central America was Nicaragua. Nicaragua was the one area where democracy could not make progress. It was right smack in the middle of everything and was a strong communist regime. The overwhelming majority of the Nicaraguan people hated the communist system. Their children were taken, they toiled in peasant work, and the Sandinista government had horrendous political prisons for dissidents who opposed the communist regime. At the time, it was estimated that at least 8,000 political prisoners were sequestered due to their political beliefs. Some were incarcerated when the Sandinistas first took power illegally. For a small country it had a high rate of political insurgency. These insurgents did nothing except oppose communism in Nicaragua.

I completely agreed with Reagan's position to support the Contras in Nicaragua. I recognized that our government made the greatest progress toward peace in Nicaragua when the Contras, or as many Americans referred to them, "freedom-fighters," were strong because of our support, and the Sandinista government had to negotiate.

At the President's request, on March 14th, 1986, at 7:45 a.m., I proudly embarked on a fact-finding mission with eight other Republicans contemporaries to Nicaragua. It was a spur of the moment trip, since Reagan realized at the last minute that he needed hands-on Congressional involvement for him to successfully support the Contras. We called it "a trip of hope," since it was basically a last minute effort to get a breakthrough deal which we believed could either lead to peace in the area, or at the very least, to strong support for the Contra rebels.

At the time, the majority of the Democratically controlled Congress was against supporting the Contras. I was selected since President Reagan knew that I was totally committed to a communist free world as he was.

President Regan proposed a $100 million aid package for the Contra rebels slated for March 20th, 1986. He wanted to provide the Contras with $30 million in non-lethal aid, such as, medicine and clothing, and $70 million that was for direct military aid. We all knew that it was an uphill battle for Reagan. Reagan wanted to give the aid so that it would force the Sandinista government in Nicaragua to come to the bargaining table with the Contras.

We flew out of Andrews Air Force Base in Maryland. The fact finding mission consisted of me, along with Congressmen Tom Delay, David S. Monson, Jim Kolbe, Paul B. Henry, Roberts S. Walker, David Dreier, Robert K. Dornan, and Congresswoman Barbara F. Vucanovich.

We arrived at Managua's Augusto Sandino Airport on a U.S. Air Force jet. We were scheduled to meet with the following people: Nicaraguan Vice President Sergio Ramirez; Bayardo Arce, who was the Deputy Coordinator of the ruling Sandinista National Liberation Front's Executive Committee; leaders of the Roman Catholic Church; the Human Rights Commission; and leaders of the Contras.

When we arrived, the first stop on our tour was the office of Nicaragua's only opposition newspaper, *La Prensa*. We met the widow of Pedro Joaquín Chamorro Cardenal who was the former owner of *La Prensa*. His widow told the story of how her husband had been murdered on the morning of January 10th, 1978, while he was on the way to work. He was shot and killed by several rounds from a shotgun. She cried as she told of how he died in an ambulance on the way to a nearby hospital. She recounted how it was widely believed that Somoza's son, "*El Chigüin*" was behind the murder.

She proudly stated that her husband Pedro had become a martyr, and his death helped ignite widespread opposition to the Somoza government. The majority of Nicaraguan citizens supported the

Sandinista insurgency after his murder. His assassination sparked off the beginning of the final mass insurrection against Somoza. Sadly though she said the new regime was as bad as the prior regime. She told us how *La Prensa* endured censorship on a daily basis due to the communist Sandinista regime. By the time we left her office, we all felt that the Sandinista Nicaraguan government was extremely repressive.

On this trip, I had the privilege and the honor to meet with Roman Catholic Cardinal Miguel Obando y Bravo. On May 25th, 1985, Pope John Paul II selected him to be a Cardinal in Central America. It was not an easy religious title to hold especially in light of residing in a communist regime. Cardinal Obando opposed what he called the "Godless communism" of the Sandinistas. He criticized many of the Sandinista's policies, including religious oppression, restrictions of press, and severe human rights violations. People were routinely beaten after attending mass. There were constant assaults against ethnic and religious groups by the Sandinistas. The Sandinistas regularly shut down the Catholic radio stations. The Sandinistas deprived the citizens of the legal right to speak, publish, assemble, or to worship freely. The government did not want the word of God to get out. Cardinal Obando felt that the constant pressure upon the Church in Nicaragua was suffocating and oppressive. He publically stated that the totalitarian Sandinista government "was an enemy of the state." The Cardinal was fearless and committed to promoting religious freedom and democracy in Nicaragua.

Cardinal Obando told me of a "Mothers' Committee" which consisted of mothers of young men and women who simply "disappeared" in the Sandinistas' prison system. The Sandinistas threatened the "Mothers' Committee" and the people who worked with them. Cardinal Obando told me about the constant public attacks on himself, his bishops, and the priests who worked for him.

The Sandinistas, in turn, felt that Cardinal Obando should have argued aggressively against U.S. aid to the Contras. The Sandinista government said that Cardinal Obando had promised the

Nicaraguan people that if human rights abuses on the part of the Contras were verifiably reported, he would denounce the Contras. Yet, the Sandinista government said that when human rights abuses were clearly documented and verified by groups established by the Catholic Church itself, the Cardinal did not denounce them as he had promised. Instead, the Cardinal travelled to the United States in January of 1986, and declared his support for the Contras in front of Congress. The Sandinistas felt that Cardinal Obando encouraged the United States Government to provide the Contras with military aid. This set the stage for a sharp confrontation between the Cardinal and the Sandinista government. Fortunately for Cardinal Obando y Bravo, his popularity was too great for him to simply vanish off the face of the Earth.

On this trip, I also met Vice President of Nicaragua, Sergio Ramirez Mercado, who served under President Daniel Ortega. I asked V.P. Ramirez, "What do you think about the possibility and prospects of peace talks?"

He quickly motioned with his thumbs down, and said, "We are going to defeat the Contras and there is no need to sit down and talk." That was the end of the discussion.

It became very clear to me that if you wanted the Sandinistas to come to the table and negotiate political reform, you had to give them an incentive. That incentive was political and financial support of the Contras. The Sandinista communist government needed to feel the pressure of possible defeat if U.S. support continued; otherwise, the Sandinistas would just continue being an oppressive communist government. I was convinced that we should not and could not abandon the Contras.

I thought it was very sad that every time the Contras seemed to be making progress Congress stopped them dead in their tracks by withdrawing financial support of the Contras. During this quick fact finding mission, I saw that the morale of the Contras was up. The Contras were fully supplied, they were going back into combat and they were making progress. The Contras were involved in some major successful attacks. I saw the prospect of peace breaking out, not war, if our support continued. I believed we had a right to be proud of the efforts our nation was taking to promote democracy in Central America.

When we returned to the United States and briefed the Reagan Administration on our findings during the mission, President Reagan addressed the nation from the Oval Office live on nationwide radio and television, regarding the situation in Nicaragua on the evening of March 16th, 1986. In closing, he pleaded with the American public to contact their congressmen and senators and tell them to vote yes for the continued support of the Contras. In closing, he stated as follows:[16]

> I have only three years left to serve my country; three years to carry out the responsibilities you entrusted to me; three years to work for peace. Could there be any greater tragedy than for us to sit back and permit this cancer to spread leaving my successor to face far more agonizing decisions in the years ahead? The freedom fighters seek a political solution. They are willing to lay down their arms and negotiate to restore the original goals of the revolution, a democracy in which the people of Nicaragua choose their own government. That is our goal also, but it can only come about if the democratic resistance is able to bring pressure to bear on those who have seized power.
>
> We still have time to do what must be done so history will say of us: We had the vision, the courage, and good sense to come together and act—Republicans and Democrats—when the price was not high and

16 *March 16th 1986 excerpt of President Speech to the nation broadcast live on nationwide radio and television.*

> the risks were not great. We left America safe, we left America secure, we left America free—still a beacon of hope to mankind, still a light unto the nations.

Disappointingly the bill was not passed on March 20th, 1986. But on June 25th, 1986, the House finally passed the Contra aid package by 123 votes. Reagan called it "a step forward in bipartisan consensus in American foreign policy." At the time, it was a major win for the President. His foreign policy of eradicating communism was taking hold.

On January 9th, 1987, I embarked on another fact finding trip to Central America with three other Congressional colleagues: Frank Wolf, Dan Coats, and Alex McMillan. This time we would be spending a full week and would visit El Salvador, Nicaragua, Honduras, and Costa Rica. The purpose of the trip was to meet with leaders of El Salvador. Suffice it to say that the effort of the United States in bringing Democracy to Central America was a daunting task. After all, Nicaragua was a third world country, but its core citizenry, "the people," clearly subscribe to independence and freedom, as opposed to oppression and suppression.

Prior to this trip, Sam Nesley Hall, the brother of Representative Tony P. Hall, a Democrat from Ohio, was arrested in a restricted area of Nicaragua and detained by the Sandinistas on suspicion of espionage. Representative Hall was a liberal who voted against all aid to the Contras seeking the overthrow of the Sandinistas. When questioned by the media about his brother's arrest Congressman Hall stated, "I do not share the same views on U.S. policy in Central America as my brother, but I love him and pray for his safety."

Before we left on the fact finding mission, I told Congressman Hall that we were going to try and see his brother. I asked Hall if there was anything he wanted me to tell his brother. Hall told me that he rarely saw his brother since they were not very close. He told me how their political beliefs were on the opposite ends of the spectrum, but he asked me to tell his brother, "I love you and our family loves you." I gave him my word that I would do my best to see his brother.

During this trip, I met three ex-commandantes in El Salvador. They were communist guerillas in El Salvador. Their objective was to topple democracy. Their enemies were the Contras. Of course, I considered the Contras "our friends." Regardless, I had supper with the communist guerillas. They were people that were used to being in the field fighting against the Contras. I learned that they had spent a year in Russia undergoing intense military training. At the time, Russia was giving approximately $300 million a year of military aid to the communist Sandinista's in Nicaragua.

When the communist guerillas were done with their training in Russia, they went to Cuba and spent another six months undergoing military training. When they were finished they went to Nicaragua. After that they leap frogged into El Salvador. So, based on their statements, I learned that the communist training of experienced military guerrillas in Nicaragua had its birthplace in the Soviet Union. When the communist guerillas finished their training in Russia, they stretched their tentacles to Cuba and Nicaragua and other communist nations. After that, it was time for them to go in the field and try to eradicate democracy in Central America. Nicaragua seemed like a microcosm of world politics at the time: the U.S. supporting democracy, and the Soviet Union fighting to crush it.

When we were on our way to Nicaragua, we took a helicopter ride to get over the border. The organizers insisted that the four of us had to separate into two helicopters. When we asked why they said, "If one copter gets shot down out of two, we only lose two Congressmen. If everyone is on the same helicopter we lose four."

Once we got to Nicaragua and met with Sergio Ramirez again, I asked to see Sam Hall. Ramirez flat out refused to let me see him. I was pissed and told him, "I was told we would be able to see him on this visit. You are the Vice President of the country. You have the authority to allow this visit, so are you going to let us see the American Sam Hall?"

Fortunately, we twisted his position and he allowed a brief visit. On Wednesday, January 14th, we visited Sam Hall. We could see that he was being held in deplorable conditions, but that was the way of life in Nicaragua. We told him what his brother said and we promised we would do whatever we could to facilitate his release. In my heart, since he was an American Citizen, I felt it was my duty to try to help him gain his freedom from an oppressive communist regime. By Wednesday, January, 28th, the Sandinista government, with approval of President Daniel Ortega, authorized the release of Sam Hall because of his "mental instability." I can only look back and think that our visit had something to do with his impromptu release. International political pressure certainly worked in this situation.

Before leaving Nicaragua, we had an opportunity to meet with the Contra rebels. One individual will always stand out in my mind. He was a typical Contra soldier, but he was missing an arm. When we were getting ready to leave he said he wanted to give me something to remember him by. He presented me with a bullet that was reshaped into a cross and attached to a cord. The Contras wore this symbol. He told me, "Even though I have lost an arm because I fight for democracy, I am willing to give up my other arm to achieve this goal. This is my life's mission. I will not stop until we are a free country."

Upon returning to Washington, I was fully on-board with Reagan's political agenda for Nicaragua. I did what I could do to sell it to the Democrats, but any kind of military action is always a tough sell for Democrats, especially if it did not directly affect America.

In my role as congressman I would do weekly news broadcast called, "*The Washington Report with Guy V. Molinari*." I thoroughly enjoyed this opportunity to fully educate the listeners on the efforts made by the Republican Party, and the rest of Congress, on behalf of the United States of America's citizenry. On July 28th, 1988, during the *Washington Report with Congressman Guy V. Molinari*, I conducted an in-depth interview with Elliot Abrams, the Assistant Secretary of State for Inter-American Affairs. He was the Reagan Administration's point man on Central American affairs. He was always spot on regarding the day to day activities within the Sandinista government and what we could do to promote democracy. I saw this as a great opportunity to educate my constituents on the importance of our continued support of the Contras and to give them a hands-on view of exactly what was going on in Central America. The feedback that I received from my constituents, specifically on this issue, was heartwarming.

Throughout my Congressional career I always fought to continue the support of the Contras. As many times as Congress kept on cutting off the support, we would somehow wriggle support back in. Through my hands on experience I became a true believer with the theory that the communists don't understand sweet talk. The only thing they understand is pressure. You have to get serious with them, otherwise you get nowhere. The "Give Peace a Chance" strategy will never work with hard lined communist regimes.

CHAPTER 34

The Rossville Jail? Not on my Watch!

ON THE MORNING OF MARCH 24, 1987, MAYOR KOCH and Staten Island Borough President Ralph Lamberti announced that they had made a "deal" regarding a jail on Staten Island. Shockingly, the "deal" involved trading homeless shelters for a jail. Lamberti publically stated that while each of the other four boroughs were receiving city homeless shelters, Staten Island would be getting a jail instead. I said to myself, "What the hell kind of deal is that?" Apparently the jail was slated for construction in the Rossville section of Staten Island without any public input.

I was shocked when I heard about this, and I knew that I needed to find out the specifics of this proposal. What I learned was that the proposed Rossville jail would in fact be a maximum security facility. New York City Corrections Commissioner, Richard Koehler, acknowledged that the inmates housed in the facility would be incarcerated for serious offenses such as murder and robbery. I remember

Koehler saying, "I never told you we'd be housing angels." Once I learned the gravity of the situation, I immediately immersed myself into the battle to end the Rossville Jail proposal.

While Mayor Koch and I had our battles in the past, we did maintain a mutual respect for each other. Still, we were political warriors at odds over our positions. Koch would always say, "Guy Molinari could run forever and he would never be defeated. He is that popular on Staten Island". In turn, I would always acknowledge that Koch did a good job as the cheerleader for the city during our dire fiscal crisis. He resurrected New York City from the 1970s fiscal crisis, and that was no small task.

But, regarding the proposal to build a jail in Staten Island that would house 4,000 violent inmates, that was inherently flat out wrong. The borough of Staten Island only generated fewer than 400 of the overall prison population on any given day, so why should Staten Island be forced to take in ten times that amount of violent prisoners? It was another case of the other boroughs dumping all over Staten Island.

I have always been committed to the concept of, "We'll take our share of anything, but only our share and nothing more." There were too many years that went by where Staten Island lacked strong leadership. It was weak in its representation, and during that time period all the other boroughs would literally dump their shit on Staten Island. Anytime that there was something that would benefit the entire city but would be a detriment to the host borough, it always wound up in our backyard.

So, as we all knew, the other boroughs felt entitled to continue this practice because, "That's the way things were done in the past." I was pissed that Democratic Borough President Lamberti and Democratic Mayor Koch made such a devastating deal for Staten Island without any input from the public or fellow politicians. They just decided willy-nilly that a jail is better than homeless shelters for Staten Island.

Wrong. Not on my watch. I had developed the reputation as an independent Republican who always fought aggressively on the side of my Staten Island constituents. I was dedicated to the concept that, "Oh, we're gonna fight you: we're gonna meet you at the bridge, or the ferry, and there's going to be a battle, because, we are not taking it anymore." Our voices would be heard through the thunderous volumes of garbage that has been consistently thrown in Staten Island's face. Under my care, Staten Island would be silent no longer. Staten Island became a powerful united voice that demanded attention.

From my perspective, Koch lost the jail issue when he stated, in effect, that Staten Islanders didn't know what was good for them without him telling them. I thought to myself, "Whoa! You don't say that to the people, and you don't say that to me. Who the hell do you think you are, God? He's going to tell us that a jail is good for us? You don't have to know very much to know that's not the case."

After fully investigating the negative community impact, I made my position known: this jail would not happen. With that, I drew the line in the sand, and I conducted forum after forum after forum: The people packed the houses and we were on a roll.

I publicized various issues that would completely destroy the Rossville jail proposal. Firstly, I thought it was ludicrous that there would be a constant flow of violent inmates being transported to and from the Rossville facility for court appearances. Second, there would be thousands of visitors traveling to the facility on a daily basis to visit the violent and dangerous inmates housed at the facility. Many of the prisoners in the facility would have been arrested for drug related crimes, and the people who visited them would obviously be associated with similar activities. It increased the dangers to local residents to have these individuals traveling through their neighborhoods. Third, there was no guarantee against escape. This we can see today with the infamous escape of two convicted murderers from the maximum security Clinton Correctional facility located in Dannemora, New York on June 6th, 2015. The entire community is at risk when something like that happens. Fourth, and of significant concern to my constituents, their home values would plummet. My constituents made an investment in their community and it was not fair for them to lose on that investment. Everyone recognized that it is almost impossible to sell a home near a jail site. Finally, it was a known fact that responsible authorities placed maximum security facilities in remote locations and not in the midst of delicate, new, and growing communities such as Rossville.

By September of 1987, I had made my position clear and publically stated, "I hope this latest development will serve to further rally Staten Islanders and their elected officials to fight this proposed jail. It is the wrong project for Staten Island and once again the city is trying to force us to carry a grossly unfair burden."

On September 28th, the swords were drawn. I went on the offensive by stating, "Mayor Koch has lied to the people of Staten Island about the size of the new city jail planned for the borough. In a letter to a national magazine he stated the jail will hold 4,000 prisoners, while he has told Staten Islanders that the city has no plans at the present time for the prison population to go above 1,000."

By December 29th, 1988, the Koch administration scrapped the option to increase the size of the proposed Staten Island Jail. If the jail ever materialized the number of prisoners would never be more than 1,000. So, the first part of my battle was won. During this controversy though, Koch referred to the opponents of the jail as "demagogues on Staten Island." He was extremely frustrated with the intense public pressure from Staten Islanders in opposition to his wishes. I knew that he meant I was the key demagogue in his world, and it was a title I would proudly hold, since I was doing what I was elected to do: which was to fight for Staten Island.

Regarding the fight against the jail, I was thrilled to have the support of my daughter, Susan. There was no better partner I could have than someone I knew to be as dedicated as myself. As a Councilwoman, she was on the forefront of aggressively fighting bad ideas. Susan stated that when Mayor Koch and Borough President Lamberti agreed to no more than 1000 inmates that, "Both the

Mayor and Ralph Lamberti were beginning to feel the fallout of such a deal, they took this position in order to insure that this would not reflect on them at the voting booth in November."

On March 28th, 1989, the proposal to build a jail for 1,000 inmates in the Rossville section of Staten Island was approved by the Board of Estimate. I was livid. There were vehement protests from the residents of the area, but the City Board of Estimate threw their power behind Koch and voted in favor of the jail 9 to 2. I argued aggressively on behalf of my community, and I told the board, "I am not here to ask you to kill a jail; I am here to ask you to save a community." I recall when Lamberti stated to the audience that, "Staten Island was the only borough without a city jail and Staten Island must do its share." When I heard that I thought to myself: "Jesus, he does not get how much abuse Staten Island has taken over the years; we have always done our 'fair share' but will never be subjected to abuse again."

Lamberti's position was ludicrous as he was blatantly allowing the city to dump their most dangerous criminals in Staten Island in a disproportionate number. Garbage is garbage no matter how you cut it, and it was the same exact concept.

By April of 1989, I had sought court intervention for the prevention of the building of the jail. I filed a suit along with Assemblyman Robert Straniere, my daughter, Susan, and the Staten Islanders Opposed to the Prison (S.T.O.P. Inc.) in the Supreme Court of Richmond County. We sought to enjoin the city and restrain the City of New York Board of Estimate, Mayor Koch, and Borough President Lamberti from taking any further action toward the selection and acquisition of the site. Additionally, we also wanted to ensure that any construction must comply with various environmental laws. If I could not win it in the streets, I would take it to the courts.

We would ultimately lose the court battle in February of 1990, but at the same exact time, the Board of Estimate was found to be legally unconstitutional by the United States Supreme Court in the 1989 case of "Board of Estimate of The City of New York V. Morris."

The court found that the Board of Estimates function was a violation of the fourteenth amendment Equal Protection clause: In essence, the "one man, one vote" concept. Looking back, it was the "fair share" principle that I always argued.

My political legacy will always be that I sent out the message that Staten Island was not going to be abused anymore. Staten Island was organized. The voting public was behind us, and we would all fight. And, despite our initial setbacks, we fought and we won. S.T.O.P. was another grassroots organization that made sure their voices were heard loud and clear. When the community believes in you, you can do anything you want within reason.

Suffice it to say, as of this date, the concept of a Rossville jail has never come to fruition. Over the course of time, the public outcry was way too much for sensible politicians to fight for. Additionally, by the end of 1989, the major proponents had lost their runs for reelection. Ralph Lamberti had been replaced, as well as Mayor Koch. The departure of Mayor Koch was not a joyous occasion in my mind though, since his replacement, Mayor David Dinkins, would turn out to be a far greater enemy of Staten Island than Mayor Edward I. Koch had ever been.

CHAPTER 35

Bush 41

The House Gymnasium has always been a very popular place for the members of Congress to unwind. Every once in a while, we would see Secret Service come down to the gym and when we saw them it was a signal that the Vice President was coming down to play paddleball. Over the course of my time in Congress, I became very friendly with George H. W. Bush, or as he is affectionately referred to in the annals of history, "Bush 41."

When we both attended events together, and I was one of the speakers, I would always tell the crowd that Bush was a great paddle-ball player, but he was afraid to play against me. It became a running joke between the two of us. In truth though, I badly wanted to play against Bush, since I thought I was pretty good. Yet, Bush would wave me off and say, "Ah come on, Molinari. You're a 'B' player," without ever seeing me play.

One day, I got to watch Bush play with three other guys in the gymnasium. One of his opponents had an emergency call forcing him to walk off the court and leave. Since there were three remaining players, Bush still wanted to play, so Lou the house jockey said, "Mr. Molinari, why don't you take his place?" Lou knew that I was a good player; otherwise, he would not have asked.

I said, "Great. I'm in." I grabbed a racket and went on the court.

The first thing I did was ask God to let me play above my level, and I did. I killed every ball that came to me. I was happy because Bush was my opponent and I was playing one of my best games ever. After all the years I wished I could do it, we were finally on the court together. Bush was a fierce competitor, and he didn't like losing. But when the dust settled, my team beat Bush's team.

The next day I received a call from Congressman Sonny "General" Montgomery who played paddleball all the time. Although he was a Democrat, he became a close friend of Bush when they served in Congress together in the early 70s. Sonny said, "Hey Guy, got a call Bush's coming down to play tonight." I said, "Really?" He said, "Yeah, guess what? George asked for you to be his partner."

I laughed and said, "Oh, my heaven. Bush asked for me to be his partner? I guess I just had to prove to him I could really play." So, thereafter, when Bush played, I would be his partner. It was fun stuff, since you really got to know a person's true character during athletic pursuits.

Bush was not a guy who fooled around. He wanted to get to the court and play the game. He played to win. I remember one time we were playing and Bush stopped the game at one point and said, "Lou could you get me my new sneaks?" The house jockey went out and got the sneakers.

As Bush was putting the new ones on, he looked at the old pair and he said, "You know there's some good rubber on these things, Lou. Why don't you see if someone could use them?"

It was fascinating that, here was the Vice President of the United States, and instead of tossing his old pair of sneakers, he recognized there was some life left in them for someone else. In hindsight, I should have taken them myself and auctioned them off to some charity, but I didn't think about that at the time.

Since 1974, Number One Observatory Circle, a house located on the grounds of the U.S. Naval Observatory in Washington, D.C., has been the official residence of the Vice President of the United States. When Bush was elected Vice President he lived there with his wife, Barbara. In October of 1987, Bush invited over thirty members of Congress and their spouses to his house at the Naval Observatory to discuss a potential run for President.

During the event, Barbara Bush came over and whispered in my ear, "George wants you to stay. When everybody leaves you stay behind. George would like to talk to you." After everyone else left, George brought me into the study and he turned on the television. There was a big story that was breaking at the time. V.P. Bush said, "Now, let me tell you what's really happening." So, he recounted what was really going on because he was privy to all the classified information. I found it fascinating that he chose me to tell the story to. I thought to myself, based upon this conversation, that V.P. Bush really trusted and respected me. I was very proud.

One of the things I loved about the Bush's is that they were really down to earth people. For example: on another night that I was invited over to their house, my wife and I were surprised there was no Secret Servicemen around when we got there. As we walked up to the front porch of the house we knocked on the front door and it opened by itself since it was unlocked. We called out, "Hello?" but nobody answered. We found ourselves in the living room and thought it crazy that there was no security around. We heard an electric razor buzzing upstairs and then we heard Bush yell down, "Joe? Is that you, Joe?"

I yelled, "No, it's Guy and my wife."

He said, "Oh, okay. I'll be right down."

When he came down he said, "I'm going to make a cup of tea. Would you like tea?" Then he offered to show us around the house. While touring the place, he brought us into their bedroom and Barbara showed up. She said, "George, what are you doing?"

He said, "What's the matter, Barb?"

She said, "I haven't cleaned up yet, and you're bringing them up? It's disgraceful."

He just sighed and nonchalantly said, "Oh, Barb, relax. They're all friends." That's the way it was with them. Very down to earth people and there was nothing pretentious about them.

So, during my years in Congress and playing paddleball with the Vice President, I got to know him really well. My admiration for Bush is as high as it could possibly be. Bush 41 is one of the greatest Americans I've ever met in my life, outside of my father. That is why, when I learned that V.P Bush was exploring a presidential bid, I jumped on the bandwagon immediately. I was the first congressman from New York to publically announce my endorsement and I became extremely involved in his presidential bid.

As a matter of fact, as a loyal Bush supporter, on January 22nd, 1987, in Washington D.C., I held a press conference with eight of the fourteen New York Republican House members, Frank Horton, Hamilton Fish, Benjamin Gilman, Norman Lent, Gerald Solomon, Dave Martin, Ray McGrath and Sherwood Boehlert where we declared our full support to V.P. Bush to be the 1988 Republican Presidential Nominee even before Bush formally announced. It was clear we were determined to make sure that Bush would become the next President.

Bush had selected a terrific campaign manager named Lee Atwater, who was a brilliant and dedicated Republican campaign strategist. Although his candidacy would not be officially announced until the fall of 1987, things were already moving forward at a very fast clip.

Campaigning is a 24 hour/365 days a year undertaking until the minute the polls close on election night. You have to work hard, have thick skin, and be quick on your feet. You have to hold your head high when the opposition tries to take you down. It is an arduous and exhausting experience, but it is also the adventure of your lifetime, especially if you are successful. You must be totally committed and cannot buckle from the pressure.

When I solidified the support for the Bush endorsement, Senator Al D'Amato was vehemently against it. D'Amato said, "The Congressmen have a right to support whoever they want, but at this time I choose to remain uncommitted." Of course George was not happy about D'Amato's lack of support, but D'Amato pleaded for neutrality until a later date. D'Amato wanted to support Senate Republican Minority leader Robert Dole from Kansas who was his Senate colleague.

Many times during Bush's presidential campaign, D'Amato and I would have heated arguments about our positions. I was as passionate as he was, so they were interesting discussions. As the race for the Republican nomination waged on, it became obvious that Senator Dole would be the biggest issue for Bush during the campaign process.

One of the key components to a successful campaign is securing firm recognizable and relevant political endorsements quickly and solidly. This is an area that I excelled in. I was a hardliner. You were either with us or against us, there was no in between.

By April 1st, 1987, I had generated forty-one Republican Congressional members who were fully behind V.P. Bush's candidacy when he was ready to announce his intention to run.

In a letter dated April 10th, 1987, I wrote to V.P. Bush regarding forty-nine congressional endorsements that I secured as follows:

> Thanks for the very kind note. Frankly, I am not as pleased as you are. I truly believe that based on your relationship with Members of the House and the help you have given many of them, we should wind up with 100 or more endorsing you. However, we have a lot of gutless wonders who are guaranteeing they will be with us at such time as it obvious that you have the nomination locked up. That is the reason why I chose to number the signatures and, more significantly, have them insert a date after their

> signature. This creates a permanent record as to when the members have endorsed you, and I sure hope that you will keep that list as a permanent reminder of those who were not only early supporters, but true believers.
>
> I am enclosing an updated list which now contains 49 signatures. You will note that Jim Leach has signed together with several others. As soon as we return to session, I will send you a list of those who chose not to sign and giving you the reasons that were cited. I have put the word out that you have inquired about those who have signed the endorsement letter and that seems to have made some of my colleagues squirm a little bit. As you talk to any of the members who have not signed yet, it would be helpful and advisable if you would ask them whether they have signed and, if appropriate, convey your wishes that they join the team.
>
> Within the next couple of weeks, we will zero in on the undecided grouping and try to firmly apply some additional pressure. Finally, as the Members now see the list getting longer and longer, I think that will help us to bring more into the fold[.]

It was during this time period that I was appointed the New York State Chairman for the presidential campaign of V.P. Bush and I was the Vice-Chairman for "Bush for President Congressional Steering Committee."

In August of 1987, Staten Island politics occupied my time as well. I was disappointed in the leadership of the County Chairman, George Hart. I felt it was time for him to go. We disagreed on a lot of issues and it wasn't good for the party. One night we had a fateful meeting. George kept hinting to me that he took offense to some phrase I used.

George said, "If you say that again, I'm gonna jump across this room and nail you." I said, "Okay, I'm going to say that again."

And I said it.

George was a big guy, but I challenged him right then and there and we came very close to exchanging blows. It was clear to me that our relationship had deteriorated, and that he was narrow minded regarding the future of the party. At the same time, Hart decided to back Senator Dole. Hart had obviously aligned himself with Senator Marchi and Al D'Amato, who had not yet endorsed a candidate, but everyone knew D'Amato was clearly leaning toward Dole. This convinced me that he was missing the mark on crucial political decisions.

So while I was involved in the Bush campaign, I was simultaneously working on the ouster of George Hart. Now, Hart was very smart. What he did was he contacted Jonathan Bush, the brother of V.P. Bush. Jonathan Bush was a New York financier who was working on fund raising for his brothers' presidential campaign. Hart told Jonathan that I was plotting his political ouster. Hart also told Jonathan that he should stop me from pursuing his ouster because he told Jonathan that it was not going to help his brothers' presidential run.

Apparently Hart pushed the right buttons since Jonathan Bush called me up and said, "Guy, I'm sorry to tell you this, but you can't run my brother's campaign and at the same time get involved in the Staten Island political controversy. You have to make your choice."

I told him that was fine and that I would just have to leave the campaign. While, he was surprised by my answer, he understood nonetheless.

A short time later, I received a phone call from V.P. Bush. He asked me, "Is my brother giving you hard time?"

I said, "No, he was very nice about it, he simply said that I couldn't continue with what I was doing in Staten Island, so he told me to make a choice. My back was against the wall, so I told him that I would leave the campaign."

I recall that V.P. Bush said, "Well, you go back and oust that George Hart guy and I'll help you do that. If my brother calls you again, just give me a call."

V.P. Bush was known as "The Enforcer" back then. Whenever problems arose in the campaign he was the one who would contact those involved and straighten them out. He was a hands-on person. So, I was able to continue doing what I was doing in Staten Island and still chair his presidential campaign in New York.

George Hart stated publically, "I think that George Bush will be the loser in this since Mr. Molinari has gratuitously started a fight because I am backing Robert Dole for the presidential election. Molinari tried to muscle me into a public endorsement of Bush and he was unsuccessful."

D'Amato got his two cents in as well when he stated to the media, "I counseled both Molinari and Hart to avoid this fight, because you don't want to jeopardize the National Republican Party in terms of local elections." Of course, at the same time, I knew that D'Amato was in cahoots with Hart regarding the Dole endorsement. I felt betrayed over the disloyalty of Staten Island Republican representation in this situation, and how it would affect the party in the future.

During the Congressional summer recess that year, I took a well-earned vacation in Florida. As soon as Congress reconvened the campaign would go full steam ahead. When the media contacted me in Florida I told them that I was solely motivated by the desire "to revitalize the party since Hart had allowed the party to go into a serious state of decline."

By August 25th, I had found a highly qualified determined candidate to replace Hart by the name of Olga Igneri. She was on point regarding the direction of the Staten Island Republican Party's future. I saw her vision as a good match for the future of Staten Island. By August 29th, I publically announced, "Me and my supporters are supporting the election of Olga Igneri as the party's county leader. When elected, she will be the first woman to head a countywide Republican organization within the five boroughs."

On Tuesday, September 29th, 1987, at our Republican Convention, an epic political battle occurred that came to physical blows between the participants. State Senator Marchi, who had George Hart on his payroll, stood on the stage shouting furiously into a microphone in support of his beleaguered candidate. Marchi then slammed his palms on the table in front of him in anger. I then stood up in front of Marchi with a throng of supporters backing me up as a slew of police officers escorted me onto the stage. It was time for me to say my piece. The entire atmosphere was tainted with anger; and violence clearly was not far away.

We then had a voice vote on the choice for chairperson. Two choruses of votes sounded from over 400 county Republican Committee Members present in the Port Richmond High School auditorium. Marchi wrongly announced that Hart had won. My supporters, who were clearly more numerous, bellowed. I stood on a chair amid supporters wearing red, white, and blue ribbons and we chanted, "We want to have a real vote, we want a show of hands or standing vote, not a voice vote." Marchi called my supporters "goons." At that point, a multitude of police officers moved in to break up the meeting. Someone pointed to me and screamed, "Arrest that man." I stood my ground and yelled, "I'm not moving."

Smartly, the police began ushering people out of the auditorium. In the rush, several brawls erupted. In one melee, Hugh Wolfe, an employee of the Corporation Council's office knocked down Joseph Madori, a party vice chairman. Madori was released after treatment in St. Vincent's Hospital. Wolfe was charged with third-degree assault. When all was said and done I was totally surprised at the actions of Marchi. In years past, I would have envisioned him playing the role of a peacemaker, not instigator. Of course, Marchi blamed me and I blamed him.

On October 5th, the debacle came to a resounding end. Again, over 400 Republican County Committee members had to wait three hours while their credentials were being checked before we could actually vote. Each committee members' hand was imprinted with a stamp to be sure there were fair and honest votes taking place. By the time the night was over, George Hart had been replaced and Olga Igneri was the new Chairwoman. Staten Island politics was always intriguing to say the least. Many times it was a fight for survival.

On January 12th, 1988, Senator D'Amato formally endorsed Robert Dole. While endorsing Dole, he accused the Bush campaign of being "pretty heavy-handed" in lining up supporters. It was a direct attack on me. D'Amato also indicated that he was disappointed in his Nassau County colleagues, County Executive Thomas S. Gulotta, and Joseph N. Mondello, the county Republican leader.

In February 1988, the first crucial primary was to occur in Iowa. Since 1972, the Iowa caucuses have been the first major electoral event of the nominating process for the President of the United States of America. Many people saw the Iowa caucuses as an early indication of which candidates might win the nomination of their political party.

Shockingly, Bush was walloped in the Iowa caucus primary when he came in third behind Dole and Pat Robertson. It was a huge wake up call for the campaign. Alarmingly, the polls showed that Dole was also leading in the polls of the New Hampshire Primary, which was next. The campaign was in a complete slump. It was clearly not off to a good start. D'Amato was pretty cocky with the Dole victory in the Iowa caucus. In response to his cocky statements, I publically said that, "D'Amato is flexing his muscles prematurely, but at the same time, he's picking up a long list of enemies. I believe he is totally out of control."

The importance of the New Hampshire primary cannot be underestimated since it generates massive media coverage. In recent decades it has been determined that the Iowa and New Hampshire primaries receive as much media attention as all other states' contests combined. Since the Bush campaign completely miscalculated the Iowa caucus, they knew they could not make the same mistake in New Hampshire.

It was at this time that Vice President Bush asked me to go up to New Hampshire. He wanted me to try and right the ship. If the tide could not be changed Bush would never be elected President. So, I went to New Hampshire and spent the last ten days of the campaign working my tail off to obliterate the twelve point lead that pollsters claimed Dole had and make Bush the winner.

I was committed to being successful in getting the people in New Hampshire to vote for V.P. Bush and I had a good idea of what I had to do.

In New Hampshire, the voting acts allowed a voter to vote in either primary, Democrat or Republican. So, a Republican could vote in a Democratic primary and vice versa. But you could only vote in one. What I found was that the people hated Doles' wife, Elizabeth, who was Secretary of Transportation. As a result, the voters thought the best idea would be to vote in the Democratic primary.

I used a unique strategy to get support for Bush. I told the voters that they were making a terrible mistake and they had it all upside down. If they wanted to get rid of Dole they had to vote in the Republican primary and vote for Bush. In essence, a vote for Bush was a vote against Dole. I impressed upon them that if Dole won in New Hampshire, it was all over, we could no longer stop him. This was the only way we could stop the onslaught Dole had going for him at the time.

Once I explained the strategy the message went over well. The next issue was how to spread the message. In New Hampshire there are only two Congressional districts. It is not a huge state voting wise. So, I went out and started campaigning for Bush. I had a meeting with all the air traffic controllers and pilots who liked me because of all the work I was doing at the time regarding airline safety. I went out to meetings to explain the strategy and generate support.

I even went to Massachusetts where there was a large gathering of Republicans that lived in New Hampshire.

Every evening when we finished campaigning we would watch the late-night news. The daily results of the pollsters regarding who was ahead in the presidential New Hampshire primary were revealed and every night the pollsters stated that Bush's campaign was still twelve points behind. It did not matter what they said, I sensed the tide clearly turning toward Bush.

The night before the primary in New Hampshire I was in my room and I heard a knock on my door. It was a Secret Service agent. He said, "Vice President Bush wants you to join him."

So I went to the Bush suite. The whole family was there and you could see they were all tired. Bush was lying on the couch. Bush said, "Hi, Guy, we're going to see the last poll that's coming in." When it came on it showed Bush twelve points down again.

I said to myself, "Son of a bitch. The election is tomorrow." Yet my political instincts told me the polls were dead wrong. I had been out with the people every single day, and one the phone with the voters. Could I have made such a colossal misjudgment?

The following day, Tuesday February 16th, 1988, was the big day: The New Hampshire Primary. In the afternoon, another Secret Serviceman knocked on my door and asked me to join the Bush's. I walked in and everybody was in sweat clothes, exhausted and trying to relax. When I entered the room everyone said, "Hi, Guy. How're you doing?" I felt like they treated me like a member of the family.

Then George said, "Come on Guy, I can't exercise, so let's go for a long walk. I need some air. Come with me."

I said, "George I would love to but the polls are still open for another four or five hours. I can't leave now! I'm used to working right up to the end, otherwise I might second guess my efforts." So, George took the walk and dopey me went back to the phones trying to muster as many votes as possible.

By the end of the night, V.P. Bush had completely turned the tables on his opponents. Bush received 38% of the vote as compared to Doles 29%. I was flabbergasted at the success of my efforts. The campaign had gained crucial momentum. Bush called this momentum that was generated on that night the "Big Mo."

The next day the front pages of most newspapers showed a picture of V.P. Bush and his wife with their hands up in the air in victory signs, and there in the corner was Guy Molinari with a big, pleasant, happy smile on his face.

One of the things that was really nice about working for a guy like George Bush, Sr. was that he always sent a note of appreciation regarding any efforts taken on behalf of his candidacy. I was amazed that for a man so busy, he would have the time to do that. They would be either hand written or typed with an original signature on the gold embossed stationary of the Vice President of the United States. These small things showed just how much he cared about his supporters.

On February 26th, 1988, V.P. Bush wrote to me and stated as follows:

> Dear Guy,
>
> There is no question in my mind that your being with me in New Hampshire made a tremendous difference. Bob Dole had gotten a big ride out of Al Haig's endorsement, and then you and the others came in and that endorsement faded into oblivion. Many, many thanks for coming and for a lot more, too.
>
> Warmest best wishes.

Lee Atwater, his Campaign Manager, wrote to me as well and said,

> Guy,
>
> You did it all – I was truly amazed watching you work during all this – and your big day in N.Y. is yet to come. Thanks for everything – Lee

On March 8th, 1988, Super Tuesday, Bush crushed his opponents. His organizational strength and fund raising leads were impossible for the other candidates to match, and the nomination was nearly his. I was hoping that we could keep the momentum rolling for the New York Primary that was on April 19th.

While we lost New York State by just 4%, if one looks at the whole national painting, our effort must be judged a successful contribution to the larger victory. In the long run, New Hampshire was the turning point and that is the state I delivered.

The Republican National Convention was held in New Orleans, Louisiana, from August 15th to August 18th. At the Louisiana Superdome, George H. W. Bush was nominated unanimously. Bush selected U.S. Senator Dan Quayle of Indiana as his running mate.

After the convention, the campaign against the Democratic nominee, Michael Dukakis went into full swing, but on November 8th, 1988, Bush won a majority of the popular vote and a majority of states in the Electoral College. Our mission was accomplished. George H. W. Bush had become the 41st President of the United States of America.

On December 9th, the President-elect called me over to his office. He said, "You're one of three people most responsible for my being elected President of the United States."

It was clear we had developed quite a bond and friendship. Obviously, that was my greatest accomplishment that year. This man that I admired so, told me that I was one of three people most responsible for his being elected President of the United States. It was an incredible thing. Can you imagine somebody telling you that?

He then said, "I have received nominations for you to become Secretary of Transportation and head of the Federal Aviation Administration. We're thinking right now friends like you should stay in Congress to help me get through some of my bills. We truly believe that you'd be more beneficial to the agenda in Congress. You know I'd love to have you in my cabinet—because there's nobody that I would trust more than you—but the same can be said about you in Congress."

It was hard to hear that I was denied a position in his cabinet, but I was honored he even considered me for such a prestigious position. That's just the way Washington works. So, on that day, I told him that I would serve any position whatsoever he wanted me to. Less than a week later, President-elect Bush announced that he would not be placing any current members of Congress on his Cabinet. It was a politically smart move since Republicans, already in the minority in the House, could not afford to risk losing any seats.

On January 20th, 1989, a year and a half after I joined his team, I was thrilled to be present at President George H. W. Bush's inauguration at the United States Capitol. I had a true friend in the White House.

CHAPTER 36

Trouble with The Advance

AT THE SAME TIME MY RELATIONSHIP WITH THE *STATEN Island Advance* deteriorated.

The final straw occurred one day when I was in my office in Washington and I received a call from my Staten Island office. They said, "Oh my God! Wait till you see today's *Advance*."

I said, "Well, why? What's on it?" They said, "The *Advance* put an editorial on the front page."

They informed me that the editorial stated that a proposed senior housing unit was going to be erected a couple of blocks away from the intersection of Castleton Avenue and Broadway. The crux of the article was that I was trying to stop the project. The *Advance* claimed I wanted to stop the project in retaliation against a Pastor of the local Protestant Church, who was also the leader of a nuclear freeze movement on Staten Island which opposed the Naval homeport. The allegations were out and out false.

By way of background, my good friend, John DePierro was President of St. Vincent's Medical Center, on the board of the Sisters of Charity health care system, and was actively involved in developing senior housing programs on Staten Island. So when Congress allocated money to my congressional district for senior housing I initially agreed with John's proposed location.

Yet when the senior community learned of the proposed location my office received many calls taking a position against the location. These calls were from constituents, police officers—most importantly the Officer in charge of the Senior Citizens Robbery Unit on Staten Island—and community leaders, including the Democratic Captain, who were extremely upset at the proposed location.

The officer from the Senior Citizens Robbery Unit said, "Congressman Molinari, you have to stop it. Don't build it there because the seniors would be a few blocks away from the biggest drug infested area on Staten Island. It is inevitable that when the senior residents go for a walk, the drug gangs are going to be picking them off day in and day out. It's so wrong. You have to pick a safer place for our seniors."

So I quickly learned that the general consensus was that we had to move the location since it was a drug plagued, crime ridden area. I called up John DePierro and I said, "John, you have to pick another location. In good conscience if you don't change the location I am not going to allocate the money to build the senior complex with this much opposition to the location. It is unsafe for the seniors. I want to do something nice for them so that they can enjoy their lives, so just find another location."

When I explained my rationale for selecting a new location John agreed as well. Yet, for some inexplicable reason, he went to the Pastor of the local Protestant Church who was a leader of the nuclear freeze movement. To this day I have no idea why John went to him, but whatever the reasons were the fallout was shocking. The Pastor went to the *Advance* and spewed a tale that the senior complex location was being changed due to our disagreement.

Shamefully, the *Advance* swallowed the whole freaking thing. It was just so stupid of them and it violated every ethical position that you could think of. Placing an editorial on the front page of the paper? I had never seen that done before! They never even bothered to reach out to me for my side of the story.

I immediately called Les Trautmann, the editor-in-chief of the *Staten Island Advance*, and I said, "I want to have a meeting with your editorial board."

Trautmann assured me that we could have a meeting the next day.

After arranging the meeting, I called the police officer from the Senior Citizen Robbery Unit and asked him to come with me, so that he could explain that we changed the location of the proposed senior complex due to the high levels of crime in the area. He wanted to, but police brass wouldn't allow him to speak to the paper. I then tried to get the Democratic Captain to accompany me to the meeting. It wasn't easy for me to swallow when the Democratic Captain called me up and told me that Les Trautmann already called him.

"I owe you an apology, Mr. Molinari," the Captain said. "Trautmann asked me if I called you and I told him no. I lied to him."

I was livid. I hung up on him, cursing him under my breath. He had the balls to call me up to intervene, but when it came to crunch time he withered away like a spineless snake. Clearly none of my witnesses would be able to come on short notice, so I was left to battle the battle by myself as I had done many times in the past.

Bright and early I walked into the room filled with the *Staten Island Advance* editorial board. There were approximately fifteen people in the room and everybody looked at me coldly. I glared at Trautmann. Fortunately, I knew when dealing with Trautmann you had to meet with him in the morning since it was common knowledge that you didn't want to see Troutman after lunch. After he had his three martinis at lunch he was extremely tough to deal with and could be very nasty.

I had the *Advance* article in my hand. I stared directly into Trautmann's face and said, "You know, I have a copy of yesterday's paper and there's nobody in the room, except me, that knows whether this story is accurate or not, and I'm telling you it's not. You did not even contact me for my side of the story. Why would you go through the trouble of doing a front page editorial - that would be so wrong?"

Well, Troutman started his usual bullshit, trying to show everyone else in the room how tough he was. He said "Well, you don't understand. It's an opinion column and we decide where we're going to put it..."

I cut him off and said, "You think your newspaper makes and defines every one of us? That's not true with me. I'm my own man. I can see that I'm not going to get any place with you. I am going to tell you that you're wrong, dead wrong. You can take this newspaper and shove it up your ass."

With that, I threw the newspaper at Trautmann and stormed out of the meeting.

As I was leaving, Troutman called out, "You want to see negative editorials? You just wait and see."

I said what immediately came to mind, "Fuck you," and went about my business.

Any relationship we had that day died. History would show that it would never be resurrected until Trautmann died.

Sure enough, the *Advance* under Trautmann's leadership began writing negative editorial after negative editorial about me. Yet in the long run it really didn't matter because the public still supported me, with or without the *Advance*.

Trautmann liked to think without the endorsement of the *Advance*, a political candidate in Staten Island had no chance of winning. Historically, they had a practice of promoting the most popular candidate, making it look like their help caused the victory. When I went to war with the *Advance*, Trautmann told me, "You're not going to get our endorsement." I said, "Stuff it, I don't need your endorsement to win, I will win on my record."

At the time, Democratic City Councilman Jerome "Jay" O'Donovan was seeking to unseat me. Before my fall out with

Trautmann, O'Donovan had several bad editorials in the Advance. They thought he didn't have much brainpower, and regularly raked him over the coals. As a result of our fallout I thought to myself, "I'm going to break Trautmann's balls. They have no choice but to endorse the guy they've already editorialized as a jerk."

By October 19th 1988 I had so irked Trautmann that he sent me a letter scolding me as follows:

> Dear Mr. Molinari:
>
> You may be pleased to know you have scored a first.
>
> You are the first public official or candidate to have declined to be interviewed by the Advance, flagship of the huge Newhouse communications empire (see recent issues of Forbes, Fortune and Parade).
>
> Of course you have the right, just as the free press has the right to question. But I would have expected the courtesy of more than a curt note.

In the long run the paper endorsed O'Donovan, who lost big time. Even without the *Advance*, my constituents in Staten Island were loyal.

I coined a very popular phrase as I made the rounds on Staten Island: "The problem with the *Staten Island Advance* is that ***we need less Trautmann and more fairness.*** " That little political ditty went over pretty well. As time went on when I was out among the public they would say to me, "Don't give up Mr. Molinari, don't give in, keep up the fight."

The battle lasted for four years until Trautmann died in 1992. News editor Brian Laline ascended to Trautmann's position. He called me up and we had a meeting. We both agreed it would be better if we had a positive working relationship. We agreed to forget the past and forge a unified future. We established a great working relationship during the rest of my time in public office.

CHAPTER 37

A Big Favor

IMMEDIATELY AFTER THE SUCCESSFUL PRESIDENTIAL CAMPAIGN OF BUSH 41, I focused all of my attention on local politics. Koch's time was up and New York City needed a new mayor. The Republican Party wanted to find a solid Republican candidate to run for mayor and I spearheaded those efforts.

Crime was rampant throughout New York City, and the crack cocaine epidemic was in full swing. By the end of 1988 there were almost 1,900 murders within the five boroughs of New York City. It was a record which demonstrated to the world how far we had fallen. The murder rate increased as a result of the inability of the Koch administration to properly address the crack epidemic. Within a six-month stretch, my wife, my daughter, and I each had our car stolen.

New York City residents and visitors couldn't go to places like Times Square without looking over their shoulder to make sure they weren't about to get mugged. Even the locals never knew if they would make it home safely. New Yorkers had to deal with fear and anxiety whenever they left the security of their homes. Daily reports of robberies, burglaries, and violent assaults, many of them associated with gangs, cluttered the front pages of newspapers. No one was immune to this blight.

At the time, there was a young Manhattan U.S. Attorney who was attracting a lot of attention. His name was Rudy Giuliani, and he had a reputation of being a tough prosecutor. I felt that as an individual with a sound sense of law and order, he was something that New York City sorely needed. I also remember that in July of 1986, Giuliani and Senator D'Amato disguised themselves and purchased crack in Washington Heights, Manhattan to illustrate to the general public just how easy it was to find drugs. This actions, as well as others, revealed to me the innovative ways Giuliani tried to address crime. I felt that Giuliani would be a natural candidate.

In my attempt to ensure that the next mayor of New York City would be a Republican, I reached out to U.S. Attorney Giuliani on December 8th, 1988, and told him how much I admired what he was doing. I suggested that he consider becoming the Republican candidate. Giuliani listened attentively. He told me that he couldn't talk politics while he was a U.S. Attorney but that he was interested enough to meet with me as soon as he left office early in January of 1989. At the time, Giuliani was only forty-four years old and he was full of intense energy. Our city needed someone driven by that vitality, and I was glad that he would consider a run for mayor.

With any political campaign, a candidate must always themselves three major questions: firstly, do they actually want to run? Running for political office is a daunting task that is a non-stop physical and emotional journey from the minute you announce your intentions to enter a race, until the time the votes are counted. Secondly, does the candidate think that they can win? And thirdly, if the candidate is successful, how will the position work for them? These are pressing issues that I believe Giuliani wrestled with between December and January.

A year prior to this, Senator Al D'Amato had asked Giuliani to run against Senator Moynihan for Moynihan's seat in the Senate,

Giuliani decided that the time was not right. Senator D'Amato was upset Giuliani didn't throw his hat into the race, but I respected Giuliani's decision; he knew he was not ready and was aware that an unsuccessful run for office could tarnish your reputation.

In early January 1989, Senator D'Amato asked me to attend a lunch at the 21 Club, located on 52nd Street in Manhattan, with Ronald S. Lauder, heir of Estée Lauder cosmetics. Lauder wanted to discuss a possible run for mayor. I had absolutely no intention of supporting Lauder's candidacy. He was too "namby-pamby," too weak of a candidate to run, but I showed up as a courtesy to Senator D'Amato.

The three of us had a nice lunch. As we were getting ready to leave, Lauder turned to me and said, "Guy, could you recommend someone to do a poll for me?"

All of a sudden, Senator D'Amato launched one of his hissy fits and started yelling at Lauder. "Jesus Christ! I don't know what the hell you think you're doing!"

Sitting directly behind us at the time was Jackie Kennedy-Onassis, and when Senator D'Amato started screaming, it frightened her so much that she jumped up in her seat. I quickly turned around to her and tried to calm her down and deescalate the situation.

When we got outside, I said to Senator D'Amato, "What the hell were you screaming for?"

Senator D'Amato said, "Oh, that dumb son-of-a-bitch. I'm sitting there telling him everything and then he turns to you and asks who to use as a pollster?"

Everything was always a big deal to Senator D'Amato. He would fly off the handle and become ballistic, ranting and raving. It was never an easy task to settle him down when he got like that.

Yet again, in a state as large as New York, being a senator is a big deal. In 1989 New York had thirty-four congressmen in the House of Representatives, but there will always be only two senators. When it came to press, a congressman could work his ass off, and the senator would ultimately wind up getting all the publicity. We see this today with Senator Schumer who does a press conference every Sunday. They are boring as hell, yet he gets the coverage just because he is a senator.

In Senator D'Amato's case, he absolutely loved being in the limelight. While he worked hard for the people of New York State, and delivered results, his ego was so inflated that if someone disagreed with him he turned into a crass bully, causing an embarrassing situation that a staffer would have to tidy up after the fact.

So, just as Giuliani had his differences with Senator D'Amato, I had my differences with D'Amato because of how demeaning he could be.

It wasn't surprising that during this time period, Giuliani and Senator D'Amato started butting heads again almost immediately. The two personalities were like oil and vinegar. They both loved the positive limelight, but they were not willing to share it. A major split between them concerned who would be selecting Giuliani's successor in the U.S. Attorney's office. The rift festered like an unattended wound. Giuliani wanted the final say, yet D'Amato felt it should be his choice since he was the Republican senator from New York.

Shortly after this luncheon, Senator D'Amato had clearly thrown his support behind Lauder for mayor even though Lauder had yet to formally announce. Lauder had been a big campaign contributor to Senator D'Amato, so it was time to pay the piper. It was clear to me that D'Amato was fed up with what he perceived as Giuliani's lack of respect toward a sitting senator. In Senator D'Amato's view, he was the "Political Boss" in New York, not Giuliani. After Lauder's formal announcement, Senator D'Amato used his political influence to aggressively back him. In the long run, they would both hold a grudge for many years over what he saw as traitorous behavior.[17]

17 *Jumping forward, on September 6th 1989 President Bush would nominate Otto G. Obermaier as the successor to Rudy Giuliani in the United States Attorney's office of Manhattan based upon the recommendation of Senator D'Amato. Rudy had no interest in Obermaier being his successor, since Giuliani thought that their prosecutorial strategies were too divergent. Much to Giuliani's chagrin, Obermaier was easily confirmed by the Senate and held the post until 1993.*

By mid-February, D'Amato and Giuliani stopped communicating entirely. I actually had to cancel a meeting between the two antagonists that was arranged to air out their differences. There was no value in holding the meeting since Senator D'Amato's actions and rhetoric indicated his unwavering support for Lauder, and I knew that nothing would change.

I felt it was now time to move away from this feud to focus on the task at hand: electing Giuliani as mayor. Giuliani knew that he had my full support. I saw Giuliani as the better qualified, more focused candidate for mayor. In Lauder's case, although he had tremendous financial support—it was estimated at the time his personal worth was over $333 million—his persona was not mayoral. Giuliani had the charisma of an up-and-comer. People liked his energy. He was a breath of fresh air. His message was one of hope. If there was a Republican primary, it would be a rich man versus a famous, energetic, and committed young man.

The day after Giuliani left the U.S. Attorney's office, I met with him at the Hamilton House in Brooklyn. Of course the topic of conversation was his mayoral bid. At the time he was uncommitted but it was clear that he was very interested. That was all I needed to know. It was enough for me to keep up the pressure. That meeting lasted almost five hours, and on the way back to Staten Island I thought to myself that I had someone who could actually win. I was proud of securing someone I thought was a viable Republican candidate.

It took a lot of vetting, but eventually I was successful with Giuliani. Sure enough by late February, he called me and said that he had made a decision that he was going to run, but he was not ready to formally announce. I was thrilled to hear that he was going to throw his hat into the ring.

With that, Giuliani began assembling his political campaign team. At my suggestion he hired Rich Bond, with whom I worked personally on the successful Bush 41 campaign. Bond was Bush's chief strategist for his presidential campaign. He also hired Russ Schriefer, who worked for me on my Congressional staff, and directed Bush

41's campaign in the mid-Atlantic states. Russ Schriefer would be Giuliani's daily campaign manager. Everyone recognized from the get go that Giuliani's weakest spot was his naiveté about the nuts and bolts of political campaigns, including handling the press and professionally addressing the other candidates. You need a thick skin to make it in politics, and this would be a baptism by fire.

As the chief Republican promoter of Giuliani, I witnessed how the buzz that was created by the prospect of Giuliani entering the race for mayor positively electrified New York politics. By early March I remember telling the press that, "Rudy Giuliani is looked at as a fellow of almost supernatural powers. People are speaking of him in god-like tones." The public loved the pictures of the young prosecutor frolicking on the Great Lawn of Central Park with his three-year-old son, Andrew, and his beautiful wife, Donna Hanover Giuliani. It was like a young Republican Camelot scenario, reminiscent of the Kennedy era.

In addition to securing the Republican nomination, we wanted Giuliani to become the fusion candidate. Everyone knew that a Republican mayoral candidate would never win the election running on one party line. Republicans were outnumbered in New York City, 5 to 1. A successful Republican candidate needed to run on multiple tickets. I would have preferred that he received the endorsement of the Conservative Party, but Rudy pursued the Liberal Party instead. By Wednesday April 5th, Giuliani learned that if he entered the race he had the Liberal Party endorsement.

Prior to Giuliani making the formal announcement that he would run, he called me and asked if I would be willing to run for borough president of Staten Island. If I was successful, I would have to give up my Congressional seat. This was a huge favor to ask of a sitting congressman, especially coming from someone who did not hold political office at the time. It could have been political suicide on my part. The reasoning behind his request was that he didn't have any background in government, and he thought that if I was borough president of Staten Island, it would make it easier for him to be more effective. In theory, he would have a reliable and experienced Republican to bounce ideas off. From his perspective it was a fantastic idea and he thought it would be a great help.

I wasn't too thrilled with the concept. Usually it was the other way around: a borough president would run for congressman. Also, I was actually looking forward to retiring from Congress after ten years, to return to my private law practice. My wife was ailing and it was time for me to get back to Staten Island full time. The rigors of being a politician traveling back and forth to D.C. were taking a toll on me.

Now, it was time for me to answer the two critical questions: could I win, and could I make it work? I thought long and hard. I would be running against the incumbent, Ralph Lamberti. I believed it would be a tough race but with my experience, I assumed I would ultimately be victorious. Borough President Lamberti had made many decisions that I disagreed with during his tenure, the most egregious being his support of the Rossville Jail site proposed by Koch. I knew Staten Island residents were livid at Lamberti for this, and other decisions, so, knowing that he had that against him, I was off and running.

I remember the day I told my Chief of Staff that I would be giving up my congressional seat to run for borough president of Staten Island. He was both confused and upset. Bob felt that I still had much to give as a congressman and he could not fathom why I would give it up to run for a position in local politics. I believe he used the words, "Guy, you are crazy!"

Since Bob was my Chief of Staff and loyal confidant, we had blunt conversations regarding my decision to leave Congress, but ultimately, the decision was mine and mine alone to make.

Based upon my conversations with Giuliani, I decided that I could do more for Staten Island at home than in Congress. I also hoped that my daughter would jump at the opportunity to fill my role so as not to lose a precious Republican seat, but I left that decision up to her.

With the Giuliani campaign in full swing I saw future possibilities of improving life on Staten Island with a Republican mayor supporting our borough. It would be an unprecedented time: a Republican mayor working beside a Republican borough president. The changes we could affect for the benefit for the city could be enormous and enduring. For the very first time in my political career, I would technically be in the majority.

Of course, no one had a crystal ball. It was all a gamble, but it was the right time for me to leave. The things that Lamberti was doing to Staten Island were irking me. Selling out the borough for the Rossville Jail? That was the final straw.

On Wednesday May 17th, 1989 Rudy Giuliani formally entered the campaign for Mayor of the City of New York. It was an exhilarating day for me and for New York as well. Giuliani announced his candidacy at the Metropolitan Republican Club on East 83rd Street, the same club where Fiorello H. LaGuardia announced his candidacy for mayor in 1933. Throughout the day I introduced Giuliani as a candidate who would, "Make our city safe by aggressively addressing crime and corruption." We traveled through all five boroughs that day with Giuliani's family in tow, spreading the word of the new fusion mayoral candidate for the City of New York.

Five days later on Monday May 22nd, on the boardwalk of South Beach in Staten Island, flanked by Rudy Giuliani and my daughter, Susan, I announced that I was entering the race for Staten Island borough president. It was a beautiful day! I told our supporters that I could not resist the "winds of change that will sweep the city this fall. Running together with Rudy Giuliani and being part of the change that is going to take place in our city is a great challenge. It is very exciting. He needs help and I think I can help him."

So Giuliani and I were running simultaneous campaigns and feeding off each other's energy. The biggest difference was that I had been there many times before; yet the last election Giuliani was involved with was twenty years earlier…when he ran for sophomore class President at Manhattan College! Yet, it was essential that we both win.

Giuliani encountered many political hurdles and committed his share of political blunders during the course of his mayoral campaign. At times, it was an out-and-out disaster. He had a tough time dealing with the press. Even the chemistry between Giuliani and his chief political advisor, Rich Bond did not seem to work well.

At the end of July, I was in a room with just three of us: Giuliani, Bond, and myself. I recall Bond remonstrated Giuliani, saying, "You're paying me a lot of money to represent you, but you don't listen to me. So, if that's the way it's going to go in the final days of the campaign, why don't you let me walk out that door and you don't have to pay me anymore?"

Giuliani stunned me by saying, "Okay, that's fine by me. You can do that."

I sat in amazement as I watched Rich Bond come over, shake Rudy's hand, and say, "I wish you well. You could still win this thing, but I think it's going to be very close."

With that, Richard Bond walked out the door and left.

It was shocking, but Giuliani had such a different way of approaching things than most. I imagined that he already had somebody else lined up to take over Rich Bond's position as a political adviser for the campaign, but I quickly learned that he didn't. This was a spontaneous decision, and that's a measure of what Giuliani is all about.

Ultimately Giuliani hired Roger Ailes, Presidents Bush's media advisor, to his staff. It did spark controversy since Ailes actually worked on Lauder's Mayoral campaign as well. It was generally agreed that Rudy had a difficult time listening to people and was spending too much time reacting to negative publicity. Sometimes in the world of politics you just have to let the story disappear and die a quiet death.

On September 12th Giuliani won a contentious primary against Lauder, becoming the fusion Republican candidate nominee for mayor. I was thrilled, but worried that on Election Day the battle would be extraordinarily close due to the issues that arose during the campaign.

As for myself, I had to jump full steam ahead with securing the position of Staten Island borough president. Although Borough President Lamberti was a formidable opponent, I was extraordinarily adept at utilizing the prison controversy as a major platform of my campaign. More importantly though I was able to fluster Borough President Lamberti every time I debated him. During our first debate, I brought along a proclamation that he presented to me in his capacity as borough president.

When I got to the debate I put the proclamation on the podium. When the debate started Borough President Lamberti went first. Then I went. I picked up the proclamation and I said, "Let me not tell you what I think of myself, let me tell you what Borough President Lamberti has said about me." The proclamation that Borough President Lamberti had given to me as Congressman Molinari stated some of the greatest accolades I had ever received: Guy Molinari has done so much for Staten Island; Guy Molinari has had so many victories; Guy Molinari is an effective leader; as such, Guy Molinari is "Staten Island's Man of the Year."

When Borough President Lamberti presented me with this title, he could never have predicted that I would use it against him.

During the debate, Borough President Lamberti squirmed while I read the proclamation. Borough President Lamberti looked like he was going to shoot himself. He was devastated, and after the debate he walked away like a dog that was kicked by his master.

Thereafter every time I went for a debate I would bring the proclamation. It was a clever little political zing. I remember one time we were getting ready for a debate at a school, Borough President Lamberti saw the proclamation and he just threw his hands up in resignation! I won without doing anything more. Borough President Lamberti was aggravated with me for merely bringing what he had written, and of course I would start off by saying, "I just want to read you something that Borough President Lamberti said about me when he declared me Man of the Year." That's all I had to say and I had already won. So every time I debated Borough President Lamberti he was dead in the water. Sometimes I did not even reference it; I would just put it on the table. It was like a subliminal warfare tactic.

Come Election Day, I won and Lamberti lost.

Although within arm's reach, Rudy Giuliani's quest for mayor would not be attainable in 1989. As Rich Bond predicted, Giuliani lost by a margin of less than 3%, which was one of the slimmest margins in New York City history. Exit polls showed that 97% of Black voters and 70% of Hispanics chose Dinkins while 66% of White voters went with Giuliani.

My success on Staten Island was a bittersweet victory. I had been elected borough president, yet I was left in the minority again. In order to elevate Staten Island to a level of equality with the other boroughs, I needed a Republican mayor. Even more disappointing was the fact that the newly elected mayor had no love for Staten Island. Mayor Dinkins wanted to continue the long standing practice of spurning and neglecting the needs of Staten Island to further advance the quality of life for the other boroughs for the next four years. It was a good thing for Staten Island that I came home, since I fought aggressively and gave Staten Island a strong voice which had worked in the assembly, in congress, and would work in Borough Hall, too.

CHAPTER 38

The Evolution of a Meaningful Staten Island Borough President

On January 14th 1990, at my alma mater, Wagner College, my good friend, Judge Dominic DiCarlo of the United States Court of International Trade, swore me in as borough president. My daughter, Susan, held the bible during the ceremony. Also in attendance were Rudy Giuliani, accompanied by his wife, Donna, and newly elected Mayor Dinkins. It would be one of Mayor Dinkins' few appearances on Staten Island during his tenure as mayor. While it was an unlikely cast of characters, it was a truly wonderful and inspiring day for my family and me. I had come back to Staten Island, and Susan had publicly announced a month earlier that she was going to run for my Congressional seat. I could not have been prouder.

The aspirations of most parents are for their children to follow in their footsteps, but it has to be the child's choice, not the parents'. In this situation I was ecstatic when she told me of her decision. She was prepared to enter the world of national politics and she was only thirty-one years old.

Regarding our political ideologies, we were pretty much on the same page regarding most issues, yet we could not agree on one major issue: abortion. At the time, my daughter was pro-choice, yet I will always be pro-life. Abortion is a very divisive political issue because it touches so many heart strings on both a personal and a moral level. Yet, even with our differences we respected each other's views, and we were fortunate enough to recognize that neither of us would be responsible for changing the others' viewpoint. Change like that can only come from within, and not through the goading and prodding of others. As a seasoned politician, you realize that regardless of your position on abortion, you will never be able to satisfy everyone. It is an emotionally and religiously charged political issue that has been argued for decades and will continue to be.

Within days of my inauguration, bad news started pouring in. The battle ship Iowa, which was slotted to be the linchpin of the new navy port on Staten Island was being decommissioned. It was not totally unexpected though because on April 19th, 1989 an explosion occurred in the center gun room of the battleship that killed forty-seven of the crewmen and severely damaged the gun turret. When I got wind of the decision I immediately contacted Defense Secretary, Dick Cheney, who told me that, "There is no discussion at this time of the Homeport being cut, and the mothballing of the Iowa is in keeping with present-day reductions of the Navy."

I was relieved to hear his reassurances since, unlike Koch who supported the Homeport, Mayor Dinkins made it clear from the get-go that he hated the idea. He was a very vocal critic of the project. He opposed spending any money on anything even remotely associated with the base. When Mayor Dinkins was asked about the decommissioning of the Iowa he said, "The decommissioning is consistent with my ambitions for the port: the sooner it goes the better." I was livid when he said that. The port was such an economic boon for Staten Island and New York City, but now without mayoral support it was possible Dinkins could ruin the entire deal.

Along with the Homeport issues, Governor Cuomo set March 20th for the special election to fill my open 14th congressional seat. My daughter's chief opponent was Robert Gigante, a forty-one-year-old lawyer who was actively involved in the Staten Island Democratic Party. I would do whatever was necessary to ensure that she was successful in her campaign, but she was running the show. She was always a skilled organizer who surrounded herself with extraordinarily competent individuals. She had done a wonderful job in the New York City Council and had generated tremendous public support. Regarding the congressional race, she had the backing of President Bush. Maintaining Republican seats in Congress was so important that George H. W. Bush came to Staten Island to attend a fund raiser for Susan at the Shalimar. This appearance alone generated record contributions for a Republican congressional race at the time. I quietly smiled to myself when I started hearing terms generated by the press such as "The Molinari Political Dynasty."

March 20th was another exciting election day for the Molinari family. By the time the results started coming in it was immediately clear that Susan had trounced Robert Gigante by a 2-1 margin. It was a landslide, and President Bush called her to congratulate her on her phenomenal victory. Our good friend Rudy Giuliani came to the victory party. At the time, everyone's eyes were on the 1994 mayoral election, which I was sure he would enter.

Amidst this joy, I was placed in a quagmire regarding my very close cousin, Ralph Molinari. As a matter of fact, Ralph's father, who was my father's brother, was best man at my wedding. Throughout my career, Ralph helped me politically by being very active in my campaigns. When my daughter was elected to Congress, her seat on the City Council opened up, and Ralph thought he'd run for it. Unbeknownst to me, the Republican County Committee met and decided that Fred Cerullo, who was a very charismatic individual and was also my daughter's legal counsel while she was in the City Council, should be the nominee of the party, and not my cousin.

Back in October of 1988 I fought an incredibly tough battle with the party hierarchy and ousted the then county chair, George Hart, replacing him with Olga Igneri. So when Igneri called me and told me that the party was endorsing Fred Cerullo, I was really blind-sided. Prior to their decision, everybody that I talked to thought that they were going to endorse Ralph. After all, Ralph had worked in the trenches for a long time. He was well versed in the political scene and in my opinion deserved the endorsement. I was placed in a Catch-22; I could never in good conscience campaign against my cousin, but on the flip side I could not campaign against the chosen candidate of the Staten Island Republican Party. The only thing I could do reasonably was to stay out of it, so I declared neutrality.

When my cousin found out that he was not getting the Republican County Committee endorsement he was very angry, and rightfully so, because he had worked really hard for it. Ralph never forgave me for that. My cousin erroneously felt that I was working behind his back, and that was simply not true.

Adding fuel to the fire were inaccurate rumors. During the election campaign for City Council it just so happened that my daughter had her office in the same building where Fred Cerullo had his campaign office. After visiting my daughter there one day, I walked out of the building and one of my other cousins saw me and apparently assumed that I was going to see Cerullo. Yet in fact on that day I was a father visiting his daughter. It is sad how some people prefer to take the poison rather than try the antidote.

In this situation though, the olive branch is always there for my cousin. Time can heal all wounds or time can fester them to a gangrenous condition. The choice is Ralph's to make. As a matter of fact, at a Molinari family reunion held on August 29th, 2009 where over 150 Molinaris gathered at the Mount Loretto CYO Center in Pleasant Plains, Staten Island, some of my relatives tried to get us back together. I was more than willing to make peace yet my cousin refused.

To this day, we've had peacemakers try to put the two of us together, but it's never been possible. After the election, at my request, Fred Cerullo called Ralph to tell him that I didn't help him whatsoever. In my heart I wanted Ralph to win because he was family, and I thought that he had a good chance. He had good political sense and he worked very hard on my campaigns, so he knew the nuts and bolts of a successful campaign. Sadly, a political victory was not in the cards for him.

When Fred Cerullo was elected to the City Council in the special election to replace my daughter, Cerullo received 3060 votes, and Ralph Molinari received 2823 votes. It was a very close race. There is nothing more I can say on this issue but *c'est la vie*.

Returning to my wonderful relationship with Mayor Dinkins, he did the unthinkable when he sent a letter to the Secretary of Defense, Dick Cheney on April 6th asking them to stop development of the Navy port. I was livid and I publically stated that, "When you have a city drowning in red ink, and the mayor is coming out every day with more and more bad news, this doesn't make sense. I think it's irresponsible on his part, and I wonder how he plans on digging us out of the fiscal plight the city is in."

In his letter to Cheney, Dinkins suggested that changes in Eastern Europe and the Soviet Union, reductions in the defense budget, and concerns about the safety of having ships that might have nuclear weapons in New York harbor outweighed arguments for the Staten Island Port.

On April 24th Mayor Dinkins spoke before the Base Closure Commission to oppose the completion of the new Naval base on Staten Island. I advocated aggressively on behalf of maintaining the plans we already had in place.

Fortunately, Susan was aggressively fighting as a congresswoman to keep the Homeport in Staten Island at congressional hearings in Washington. Between the two of us we were a formidable force for

Mayor Dinkins to deal with, and frankly it frustrated the hell out of him. I would stage well-organized protests on the steps of City Hall faulting Mayor Dinkins for lack of support for the Homeport as well as enlightening the general public regarding the benefits the city could reap. I brought the fight right to the doorstep of his office since he would rarely come to Staten Island. If he would not come to my borough, I would go to him.

Regardless of our bitter battle, the event that allowed the Homeport to survive in 1990 was the Persian Gulf War, otherwise known as Operation Desert Storm. When the Iraqi Army occupied Kuwait, international condemnation was immediate and President George Bush deployed troops to Kuwait promptly.

As a result of Iraq's invasion of Kuwait, the House of Representatives, by a vote of 230 to 188, rejected a plan that would have cancelled financing for the Naval Base on Staten Island. My daughter's aggressive fight in keeping the homeport was perceived by many observers as an "upset victory" for the young Republican congresswoman from New York. She was emerging as a real force to be reckoned with in Washington. A strong Molinari voice was heard in Washington and Staten Island.

Somehow I still found the time to throw myself whole-heartedly into the improvement of Staten Island. One of the first things I did when I assumed the borough presidency was to actively engage our teenage population by providing fun activities that would keep them away from the rampant crime and illegal drugs on the streets. I started the Staten Island "Teen Rock Concerts." I brainstormed with my staff and I pushed controllable teen get-togethers. We organized these highly successful concerts in parks across the borough every Wednesday night in the summer, allowing our young people to have an opportunity to get together with their peers and dance, sing, and just have clean teenage fun. The concerts gave teens a safe place to go with their friends, while also affording local musical acts a little exposure. They were extraordinarily well-attended events; even the teenager's parents loved them. As a testament to their success, these concerts continue on Staten Island to this day.

I would go to the "Teen Rock Concerts" every Wednesday night whenever my schedule permitted it. I loved mixing with the kids. Many times after a long day at work, I came to these events to let off steam, loosen my collar, and have some fun with my younger constituents. There was a lot of positive energy emitted by the youth of Staten Island.

My staff, especially Eddie Burke, was excellent in coercing me to humiliate myself on stage. I would usually get up on stage with little prodding and do what I was asked. The kids loved the presence of the energetic old politician making a fool of himself. I was not averse to dressing up as, say, Bruce Springsteen. In that instance, my staff had a bandana and a torn shirt that they made me wear on stage and lead a chorus of "Hey Jude." That appearance would bring the down the house!

One of the great pleasures of my first year was being able to appoint someone to the New York City Board of Education. Each borough was given one slot, and the mayor was given two. I had chosen my good friend and highly qualified political ally, Michael Petrides, who was the current Dean of Administration at the College of Staten Island. He was the former chairman of Community School Board 31, and was my educational advisor for years. It was always his dream to serve on the Board of Education and I was thrilled to provide him such an opportunity. He was totally committed to the public school system. At the time, Mike's youngest child was attending public junior high school in Staten Island. Mike Petrides was just what the school board needed: a parent with a child in the public school system that had devoted his life to public education.

I was full of energy since I was back in my hometown. I kept my office operating at full speed. That was the beauty of the job: based upon the previous role established by my predecessor, there were not many mandatory items that I had to take care of. So I was able to reinvent the role of Staten Island borough president by making it a relevant public office that professionally, quickly, and efficiently addressed pressing Staten Island issues in order to improve our borough.

I was tired of people griping but not trying to solve anything. I vowed not to be like those bastards sitting around doing nothing. It would no longer be business as usual at borough hall where everything shut down during the summer and people hung out on their boats or played golf. I was there to work. Under my watch, the office of borough president would be a 24/7/365 operation. In the beginning there was some resistance because I expected my staff to work hard and go to public events to reach out to the people. I wanted them to know that we would work with everyone. Our door would always be open, and if somebody wanted to talk to me they would have access. My secretary, Lorraine Whitzak, a dynamite lady, knew how I operated from my years as a young lawyer and my assembly days and she knew that access was to be granted to all regardless of political affiliation, race, residency, or whatever.

When I was elected borough president, the Conservative Party asked me to appoint James Molinaro as my deputy. Since the Conservative Party was my margin of victory, and Jimmy was my friend, he came with me when I was elected. He was kind of a "dem, deese, and dose" type of guy. Some people thought that he was a not educated by the way he spoke. I didn't agree. He was a pretty smart guy; he just didn't have any formal schooling.

When I started to drastically change the role of the borough president, Jimmy Molinaro came to me and said, "I don't get it. You're working so hard. This is supposed to be a job where you can take it easy." I said, "Jimmy, I'm not asking you to work as hard as I do. The fact is, you can do whatever you want, but I didn't leave congress to relax and play golf. I want to accomplish something."

We left it like that. At the time his wife was ill and it was important that he be there for her.

One of my favorite things about my borough presidents' office was my cats. If someone came to me with a stray kitten, I would just adopt them, and they became part of my office staff. So when someone was nervous to meet me, as they were waiting they would invariably be questioned by one of my cats. They either relaxed the person immediately or put them on edge. I loved to see the different reactions people had. These little things made the office fun to work in on a daily basis. When I got my full-time staff settled in, we were a well-oiled machine that knew how to achieve things, yet have fun at the same time.

I remember one time in my office while I was being interviewed by the national news on aviation safety, when the newsmen came into my office there was a fly in the office buzzing around. I said to Eddie Burke, "You'd better get rid of that fly or it's going to be in the film." Well, Eddie failed in the mission that I had assigned to him. While I was being interviewed I got on a roll talking about aviation safety and how people's lives were at stake and suddenly the fly starts to buzz around. Right in the middle of the interview the fly lands on my nose. I continued talking, but it was impossible to finish the interview with all the laughing going on. So we had to stop the interview, and restart the cameras promptly.

One of the major changes I made when I assumed the role of borough president was the fact that I was willing to conduct active investigations to root out the causes of problems rather than wait for others to report. I felt extraordinarily comfortable in this capacity due to almost ten years of extensive investigative experience on a first hand level while in Congress concerning aviation safety, toxic waste exposure, medical issues, international fact finding missions, and more. So I looked at the borough presidency as a unique opportunity and an effective tool to bring important issues before the electorate since I was able to make it what I wanted.

CHAPTER 39

Yankee Doodle Dandy

I REMEMBER WHEN I WAS IN KOREA, THE TROOPS kept hearing rumors that when we returned to the States, they were going to give us a ticker-tape parade and we were going to be marching down the "Canyon of Heroes" on Broadway. Everybody was excited. Whether you were from New York or Oshkosh, you wanted to march down Broadway. If we were going to survive this bloody war, that's what we wanted to do, and frankly, that's what every member of our armed forces deserves.

Shortly after President Bush declared a ceasefire ending the Persian Gulf War in 1992, Mayor Dinkins announced that due to the city's fiscal crisis, there was no money for a ticker tape parade down the Canyon of Heroes for our returning Gulf War Veterans. When I heard about his decision I thought that was a tasteless statement. Money shouldn't be an issue when you're honoring our heroes and showing our American pride.

I publically criticized Mayor Dinkins on his poor decision and said that I was going to raise the money myself. By hell or high water, our troops deserved the recognition for risking their lives on behalf of our entire nation.

As everyone knows I have been a die-hard Yankee fan my entire life. The Yankees will always be very much a part of my life. I remember when things were difficult in Korea, how reading about the Yankees was a morale-lifting experience. I would always write to my father and tell him about the few bucks that I was making by betting on the Yankees. They were my pride and joy.

So when I decided to start raising money for a publically financed parade, naturally the first person I called was "Mr. Yankee" himself, George Steinbrenner. As the owner of the Yankees, he understood the pride that is associated with a ticker tape parade. In 1977 he had his first ticker tape parade down the "Canyon of Heroes" when the Yankees won the World Series against the Los Angeles Dodgers.

I felt confident that he would make a significant donation to have a ticker tape parade. In my own mind I thought that I'd ask for a commitment of $25,000 from each person I contacted. I estimated that if I had enough commitments, we would be able to fund the parade regardless of Dinkins' decision not to honor our returning war heroes.

"Mr. Yankee" already knew that when I went to opening day as an elected official and sat in the owner's box, unlike the other elected officials who went to see and be seen, I was not there to conduct social niceties, I wanted to watch the Yankees play hard and I wanted to see them kick the other teams' ass and win.

When I spoke with George Steinbrenner and filled him in on the situation, George said, "Ah, that son of a bitch liberal bastard."

I said, "Well, I'm trying to raise the money." George said, "How much do you want?"

I responded, "$25,000." I was thrilled when he said, "You're on."

It warmed my heart. He got the ball rolling on the parade, and I couldn't thank him enough.

After Steinbrenner's commitment, I did really well in soliciting commitments for large donations for a publically funded ticker-tape parade. Everyone that I called wanted to contribute to this great cause. I had additional commitments from: *New York Post* owner, Peter Kalikow; Long Island builder, Fred Dematteis; and even former mayoral candidate, Ronald Lauder. So within a matter of hours, I had commitments for over a hundred thousand dollars and it was clear that the parade honoring our Gulf War vets would happen with or without Dinkins' support. Within days of Dinkins hearing about my success, he reversed his initial decision because he realized that my donors were going to make him look bad.

On March 4th Mayor Dinkins held a press conference at Gracie Mansion announcing that the City of New York would in fact host the parade. I was invited to the press conference but it was clear that my physical presence was like acid on the mayor's skin. It was complete reversal of his original position.

He stated, "New Yorkers love a parade, and I can assure you, the biggest welcome of all, the greatest ticker-tape parade in this or any city's history awaits the American and allied forces upon their return from the Gulf."

Mayor Dinkins created a commission of business, civic, and political leaders to raise money for, and to organize the parade. The several hundred thousands of dollars in donations that I had raised were given over to the commission. In a roundabout way, I got everything that I wanted. I needed to know that the right thing was being done for our heroes.

On June 10th, 1992, thousands of Desert Storm veterans converged on New York City on a beautiful sunny day and paraded through the "Canyon of Heroes." Tons of ticker tape and confetti poured from the sky. Several million people attended "Operation Welcome Home." Proudly attending were: Secretary of Defense, Dick Cheney; Chairman of the Joint Chiefs of Staff, Gen. Colin L. Powell; and Operation Desert Storm Commander, Gen. H. Norman Schwarzkopf, AKA "Storming Norman," all riding in open vintage convertibles to a thunderous, nearly deafening ovation. Behind them, tens of thousands of marchers, more than half of them veterans of the Gulf War took part in the largest ticker tape parade ever.

Looking back, I know that Mayor Dinkins never really understood what the parade meant to the returning veterans. Although Dinkins enlisted in the military he never actually served during wartime. Having served during wartime I recognize that honoring our heroes is one of the finest things that the greatest city in the world can do. Let them March down Broadway and have their moment of glory that will be with them for a lifetime!

Unfortunately, under Mayor Dinkins' administration's liberal philosophy the anti-military sentiment would always slam the door shut on our war heroes. It would be the only time I was successful regarding a military issue with Mayor Dinkins. His disdain for our military was legendary and it hurt me deeply.

It is the same liberal anti-military philosophy that is ruining our city right now under Mayor DiBlasio. The first thing a liberal mayor does is cut down the powers of the police and empower the people at the expense of the personal safety of the law enforcement community. The only time that our liberal politicians understand the need for police or the military is when a relative, close friend, or they themselves are victims of a crime or a casualty of war. Then they start screaming for more policing, more security, and more justice.

Immediately after the Persian Gulf War came to a swift end, the issue of the closure of the Staten Island Homeport became the topic of conversation again. The federal government needed to cut the military budget so the Base Closure Commission was reviewing every Naval base in the country. They would then conduct hearings on whether a Naval facility should continue to operate or be closed down. Dinkins immediately let everyone know he was again targeting the Staten Island Homeport and had all intentions of killing it once and for all.

In order to be successful in the battle, my daughter and I asked former Congressman James Courter, Chairman of the Base Closure

Commission, to tour the Homeport prior to a scheduled hearing. On June 11th Chairman Courter spent three hours at the facility being briefed by Port Commanders on real economic and military facts regarding the location. It was clear that he gleaned new and important information that would be relevant in making the decision on whether or not to close the base.

At the conclusion of his tour, Chairman Courter assured community residents who supported the Homeport that, "The commission will be even-handed and open-minded and be assured that the Commission is legally bound not to look at politics." Before Courter left, Susan told the crowd of supporters, "We are not going to lose the sailors now. If we didn't lose them to Saddam Hussein, I'll be damned if we'll lose them to David Dinkins." When those words came out of her mouth, I beamed and thought to myself, "She is a chip right off the old block."

On Monday June 24th, 1991 I was scheduled to appear before the Base Closure Commission. I would be arguing aggressively against Mayor Dinkins and New York City Comptroller Elizabeth Holtzman. Their only goal was to have the homeport closed forever. Holtzman was Dinkins' lackey at the time.

Nowhere else in the country did such a show of stupidity occur. Dinkins and Holtzman were the only two elected officials, nationwide, to ask for the closure of a base, while all the other bases on the list for possible closure had public officials pleading to keep their base open. Unfortunately, that was not the case for New York City. Worst of all, I knew that the government was more likely to close a base that had substantial opposition than one with strong local support.

As you can imagine, I was angry. Angry because I worked so hard to bring the Homeport to Staten Island and these dumb sons of bitches were turning it down, even though the city was drowning financially. After pulling off a slight miracle in Congress, to think that my mayor was publicly going to testify before this Base Closure Commission and say he didn't want the Navy there and wanted the facility closed, I was heartbroken to say the least.

When I was a congressman, every year when the budgetary process took place in Congress the Liberal Democrats would invariably vote against any increases in military budget. It's an annual battle. It's a tough thing to watch year after year, especially having served in combat myself. I'm acutely sensitive to the fact that there has to be enough money in the military budget to protect our country. I will always believe that there is no time better than today to worry about what tomorrow will bring to our shores.

Before the hearing, someone gave me a copy of Holtzman's written speech before she testified. Since I was testifying first, I made reference to what she was going to say in an effort to blow her out of the water before she spoke. I was a fortunate politician in that I always had extraordinarily reliable informants regardless of their political affiliation.

Immediately after we both testified, I stood outside the House hearing room and Holtzman confronted me like a rabid dog. She was furious about the fact that I got a copy of her testimony beforehand. She followed me and started yelling at me and of course I started yelling back, and before you knew it we had a real shouting match going on. She was screaming that I didn't know what I was talking about when I testified that, "The comptroller has never even asked for a classified Navy briefing on the port."

When she confronted me I yelled, "Well, let me ask you this: have you asked for a briefing? How can you take any position without asking for a briefing?" She was flustered and whimpered, "I'm not sure the Navy would be willing to supply it." I said, "Oh, come on. The Navy has provided it to anyone who has asked for a briefing."

She then said, "Listen, you didn't know what you were talking about and you said it anyway." I promptly responded, "I'm pretty sure based upon my extensive experience I know a lot more about the Homeport than you do. You should be embarrassed to make the outrageous statement that you have made here today."

She then turned away with her tail between her legs and left.

At the time, neither one of us knew that, nearby, TV cameras were recording, capturing the whole screaming match. Everything was on television that night: the fight between "the Congressman and the Comptroller."

By the grace of God, a small miracle occurred when the Base Closure Commission formally announced on July 1st its decision to keep the Homeport open. The commission stated that the port was one of the Navy's most modern facilities. That was the major consideration that outweighed all arguments put forth by Mayor Dinkins and his cronies.

To everyone's surprise, we had raised a sinking ship one last time. My daughter had done a wonderful job advocating on behalf of the port in Washington and I had had kept the fight alive in New York. It would not be "anchors aweigh" for the Homeport just yet. The ships would be staying.

The Homeport has always been a rollercoaster for me. But the final dip occurred two years later. I was in Washington again fighting the same old devils when, during a break, one of the members of the commission came up to me and said, "Mr. Molinari everybody wants the Navy to stay in their State except New York City. How do we justify keeping your facility open when the Chief Executive, your mayor, and the comptroller both testify that they want it closed? Your leaders are saying they don't want us there, and we've got to close some bases, so it's going to have to be here."

There was nothing more I could do. On June 25th, 1993 the Commission voted to close the base forever. As a result of this decision there would be no military base in New York harbor. I know they made the right decision, and I couldn't fault them for that, but it was a shame. It would be the first time in more than two centuries that New York would be without a Naval base.

After the tragic events of September 11th, 2001, I would always look back and wonder if we had the Homeport in New York Harbor if it would have changed the targets of the terrorists. Our City lost almost 2,800 beautiful people on 9/11 because of terrorist attacks on our own soil, and there's no question in my mind that our ability to protect ourselves was impaired by the action of local officials.

CHAPTER 40

The Attempted Destruction of INS Agent Joseph Occhipinti

I LEARNED OF THE PLIGHT OF JOSEPH "JOE" OCCHIPINTI from his sister who lived on Staten Island. She came to me after Joe was convicted in federal court of civil rights violations on June 28th, 1991. He was going to be sentenced within days and she was desperate for help. She told me the tragic story of what happened to her brother, and she asked if I would meet with him even though he lived in New Jersey and was not a constituent of mine. She knew I was firm supporter of law enforcement and had nowhere else to go. I agreed to meet with him since his story sounded like a terrible injustice if what she was telling me was accurate.

Although people thought it was strange that I would become the primary political advocate for Joe Occhipinti, it did go along with my political mindset and the new expanded role of the borough president of Staten Island. I recognized that many times politicians avoided getting involved in a sensitive issue that has nothing to do with their district, but I instinctively believed that the Occhipinti case could affect law enforcement personnel throughout the city, not just in Washington Heights. When I assumed the role of borough president, I specifically created a unique office where I could handle everything that borough presidents needed to handle yet do other things as well, such as the Occhipinti case.

To correct injustices was my charge to myself. Even to this day I want to be part of the solution to make life better for everybody. I believe that if we use the brains that God gave us we can make life better. Whether it's in our communities or outside of our community, if you can help you should. Although Joe lived in New Jersey, he worked in New York City as an INS agent. I felt that I had a duty to seek the truth and if he was railroaded he needed a strong advocate. As an elected official of New York City I would be that voice.

When I met Joe I learned that he was the most decorated immigration agent in the agency's history. During his career he had received over seventy commendations. I found him to be a likable and very personable guy. Joseph Occhipinti came off very credible. He had a devoted wife and three lovely daughters. Yet, the man I saw before me was an emotionally shattered man who could not believe that his life was destroyed for doing his job and enforcing the laws that he was sworn to uphold.

The charges stemmed from searches that Occhipinti conducted while running "Project Bodega" and "Project Kuala Lumpur." These were two programs that he had specifically organized while an INS agent to target illegal aliens from the Dominican Republic and Malaysia who were involved in illicit activities. Basically he was doing exactly what we would want and expect our INS agents to do.

He told me how he was the first law enforcement agent ever tried and convicted on federal civil rights charges for unlawful search and seizure. He was not accused of brutality or racial bias. Dominican bodega owners in Washington Heights alleged Occhipinti illegally searched their premises and then made the bodega owners sign "consent to search forms" after the search was done. This made no sense whatsoever. Why would someone sign the consent *after* Occhipinti found illegal contraband?

The charges stemming from the consent to search forms didn't sit well with me because Occhipinti was the man that the INS relied upon to the train others how to do searches properly so that the searches would legally stand.

After I interviewed Occhipinti, I asked my chief investigator, Raymond Hagemann and his partner, Bill Franz to spearhead an intensive investigation to verify Occhipinti's facts. Hagemann was a former federal narcotics agent and knew the ins and outs of illegal drug trafficking. Before I jumped on the bandwagon, I wanted to make sure that everything checked out. As our investigation moved forward, it was clear there were many areas of the justice department's investigation that reeked of improprieties.

I learned that in March of 1989, about a year prior to Occhipinti being targeted by the justice department, a woman by the name of Alma Camarena, a former assistant in the law office of Aranda and Guttlein, heard Andres Aranda and Jorge Guttlein talking about how they would like to have Occhipinti "eliminated" or at a minimum "set him up - to get rid of him."[18]At the time Occhipinti's success in Project Bodega was dramatically decreasing the illegal Dominican drug cartel's monetary intake in Washington Heights.

Alma actually went to the U.S. Attorney's office at the time and told U. S. Attorney Jeh Johnson about the threats to Occhipinti's life. Remarkably nothing was done. Instead, nine months later, the U.S. Attorney's office decided to prosecute Occhipinti for civil rights violations.

When I heard what Alma said, I was shocked. The system seemed upside down. Her testimony corroborated the fact that there was a pattern in Washington Heights. If a law enforcement officer was giving a homicidal drug cartel problems, there was a new and

---

18 Alma Camerena was interviewed by multiple agencies over the course of the Occhipinti case and she never wavered from her statements. She was adamant that Occhipinti was targeted and set up.

better way of dealing with the officer: set them up, and get rid of them.

It turned out that the law office of Andres Aranda and Jorge Guttlein generated their business income from representing drug dealers, many of them associated with the Dominican drug cartels. The majority of the bodega owners who accused Occhipinti were members of the Federation of Dominican Merchants and Industrialists, which was a front for the Dominican drug cartel. Not surprisingly the Law firm of Aranda and Guttlein represented The Federation of Dominican Merchants and Industrialists.

I was dismayed to learn that shortly after Mayor Dinkins' Inauguration, he actually hosted a party at Gracie Mansion for the Federation of Dominican Merchants and Industrialists to thank them for their contributions and support during his election. Dinkins knew that without the support of the Dominican community, he would not have been elected mayor. The Federation was reported to have generated a large numbers of critical votes in 1989.

Several months later the Federation of Dominican Merchants and Industrialists held a protest on the steps of City Hall protesting the highly successful police operation, "Project Bodega." At the protest, Mayor Dinkins, in support of the Federation, called "Project Bodega" a "Republican-backed conspiracy," and demanded a federal investigation against Occhipinti based upon civil rights violations. Founded upon Mayor Dinkins conversations with the members of the Federation, Mayor Dinkins believed that the purpose of "Project Bodega" was to disrupt the census and eliminate crucial Dominican votes in the next election.

Immediately after this protest, as demanded by Mayor Dinkins, Joseph Occhipinti became the target of a justice department investigation into civil rights violations. Lo and behold, several months later Occhipinti was indicted.

On March 6th, 1991 Occhipinti was indicted by the United States Attorney's office for the Southern District of New York. Normally a trial would take over a year to commence. In Occhipinti's case he went to trial by May 17, 1991. Norman J. Mordkofsky, who had a nervous breakdown before trial, represented him. Mordkofsky begged the judge to be recused from the case, but Judge Constance Baker Motley refused. This was not surprising since, Judge Motley was a close friend of David Dinkins and Jeh Johnson, the prosecutor for the U. S. Attorney's office, was Motleys' former law clerk. With the cards that Occhipinti was dealt there was never going to be any justice for him in the court room.

Six weeks later, June 28th, became a day that will live in infamy for law enforcement everywhere: Joseph Occhipinti, in a mockery of a trial, was convicted of civil rights violations and was sentenced to thirty-seven months in a federal prison by Judge Motley.

By November of 1991 I publicly announced that I wanted the justice department to investigate what happened in the Occhipinti case and reopen the case. My investigative team had compiled affidavits and audio testimony refuting much of the information that was put forth during the trial.

The perjured testimony of the bodega owners who were all represented by the law firm of Aranda and Guttlein were boilerplate: "Occhipinti searched my premises without my permission. Then, after he searched my store and found illegal things, he wrote up consent to search form and had me sign it, but he did the search first." That was the basis on which he was convicted. Yet, there was another group of Bodega owners that were searched by Occhipinti that my investigators interviewed that did not testify at trial. None of them belonged to the Federation, and every one of them stated that they signed the consent first, and then Occhipinti searched.

It really pissed me off since the job that Occhipinti did for the government was dangerous. Even as we tried to clear his name, the savagery of the drug cartels was ever present. In Washington Heights there was an individual named Miguel de Dios, a Hispanic journalist who made it his mission to expose the Dominican and Colombian drug cartels in Washington Heights. He was an extraordinarily committed journalist who wanted to free his community of the scourge of these homicidal drug cartels.

Occhipinti wanted me to talk to de Dios since he was trying to help exonerate Joe. One day, we had a three-way conversation on the phone and Miguel said to me, "Mr. Molinari, I'm happy you're trying to help Joe out, but you have to explain to Joe that this is this is very dangerous for me. The Dominican mob is not like the Italian mob. The Italian mob, if you cross them, they will kill you. The Dominican mob, they are going to kill you, your mother, your father, and everybody else. They'll kill your canaries, they'll kill your dogs, they'll kill everybody, so I have got to be very careful, or I'm going to get everyone I love killed."

That was the only conversation that I had with the scared, but courageous man. It was brief, but stirring.

Miguel knew exactly what he was talking about. On March 11th, 1992 de Dios was sitting at the bar in Meson Asturias Restaurant in the borough of Queens. De Dios was approached from behind and shot twice in the head by an assassin. He died instantly. The assassin was later identified as Wilson Alejandro Mejia-Velez, an illegal alien affiliated with the Cali drug cartel.

After Occhipinti's appeal was denied on June 12th, 1992 he surrendered to the authorities and he was sent to Oklahoma's El Reno Federal Penitentiary. Joe would spend his entire time behind bars in solitary confinement since he was a former law enforcement officer and some of the individuals he arrested were in that facility. At the time of his surrender I held a rally of support for him outside the Federal Court at Foley Square, Brooklyn. I publically criticized U.S. Attorney Otto Obermaier, the same individual Giuliani did not want to take over the U.S. Attorney's office, for prosecuting the highly decorated officer. I knew that if Giuliani was the U.S. Attorney this case would never have happened. At my side was PBA President Phil Caruso, Roy Innis of the Congress of Racial Equality, as well as Curtis Sliwa. They all spoke in support of Joe, as well as his wife, who was on the verge of a nervous breakdown.

To the police, law-abiding citizens, and me, Occhipinti had become a political martyr. He successfully rooted out drug dealers and illegal aliens in dangerous neighborhoods and his reward was to be incarcerated in a federal prison. It made me sick to my stomach. The city was going down the toilet, because the liberal politicians were letting the drug dealers flourish and handcuffing law enforcement.

On June 14th, I quit the presidential campaign of George H. W. Bush and Vice President Dan Quayle. I told the press that I was resigning not because of "my lack of affection for George Bush, but for some of his appointees." I was specifically referring to the justice department. By that time, I had over forty meetings and phone conversations with the justice department officials yet nothing happened. I was convinced that an innocent man was behind bars because of their refusal to consider the information we compiled, and it broke my heart. I gave them affidavits and audio tapes from prosecution witnesses who admitted to perjury, yet the justice department did nothing.

I was pleased when I learned in August 1992 that the justice department publicly acknowledged that they ordered the F.B.I. to take another look at the Occhipinti case. When the government agreed to review the case, the hope and expectations would be that we would be able to set aside the conviction. The F.B.I. would be conducting the actual review. I did not want the F.B.I. office from Manhattan to conduct a review with us since they were the same officers that helped convict Occhipinti in the first place and I knew that they could not be impartial. So, the justice department then suggested using a group in Queens that was a civil rights F.B.I. group. I said that it was fine, as long as it wasn't Manhattan. In retrospect, it was a total mistake on my part. I should have asked for an outside independent agency to review to the case.

Unfortunately, it became readily apparent that we had been duped into believing that the Queens group was anything other than a total farce. The investigators and anyone assigned to the case did not have their heart in seeking the truth.

There was a red-headed F.B.I. special agent who was in charge of the group. Without any formal contact, his group spontaneously showed up at Borough Hall one day. The lead agent came into my office and started talking to me. While he was talking to me I learned that my investigators, Ray and Bill, were each being interrogated by two F.B.I. agents separately. I was livid. We had now become the targets of an F.B.I. probe, for what, seeking the truth?

It became totally clear to me that day that they were there to investigate my people, not what happened to Occhipinti, and that led to some really hard feelings. The focus of their investigation was not the evidence that we had produced, but was instead the involvement of the investigators I acquired to examine the matter. The case agent inferred that they would criminally prosecute anyone responsible for fabricating evidence concerning the drug cartel conspiracy. They wanted to entrap my investigators and me. My God how low the F.B.I. had fallen in this situation. Here I was, seeking to redress what I saw as a total miscarriage of justice, and finding that I had become a target of an F.B.I. probe. Little did they know that I was not a man that can be intimidated by rogue agents.

The final straw was when I anonymously received in the mail a sworn affidavit of Alma Camarena. In the affidavit, she stated that on August 28th, 1992 she was asked to come to the F.B.I. office in Queens to meet with the agents. During the meeting the agents wanted her to wear a wire so that the F.B.I. could set me up. The agents wanted Alma to come see me at Borough Hall and try to get me to offer her a job in exchange for tainted testimony. They even talked to her about having a helicopter fly over Borough Hall while she was in the process of trying to entrap me. They said when they heard what they wanted they would swoop down and arrest me, like something out of a Hollywood action movie.

After this rather bizarre turn of events, I called up the main FBI field office located in Manhattan since it was clear that the investigation was a total sham. When I spoke to the Director of the New York Regional Office, William Gavin, I said, "I received a very disturbing affidavit in the mail." He said, "Oh, we were expecting your call, but the number two guy knows this subject better than me, so please hold on."

The other guy gets on the phone and he started condemning Alma saying, "She is a God damned liar, and she doesn't know the fucking truth of anything."

It was not a pleasant set of circumstances and the conversation eventually developed into nothing more than us cursing each other out.

I learned that Alma had left New York and moved to Philadelphia. So I contacted law enforcement people in Philadelphia and I got a totally different picture of her credibility. In Philly she was like a heroine: she was almost killed because of the testimony she gave regarding mob guys in Philadelphia. So, she was a courageous lady with a stellar reputation in Philadelphia.

I was livid that the F.B.I. would try to set me up when I was pursuing justice on behalf of another law enforcement officer. I immediately called up the F.B.I. Office of Professional Responsibility and demanded an investigation into their agent's corrupt behavior. I told them, "Your agents actions are outrageous! If they will do this to me, an elected official, I hate to think what they might do to a member of the general public!" After a year, the Office of Professional Responsibility simply stated that the supervising agent and U.S. Attorney did not authorize such action against me. Essentially, a white wash of the egregious actions of the agents that plotted to set me up.

On December 9th, 1992 I received a letter from Deputy Attorney General George J. Terwilliger stated that after a five-month investigation, the material reviewed in defense of Occhipinti defense was fabricated. Again I was exasperated. When the press asked for my comments, I could only say that the letter from Terwilliger was "pure garbage." It was a bloody shame that certain agencies within the justice system could get away with such crap. They blatantly ignored all the evidence we submitted. It was clear to me that it was a bullshit investigation and they never intended to search for the truth. At the time and to this day I considered Obermaier and his cohort's actions an "absolute disgrace."

Unfortunately, President Bush lost his bid for reelection to President-elect Bill Clinton. Yet I knew that he had the power to ultimately correct a terrible miscarriage of justice before he left office. During the week of January 4th, 1993 I went to Washington to meet with President Bush in the Oval Office. I pleaded my case for Joe Occhipinti's freedom. President Bush told me that Terwilliger actually recommended a commutation of the sentence, since it did not fit the crime. I was so surprised when he told me that Terwilliger recommended the commutation in light of the scathing letter he wrote regarding the reinvestigation of the Occhipinti case.

Such complaints would normally result in discipline or dismissal but not a prosecution resulting in prison. When I left the meeting with Bush 41, I was convinced that he would commute his sentence, but I could not share this conversation with anyone until the actual order came out.

On January 15th, 1993, five days before he left office, President Bush formally commuted the sentence of Occhipinti. I was at the airport along with dozens of police and union officials to greet him home. When Occhipinti disembarked from the plane and ran into his wife, Angela's arms they both cried, I knew things were going to be O.K. for Joe and his family.

I will always be eternally grateful to President George H. W. Bush for commuting Joe's sentence. He did the morally right thing as the chief executive.

Fortunately, this story has a good ending. Joe Occhipinti is doing what he does best by serving the law enforcement community. He survived a terrible ordeal and turned it into a great legacy. He now runs the National Police Defense Foundation (NPDF). The NPDF is a nationally renowned organization that that provides free medical and legal support services to the law enforcement community, as well as providing funds for a variety of public safety and law enforcement initiatives. His foundation helps other law enforcement people who had somewhat similar problems in their lives by giving wrongly accused officers a place to turn.

I know that I did the right thing by supporting Joe. Honest people such as Joe do the right thing and find themselves convicted of something that they didn't do. I will always have a very strong feeling that we must support our law enforcement personnel. These people give their all every day and deserve no less than the "fair and impartial" treatment we so liberally hand out to drug kingpins, rapists, and murderers on a daily basis. If we don't support law enforcement officers, all the law enforcement personnel will hear that message loud and clear: "Don't be vigorous in your job. Your liberty can be at stake." I have seen too many cases where law enforcement personnel were convicted and incarcerated unjustly, and I am proud I was able to play a vigorous role to try to correct the wrongs that were done to people like Joe.

CHAPTER 41

All Hell Broke Loose

ON JULY 3, 1992, NEW YORK CITY POLICE OFFICER Michael O'Keefe, a plainclothes officer assigned to the 34th Precinct in Washington Heights, became involved in a violent struggle with an armed drug dealer named, Jose "Kiko" Garcia. Officer O'Keefe was trying to arrest Garcia for being in possession of an illegal gun. Kiko was high on cocaine at the time and the struggle went on for almost four minutes. In defense of his life, O'Keefe shot and killed Garcia. Justice! Yet, chaos followed and it was propelled by the actions of the media and the mayor.

In the ensuing days, the liberal media fueled a fabricated story that O'Keefe executed an unarmed Garcia based upon the statements of alleged eyewitnesses. During the hot summer nights, the community heard countless recitations of the false story that a White cop had beaten Garcia, a hard working bodega clerk with no criminal record, to the ground and executed him at point-blank range.

Garcia was painted as an altar boy by the media, when in fact Garcia himself was a coke addict and part of an elaborate drug organization. He was armed with an illegal firearm at the time and by the grace of God, Police Officer O'Keefe was lucky to have been able to walk away alive.

These false rumors, concocted by the drug gangs, sparked the Washington Heights riots which went on for three days. During this time, Mayor Dinkins visited the drug dealer's family, invited them to Gracie Mansion, and paid for the drug dealer's funeral and airfare to return the criminals' body to the Dominican Republic. When all was said and done, another man died during the riots, almost sixty cops were injured, and Washington Heights was smoldering from the fires that torched the neighborhood.

The Washington Heights riots came on the heels of the Crown Heights riots in August of 1991. During the Crown Heights riots, the police rank and file felt that Police Commissioner, Lee Brown and Mayor Dinkins held back a uniformed presence so that the Crown Heights Black community could "grieve" after the accidental death of seven year-old Gavin Cato when he was hit by a car driven by a Hasidic Jew. The riots ultimately led to the murder of Yankel Rosenbaum, a Jew who was stabbed to death by a black teenage mob.

Never once during the riots in Washington Heights did Mayor Dinkins call Officer O'Keefe and say, "Thanks for putting your life on the line for the city of New York. Thank God you survived." The mayor's actions were seen by New York City Police Department as catering to the drug dealers. To Mayor Dinkins, Kiko Garcia the drug dealer was a martyr and the dedicated police officer Michael O'Keefe was a demon.

Two months later when the investigation was completed it was revealed that the story was completely fabricated. In fact, Garcia was an illegal immigrant and a convicted drug dealer. The two eyewitnesses who were sisters, Juana Madera and Anna Rodriguez, lied and were intricately involved in the illegal drug trade in Washington Heights. These sisters never saw the violent struggle at all. To top it off, Anna Rodriquez's son, Jose Rodriquez, ran the ring Kiko worked for. It wasn't until the world saw a videotape of Kiko Garcia with his boss, Jose Rodriquez holding bags of cocaine and gloating "It's legal here," that world opinion changed and Michael O'Keefe was finally vindicated. A picture is worth a thousand words and in this case that was the only thing that changed public opinion.

It was determined by the Manhattan District Attorney's Office that Michael O'Keefe justifiably shot Kiko Garcia in self-defense after Garcia pulled a gun on Officer O'Keefe. Yet in the end the drug dealers won since the morale of the police department plummeted to an all-time low due to the mayors' actions. The damage that was done to the relationship between the mayor's office and the police department was extensive. It kind of rings a bell similar to the things that we're experiencing today with Mayor DiBlasio, especially after the assassinations of Police Officers Rafael Ramos and Wenjian Liu in the Bedford-Stuyvesant neighborhood of Brooklyn.

I felt awful for Officer O'Keefe and his precinct. I knew that they risked their lives on a daily basis. I was already very familiar with the neighborhood since I was actively working on the Joseph Occhipinti case.

One of the benefits of being back in Staten Island was that I was able to concentrate my energy on local city issues. I have always had a wonderful relationship with police officers and other public servants. They will always be heroes in my eyes. Although I was borough president, I could not ignore the cold hard fact that officers valiantly serving our city in other boroughs were under attack. So I did what I do best, I spoke up.

On July 14th, 1992, I wrote a letter to the police officers of the 34th Precinct. I wrote, "I know that your morale has taken a beating in recent weeks and the actions of Mayor Dinkins have undoubtedly contributed to your present feeling. However, I did want you to know that there are some of us in government who will hold you in the highest esteem." I was told that when the letter was read to the officers in the 34th Precinct, prior to them starting their shift, they applauded. They needed to know that although the mayor failed to support them, there were elected officials such as myself who would publically back them up.

When Dinkins was campaigning for Mayor he made a commitment that he would be the mayor of all boroughs not just Manhattan. He promised that if he was elected he would relocate his mayoral office to each of the boroughs for one week in an effort to show his sincerity. When he relocated to the other boroughs he would ask the borough president to provide their private offices for the week that he was spending in their borough.

After the Washington Heights riots, he was scheduled to relocate his office to Staten Island. As a direct result of my letter of support to the officers of the 34th Precinct, my office was informed that the mayor would not be using my private offices because he was upset over the criticism that I had directed at him.

On Monday July 27th, a contingent of my staff and other elected officials stood on the steps of Borough Hall to meet the mayor when he arrived on Staten Island. I wanted to give him a nice greeting even though I disagreed with the man. After all, I am a politician. My daughter took the opportunity to bring attention to the Fresh Kill's landfill. My daughter stated, "Mr. Mayor, typically individuals will get a key to the borough but I would like to present you with this." Susan then pulled out a large poster which said "MOLINARI LANDFILL LOCK." She expected him to laugh and take the poster.

Unfortunately, the exact opposite happened. He did not take it very well. He took it as something mean on our side and started yelling at Susan. I went over to him and said, "Welcome to Staten Island." I was trying to do the right thing and I said, "We've got a nice set up for you and—"

Dinkins interrupted and said, "No, I will be using the other offices that are used by my city agencies." I rolled my eyes, and then gave him a book about the history of Staten Island.

When the mayor visited each borough he would typically visit the unique sites in the borough. Of course in Staten Island at the time it was the garbage dump. How flattering it was for Staten Island's main contribution to the city to be identified as taking everyone's garbage. So during the mayor's visit I got a call from his staff saying, "The mayor is going to see the garbage dump. He'd like to extend an invitation to you if you want to go along with him." I said, "Of course." So, I hopped in the mayor's van and we drove to the garbage dump. What followed there was very amusing.

Mayor Dinkins always had expensive suits. He was a man who liked good clothes. When we got to the landfill, everybody was lined up, including me, and they were ready to take the pictures. One of Dinkins' staff went over and whispered to him. I heard Mayor Dinkins say, "You know, you're right. I don't want to take the picture here." I said, "Why, it's a nice shot?"

Mayor Dinkins said, "No, because it shows the garbage in the background." I looked at him stunned and said, "What do you expect to find at a garbage dump?"

He refused to take pictures with garbage in the background at the Staten Island garbage dump. We all had to move and take pictures where there was no garbage. So, the artificiality of the whole thing was amusing, really, if not pathetic.

In September, the Patrolmen's Benevolent Association, President Phil Caruso invited me to be the keynote speaker at their annual luncheon in the Catskills scheduled for September 10th, 1992. All the delegates of New York City's largest union, representing over 20,000 police officers, descended upon the Catskills for a week of family fun.

Mayor Dinkins was not invited. Instead, his biggest critic at the time, Guy V. Molinari, was asked to say a few words. This was major slap in the face to Mayor Dinkins. The keynote address in the past was typically given by the then sitting mayor. It was a bold statement on the part of the PBA. Caruso needed to boost the morale of his police officers and he tapped into me to be that booster. I was honored. With the invitation I knew that law enforcement personnel could tell that I would be their political voice in a dark era of anti-law enforcement.

The media immediately contacted me when they heard that I was the keynote speaker and asked me what I would be saying. I responded that, "I have very serious concerns about the low morale that affects the police community today and I think it's primarily the fault of the guy in City Hall, Dave Dinkins. He talks about 'Safe Streets, Safe City', but it doesn't do much good to hire thousands more police if you take away their ability to do their jobs. I will let the officers know that I support them wholeheartedly."

On the day, I addressed a crowd of over 1000 attendees at the Concord Hotel. I applauded the brave young men and women who selflessly put their lives on the line on a daily basis. I assured them that the city would never pay for the funeral of a drug dealer again. My remarks brought on thunderous applause and a standing ovation. They were moved to know that they had at least some support in the political arena of New York City.

While at the convention, we learned that the Manhattan D.A.'s office made the formal announcement that Grand Jury had declined to indict Michael O'Keefe. The Grand Jury found that Officer O'Keefe was justified in killing Kiko Garcia in defense of his own life. It was an uplifting experience to be at the convention when word spread of the Grand Jury's decision.

On Wednesday September 16th, immediately on the tails of the convention came the most shameful examples of media exploitation that I have ever witnessed. After months of growing tension between Mayor Dinkins and the police, over 10,000 off-duty officers and their supporters gathered outside City Hall to protest Mayor Dinkins' support of the formation of an all-civilian review board to investigate police misconduct, the appointment of a mayoral commission to investigate charges of police corruption, and finally the mayor's refusal to approve the issuance of semiautomatic pistols. Yet, the real underlying tension revolved around the Mayor's handling of the Washington Heights riot and the mayor's support for the family of Kiko Garcia.

The demonstration began shortly after ten o'clock a.m. when the officers started marching around City Hall Park. There were so many cops present that the crowd stretched throughout the entire park all the way out to Broadway and Park Row. In direct reference to Al Sharpton's divisive chants at anti police rallies of, "No Justice, No Peace", the cops chanted, "No Justice, No Police." Many officers wore t-shirts saying, "Dinkins Must Go!" They had signs, one of which I remember said, "Dear Mayor, have you hugged a drug dealer today?"

The demonstration began calmly enough, as the speakers gathered on a platform about a block west of City Hall on Murray Street between Church Street and Broadway which was the designated area to address the demonstrators. The protesting officers listened intently to blunt speeches from Phil Caruso, Rudy Giuliani, and me. Police Officer Michael O'Keefe gave the final speech.

Regarding Rudy's speech, he picked up exactly where I left off and ran with it. Rudy repeated what I said. We both harped on the fact that Mayor Dinkins made the tragic mistake of treating a drug dealer as a hero. Rudy was animated as I was at the time and we both gave fiery speeches, and that was why we were there: to drum up support for the cops and to let them know that they were not alone. We were all on the same team. Several times during his speech Rudy called the mayor's proposals "bull shit," and the media crucified Rudy over his use of it.

Apparently a few of the off-duty cop demonstrators went over the barriers in front of City Hall and then marched onto the Brooklyn Bridge, blocking traffic in both directions for several minutes. Everything was over with by 12:20 pm. With the exception of a traffic tie-up, it was a peaceful demonstration and no one was hurt. When we left, I felt that Rudy had hit a "grand slam." Our message was heard loud and clear. The police needed our support.

Unfortunately, the media reports that came out the following day were so wrong that they would have angered anyone who was there. They painted the entire police department as a bunch of rowdy drunk cops who were racist. Nothing could be further from the truth. I was there: I watched the demonstration, and never saw a single person with a can of beer in their hand. The media portrayed Rudy as the inciter to the media described "riot." To me it was a total distortion of the truth. Mayor Dinkins publically came out and said, "Rudy was out there inciting White cops to riot."

Yes, we had a passionate crowd, but it was not riotous. For the media to use that word was ludicrous. Washington Heights and Crown Heights were riots; the police demonstration was an emotional affair for the officers attending but it never reached the level of criminality like what Dinkins allowed to happen in Crown Heights and Washington Heights. This was yet another example of Dinkins bigoted behavior toward the police.

I believe the media went after Rudy because he was going to be the Republican candidate for mayor against Dinkins in 1993 again and the liberal media was not about to give Giuliani a pass. As I said before, Giuliani said nothing more or less than what I said.

Regarding what happened at the steps of City Hall, nobody was aware of it. That was a splinter group of demonstrators. When we did hear about it, Phil Caruso, Rudy, and I tried to calm the crowd and restore order.

Sorry to say, but that's the way it was back then. A complete anti-cop media distortion. Obviously after all this, there was no relationship at all between the PBA and the mayor. This time the damage was irreparable. The PBA was anxious to see a new mayor, as I was.

CHAPTER 42

Secession Fever

By 1993, praise the Lord, a hotly contested mayoral race was brewing again between Mayor Dinkins and Rudy Giuliani. As before, I was a die-hard 'Rudy for Mayor' politician, as was my daughter. I knew that it was essential for Staten Island's benefit to get Rudy into City Hall and to get rid of Dinkins. This time around, Rudy hired David Garth as his adviser. Garth was instrumental in the elections of prior mayors such as John Lindsay and Ed Koch, as well as Governors Hugh Carey and Brendan Byrne. Garth was often referred to as a political genius and so it was hoped that Rudy would blossom under his guidance.

When asked about the addition of David Garth to his campaign I responded, "Garth can get Rudy to do tough things that Guy Molinari can't and that's important. Garth can give him hell." Garth was a great political analyzer and strategist who knew how to goad the other side into making spontaneous, rash statements, while at the same time make his own candidate maintain a calm professional demeanor. That was important this time around for Rudy: he could not let his feathers get ruffled and he had to stick to the issues.

Up until Election Day, I was on the campaign trail for Rudy whenever necessary. Everyone knew that Staten Island was going to be key to his victory. By slaughtering Dinkins in Staten Island, he would improve his chances of winning the overall election. Because it was so important, Rudy made sure that he spent plenty of time in my borough. I remember marching with him and my daughter in the St. Patrick's Day parade in Staten Island where mayoral candidate Giuliani received a hero's welcome. The crowd chanted, "Save us Rudy!" Susan turned to me and said, "It's like we are with Elvis, for God's sake. This isn't a political response. This is a real emotional response." She was right. My borough knew they needed Rudy on their side since Dinkins never would be.

A big issue during the campaign involved Staten Island and the possible secession from New York City. Staten Island has always had a problem with a lack of respect from its sister boroughs and their politicians. Over the course of my lifetime as a Staten Island resident, the politicians or the citizens of Staten Island would occasionally take up the cry of secession from New York City. The arguments were many and varied: we're different from the other boroughs; the taxes are too high; commuting is terrible; they throw coal burning power plants at us; they want to build prisons here; the LNG tanks could have wiped out half of Staten Island; they want to give us all the homeless; they want to give us all their garbage; etc.

Initially I took the position that secession was never going to occur because, having walked my way through the New York political landscape for decades, no matter what Staten Island wanted at the time, I believed that Albany, specifically Sheldon "Shelly" Silver, the Democratic speaker of the assembly would never let Staten Island secede from the city. I liked Shelly, and he was very good to me over the years, but one has to be a realist. I knew that Staten Island was more important to "The City" than "The City" was to Staten Island. In those days we had the God forsaken garbage dump. If for no other reason, that was reason enough for Albany to deny secession to go through. Additionally, the state did not want to see New York City reduced in size.

As far back as November 6th, 1990 Staten Island's residents voted overwhelmingly in favor of a referendum that created a charter commission to explore the feasibility of Staten Island seceding from New York City. The commission, consisting of eighteen Staten Islanders, studied the fiscal and political consequences of secession. In 1994, a new charter would be submitted to Staten Island voters, although the state legislature and governor would have final say. From the beginning I was a quiet opponent of secession since I believed that the cost for services to Staten Islanders and property taxes could quadruple.

As late as March of 1993 I was still skeptical about the issue of secession, because we have no real commerce or significant industry; the need for new revenues would be borne by homeowners. However, after representing the people for quite some time, they learned to turn to you for advice when they have doubts, and secession clearly was such an issue. As borough president, I had an open town hall meeting, and a gentleman in the rear of the auditorium stood up, raised his hand and addressed a question to me: "Mr. Borough President, you haven't told us your position on secession. I think that you have an obligation to tell us so that we can know what we should think about when we take a position on it."

I gave a smart-ass response when I said, "Oh, now I know why I came here, so that I can learn what I have to do!"

At the conclusion of the event, the man was waiting for me and I remember thinking it would be one of those serious arguments, but I was wrong. The man came up to me and said, "I apologize, Mr. Molinari. I didn't want you to think that I was trying to put you on the spot or anything, but what I really meant to say was that I trust and respect your judgment. I don't know whether secession would work or not, but if you said that it would work, I would vote for it, and if you said it was not a good idea I would vote against it. It's that simple."

I told the man, "I'm sorry, I must have been tired, you're right. I will have to take a solid position on the issue." I told him that even though I thought it would not work, that I agreed that I had an obligation to give my constituents a knowledgeable, fact-based position on such a critical issue. From this conversation, I knew that I could not ignore that secession under Dinkins was a concept that appeared to be gathering steam. I said, "I'm not going to be a supporter or a detractor of it. I'm going to study it. After studying it, I will announce my opinion."

After this conversation I went out and hired two consultants to study the issue on the true viability of Staten Island seceding from New York City and becoming independent. In addition, a private organization donated their time to study the issue for free. When all three studies came back they all concluded that secession could work. Staten Island could survive as a separate entity.

After all the research and several extensive reports, in October of 1993 I publicly came out in favor of secession. I told Staten Islanders that they had to go out on Election Day and cast their vote in favor of secession. When I came out in favor of secession, both Rudy Giuliani and Mayor Dinkins opposed secession. Nonetheless, I knew that if Dinkins was successful in his reelection efforts, I would wholeheartedly lead the effort for seceding. Yet if Dinkins lost, I believed the cry for secession would diminish because Giuliani would be a friend to Staten Island.

So, when I came out in favor of secession I stated, "I believe that it a risk worth taking now, since we have irreconcilable differences with the rest of the city. An independent 'City of Staten Island' would be better off, despite the higher taxes we will pay at the outset. My change of heart is primarily driven by the historical mistreatment of Staten Island by city administrations, of which the greatest offender is Mayor Dinkins." I had had it with Dinkins. The thought of having him for mayor for another four years made me want to throw up. I blasted Dinkins on destroying the Naval Homeport, cutting rush hour Staten Island Ferry service, forcing homeless shelters onto the Island, opposing toll reductions, and although we made up only 5% of the population of New York City, we received virtually 100% of the garbage!

Every politician knows that the hardest thing to do on Election Day is to get the voters to actually physically go to the polls and vote. Of all the boroughs Staten Island was the most important for Giuliani. This was the swing borough. Without us he would not get elected.

I had my staff out every day immediately after I announced I was endorsing secession. Wherever you looked on Staten Island, you saw a sign, poster or flyer supporting secession. With this strategy, every Staten Islander knew it was important to cast a vote in favor of secession. As a result, we worked Staten Island up into froth. By Election Day I guaranteed a better turnout than 1989. Over 25,000 more Staten Islanders went to the polls on November 2nd, 1993 than did in 1989. As Staten Islanders flocked to the polls that day, they were essentially casting two votes against Dinkins. The issue of secession brought them to the polls, but every vote for secession also included a vote for Rudy Giuliani to be the next mayor. It was a great political strategy to rally the citizens to make a difference for the entire city.

November 2nd, 1993 was an incredibly important day for Staten Island. Rudy Giuliani was elected mayor of the New York City. In 1989 he had lost by 2% of the votes, yet in 1993 he had won by 3%. Both times I had delivered Staten Island, but this time we delivered 25,000 extra voters. Everyone agreed when the polls were closed, had it not been for the votes of Staten Islanders, Dinkins would have been mayor again. The tides had changed.

Giuliani's victory party at the penthouse suite of the Hilton Hotel in Manhattan was the place to be that night. It was the "who's who" of the next mayoral cabinet in the city. Peter Powers, Dennison Young, Randy Mastro, Randy Levine, Cristyne Lategano, Bill Powers, Susan, and myself to name a few. It was a thrilling victory and I felt for the first time in four years that things were going to change for the better for my constituents in Staten Island. I was thrilled that the smallest borough had achieved such a great outcome. I had worked hard since 1989 to help Rudy become mayor, and I expected him to remember where his loyalties lie.

In addition to Rudy's win, secession had passed overwhelmingly, yet there were other steps to be followed. Within two days after the election I got Civil War reenactors to set up an authentic Civil War cannon at Fort Wadsworth right by the Verrazano Bridge. We fired four shots from its cannon at the other boroughs. The first shot was symbolically aimed directly at Manhattan. The message sent was that the secession vote passed and we were ready to move forward if we had to. Although I did not believe secession would come to pass, I wanted to let everyone know that Staten Island would continue to defend itself no matter what. I told everyone that the cannon symbolized the spirit of revolution. That is what Staten Islanders are about.

Of course, secession never did happen, because when Giuliani was elected life got a lot better for Staten Islanders. Secession, while it may have been a viable alternative under Dinkins, would also have been a difficult one. Once Mayor Giuliani took office Staten Islanders recognized that with a supportive mayor there was a lot to be said about being part of the Big Apple. As long as the city didn't dump on us again, there would be no reason to speak of secession.

However, succession is the kind of issue that could come back, especially if the city reverts to past policies. Living under Mayor DiBlasio's rule, it has always been a possibility since his mayoral term seems to mirror that of Mayor Dinkins in many respects.

Shortly after the election of Rudy Giuliani, many people vetted my daughter about a potential run for Governor of the State of New York. On the weekend after Thanksgiving we had a family summit where we seriously discussed the pros and cons of running for governor. By the end of the weekend, our family and Bill decided that if Susan wanted to throw her hat in the ring she would decide by Christmas.

On November 30th, on the steps of City Hall, my daughter announced that she was considering a race for governor in 1994. She informed the press that she would make her decision within two weeks. During those two weeks, Susan's phone did not stop ringing. Politicians and citizens from all over New York State were calling her office and urging her to run. It was overwhelming. Never in her wildest dreams did she expect such statewide acceptance of her potential candidacy.

Ultimately Susan sat down with me and said, "Dad, I've decided that I don't want to run. I can't take any more of this stuff." I said, "Alright, just play it for a while and get your name out there for the future, maybe."

She said, "No. I don't want to do it. I want to announce right now that I'm not running and I'm not a candidate." I respected her decision because she knew that her plate was full and she was committed to serving New York from Washington.

So true to her word on December 14th, my daughter formally announced that she would not enter the race. The cons had outweighed the pros. The three biggest cons were her commitment to her congressional constituents of Brooklyn and Staten Island, her power base in Congress, and finally, personal reasons especially the fact she was getting married and wanted to start a family.

The holiday season was upon us, and great gifts were bestowed upon our city. The upcoming year showed great promise. I know that I was the most ebullient of all borough presidents since I had done the most work to elect our Mayor. When the press interviewed me at Christmas time I told them, "Since you asked me what I want for Christmas, I will answer by telling you, I have got it: Rudy Giuliani! Staten Island's stocking will stay up all year."

CHAPTER 43

Rudy the Chameleon

In 1994 the Republican Party had the best opportunity in twenty years to recapture the Governorship of New York State and it was important not to squander the chance at victory over petty politics. We needed to find the best possible candidate who could actually win against Cuomo. In the early vetting process, I received a call from Senator Al D'Amato who said he was on the verge of backing State Senator George Pataki from Westchester as the gubernatorial candidate.

At the time I had never heard of a guy named George Pataki. I laughed at first because the name Pataki sounded like a Polish pastry. Within a short period of time Senator D'Amato arranged a meeting. When I met Pataki I thought he came off very genuine and intelligent. Most importantly we agreed on almost all Republican issues, specifically the death penalty, we were both ardent supporters. I would learn that he also surrounded himself with an excellent staff.

In the early gubernatorial candidate selection process, there was a lot of infighting between Senator D'Amato, and State Senate

Majority Leader Ralph Marino from Nassau County. They were considered friendly rivals since they both came from the highly influential Nassau County Republican machine overseen by Nassau County Party Chairman Joseph Mondello. Friendly is a politically correct term, since they did not seem to like each other.

Senator Marino hated George Pataki ever since Pataki won election as a New York State Senator in 1992. Pataki was supported by an anti-tax organization called PACK-UP/CHANGE-NY. This same organization had actively campaigned against Senator Marino in his reelection campaign that year, and Marino despised Pataki for taking money from a group that tried to overthrow him.

I was annoyed that we, the Republican Party, did not have a definitive candidate by March. I felt that if the impasse was not broken soon, the Republican Party would lose a great opportunity to pick up the coveted Conservative Party endorsement and we would not be able to raise the cash necessary to mount a campaign against Cuomo. I knew that in order to have a successful campaign against Cuomo we needed Republican unity.

At the Republican Party State Convention on May 23rd, Pataki was finally endorsed as the Republican gubernatorial candidate. Shortly after the convention, New York State's Conservative Party endorsed Senator George E. Pataki for governor. This was a major step toward cementing a Republican-Conservative alliance against Gov. Mario M. Cuomo that had been four years in the making. It was a long hard journey, but with Pataki as our candidate, I could finally see the light at the end of the tunnel.

I became Pataki's New York City campaign chief. It only made sense since realistically his entire voting base in the city would be from Staten Island. I would campaign with him when necessary. One of the funniest times I had with him was when we were campaigning in Brooklyn. We went to an Italian deli where they had these big dried meats hanging off the top of the wall and I took one and I put it on my shoulder. I knew that when I walked out, the press was going to be there and they were going to take pictures. I gave Pataki one as we walked out, and everybody was taking pictures. It was a good prop for the campaign.

Pataki's campaign was more wholesale than retail. What I mean by that is if you have the money, you do a lot of the advertising by TV, mail, radio, etc., to get your name out. Pataki's campaign was well-funded. The Republicans wanted to win. If you don't have money then you have a retail kind of campaign where you ring doorbells, go to functions, summer block parties, constant events: basically the kind of campaigns I was consistently involved with in the beginning of my career. Abbreviated, if you don't have money, you're shopping retail.

June 30th 1994 was an extremely sad day for Staten Island and me. My good friend and political advisor Mike Petrides passed away from lung cancer. He was only 53. As you know when I was elected borough president one of my proudest acts was to appoint Mike to the Board of Education slot. It was his dream job and I knew he was born for the job. Mike was a devoted member and he addressed controversy head on. He was not afraid to follow his educational vision and that is why he had no problem chastising then School Chancellor Joseph Fernandez over his plan to distribute condoms. Mike immediately went public against the policy and voiced his very realistic concern that the next step of the public school system might be to "distribute hypodermic needles." This very blunt statement obviously gave the public realistic cause for concern for their children, especially in light of the proliferation of AIDS primarily due to intravenous drug use.

Mike was the sole Republican on the board yet due to his commitment he ultimately became known as the leader of the "Gang of Four" majority consisting of board members Ninfa Segarra (Bronx), Carol A Gresser (Queens), and Irene H. Impellizzeri (Brooklyn) which led to Fernandez's demise in February of 1993. Essentially Fernandez was canned and Mike led the charge. Obviously Fernandez' ouster was embarrassing and annoyed the hell out of Dinkins. I personally enjoyed the whole debacle.

At the tail end of his life, Mike was a close political advisor to Mayor Giuliani regarding educational issues. He was an amazing strategist, always thinking ahead and never looking backward. I will always consider him a genius in the fields of politics and education.

As a testament to his educational dedication to the residents of Staten Island as well as the City of New York I had a school named after him in 1994. He was the most devoted educator I ever met. The school, located in the Sunnyside section of Staten Island, was formerly part of the New York City College of Staten Island campus (hereinafter "CSI"). In 1993 CSI moved to a larger campus. As a result, CSI no longer needed the property located on Ocean Terrace so the city was thinking about selling the property to the private sector in order to generate money.

Initially, Rabbi Rappoport, of the Congregation B'nai Israel synagogue located at 45 Twombly Avenue in Bay Terrace wanted to obtain the property for his congregation. At the time Dinkins was Mayor and he was all for the private sale of the property, therefore his administration was pushing for Rabbi Rappoport's proposal. As circumstances would have it, one day while meeting with several parents in Borough Hall they asked me, "Why don't we make the CSI campus a public school for our kids?" The parents felt that the overall community needs of the children should be the first priority. When they explained their proposal I Immediately agreed that it was a good idea worth looking into. After doing research, I decided that the property should be converted to a public school. Mike spearheaded the Board of Education's efforts to obtain the property.

When Rabbi Rappoport heard that I wanted to convert the property into a public school he went crazy. He went all around Staten Island saying that I was anti-Semitic. It was a ludicrous and totally illogical conclusion but that is what happens when a public official takes a position that is contrary to that of the opposition. Fortunately, the war between Giuliani and Dinkins was in full swing for the next mayoral election so the issue of the ultimate conversion of this part of the CSI campus fell by the wayside.

I remember after Giuliani was elected, he swore me in for my second term as borough president at the Williamson Theater on the former campus of CSI. It was his first week as the newly elected mayor. At the ceremony, Mayor Giuliani declared, "I am now the mayor, Guy is again reelected borough president, and as my first act here on Staten Island, I am declaring this a public school and the property is transferred to the New York City Board of Education. We're saving this school." You couldn't get more dramatic than that regarding the birth of a fantastic public school. Mike was present at this moment and I could literally see his heart swell with pride on how far his vision had come for Staten Islanders.

Unfortunately, a few short months later Mike was at the end of his life. He was terminally ill with lung cancer. By the early 90s the dangers of cigarette smoking were finally being revealed yet it was too late for Mike. The damage was already done and cancer was ravaging his body. Although he was extremely debilitated from the disease he still wanted to serve New York City and the Board of Education. I gladly reappointed him to his coveted position.

We held Mike's reappointment ceremony on May 24th 1994 in my office. I remember Mike thanking me for giving him a seat at the table. I was dumbfounded. I told Mike, "You want to thank me, but I want to thank you for being such a great guardian of our students. It goes both ways. No one could do the job that you did in such a flawless manner. You followed your heart regarding our children and there is no greater gift that you can give us."

Immediately before the ceremony Mike whispered to me, "When you bring me up to the podium let me hold onto a piece of the dais to keep my balance, otherwise I will fall." At the time I really did not get what he was talking about, but now that I am frail and have difficulty keeping my own balance I can truly appreciate what he meant. It does not require a lot. Just that little touch that gives you the balance you need.

After we were finished, I looked at my great friend and I knew that he had lived a dream come true as I have lived my dream come true. We were both lucky to have served Staten Island.

When the school formally opened after Mike's untimely death, as a testament to his dedication it was named the Michael J. Petrides School. It stands as a tribute to a man who dedicated his life to the education of our young children. Today, the Petrides School is a highly competitive and successful school. The school prepares children for the rigors of college life, and will always be a great gift for the children of Staten Island. Additionally, in memory of my great friend I established the Michael J. Petrides Award. Since Mike was dedicated to promoting superiority in math and science, the award is given to annually to a graduating student who excels in those disciplines. It is a great legacy for a great man.

Shortly after Michael's death, the Congressional Republicans successfully defeated a passage of President Bill Clinton's anti-crime bill for a multitude of reasons. Stunningly, immediately afterward, going behind every Republicans back, Mayor Giuliani reached out to Clinton and asked if there was anything he could do to resurrect the bill. He never even bothered to contact me, but more importantly he never reached out to my daughter Susan, the Republican congresswoman who fought aggressively against the bill. Rudy indicated to Clinton that he could possibly sway peoples' minds. Now, I get the fact that there was $800 million for New York City on the table, so I could understand Rudy trying to break bread, but political courtesy goes a long way in the world of politics. The chameleon was starting to expose his true self. A lot of Republicans were very uneasy seeing Giuliani cross party lines so easily and many of us felt that it certainly would have been better had he discussed it with key allies in the party before he jumped into the fire.

By the end of August, the anti-crime bill passed. Susan drafted the "Molinari amendment" which included important concessions regarding sex crimes and other Republican issues.

I was beginning to see that the real Rudy Giuliani was a man blinded by ambition. I was very frank when I spoke to the media and said, "I absolutely feel a sense of betrayal. There was a total lack of sensitivity toward my daughter who considered herself a very good friend of the mayor. There is something called loyalty in politics, and the mayor has not followed that practice."

At the same time George Pataki was running for Governor, Republican Dennis Vacco, a former A.D.A. for Erie County and U. S. Attorney for the Western District of New York, was running for NYS Attorney General. At the time, Dennis Vacco was not well-known throughout the State. After all the primaries were done Dennis Vacco was running against Democrat Karen Burstein, and apparently both Vacco and Burstein made an agreement that neither side would use the fact that Burstein was a lesbian in their campaign. In essence her sexual preference would be a non-issue.

Yet as Burstein campaigned she printed up campaign literature that she was disseminating primarily in the gay areas of her district in Manhattan. In the literature she acknowledged that she was gay and would be an advocate for the gay community. Her literature would make statements such as, "I will help lead the fight for lesbians and gay men in New York and across America." So she was violating the agreement that they had. In fact, she was taking advantage of the fact that she was lesbian where she could, but she would hide that fact that she was lesbian in upstate New York and other more conservative areas of the state, but she would learn that it was a flawed strategy especially with somebody like me.

On Monday October 10th, 1994 I marched in the Columbus Day parade up Fifth Avenue. My daughter Susan joined me. As an Italian-American I loved marching in the Columbus Day parade. This year, however, the parade was filled with political tension since Giuliani had not yet formally endorsed Pataki and my other Republican counterparts were pissed. To throw more salt onto the wound, rumor had it that Giuliani intended to march with Governor Cuomo. This was something that we could not tolerate. It was a matter of party loyalty. Cuomo was not going to be given the honor of marching with Republicans endorsing his challenger.

In past years I would meet my Republican counterparts at 44th Street and 5th Avenue where we would normally start marching. Due to Giuliani's intention to march with Governor Cuomo, I gathered with my Republican counterparts, Senator D'Amato, my daughter and, others who were committed to George Pataki at 46th Street and 5th Avenue. When the parade started, we were up front since Mayor Giuliani and Governor Cuomo started two blocks behind us.

It bothered me since the night before the parade Pataki had finally met with Mayor Giuliani for the first time at Gracie Mansion. I was working very hard to have Giuliani endorse Pataki, and not Cuomo. That could have been seen as heresy in politics. So since the Mayor met with Pataki the night before and in the spirit of Republican solidarity, after we were marching for a few blocks I fell back for a short period of time to march with Giuliani. I said at the time that, "Columbus Day is a good day for everybody to get together, at least for the day, and forget their differences. That is how good friendships endure."

When the parade was over I mentioned to my daughter that the New York City Police Department's Columbia Association invited us over to the Church of St. Ignatius Loyola located at 980 Park Avenue at the corner of 84th Street for lunch. It was expected, especially during an election year, that politicians would make an appearance and hopefully speak. The endorsement of Police Unions will always be important to any politician's election campaign.

Susan and I went over to Wallace Hall which was part of the Church of St. Ignatius Loyola. The hall was packed with hundreds of police officers. At a certain point, the Columbia Association invited public figures to speak. Rudy Giuliani was there with his wife, Donna Hanover, and Dennis Vacco was present with his campaign people.

Vacco spoke first and he talked about his campaign and the things he did. Then Rudy spoke. Rudy went off on a tangent by saying, "What Dennis Vacco hasn't told you was this…and Dennis

Vacco hasn't told you this…" So by the time I got up I started my speech and I bluntly said, "Yeah. What Dennis Vacco and Rudy Giuliani didn't say is that the next Attorney General should not be a lesbian, but I will say it: Karen Burstein is a lesbian!"

The place went crazy wildly applauding. I wanted to explain why I said what I had just said but it was impossible because the crowd would not settle down. This statement would be the difference between winning and losing regarding the race for NYS Attorney General in 1994. I had wanted to explain to the crowd that it was agreed-upon between Vacco and Bernstein that her being lesbian would not become part of the campaign, yet she had made it an issue by her campaign literature and actions.

The media was there and they ran with what became a big story for next several weeks. My statements were on the front page of all the major newspapers the following day. I received a phone call from the New York State Conservative Party Chairman Mike Long, and he said, "Guy that was great publicity for Dennis that you engendered yesterday. Can you keep the story going for another two or three days?" I told Mike, "I won't have to do anything, the story will keep running for at least another five days. You watch. I know how the media operates."

Sure enough, before that event took place, Vacco was losing in the smallest districts upstate New York. Shortly after my statements, the polls suddenly showed a different story; Vacco's numbers soared and the campaign made a complete turnaround. Even to this day when Dennis Vacco talks about his campaign he acknowledges that my frankness on a touchy issue was what got him elected.

I publically stated that I did not regret making my comments and would continue to speak about Burstein's sexual preference. I told the press that Vacco had no idea what I was going to say when I stepped up to the podium. It was totally unsolicited and it surprised him as much as everyone else in the room.

Immediately after this speech, LGBT groups everywhere were after me. They demanded that I publicly apologize for my remarks.

I absolutely refused to apologize for what I knew was a correct statement. I was heavily criticized for my stance yet I held my ground. I vehemently repeated, "The fact that she is lesbian is not being divulged to people in the rest of the state, and if it were, it would cost her politically. So I say loud and clear everyone should be aware of her sexual preference since she made it a campaign issue even if it was only in select districts."

Of course I was labeled a bigot and anti-gay. I'm sorry that my name had be attacked as it was, but nevertheless I'm big enough not to take those kinds of things personally when I know that my statements weren't intended to be offensive toward any group of people regardless of their sexual preference. Even though it appeared to be an attack on a woman who was a lesbian, such was not the truth.

George Pataki thought that my statements were "inappropriate and a mistake," and that I should probably apologize, but even though I refused, I still remained his New York City Campaign chair. Again, it's all politics.

On Monday October 25th, to my dismay, Rudy Giuliani publically endorsed Democratic Governor Mario Cuomo. When the announcement was made I was shocked and hurt. I told the press that my daughter and I had spent almost six years supporting Giuliani, and that we placed a heavy emphasis on loyalty. Staten Island felt duped by Giuliani's endorsement. Staten Island after all, put Giuliani in Gracie Mansion, and this was our reward.

It hurt to see Giuliani immediately before the election going out to campaign for Cuomo. I will always believe that Giuliani's endorsement of Cuomo was meant to finish off D'Amato if in fact Cuomo won. It was a huge and dangerous gamble that Giuliani was taking at the time. I was livid that he would go to such lengths due to personality conflicts. I thought he was better than that, but I was wrong. Apparently Giuliani was pissed when he heard that D'Amato threatened to show Giuliani, "The difference between a United States senator and a first-term mayor." The egos between the two were so huge that there was no room for reason. I was so upset that I stated at the time that I would not endorse Giuliani for reelection. It seemed as if I had created a monster. This was the second time in a matter of months that Giuliani exhibited traitorous behavior, and I would have no more of it.

Immediately before the election there was absolutely no way to be sure who had the upper hand. The race for governor was tight as well as the race for attorney general. It would be all about getting the right people to the polls. The Republicans were labeled the fear monger party based upon my refusal to recant my statements and apologize to Burstein.

On Tuesday November 8th, the battle was over. The results were a grand slam for the Republican Party. George Pataki had been elected Governor with 48% of the vote compared to incumbent Governor Mario Cuomo 45%. It was a huge victory for Pataki, D'Amato, and me.

Most surprisingly, though, was the win of politically unknown Dennis Vacco. He won the position of New York State Attorney General with 50% of the vote compared to Burstein's 47%. In the end, both races were nail biters. The press asked me how I felt about Vacco's results and I stated, "By the time the election rolled around, I don't think there was tiny hamlet in the state that wasn't aware that not only was Burstein a lesbian but that she had some very bad votes when she was in the senate and that she had a gay and lesbian agenda. Many people told me, 'Thank you for letting me know, Guy. It does make a difference to me and now I know how I will vote.'"

The political fallout for Giuliani was quick and immediate since many members of the Republican Party vowed vengeance against Giuliani for his rash and poor decision. Giuliani needed money, yet he had to face a Republican governor who owed him nothing. Giuliani had called Pataki two times to congratulate him, but Pataki did not return the call. I would have done the same thing myself. I know It was hard for me to watch Giuliani campaign for Cuomo, and I can only assume it was harder for Pataki. But by the grace of God, the right man won again.

The only thing that Rudy had going for him immediately after the election was the fact that American politics changed so quickly. It would be foolish to try to assume what Giuliani's true political legacy would be at the time. Yet the only one to blame for the plight that Rudy was in was Rudy himself. No Republican envied him. On the flip side his nemesis D'Amato was in his glory. He continued to beat down Giuliani.

The rift would continue for a long time. Pataki asked me to set up a meeting of city officials on Staten Island so that we could work out a plan for the city. Staten Island was the only portion of the city that delivered for Pataki, so of course he would want to come to my borough. It was friendly territory. Time and time again, in the election process Staten Island was the friendliest territory to a Republican. So, my people called up Giuliani's people and invited the mayor to a November 28th meeting on Staten Island. His Press Secretary, Cristyne Lategano, said the problem with the meeting was that it was partisan and petty. We even moved the meeting to Manhattan, yet Giuliani still did not come.

Regardless, it was a very productive meeting. In attendance was Governor-elect Pataki, Lieutenant Governor-elect Elizabeth McCaughey, Comptroller Alan Hevesi, Public Advocate Mark Green, Bronx Borough President Fernando Ferrer, Brooklyn Borough President Howard Golden, Manhattan Borough President Ruth Messinger, Queens Borough President Claire Shulman, Republican Councilman Thomas V. Ognibene of Queens, as well as myself.

Many of the attendees, especially the Democrats, did not know Governor Pataki at all. After the meeting it was generally agreed that they found Pataki to be approachable and knowledgeable on the issues, as well as being committed to appropriate beneficial resolutions to all parties involved. Everyone in attendance agreed that Rudy should have swallowed his pride, fessed up to a colossal blunder on his part, and showed up at a meeting that was all about New York City since after all he was the mayor.

The following day, November 29th, Governor-elect George Pataki met privately with Rudy Giuliani. It was a telling sign at the time that Rudy trusted no politician in the city and many politicians such as me held Rudy in contempt for his traitorous behavior.

Politics being politics, I had to ultimately bury the hatchet so to say with Giuliani for the benefit of Staten Island. I recognized that with the election of a Republican governor and mayor, real miracles could occur for my borough. On February 7th 1995, Rudy attended one of my Town Hall meetings held at Susan B. Wagner High School on Staten Island where we publically put an end to our personal tensions for the benefit of the city. I remember saying to the over 500 Staten Islanders in attendance, "We have a serious problem, the mayor and I, we have been fighting for some time, and now we are trying to discern what the best pizzeria on Staten Island is." Everyone laughed. Then I said, "On a more serious side, me and Rudy may have had some differences, but he has been a damned good mayor and he's been good to Staten Island."

In return Giuliani said, "Guy has been so supportive to me and he is always fighting for the interests of Staten Island. You are lucky to have him and I am lucky to have him." When the meeting was over, we headed to Goodfella's Pizzeria. In the back of my mind though Rudy would forever be considered a chameleon.

CHAPTER 44

The Marriage of Susan and Bill

On August 5th, 1993, I received a wonderful call from New York Congressman Bill Paxton. He asked for my permission to marry my daughter Susan. I was impressed that he did it the old fashioned way, by asking for parental permission first. They had been dating about three years. Of course I said yes. I knew they had a terrific chemistry and got along so well. When Bill called my wife Marguerite she was thrilled. I remember Marguerite telling Bill, "If Susan doesn't accept, I will hold Susan's dog George hostage until she does accept." As with the Bushes, Susan is a dog fanatic, and actually named her dog after President Bush, Sr.

Immediately after he spoke to us, when the House was in session, Bill Paxton planned to propose to Susan on the house floor. It was to be the first such proposal in the history of Congress. On that evening between votes, Bill pulled Susan over to the seats in the back of the chamber under the pretense that he had something important to tell her. It was not unusual for them to do this since they were always sharing news with each other about what they had done during the session.

Susan told me that Bill looked at her and said, "Boy, have I had a day. I've been on the phone with your parents." She told me when Bill said that, she got worried that something might be wrong with Marguerite or me. Bill said, "Nope, they are fine, but I wanted to tell your parents that I want to give you this." Bill then handed Susan a box containing a 2-carat-plus diamond ring. He immediately dropped to his knees and formally proposed to my daughter in the house chamber. Thankfully she said yes. So in addition to being the young congresswoman from New York, she was now the newly engaged congresswoman. As parents we were thrilled, and Marguerite didn't have to resort to kidnapping a dog.

Susan had been married once before but the marriage did not work out. They were both very young, had no children, and as soon as she moved to Washington she got divorced. So this seemed to be a match made in heaven since she and Bill were both in love with the political world as well as each other. They were both seen as up and comers in the Republican Party and Bill wanted to shepherd Susan's career in Congress.

CHAPTER 45

The Feerick Four

I CAME TO KNOW ABOUT THE HEARTBREAKING CASE OF Lieutenant Patricia Feerick and her officers from Tony Garvey, who was the President of the Lieutenants Benevolent Association. He was outraged that Pat and three of her officers were convicted in a sham of a prosecution based on an investigation she conducted while she was the lieutenant in charge of the Street Narcotics Units in the 25th Precinct located in Harlem. The investigation concerned a stolen police radio that had fallen into the hands of a homicidal drug organization called "Purple City." This crack gang, known for its deep purple crack vial caps, was responsible for at least seven murders in their pursuit to maintain their $14 million a year drug empire.

In a total travesty of justice, on October 3rd 1994, Lieutenant Feerick received an unprecedented two-year jail term on misdemeanor convictions in relation to the investigation she oversaw. The officers' sentences were stayed pending the outcome of the appeal, but if unsuccessful Pat would be serving her time on Rikers Island, a hell hole of a prison for a young, White, female police lieutenant.

On October 6th, 1994 Pat and her officers, against the advice of their attorneys, spoke out for the first time after their sentencing. For three years their voices had been silenced and they had lost everything as a result. They held a press conference at the PBA headquarters. For the first time, the public saw a video tape taken on May 3, 1991 of the main prosecution witness, Ben Stokes selling crack while cooperating with the Manhattan District Attorney's office. Yet, during the trial Stokes testified that he was no longer involved in the "Purple City" gang. In direct contradiction to his testimony the tape clearly showed Stokes selling crack to a woman pushing a baby in a stroller and making dozens of crack drug sales in broad daylight. Also seen on this tape were two other main prosecution witnesses, Maribel Delgado and Monty Jimenez, purchasing drugs from Stokes. Delgado, a felon drug dealer and crack addict was Stokes' girlfriend. Jimenez was a sixty-year-old crack head who testified at trial that he did not know Stokes.

Jurors in the trial did not see that videotape since the attorneys for the police officers put up absolutely no defense. It will always boggle my mind how they could be so stupid not to introduce this tape into evidence. Only after the trial was the truth exposed. Even still, from a legal perspective, it was too late. The damage was already done.

Judge Milton Mollen, the same man who oversaw the Mollen Commission was outraged with the convictions. The Mollen Commission investigated corrupt officers from the 30th, 9th, 46th, 75th, and 73rd precincts who were caught stealing and selling drugs, beating suspects, stealing guns, etc., during the same time period. When Judge Mollen heard about Pat's case he was flabbergasted. Judge Mollen asked his good friend, Jack Newfield a very liberal—typically anti-cop reporter—to check out the story. Again, against their attorneys' advice, Pat and her cops sat down with Newfield. They had been quiet for too long. On October 14th Newfield's story hit the newsstand titled, "Drug Gangs Wild Tale Puts Good Cop in Jail." It sparked tremendous publicity.

Everyone knew that for Jack Newfield to be a believer in Pat's story, something had to be seriously wrong. His story added a lot of credibility to Pat's case. It was evident that something was dangerously wrong with the system. Milton Mollen himself said that the whole thing was a disgrace and that their case should have never been criminally prosecuted.

Jay Diamond, a radio show host on WABC, read the article written by Jack Newfield and dedicated an entire radio show to the tragedy. I remember Pat telling me how her mother, Joan, heard Jay Diamond talking about the case on his radio show at two in the morning on October 18th. Jay Diamond wanted to know if anyone had any information about the story. Joan called Pat immediately. Her husband Joe answered the phone, since Pat, who was pregnant, was sleeping. Joan told Joe to call WABC radio immediately Joe called up Jay Diamond but Jay did not believe that Joe was actually Pat's husband. It was really quite funny no matter what Joe said Jay did not believe him. Joe finally woke up Pat and the rest was history.

Throughout the whole debacle, Lieutenant Tony Garvey was the staunchest Police Union President completely dedicated to reversing this gross injustice. After their convictions Tony asked for my support since he personally knew that I was extremely supportive of our police officers and that I fully respected honest, hardworking cops. I was one of the few New York City public officials who supported police officers during the Dinkins era debacle, so it was only natural that he would contact me.

After I spoke to Tony I immediately met with Pat and her officers. I was impressed with their professionalism and genuineness in telling their story. I would have to say it was the most interesting and cohesive group of officers that I had met. They represented a true mosaic of the NYPD: Mayra Schultz was Dominican and born in Washington Heights; Orlando Rosario was Puerto Rican and born in the Lower East Side; John DeVito was Italian born in Queens; and Pat was Irish/Lithuanian living in Queens. They were crushed by the convictions yet they were totally committed to clearing their good names.

In the summer of 1990, Pat was a Lieutenant with the NYPD assigned to the 25th Precinct in East Harlem. The residents of Taino Towers, a low income housing project consisting of four thirty-five story towers, were having their lives sucked from them, as they were terrorized by the crack dealing gang known as Purple City.

After the local residents approached the 25th Precinct Commander Officer Deputy Inspector William Friedlieb for help, he assigned Pat the duty of coordinating efforts to eliminate the Purple City gang. Her units did a tremendous job of affecting the arrest of hundreds of drug dealers, buyers, and most importantly, high-level members of the organization. Due to their efforts, life had significantly improved for the residents of Taino Towers, and as a result the Purple City hierarchy loathed Pat's unit. Yet, as with any massive drug organization, Purple City was able to rebound to continue peddling poison in the area. In order for the good to prevail, it had to be a continuing effort to eradicate the drug organization.

On the night of September 22nd, 1990, Pat, Orlando, Mayra, and John were making routine drug arrests in the area of Taino Towers. The cops could see that business was booming for Purple City. While they were effecting narcotics arrests in front of Taino Towers, a riot ensued, and the drug gang stole a police radio from Officer DeVito.

An active investigation was initiated regarding the stolen police radio. Over the course of the next four days, the Purple City gang utilized the stolen radio to transmit threats directed at the narcotics enforcement officers, as well as interfering with critical police transmissions. In order to try and get the radio back, intense pressure was put on the drug organization. Multiple nonstop arrests were made until Purple City was basically shut down.

As a result of the arrests, one of the drug dealers became an informant. She stated she was in a "stash apartment" located in Taino Towers complex on September 24th, 1990 and heard a police radio.

She also said she saw a high ranking member of the Purple City gang named "Ben" in possession of thousands of vials of crack and guns. Based upon her information, a search warrant was obtained by Manhattan North Narcotics, and when it was executed under the supervision of Lieutenant John Comparetto of Manhattan north Narcotics, they came up dry, since the informant gave them the wrong apartment number.

The investigation continued. On the afternoon of September 26th, 1990, Lt Feerick with her officers conducted a canvass of the Taino Towers complex. During the course of the canvass they knocked on a door which was answered by a woman identified as Denise Jackson. Not wanting to be seen by her neighbors, Jackson told the officers to come into her apartment.

The officers immediately knew it was a crack den, as the place was filthy and littered with empty crack vials. They asked Jackson if she knew anything about a stolen police radio. She said that she did not, but that maybe "Ben," a drug dealer that rented one of her bedrooms, might know something about it. Pat and her officers then finished their building canvass and exited the building.

Upon exiting the building, they saw Ben Stokes, a Purple City "lieutenant," in the rear courtyard. He was carrying a bag and walking toward the tower that the officers were exiting. Seeing four police officers in uniform, Stokes dropped his bag and ran.

They were unable to apprehend him but recovered the bag, which contained almost 600 vials of purple capped crack vials and cash. They vouchered the drugs and money, and made out a complaint report for the arrest of Benjamin Stokes. Miraculously as a result of the increased pressure, the stolen radio was anonymously returned at 10 p.m. to security guards in Taino Towers.

Yet unbeknownst to Pat and her officers, just as in the Occhipinti case, a hoax with terrible consequences was being perpetrated against these dedicated officers. Nikki Jackson and Ben Stokes decide to kill two birds with one stone: that is, they would account for the missing crack to the gang, and get rid of the officers that had become such a nuisance to Purple City.

Stokes and Jackson put together what eventually became a story that could only be believed by gullible and incompetent individuals with no discernable street experience, specifically NYPD's Internal Affairs Division (IAD) Lieutenant Kim Foley and Detective Robert Miller. Miller was a twenty-nine-year veteran and Foley, his immediate supervisor, a thirteen-year veteran. They were both career pencil pushers. The 30th Precinct scandal fell under their jurisdiction, and yet, neither of them could find a single crooked cop in the whole precinct. It was clear that the "Dirty Thirty" cops flourished under Foley and Miller. For some inexplicable reason, Foley and Miller turned a blind eye to real corruption, and instead focused their attention on officers who were legitimately fighting the war on drugs.

Hours after the officers had left her residence Jackson set the wheels in motion and filed a false complaint against the officers. When Miller arrived at the scene he met Jackson, who changed her story constantly throughout the entire process. At the time she was the only one to report the fabricated story to IAD. She said that a bunch of unknown police officers forced their way into her apartment and held her hostage.

Stokes went into hiding for several months. On January 5th, 1991, the next time Stokes was observed on the street, Officer Rosario promptly arrested him for the previous crime of possession of almost 600 vials of crack. At the time of his arrest, Stokes was again in possession of purple capped crack vials. On January 11th, 1991, a grand jury indicted Stokes on the felony charge of possession of narcotics with the intent to sell. As far as the cops were concerned, they had done a great job in recovering the radio, and the arrest of the drug dealer Stokes. As far as the cops were concerned, the case was closed. Yet for Foley and Miller this was only the beginning.

On January 7th, 1991 the Manhattan District Attorney's office sent formal notice to the Police Department that they would not prosecute the police officers criminally, and any disciplinary action should be handled internally through an administrative investigation. Their actions, however, did not support this statement. In January, each of the officers was interrogated by the IAD.

In New York State when police officers are questioned in an administrative hearing, they are compelled to answer questions or face immediate dismissal. It is for this reason that any information obtained from these compelled interrogations cannot be utilized in a criminal prosecution, in order to preserve an officer's Fifth Amendment rights.

In complete disregard for the laws of the state, IAD used these interviews as a scheme to generate leads and witnesses for a criminal prosecution. During the course of their interview investigator Foley was informed that Officer Rosario had arrested Stokes for possession of almost 600 crack vials. They were humiliated to learn that Orlando had legally arrested Stokes.

Foley immediately informed the A.D.A. Larry Stephen, the chief of newly formed Anti-Corruption Unit of the Manhattan District Attorney's office who had initially declined to prosecute the officers. The Feerick case was the first one they ever investigated. Stephen's office reached out to Stokes. The D.A. made a deal with Stokes, an admitted drug kingpin, and set him free in exchange for his fabricated testimony against the officers. The D.A. dismissed the felony indictment against Stokes, for which he could have been sentenced to twenty-five years to life.

Over the course of the next four years the drug dealers' and crack heads' stories continued to change until Miller, Foley, the drug dealers, and the D.A. were happy with the final contrived, yet still inconsistent, version presented at their criminal trial. During this time, Stokes was given free rein to poison the community with crack, as was shown by the videotape.

In 1992 Pat and her officers were arrested on an absurd thirty-one count indictment and placed on modified assignment. Two years later, they went to trial.

One of the most disheartening and traitorous events that occurred was that Inspector Friedlieb never advocated on behalf of his brave officers. Had he done his job as a Commanding Officer and defended the excellent police work of his officers, this case would have been nipped in the bud. Instead when Pat confronted Friedlieb and asked him, "What are you doing to protect us from this outrageous investigation? We were only doing the job you asked us to do!" Friedlieb's response was, "Let IAD do their job." He will always be a coward in my book. They did a dangerous job and when the shit hit the fan the man who sent them into it abandoned them. Duty, honor, and loyalty were clearly nonexistent traits of Inspector Friedlieb.

In May of 1994, they had a jury trial before Judge Bonnie Wittner. It was sad to see how wickedly twisted the D.A.'s perception of corruption was. The pathetic A.D.A.s prosecuting the case, John Dormin and Thomas Hickey, were relentless in their defense of the integrity and credibility of drug related criminals, yet vilified the courageous police officers. At trial all the main prosecution witnesses were admitted drug users and/or dealers associated with the Purple City gang. Each witness gave contradictory testimony to events. In A.D.A. Dormin's closing statement he asked the jury to disregard the testimony of the chief investigator Miller, and rely solely on the testimony of Jackson and Stokes, convicted felons and drug dealers.

It was clear that Miller and Foley had ignored the most rudimentary investigative steps in a criminal investigation. They based the investigation solely on the statements of Jackson, a convicted felon and crack head, who at the time of the incident had her children placed in the custody of the Bureau of Child Welfare, because she had given birth to a baby addicted to crack. Miller never canvassed the building for an objective witness who was not associated with Purple City. He ignored glaring inconsistencies in the witnesses' interviews, took no fingerprints at the crime scene and vouchered no objective evidence. Had he taken fingerprints in the second apartment, it would have clearly shown that they were never there.

If Miller had interviewed building residents, he would have found unbiased witnesses who would have verified the officers were in fact canvassing the entire building, and were not in Jackson's apartment for ten hours.

Tragically the cops' attorneys did not want anyone to testify at trial since they were adamant that it was not necessary. It was a horrible misjudgment on their part. The attorneys were of the mindset that no one would ever believe a drug dealer or a crack head. Pat argued aggressively to testify since she was the supervisor, but since it was a joint trial she had to go along with what the attorneys for all the cops collectively wanted. The attorneys put up absolutely no defense. They never admitted the tape that showed major prosecution witnesses dealing and using crack, which was a tragic decision on the part of the attorneys. The attorneys took a crap shoot with four cop's lives and lost.

I know in my heart and soul that had the officers testified they would never have been convicted. They are all honorable and credible hard working individuals. All of them had stellar backgrounds. They were the type of cops we wanted patrolling our city streets. It drove me crazy when Pat told me how the lawyers always said, "You can't say anything. You can't testify before the grand jury. Don't worry about it, don't do this, don't do that," just because it was standard operating procedure for cop lawyers at the time.

Yet on May 25th 1994 they were found guilty of several crimes in relation to the investigation they conducted. The attorneys walked out of the courtroom free men, and Pat and her officers left as convicted criminals. A poll of the jury after trial showed that they made a compromise verdict. After three days of sequestered deliberation, they wanted to get out of the courtroom for Memorial Day weekend and sold their souls. Three jurors wept as they read the verdict.

In October 1994, when Judge Bonnie Wittner sentenced them, she inferred that because of their impeccable backgrounds she would judge them more harshly than the common criminal. She wanted to send a message out to the law enforcement community. Well, the message was never received. Instead, the phrase "20 and Out" became the call of NYPD officers; that is, serve your twenty years on the force and then get out before you got screwed.

After I met with them, I asked my staff to investigate the case and try to find exculpatory evidence that could help on their legal appeal. Chris Johns, one of my investigators at the time, went to Taino Towers and interviewed the prosecution witnesses. Although it was three years after the incident, nothing had changed for the neighborhood or the complainants. Everything that Pat and her officers told me checked out. It was a terrible miscarriage of justice.

I immediately decided that we would hold rallies to support them and do whatever we could to help reverse the convictions. I had Dan Master, my counsel, contact the appellate attorneys and we started on the long and arduous path to trying to reverse the convictions.

On Tuesday November 15th, 1994 the Lieutenants Benevolent Association took out a full page ad in the New York Post as follows:

**WHEN WE TRUST CRIMIALS OVER COPS,
THE FIGHT AGAINST CRIME IS OVER**

> Each day we ask our police officers to face-off against criminals in our city. And each day they heed the call. But when the time comes to support our police officers, we turn our back.
>
> It sounds incredible, but this is what happened with the recent conviction of three New York City Police Officers and one NYPD Lieutenant. Following an investigation for a stolen police radio, these officers were accused of mistreating several residents of Taino Towers on East 122nd St. in Manhattan. The greatest insult came when the judge sentenced three of the four officers to jail time. Shockingly, the Lieutenant

> was given two consecutive one year terms for misdemeanors. This sentence came from the same judge who released a man with convictions for two separate gun felonies, crimes which demand mandatory one-year jail sentences.
>
> **SIMPLY PUT, OUR POLICE OFFICERS DESERVE BETTER THAN THIS.** Especially individuals as highly accomplished as Lieutenant Patricia Feerick and Police Officers Mayra Schultz, Orlando Rosario and John DeVito. Lieutenant Feerick, who is a registered nurse, was at the top of the Captain's list at the time of the incident. In her 13 years on the force, Feerick received 12 commendations, earned a law degree and taught search and seizure at the Police Academy.
>
> How can we expect Police Officers, who willingly perform the worst jobs under the worst conditions to respond to betrayal? How can we expect them to aggressively pursue drug dealers and felons when they know the criminal justice system will not back them up? There is no doubt that if upheld, theses convictions will have a chilling effect on every law enforcement officer in the New York City.
>
> New York has one choice in our struggle against crime, drugs and the collapse of our quality of life. We must work as a team with the police officers who protect us. We must fight alongside them against crime. Above all, we must support them.

Tony Garvey and I were unwavering in our support of Pat and her officers. It could be interpreted as too late, but we were there emotionally for a fractured police department and its members. Tony Garvey learned many valuable lessons from Pat's case that would benefit his officers in the future. The key one being sometimes you have to say to hell with the lawyers; if you are innocent, you have to speak up and be heard. Tony was that voice and so was I.

On Friday October 27th Curtis Sliwa took his Guardian Angels to Taino Towers and he had petitions signed in support of Pat and her officers. As part of Curtis's mission, I had members of my office go up to Harlem to get signatures as well. Thousands of people signed the petitions on that day. The drug dealers receded into their dark dens while the good residents of Taino Towers came out in support of the officers.

On December 3rd, 1994 I held a massive rally for Pat and her officers. Chief Kevin Farrell sat on the dais in support of the officers. Hundreds of supporters showed up. Curtis Sliwa, Assemblyman Tony Seminario, Steven McDonald, Joe Occhipinti, Michael O'Keefe, countless other public officials, but most importantly the residents from Taino Towers made the trip to Staten Island in support of Pat and her officers. At least they knew that they were supported for their efforts and the good people recognized that the case was a disgrace.

In the latter part of my involvement in the case I received a letter from recently retired Lieutenant John Comparetto. During trial, the prosecution said the officers wrote, "We want the fucking radio back" on Jacksons living room wall. Lt. Comparetto was the Lieutenant who supervised the search warrant that was executed that emanated from the informant that was arrested. While executing the search warrant Lt. Comparetto saw the same exact writing in a different abandoned apartment in the Taino Towers complex that was used by the drug dealers. That wall had written on it, "We want the fucking radio back." Feerick's team had never been in the part of the Towers. So it was clearly not the "Feerick Four" who wrote on Jackson's wall. In fact it was the hierarchy of the drug organization that wanted the stolen radio returned because the pressure that was put on their operations was crippling their crack dealing business. They wanted to get the officers off their backs.

While on the force, Lt. Comparetto asked permission from the New York City Police Department hierarchy to give that information to me to use in court, and he was turned down. They wouldn't let him do it. I was stunned that they would deliberately refuse to give something that was going to help prove the officers' innocence. When Lt. Comparetto retired he submitted an affidavit attesting to what he saw, yet the courts ultimately ignored it. Lt. Comparetto tried multiple times to do the right thing to no avail.

At the time no one would have guessed that it would take over five years for the appellate process to be over with. Pat's case was the epitome of the wheels of justice grinding slowly, or in Pat's case, not at all.

CHAPTER 46

A Breath of Fresh Air

One of the greatest accomplishments of my political career was the fact that I was able to permanently close the Fresh Kills landfill, more commonly known as the Staten Island Dump. People today forget how bad it really was. In order to understand what a great triumph it was, one has to look at the entire history of this horrendous eyesore that stained the whole landscape of Staten Island for over fifty years.

As you know, when I was a teenager, my father, S. Robert Molinari, was an assemblyman from 1943 to 1944. I remember him fighting vigorously to stop what then was being proposed as a temporary landfill which was to be located on the west shore of Staten Island. My father adamantly said at the time that, "It will never be here for a year or two. It will be here forever! It is a terrible idea and we should do everything in our power to stop it." In the 1940s our borough was seen as insignificant. At that time the population of Staten Island was only 175,000, while the rest of the City encompassed over 7,000,000 people. By sheer numbers alone it is easy to see how the other boroughs stifled Staten Island's voice. The rest of the city saw Staten Island as the perfect place to hide a massive garbage dump.

As much as the garbage dump consumed my father's attention, there were pressing matters of national security in relation to World War II that preoccupied the nation and the residents of New York City.

Politicians from the other boroughs who fought for the garbage dump to be in Staten Island harped on the fact that the proposed site for the landfill was remote and not surrounded by residential communities. At the time that was true, but as decades passed and the population of Staten Island almost tripled, the area surrounding the landfill became populated.

Unfortunately, the alleged "temporary" Fresh Kills landfill formally opened on April 16th, 1948. Well, as we all know, these few years turned into over half a century. Since the beginning, the horrendous stench from the landfill was an everyday nightmare for the residents of Staten Island. In the sweltering summer the smell assaulted a person's respiratory system making the prospect of being outdoors in that area or downwind from the area unthinkable. In addition, packs of feral dogs roamed the dumps and the surrounding areas became hazardous. Finally, the rat population exploded in the dumps and spread to nearby neighborhoods, so much so that people believed the rats would take over the island.[19]

Anything associated with the landfill was completely ignored by the other boroughs for decades even though it was clear that it was an ecologic disaster for the residents of Staten Island. No state or federal environmental group gave a damn about the impact on the community and the only people who cared about the effects of this

---

19 *At that time, some genius came up with a novel idea to handle the rodent problem: They brought in specific predatory birds to eat the rats such as hawks, falcons, and owls. There was a significant reduction in the rat population as a result of the predatory birds. A comedic irony of this festering eyesore was that the entire area encompassing this massive garbage dump was categorized as an actual bird sanctuary during this time to protect the birds.*

disaster were the people who lived under the acrid clouds of smoldering decomposing garbage on a daily basis.

The landfill itself was over 2,200 acres and was composed of four sections. These sections ranged in height from ninety, to approximately two hundred twenty-five feet. It was the world's largest landfill. At its peak, almost 16,000 tons of garbage were dumped into the landfill on a daily basis. The facility became so large that the workers navigating the dump had to create a new infrastructure to continue to get rid of the waste. Garbage trucks and barges continuously brought trash in 24 hours a day, 365 days a year. As a result, it spewed poison onto Staten Island. The smell, like the endless stream of incoming garbage, was omnipresent.

It was a constant embarrassment to all the residents of Staten Island no matter where they lived. When people came to visit Staten Island residents, many of the visitors had to drive along the West Shore Expressway. This expressway cut right through the Fresh Kills landfill. Invariably the drivers would have to close their car windows because of the gross stench. The memory of their visit to Staten Island was always overshadowed by the massive mountains covered with tens of thousands of seagulls flying around. If you took your visitors to the Staten Island Mall you would have to run with them from your car into the mall because the stench was so overpowering.

To add insult to injury, plastic bags and debris flew all over the dump into the surrounding community. The city had erected tall garbage retention fences, but once the bags flew over the fence no one cleaned them up because no one took responsibility. You would see thousands of trees with branches filled with empty plastic bags hanging from the limbs instead of green leaves.

I remember one day in the summer, my wife and I got out of our car in front of our apartment in Bay Terrace and the odor was so bad that we couldn't breathe. Bay Terrace was quite a distance from the dump yet we had to actually run to the entrance of our home. We were both choking when we got inside. That was the kind of thing that was assaulting our residents on a daily basis. Not a soul should have to live under those conditions, but that's the way it was. Nobody cared about the consequences of the dump except the residents of Staten Island.

Although I had tried numerous measures to address the closing of the dump as a state legislator, congressman, and finally borough president under Mayor Dinkins, my attempts fell on deaf ears. It may sound ridiculous Staten Island was continually dumped on because of the dump. In other words, Staten Island lost a lot of political respect because of the Fresh Kills landfill.

When Rudy Giuliani beat Dinkins in 1994, Staten Island was now in the hands of a mayor who actually cared about Staten Island and respected its residents. I had also just chaired the New York City campaign for our new governor, George Pataki who took office on January 1st, 1995. I knew in my heart and soul that if we all put our heads together on many issues, things could take a 180-degree turn. It was a perfect scenario and now I thought perhaps some real miracles could be done for Staten Island and its residents.

That is when the "what if" issues became a reality. "What could we do if Giuliani won?" What could we do if Pataki won?" Well, Giuliani and Pataki won. So now Staten Island was at a crossroads. There were a whole host of issues at the time, yet in my mind, most paramount was the infamous dump. In fact, by the 1990s it had become so huge that it could be seen from satellites in outer space. My staff and I had many meetings to put forth items on a so-called "wish list" that we wanted to accomplish. Regarding the dump, the more people who said we couldn't get rid of it, the more I said we could. We just had to figure out how to do it.

The spark that lit the ultimate fire was in February 1996 when I learned that the city was actually spending valuable money on printing tour brochures to help the curious tourist navigate the world's biggest garbage dump. Apparently a deranged consultant suggested to the city that allowing visitors to the landfill might make the landfill more palatable to Staten Island residents. I went ballistic when I heard this proposal. This was the final straw.

Assistant Commissioner of the Sanitation Department Lucian Chalfen actually stated to the press, "The tour is meant for people to get a broader understanding of the landfill, and we encourage people who live around it to tour it also." In response to the Department of Sanitation's godforsaken thought process I had Daniel Master, my legal counsel, write a scathing letter that was printed in the *New York Times*. In the letter he debased the Department of Sanitation and concluded the letter as follows:

Mr. Chalfen's suggestion about the dump, that "people who live around it" should "tour it," is, for Staten islanders the last straw. Might I suggest that those like Mr. Chalfen who tour the dump should live around it for a few years. Maybe then city administrators like Mr. Chalfen will wake up and smell the methane.

Around that time, I had a secret meeting with my senior staff early in the morning and told them that with Mayor Giuliani and Governor George Pataki, I knew if we were ever going to be able to accomplish anything with regards to closing this dump, that was the time.

We looked at the Federal Clean Air Act. My Chief of Staff Dan Donovan, and my counsel, Daniel Masters, came up with a novel plan where we would institute a lawsuit in both federal and state courts. The federal suit would be based on the Federal Clean Air Act because of the five tons of methane gas the dump emitted daily.

The state suit fell under the "fair-share" provision of the New York City Charter. Over the course of several years, due to environmental regulation violations, all the other boroughs were able to get their incinerators and landfills closed. As a result, Fresh Kills received 100% of the city's residential garbage violating the provisions in the city charter, which required that the five boroughs share equally in the city's burdens. A common phrase regarding our predicament was, "All the garbage New York City makes, Staten Island takes."

Under the provisions of the Federal Clean Air Act you had to give sixty days' notice to the authority that you were suing. So I called up Peter Powers who was the First Deputy Mayor under Giuliani and

I said, "Peter, I just want to give you a heads up. We are suing the mayor."

Peter was pissed and said, "Why are you doing this? Why are you suing the mayor? Rudy is your friend." I said, "Yes, we are friends, but I have to sue on behalf of my Staten Island constituents under the Federal Clean Air Act. It is a friendly lawsuit. If I take this approach I believe that we will be able to get rid of the Fresh Kills Dump. I do not want Rudy to take it personal."

On March 25th, 1996, as promised, I tried something new and asked a federal judge to shut down the landfill permanently by formally filing the lawsuit. I sued New York Mayor Rudolph Giuliani, New York City Sanitation Commissioner John Doherty, Gov. George Pataki, and State Environmental Conservation Commissioner Michael Zagata. I was encouraged when the press interviewed Mayor Giuliani immediately after the suit was filed and Rudy stated, "I understand the problems that people in Staten Island have about the dump getting larger and larger, and it's going on what appears to be endlessly, and we'll work with them to try to find a rational solution." Unlike his predecessors at least he gave a damn.

No one knew this at the time, but in the back of mind I thought that if I could the dump closed within ten years I would consider it a great accomplishment. This monstrosity could be dealt with. The key was to get everyone to finally agree to close it. So we started negotiating with the mayor and his administration. Things then took a positive turn and we got real serious about how we would do this.

Immediately after filing the suit, on April 2nd Mayor Giuliani publically stated the landfill would not be a tourist attraction. He did this after I told the mayor that Staten Island was repulsed with the Sanitation Departments' proposal to offer regular tours of the world's largest garbage dump. My constituents were outraged rather than shutting it down, it would instead be promoted as a tourist attraction. Mayor Giuliani grasped the negative aspects immediately and assured me that it would never come to pass. As such he formally announced that public tours were never going to happen. It is amazing how detached the Sanitation Department was to the residents of Staten Island.

Regarding the actual closing of the dump, there were still major issues for the mayor to tackle, especially figuring out what to do with the almost 16,000 tons of garbage generated each day? You couldn't just close the gate and walk away. Closing the 2,200-acre landfill would cost the city more than $1 billion. Covering and sealing the vast trash heaps would take about five years. Also an intricate network of sophisticated equipment would have to be constructed to protect surrounding neighborhoods from the foul gases and water emanating from the rotting refuse.

So there were many obstacles to overcome, but Mayor Giuliani, true to his nature, said to his staff, "We were put here to do miracles, so let's do this." Every day my staff worked with Giuliani's staff to work out the difficult details of such an enormous task. We had to work with other States to get them to accept New York City's trash. Eventually after intense negotiations all the details were worked out.

It wasn't an easy process; there were times when tempers flared. I remember a specific time involving Randy Mastro, Rudy's Deputy Mayor of Operations. Randy interestingly was a registered die hard Democrat serving a Republican mayor. I wanted specific steps to be followed before the final closing in 2001. Each year I wanted sections of the dump to be closed prior to the final closing. In other words, the city would dump less and less garbage there each year. I did not want five years to go by and at the end of five years nothing was done. The city didn't want to go along with the gradual closing proposal, yet I was representing the Island, and I had to push for it. God forbid Giuliani or Pataki was not reelected and another administration came in. I needed to know that the plan would move forward no matter what.

On the day in question, Randy was negotiating with Dan Donovan. I was home sick with the flu. Danny called me and said, "I'm here with Randy Mastro and..." I said, "Put him on." Even though I didn't want to talk to anybody because I was feeling terrible, I knew I had to speak to him since the issue was so important.

I said, "Randy, what the hell is going on?" Randy said, "I understand what you're asking for, but it's unreasonable. You can't tell us what we have to..."

I cut him off and screamed, "Randy, I'm not gonna ask you, I'm telling you. It's got to go in there. I don't care how you do it, just get the fucking thing done." With that, I slammed the phone down since I did not want to hear anymore. Immediately afterwards, of course I was wondering what was going on at the meeting. Within a few hours Danny called me up and said, "It's done. You got it."

After all these negotiations a solid initial plan was finally agreed upon. We came up with five years, not the ten years that was always in the back of my mind. So it was even better than I expected.

On May 29th, 1996 a press conference consisting of all Republicans was held. Present was Mayor Rudy Giuliani, Governor George Pataki, my daughter, Susan, and myself. The Democrats were pissed, but the fact was to be history: Republicans would ultimately be responsible for closing the dump. At the press conference, Mayor Giuliani and Governor Pataki announced that they had reached an accord that they would definitely close the Fresh Kills Landfill by December 31st, 2001. They both stated they would create a task force of city, state and federal officials who would devise a viable plan to close the dump by the established date. They said that the task force would report back to their offices by October 1st, and present feasible alternatives to disposing of New York City's garbage as well as a realistic closure plan.

When I heard their words publicly spoken, I remember thinking Staten Island's toughest fight has been won against the nation's worst environmental nightmare. There is no greater gift that we can give to the people of Staten Island than what we are giving them today: the covenant that the landfill will be closed. With a Republican governor and a Republican mayor, we were able to do things that we only dreamt about before. That's the way party politics works.

Rudy Giuliani, George Pataki, and I created what is now known as "the perfect storm." Without one of us, the dump would never have been closed. In this situation, instead of "People Power" it was "Political Relationship Power" that got the job done. In Giuliani's words, "If you didn't have Guy Molinari, you would not have the driving force for decades to get it done." Rudy was right; I saw the perfect opportunity after decades of trying to deal with this catastrophe. We were able to move barriers, and then create this miracle for the residents of Staten Island

Immediately after the announcement, as a consequence of being the driving force behind the deal, I would play a pivotal role in almost every city decision involving the future of the disposal of the city's garbage. I conferred with the Deputy Mayor for Operations, initially Randy Maestro and then Joe Lhota, four or five times a week on the issue. I hired consultants to monitor city garbage policies. I talked frequently about possible disposal sites with political leaders and landfill owners. I also conferred on a weekly basis with new Sanitation Commissioner, Kevin Farrell. It was based upon my recommendation that Farrell became the New Sanitation commissioner. Farrell often said, "Fresh Kills will close even if I have to close it myself." So it was clear that we were on the same page. The process for final closure was not an easy path, and many hurdles over the ensuing years would occur. Yet the fateful highly anticipated day would inevitably come since the key political players were still in power.

Fast forward to March 22nd, 2001. That date can be described as one of the greatest days of my political career, if not the greatest. I succeeded in completing a task which other Staten Island politicians didn't have the nerve or stamina to complete. The dump was finally closed. The city had in fact exceeded the milestones that were written into the original agreement and the dump closed early. It was closed in four years and three months, even better than the five-year deadline which we agreed upon.

There was a big ceremony at the garbage dump. One last garbage scow came into port. I stood together with my daughter, Mayor Giuliani, and Governor Pataki in the rain as we watched the final barge of trash float down the Arthur Kill. Instead of being dumped on our Island, New York's almost 16,000 daily tons of trash would now be sent to landfills and incinerators outside the city.

We all stood under a banner which said, "A Promise Made, A Promise Kept." Now Staten Island would be known for its beautiful parks, golf courses, and great views of Manhattan instead of its garbage dump. Joe Lhota was the master of ceremonies. Only three people spoke on that day: Mayor Giuliani, Governor Pataki, and me. My heart swelled when Mayor Giuliani stated, "I've already determined I want to retire here."

I could only think how far Staten Island had come in my lifetime. It was just a wonderful day. That was probably one of the happiest days in the history of Staten Island.

Today people who are looking for a different way of life in New York City now look at Staten Island again. We see people buying homes that are very expensive and we see the better side of Staten Island coming forward. I think since the day that the Fresh Kills Dump closed it's a different borough. It's a better borough. We've still got a long way to go, but the closure of the garbage dump has to be one of the most positive events that ever took place here.

And, as a side note, I'm still waiting for Rudy to buy a home here.

CHAPTER 47

Thank You, Susan

On May 10th 1996 at 10:15 p.m. my beautiful granddaughter, Susan Ruby Paxton, was born at Staten Island University Hospital. She was named after my wife's mother Susan, and Bill's mother, Ruby. As a result, the families have affectionately called her Suby for the majority of her life.

On Saturday July 15th, 1996, my granddaughter was christened in Akron, New York a small town outside Buffalo. It was a small intimate affair consisting of close family and friends. After the luncheon honoring Suby, I made the long drive home to Staten Island with my wife. It was a serene ride home since we both felt so proud that our family was growing. Marguerite rarely left the house by this time due to her illness but we both knew that she had to go to her granddaughter's christening. Being new grandparents is an experience that mimics the miraculous birth of your own children, yet it is different in a special way, since it is your own child who has now emerged as the all-important parent in their world. On the long drive home our time was consumed with talking about how happy and proud we were of Susan's embracement of motherhood, how cute Suby was, and how far Susan had risen as an important Republican congresswoman. As such, the long drive disappeared as we basked in our good fortune. In fact, we did not think we could be any prouder on that day. Well, we were wrong. Susan's life was always full of surprises.

When we left to go home my daughter and her husband took a rare night off, and left Suby with Bill's parents to go out to dinner with friends in a local tavern in Williamsville, New York. In the event of an emergency Bill's parents had their beeper numbers. Lo and behold during dinner Bill's beeper went off. Susan told me that they both immediately panicked because they thought something happened with their daughter. Fortunately, when Bill looked at the number on his beeper it was a number from someone in Bill's staff. They both breathed a sigh of relief since it was just a "political crisis."

When Bill called his office they yelled into the phone, "I'm listening to Larry King Live and I think Bob Dole just announced that Sue is going to be the keynote speaker." Susan's jaw dropped when she heard the news that presidential candidate, Robert Dole announced to the nation on live TV that he had a dynamite keynote speaker selected for the Republican Convention, to be held in San Diego California in less than a month, named Susan Molinari.

Wham! Just like that another whirlwind event started with a simple chirp on a beeper. Susan actually accepted the invitation over a pay phone from the bar while Bob Dole was being interviewed on the Larry King Live Show. It is funny to think how far technology has come in only twenty short years—beepers and pay phones seem so outdated today—yet back in the day they could change your world in a flash.

The general consensus at the time was that Bob Dole's campaign wasn't going very well and everyone kind of felt that the selection of Susan was a good shot in the arm for him. Immediately after the announcement the *New York Post* ran a front-page story headlined, "Susan to the Rescue." I was amazed at the degree of support that she engendered as a congresswoman in such a brief period of time from

New Yorkers. It was abundantly clear that not only did Staten Island love Susan, New York State was super proud of her as well.

People saw my daughter as the "sweetheart" of the Republican Party. She was young, energetic, a new mother, and she was juggling so many plates at the same time, with what seemed like flawless ease, that the public became captivated by her persona and she endeared herself to the public. She had risen in Congress with meteoric speed to a position of power fueled by her personal warmth and the innate ability to cross party and ideological lines in an effort to represent her generation of moderate, pro-choice, Republican women. At the time Susan was considered the most powerful woman in Congress. It was the bolster that Dole's campaign needed at the time. Fresh young blood to heat up the presidential race.

The Dole campaign supplied a suite of rooms at the Marriott Hotel and of course as her father I was afforded the privilege of staying at her side. Several days before the speech we arrived at the Marriot. Susan was then charged with the incredible task of writing a memorable, down to earth keynote address that would energize Dole's campaign.

I had been involved in so many campaigns over the course of my career, yet l was amazed with the racket that was taking place within this suite of rooms: typewriters clicking like crazy, computers buzzing, faxes coming in, and the constant ringing of telephones throughout the chaos. It was a beehive of activity with no break for relaxation. I thought to myself how the hell anyone could get a bit of sleep in the bloody place. As a father I was concerned for my daughter, but as I watched my daughter very closely I was amazed at the way that she was able to operate with all that confusion going on. When I looked at Susan she was a cool cat. I was nervous...she wasn't.

Since my wife was unable to attend the event due to health concerns, Susan made sure that Marguerite was part of this epic event. Susan religiously called Marguerite to update her on the events of the day and also to fill her in with Suby stories. These calls were the highlight of my wife's day.

Susan's accomplishments always gave Marguerite something positive to focus on. On this night, the entire nation would be listening to her daughter as she was given the coveted spot to deliver the keynote address.

So, on the evening of August 13th, 1996 I experienced the greatest day of my life. It is a night I will never forget. My only child was going to deliver the keynote address at the 1996 Republican National Convention. When the time came for us to leave the hotel and go to the convention hall, we walked together and we sat together. I will never be able to adequately express the intense feelings that I had as a father walking with her from her hotel to the convention hall. Yet Susan didn't seem to be nervous at all and walked with great confidence. I was so proud to be at my daughter's side.

The only thing that really pissed me off that day was the person who preceded her speech, Congressman John Kasich, now Governor John Kasich of Ohio. His speech went over time and it seriously disrupted the itinerary.

I knew that the Dole campaign had done a wonderful video story about Susan. It was to be shown just before she spoke, but because Kasich took so long they had to scratch the video. The keynote address was specifically slotted for the most coveted time period in prime time TV. Susan was scheduled to speak at precisely 10:42 p.m., immediately before the 11pm news. Yet because of Kasich's disregard for the schedule he disrupted the meticulous schedule to bolster himself. It was not received well by the Republican Campaign at the time. They had put a lot of work into the video they couldn't show because of his selfishness.

As we watched Susan deliver her speech, at a certain point in time Bill left his seat so that he would be at Susan's side on the podium immediately after she finished her speech. When he left, Bill handed Suby over to me. As I held Suby in my arms my heart swelled. It was a crazy feeling to have the joy of my life in my arms and at the same time to watch her mommy, my daughter, give such a great speech. So, even though Kasich caused the video to be scrapped, and believe me, I was furious since I was looking forward to it, I was still sitting on top of the world. I had my granddaughter in my arms and my wonderful daughter speaking to the world. It doesn't get any better than that. I believe my daughter did a beautiful job in delivering her speech. My wife said that Susan sparkled on the television screen. When Marguerite watched Susan on TV she cried because she was so proud. So, regardless of the Kasich transgression it was an extraordinary event for our family, particularly for me to see the daughter I love so deeply perform at her absolute best. After her speech we all gathered together on the podium and basked in the excitement of the glorious moment.

After the event I learned that Kasich wouldn't listen to then Governor Christine Whitman from New Jersey to stop his speech since he was going over his allotted time. Governor Whitman did her best to get Kasich to shut up and end his speech, but Kasich ignored her. Susan then showed us the teleprompter. She explained how she was able to avoid a disaster. The teleprompter had been raised for John Kasich the previous speaker who was much taller than Susan. When he finished his speech he "forgot" to bring it down. In my opinion he will always be considered a complete ass for what he did. As an experienced politician you don't make blunders like that.

So when Susan got to the podium, the teleprompter was not positioned properly and she couldn't see it at all. Fortunately, she wrote the speech herself so she knew the words off the top of her head. My daughter had to deliver her speech from memory. So in retrospect her speech was even more amazing since we all assumed that she was looking at the teleprompter, but that wasn't the case. I was completely impressed with how my daughter was able to deliver such a historic speech without the assistance of modern day technology. She will always be a person who can rapidly adjust to unforeseen circumstances without blinking an eye.

As a side note, to this day every time I saw Kasich on TV running for president in 2016, which I never believed he had a chance of being successful, I can only say to the Republican Party, be wary of putting him on the convention itinerary, it could turn into a colossal disaster for the person following him since they may not be as quick on their feet as my daughter was.

CHAPTER 48

Prostate Cancer

I BELIEVE THAT "PROSTATE CANCER" IS A WORD THAT strikes fear in every man's world. It goes to the heart of our manhood. Yet, as important as prostate cancer awareness is, many men will refuse to think about it until the symptoms are unavoidable. I was one of them. Then it is like a sledge hammer hitting you in your gut.

For me the hammer starting falling in 1997. At the time I was starting to have urinary problems, specifically going often and the occasional loss of control. The final straw that opened my eyes was when I was in my car and a driver was taking me to the south shore of Staten Island for a meeting. On the way there I suddenly had to urinate badly. I said to my driver, "Quick! My daughter lives here. Let's go to her house so that I can pee." Well, we pulled up in front of the house and I couldn't hold it any longer and I urinated in my pants. Susan had people in the house, and when I walked in I was wet all over. I was totally humiliated. It was then I knew that it was time for me to consult with a doctor.

The doctor did a Prostate-Specific Antigen test and it came back as "6," which was on the high side. The PSA is a protein produced by cells of the prostate gland. Unfortunately there is no specific normal or abnormal level of PSA in the blood. In 1997, and this is pretty much true today, if a man had a PSA level above 4.0 the doctors would recommend a prostrate biopsy to determine if prostate cancer was present. Since mine was 6 we did a biopsy.

On Monday June 30th 1997 I received a phone call from my doctor regarding the results of the biopsy. He said, "I have bad news for you. You have prostate cancer." So the hammer fell and I heard the Big "C" word. Being practical my next question was, "Well, okay, what do we do?" The doctor told me to come in right way so we could discuss my options such as surgery, seed implantation, chemo, radiation, etc.

The following day, the doctor called me again and gave me more bad news. He said that the cancer was very aggressive and there was no time to lose. We had to act immediately. The doctor had already scheduled me for surgery. I was shocked and said, "Well, wait a second. Yesterday you told me that I should read books to determine the course that I wanted to follow." He said, "Well, if you want to do seeds instead, we'll do seeds. I'll just have to call the hospital."

I didn't feel comfortable with how the doctor was treating me. I didn't want to jump into surgery if it wasn't necessary. I did want to look at options and know what the risks and benefits of each option were. So I said, "No, I don't know what I am going to do, I need a few days to think this thing through." I was wondering why anybody would want to opt for such invasive surgery when you could possibly get the same kind of results from alternative treatments.

I called up Dr. Gil Lederman who was a friend of mine and the Director of Radiology at Staten Island Hospital. He reviewed the results and suggested that I should take a serious look at Brachytherapy or radioactive seed implantation. He was a surgeon himself and he indicated at the time that the implantation of seeds was still relatively new but the results at that time were equally as good as the results being reported from surgery. Dr. Lederman explained that the only problem was that they could only look at about ten years' worth of data as to how Brachytherapy was working. He said so far the results were great, as successful if not more than radical prostate surgery. Additionally, the potential side effects, specifically incontinence and impotence, were significantly less than with radical surgery.

So I had to make a major decision but I also had to deal with the rumors. By that time, it was leaking out to the public that "Guy Molinari has prostate cancer." Being a politician I knew the best course to follow would be to call a press conference and let the world hear it from me to stop all the speculation as to what was going on. As much as I would have liked to have privacy especially in the beginning of an illness, if I didn't have a press conference, I knew the next thing that would happen would be that the press would have me on my deathbed. So, I called a press conference and I explained what was happening and that settled things down.

Of course at the time I was involved in my reelection campaign against Democrat Steve Higgins. Additionally, my daughter's congressional seat was up for grabs since she was stepping down to be a co-anchor of a new Saturday CBS TV news program. The filling of Susan's congressional seat was a hotly contested battle. The Republican candidate, Vito Fossella was selected by the executive committee of the Staten Island Republican Party to run against Democratic Assemblyman Eric Vitaliano. I was actively involved in both races. As I was always an active politician I needed to let everyone know that this disease was not going to slow me down. I would take care of the health issues, but I would continue to be totally politically involved.

I remember my wife being furious that some people were using the prostate cancer to knock me out of contention for continuance in public service. Although she usually stayed in the background since she was physically unable to do a lot of things due to her chronic illness, she felt compelled to write a letter to the *Staten Island Advance* when somebody questioned whether or not I would be able to fill out my term as borough president. In the letter she wrote:

> Like many Staten Islanders who love Guy Molinari, I never expected that his bout with cancer would be raised as a campaign issue. Most would consider that an extremely low tactic...I have watched him working as hard as ever, day and night, seven days a week, doing what he loves to do as borough president...In fact, since the beginning of this entire ordeal, I cannot recall Guy missing a single day of work.

So I went to Staten Island hospital to do some preliminary tests and I ultimately decided upon Brachytherapy (seed implantation). When I underwent the procedure two doctors were doing the implantation of seeds, Dr. Gill Lederman, and a colleague. Although I was under anesthesia during the procedure I can clearly remember one doctor was singing opera. He was awful! I always look back and say I don't know which was worse, seed implantation or being forced to listen to bad opera.

After the procedure was done and I was in the recovery room loaded with ice packs, the original doctor who insisted that I do the radical surgery happened to walk by my stretcher. He asked how I was doing, and wanted to know how many seeds I received. I told him I thought it was around 110. He started joking with another doctor nearby about how Dr. Lederman hit me heavy. Obviously I had no reference as to whether this was a lot or not. Funny thing is almost seventeen years later, it's clear Dr. Lederman and I made the right call since I have not had another problem with my prostate.

While I was in the recovery room there was a guy next to me in a hospital bed and he looked over to me and said, "Hey! Mr. Molinari! I want to thank you." I didn't know who the hell he was since I didn't recognize the guy, so I said, "For what?"

He then proceeded to tell me, "I know they gave you the false name of Fitzgerald when they checked you into the hospital for security reasons. Well my name is actually Fitzgerald, and I was going to have to wait six weeks to have this done. Yet they called me yesterday and said that they had me scheduled for today. It was only after I got here that they realized that I was the wrong Fitzgerald. I got my procedure moved up six weeks because of your pseudonym. I can't thank you enough." We both laughed that it worked out better for him just because of the phony name.

When Dr. Lederman checked up on me after the procedure I asked him when I could go back to work. He said I could go to work the following Monday which was the third day after the procedure. He said, "Just make sure you have a bathroom nearby." Well I had a bathroom in my office in Borough Hall so I met that test.

Unfortunately, on that Monday when I went to my office to work after the implantation I had another embarrassing situation. I was on my way to work and I had another accident. Ugh. So when I got to work I was a mess. My Executive Assistant Eddie Burke took all my clothes and brought it to a nearby laundry. I didn't have anything else to wear at the office. In hindsight I learned a great lesson: always have a "spare pair to wear." Obviously it was not a great experience but thanks to my staff we all got through it okay. Most importantly office morale was high since everyone had a good laugh on me that day.

Fortunately, the public appreciated my candor about my illness and, true to my word, Vito Fossella won with 61% of the vote. It was a landslide. And of course I won with almost 70% of the vote and was reelected to another term as borough president. As I was always loyal to my constituents, they were extraordinarily loyal to me.

Since I was a public figure and publicly acknowledged the fact that I had prostate cancer I received hundreds of phone calls in succeeding years from terrified people that were diagnosed with prostate cancer. Sometimes the doctors would have their patients contact me and I would walk them through it, if they chose to take the same path as me. I would tell them not to worry about it since it was a simple enough procedure. Looking back, it was rather easy in terms of the treatment and I lost very little time. For people that are worried about their jobs and what not, in my opinion it was really not that disruptive.

I continue to run into people who tell me that they had prostate cancer and went for seeds because they learned in the paper that that is the procedure that I had chosen. I guess they figured that had to be the best thing. I should have had stock in the company since I sold a lot of seeds indirectly. So for me I was able to help other people who were diagnosed with the same disease.

They used to call me, "The poster boy for prostate cancer." I attended a number of conferences and talked about my experience. I wanted to help people understand the importance of having the PSA test. Early detection is the key to a successful outcome in almost any cancer. A simple blood test can reveal whether or not you have a high PSA and as such may have a high potential for having prostate cancer.

In August of 2000, Mayor Rudy Giuliani contacted me shortly after he was diagnosed with prostate cancer. He was distraught because everybody was calling him and giving him different ideas as to what he should be doing. His head was full of so much information that he couldn't deal with it. I felt really sorry for him because as the Mayor of New York City, he had a tremendous amount of pressure already on his shoulders. And now with diagnosis of prostate cancer it's not something most people would be able to deal with. People wanted to help, but everyone thought that their treatment was the best, no matter who they were. Because of that, his head was full of too much information, and he was truly a mess: I had never seen him like that before. He wanted to know what I did with the seeds and how it worked out for me.

There was a major difference though between Rudy's cancer diagnosis and mine. Rudy's father had been diagnosed with prostate cancer at a late stage and ultimately died from it. So he had a genetic history of fatal prostate cancer. As a result, Rudy decided to pursue a three-prong approach to the treatment of his cancer. He chose hormone therapy, external radiation beam therapy, and finally the seed implantation.

On Friday September 15th, 2000 Rudy had the final stage of his treatment the seed implantation surgery at Mount Sinai Medical Center. He came home early that evening and I greeted him at Gracie Mansion. We talked about the procedure that we both had and relaxed. I gave him some good advice that he should have an extra set of clothes when he goes back to work, just in case. We both laughed over that. Judith Nathan, his current wife, was there at the time. She was a nurse, and we all took a leisurely walk around Gracie Mansion. He was relieved to have the surgery over with and wanted to move on with his life. When I saw him at Gracie Mansion I knew that he had weathered the storm and was back to the old Rudy that we all loved. As I did, Rudy became a great spokesman for early detection of prostate cancer.

CHAPTER 49

An Innocent Man Taken Down by a Vindictive Prosecutor

In the early morning hours of August 9th, 1997, the life of a dedicated New York City Police Officer and a great Marine who courageously served in Operation Desert Storm, Charles "Chuck" Schwarz would be changed forever, based upon the trumped up perjured testimony of prosecution witnesses in order to satisfy the prosecutors' lust for blood. Based upon my investigation, knowledge of the transcripts, and personal observations of the court proceedings I am convinced beyond a reasonable doubt that the government convicted an innocent man. In my opinion the vindictiveness of a federal prosecutor by the name of Alan Vinegrad, coupled with the perjurious testimony of Eric Turetzky, and a multitude of blunders, sealed the fate of an honorable man and subjected him to a life of missed opportunities due to his wrongful conviction.

On that fateful night Abner Louima, a thirty-three year-old Haitian immigrant, visited Club Rendez-Vous, a popular nightclub located in East Flatbush. At approximately 4:00 a.m. after a night of dancing and drinking at the club, Louima and several other men intervened in a fight between two women. The fight quickly escalated and spilled out onto the sidewalk. It attracted a crowd of rowdy onlookers, many of whom had been drinking. When things got out of hand, police officers from the 70th Precinct responded.

At that time a riot ensued between the police, club patrons, and bystanders involved in the scuffle outside the club. During the riot, Officer Justin Volpe was sucker punched on the side of his head twice. Officers Charles Schwarz and Thomas Wiese were partners that night. They believed Abner Louima was responsible for the assault on Volpe, so they arrested him.

Schwarz and Wiese transported Louima to the 70th Precinct for arrest processing. They stopped at the desk and told Sergeant Jeffrey Fallon that they had a suspect to book. When Volpe arrived back in the precinct with his partner Officer Thomas Bruder, Volpe immediately went to the front desk, where Louima was being searched and processed. Volpe was adamant about taking the arrest because he believed Louima was the guy who had sucker punched him in the head.[20] Sergeant Fallon gave the arrest to Volpe. In hindsight had the arrest never been reassigned to Volpe one can only wonder if any of the ensuing horror would have ever occurred?

Volpe then took Louima into the bathroom and would commit an atrocious act that would forever scar the reputation of the New York City Police Department. Volpe, acting alone while Louima's hands were cuffed behind his back, sodomized Louima with a broken broomstick. Volpe then confided to Sergeant Kenneth Wernick that he "took a man down tonight."

Louima was eventually taken to the emergency room at Coney Island Hospital and the rest is history. The attack by Volpe left Louima with severe internal damage to his colon and bladder that

---

20 *It would later be learned that Abner Louima did not punch officer Volpe it was Louima's cousin, Jay Nicolas who actually punched Volpe.*

required major operations to repair. He was hospitalized for two months after the incident.

The Internal Affairs Division (I.A.D.) interviewed Louima at the hospital. Louima was shown a photo array in order to identify his attacker. Schwarz picture was in the array. Abner Louima did not identify Schwartz as his attacker. Inexplicitly missing from the photo array was a photo of Weise.

On August 15th, 1997, Volpe and Schwarz were indicted on charges of aggravated sexual abuse and first-degree assault by the state. Eventually Wiese and Bruder were charged by the state with beating Mr. Louima in their patrol car. Subsequently on February 26th, 1998 the federal government, which had taken over the case due to the intense public outrage, indicted the four officers on a variety of civil rights charges.[21] The federal grand jury added additional charges of conspiracy and obstruction of justice to the cases against Schwarz, Wiese, and Bruder.

When I first heard about the case in the media I was repulsed by what I read, as was the rest of the city. I could not understand how such a brutal and sadistic act could be inflicted upon a prisoner in the 21st Century. Never in my wildest imagination would I have foreseen myself getting involved in a case that seemed so barbaric and brutal. The case would rightfully turn out to be one of the most shocking police brutality cases in the city's history.

In fact, shortly after this incident I was part of a task force that Mayor Giuliani assembled to examine the relations between the city's residents and the Police Department in the wake of the Louima travesty. Mayor Giuliani appointed: Tom Repetto, Director of the Citizens Crime Commission; Norman Siegel, Director of the New York Civil Liberties Union; Curtis Sliwa, a Conservative radio talk show host; Eric Breindel, an editor from the *New York Post*; Rabbi Shea Hecht; Christine Quinn, Director of the New York Gay and Lesbian Anti-Violence Project; members of his own staff, and me.

---

21 A fifth officer was also indicted - Sgt. Michael Bellomo

We put our hearts and souls into trying to figure out how to improve police and community relations and put together an expansive report that outlined over one hundred recommendations. We all worked without compensation. It was an arduous task, yet by March of 1998, we had compiled a succinct report.

Almost a year later, on May 4th, 1999, the trial of the five police officers indicted in the Abner Louima case began before Judge Nickerson in Federal District Court in Brooklyn. On May 12th, newly promoted Detective Eric Turetzky who was now assigned to the Internal Affairs Division falsely testified that when he saw Schwarz in the precinct he was turning right into a dead-end hallway that led only to the bathroom. One would think that logically the jury would see that his testimony was bought and paid for by the Internal Affairs Division of the N.Y.P.D. since Turetzky was promoted to detective and assigned to I.A.D. immediately before the trial in anticipation of the testimony that was given during trial. At the time of the actual riot in front of Club Rendez-Vous, Turetzky was still on probation and he had threatened to kick a pregnant woman in the stomach if she did not move on. In my opinion, it is crystal clear that Turetzky cut a deal to save his career.

Shortly thereafter, on May 25th, due to the overwhelming evidence presented during the trial that Volpe was the sadistic officer who clearly sodomized Louima, Volpe copped a plea of guilty in the middle of the trial.[22] At the time of the plea, Volpe told federal officials that the second officer in the bathroom when Volpe attacked Louima was Wiese, not Schwarz. The jury would never hear this information. The proper course of action would have been for the judge to accept the plea and call a mistrial for the other officers at this point but such was not the case. Tragically, on June 8th, 1998 Schwarz was convicted of being in the bathroom while Volpe sodomized him. Schwarz' attorney, Steve Worth, did not want Schwarz to testify at trial. As a result, members of the jury were never given

---

22 *On December 13 Judge Nickerson sentences Volpe to 30 years in prison.*

the opportunity to hear Schwarz testify to the fact that he never took Louima to the bathroom. Wiese and Bruder were acquitted of beating Mr. Louima on the way to the precinct.

Schwarz was immediately taken into custody. He was held in the maximum security Manhattan Correctional facility on a special unit on the ninth floor awaiting his second trial on obstruction of justice charges. On Feb 7th, 2000 the second trial began against Schwarz, Bruder, and Wiese regarding the theory that they conspired to cover up the attack. On March 6th, they were all wrongly convicted of covering up the assault on Mr. Louima, even though the torture inflicted upon Louima was an awful act of one clearly deranged police officer, Volpe. It was Volpe and Volpe alone who perpetrated the most heinous act on Louima. Everyone else that went down that night was collateral damage and another notch on the belt of an unscrupulous prosecutor – Alan Vinegrad.

After the second conviction, the Schwarz family, all Staten Island residents, requested a meeting with me to discuss Schwarz's case. As borough president, I met at Borough Hall with Chuck's wife, Andra, his mother, Estelle, his sisters, Eileen and Catherine and their husbands, Richard and Jack, and his brother, John.

Although I was disgusted and outraged by the assault on Mr. Louima, during the course of the previous two years I had heard nothing but good things about Schwarz from fellow Marines and police officers on Staten Island. The resounding theme was that Schwarz was a great son, husband, brother, neighbor, Marine, and most of all, police officer. Anyone who knew Schwarz personally said he was marvelous. There was a very strong sentiment amongst the police department that the government had railroaded Schwarz. It was because of these observations that I agreed to sit down and listen to what they had to say.

When I met them I immediately knew that Schwarz had married a truly devoted and loving wife, and he had a dedicated family. They would go to their graves trying to prove his innocence. He was a good, hardworking American who served his country honorably.

The story they told me broke my heart. Even before the Louima incident, the Schwarz family was struck by tragedy. I learned that one year before the incident Schwarz's younger brother John, who sat before me in a wheelchair, was critically injured diving into a pool. The accident left John a quadriplegic, paralyzed from the neck down.

I learned that in order to take care of his brother, Schwarz switched his shift from days in the coveted anti-crime unit at the 70th Precinct to the midnight-to-eight shift. After working the night shift, Schwarz would take John to the Kessler Institute in New Jersey for therapy three times a week. He devoted all his free time to helping John recover.

They told me that Schwarz was the glue that held the family together. Now that Schwarz was incarcerated there was no one else that could take care of his brother the way that Schwarz did. The case had taken a devastating physical, emotional, and monetary toll on the family. I could see that they were a loving family that had been destroyed.

As you are aware, by the time I had met them, I had extensive investigative experience during my career regarding investigations concerning aviation safety, medical breakthroughs, toxic waste issues and most recently the wrongful convictions of Joseph Occhipinti and the Feerick Four. The family went through the facts of the case, the tragic legal mistakes made, and the malicious illegal prosecution tactics used to obtain the unlawful conviction. When they were done I believed there was a good possibility that an innocent man was sitting in jail and I knew I could not idly sit by. I had to do something to try to correct this injustice. So I told them that I would conduct my own investigation and get back to them shortly.

During the course of my investigation, I learned that what never came out at any trial was the fact that shortly after the incident, Thomas Wiese, the 70th Precinct PBA delegate, told prosecutors that Volpe was the one who rammed a broken broomstick into Louima's rectum and Schwarz was not in the bathroom. Weise knew this, he said, because he saw Volpe immediately after the assault.

Weise told prosecutors that he was chasing a puppy the cops had picked up in the street when the puppy ran to the back of the precinct by the bathroom. Weise followed the puppy, heard a noise inside the bathroom, and opened the door. There was Volpe, he said, standing over Louima, with a stick in his hand. Wiese said Volpe told him, "He shit himself." Bruder backed up Wiese's statement and said he saw Volpe take Louima into the bathroom and saw Wiese near the door.

For some unknown reason the government and prosecutors dismissed these accounts from the beginning. Why would Weise put himself in harm's way when the city was crying for the crucifixion of any officer even remotely involved in the case? The last place any sane cop would place themselves was at or even remotely near the bathroom. Yet that is exactly what Weise did. He told the prosecutors it was him in the bathroom and Wiese's admissions were blatantly ignored and dismissed outright by prosecutors.

Secondly, in my opinion during the joint trial the animosity between Schwarz's lawyer, Steve Worth, and Volpe's lawyer, Marvin Kornberg, distorted the proceeding. Their hatred for each other impaired their abilities to zealously defend their clients. The animosity between the two lawyers was initially based on one main issue that corrupted both attorneys: money. Worth had the coveted Patrolmen's Benevolent Association contract to represent cops, a deal worth more than $5 million a year at the time. Kornberg didn't. Kornberg had spent a good portion of his career defending cops who opted not to use the PBA lawyers. He let the cops know that although he was expensive he was infinitely better than the lackluster PBA lawyers. This was a battle of egos that would contribute to the tragic incarceration of an innocent man - Chuck Schwarz.

The third issue revolved around trial strategy. From the beginning it was quite clear that virtually all the physical evidence against Volpe was overwhelming. Yet Kornberg made a colossal mistake in his representation of Volpe. He publicly went after the victim, Abner Louima. Kornberg stated publicly months before the trial the theory that Louima was a homosexual who engaged in violent sex and that's what caused his injuries. Volpe did not sodomize Louima with a stick. It was a crazy and outlandish path to follow, and it was a tactic which sickened the general public.

In my opinion, Kornberg had a strong legal obligation to represent his client zealously, yet sometimes cutting a deal for a guilty man is the best path. He could have offered mitigating circumstances such as temporary insanity, due to the trauma to his head from being sucker punched, to get a decent deal. Yet Kornberg never followed that path, and as such he took a slew of non- participating officers down with his client.

When Volpe pled mid-trial, the government's case against him was airtight and Volpe had no leverage to cut any significant deal. In fact, the prosecution wouldn't even accept Volpe's first plea, in which he stated that he alone committed the sodomy of Louima in the bathroom. The government would not accept a plea until Volpe swore that there was a second cop in the bathroom. So, Volpe said there was another cop in the bathroom that didn't participate in the attack but stood by the door and did nothing. Of course the jury would never hear this. Kornberg did tell the government, and Schwarz's lawyer, that the other cop Volpe was referring to was Wiese, yet Wiese wasn't named in the plea because the prosecutors refused to include his name.

In my opinion, the final colossal blunder in the trial occurred when Steve Worth failed to call Volpe to testify. This was the key decision Worth had to make in the trial. Stupidly when Worth looked at the case he had presented for Schwarz, he thought he had put together a strong reasonable-doubt case. As in the Feerick case, where Worth put up absolutely no defense on behalf of his client DeVito because he thought he had a "pretty good" case, he did the same exact thing with Schwarz. "Pretty good" does not cut it when an innocent life is on the line. In my opinion, Worth never learned from his past mistakes.

Worth claimed that he did not know what Volpe was going to testify to, so never called Volpe. Yet, Worth could have easily interviewed Volpe beforehand to find out what he would say, but he did not. Why? Again, only God and Steve Worth know the answer to that question. Even now, everyone knows that Volpe would have said it was Weise in the bathroom and not Schwarz.

In my opinion, it was abundantly clear to me that prosecutorial misconduct coupled with attorney malfeasance, and finally the massive egos of the attorneys involved ultimately destroyed an innocent man's life. Schwarz placed his life in the hands of a lawyer and assumed he'd be acquitted because he was innocent, yet such was not the case.

Once I had done my investigation and determined that an innocent man was sitting in prison I didn't just offer verbal support; I took it as a mission. The fact that Schwarz was a Marine had significant bearing, since Marines always give it their best effort to make sure that you get back in one piece. As such, I went in full steam ahead. I got to know his new defense team, trial lawyer Ron Fischetti, and appellate lawyer Diarmuid White, really well. I did fund raising drives. I even ran articles in the paper asking people to contribute to his legal defense.

On Saturday June 24th, 2000 immediately before Schwarz's sentencing I held a rally to express outrage over the miscarriage of justice and to condemn the prosecution and incarceration of an absolutely innocent man, Chuck Schwarz. The rally was held at the Michael J. Petrides School. Hundreds of off duty police officers, Staten Island residents, and ardent supporters showed up in support of Schwarz. My message was getting out loud and clear. Schwarz was innocent. He had nothing to do with the unconscionable torture of Abner Louima.

Other wrongly convicted officers that I had helped in the past such as Joe Occhipinti, Pat Feerick, Orlando Rosario, Mayra Schutz, and John DeVito showed up in support of Schwarz. They all told the crowd that, "We are living proof that police officers can be wrongfully convicted." Feerick said, "Schwarz is a sacrificial lamb for inept prosecutors. He is an innocent man and needs to be set free."

I remember the crowd was completely silent as the heroic, paralyzed police officer, Steve McDonald, spoke passionately about the perversion of justice orchestrated by Alan Vinegrad against Schwarz, all while sitting under a banner that stated, "Evil prevails when Good men stand idly by." McDonald called it a "crime of the gravest magnitude." Tears came to the Schwarz supporters as they watched Steve, a man whose life had changed dramatically when he was paralyzed after being shot three times by a fifteen-year-old thug, struggle to grasp a breath while breathing on a respirator to get the message across: "Chuck Schwarz…is an innocent man…, set…him…free."

Finally, Schwarz's wife spoke and let the crowd know that her husband had been interned in solitary confinement for more than a year for something he did not do. While incarcerated Chuck told Andra that, "I would rather have been shot dead as a Marine, than been accused of this crime." You could see that every person in the crowd believed her and wept with her.

The famous Australian police supporter, Steve Dunleavey, chronicled these events dutifully in the media. He, like myself, was not afraid to publicize the truth about unpopular cases. Without reporters like Steve, falsely accused officer's stories would never get out.

Over the course of the next several years I would attend many of the "Free Chuck Schwarz," fundraisers that were held. These events were held in every borough of the city. His ardent supporters donated their services to ensure the success of the fundraisers such as: rocker Eddie Money; comedians John DiResta and Colin Quinn; the National Police Defense Foundation; The Law Enforcement Legal Defense Fund—of which Edwin Meese, the former attorney general, was director; The Reverend Bill Kalaidjian, and his devoted wife Val; Father Brian Jordan; and the list would go on and on. I would attend and speak passionately about the need for the truth to come out and that Schwarz should be freed.

Andra Schwarz was relentless in pursing justice for her husband and got Schwarz's story out via distinguished talk show radio hosts such as Sean Hannity, Bob Grant, and Steve Malzberg, reporters Steve Dunleavey, Nat Hentoff, Jeffrey Toobin, CBS correspondent Ed Bradley, and a slew of others. She and Chuck's family worked 24/7/365 in their pursuit of justice.

Yet tragically on June 27th, 2000 in Brooklyn Federal Court, Judge Eugene Nickerson shamelessly sentenced Schwarz to fifteen years and eight months in prison for the attack and conspiring to cover it up. The judge sentenced Bruder and Wiese to five years in prison for conspiring to obstruct justice. When sentenced, Schwarz addressed the court and vehemently stated that the assault Louima endured was an unthinkable, horrendous, and inhumane act committed by Volpe. Schwarz had no knowledge prior to, during, or in the hours after this horrendous act, nor would he have ever condoned it or taken part in it. His prosecution was a misguided witch-hunt on the part of prosecutor Alan Vinegrad.

On one side of the packed courtroom sat Rev Al Sharpton and his cohorts and on the opposite side were Steve McDonald, myself, and Schwarz's supporters. I remember when Sharpton and I walked out of the courthouse Sharpton was swarmed by the press. As Sharpton held court with the press bellowing his race-baiting rhetoric, you could see he was clearly basking in his glory. It tore my heart apart as I stood by myself because there wasn't any room due to the swarming of the press to interview Sharpton. Sharpton looked toward me and with venom in his eyes he blurted out, "Repent, Molinari. Repent." I told him flat out, "Fuck off."

I remember having a conversation after the press dispersed and Sharpton said, "The assault in the bathroom could not have been conducted by one person." I said, "Maybe so, but doesn't it bother you that it might be somebody else other than Chuck Schwarz?" His reply was cold and calculated, "No. It doesn't bother me." I was stunned. I couldn't believe what I was hearing out of Sharpton's mouth, but the Sharpton of yesterday is still the Sharpton of today.

The only difference now is that he seems to have hit a home run since he can get the President of the United States to be the keynote speaker at the racially charged National Action Network convention.

The next few years would be hell for the Schwarz family with legal setback after legal setback. Judge Nickerson had no interest in seeking the truth and ruled against everything the appellate defense team submitted. The team ultimately appealed to the United States Court of Appeals for the 2nd Circuit.

On February 28th, 2002 after a zealous appellate representation by Schwarz's new legal team, the United States Court of Appeals for the 2nd Circuit miraculously overturned the convictions of Schwarz. The court also threw out the obstruction-of-justice convictions of Schwarz, Wiese, and Bruder. It was music to my ears when I heard the decision. Finally, justice was being served for an innocent man. Now, we needed to get him out of prison as soon as possible.

The Schwarz family was financially drained due to the case and I knew making bond would be very difficult. I felt I had a duty as a Marine to get Schwarz out. I went home that night and told my ailing wife that I wanted to put up our condominium as bail for Schwarz. Marguerite rolled her eyes and said, "I believe that Chuck is innocent also, so do what you have to do as one Marine for another. I expect nothing less from the man that I married. You have lived your life true to the Corps and you know I totally respect and support your decisions. So put up our home for him, it is the right thing to do."

When Andra and Schwarz' family heard about my offer she was thrilled and speechless. I knew that my efforts had offered comfort, support and hope to a family that was placed in a desperate position through no fault of their own.

When the press asked me if I would regret this gesture I remember adamantly telling them, "Of course not, It's Chuck's decency as a Marine, his discipline as a Marine, that kept him going inside solitary confinement when he knew, you knew, the world knew he had nothing to do with what happened to Abner Louima. That is Marine

Corps discipline, the ability to carry forward under insurmountable odds. No, I have no worry about my home. He is a Marine and a hero in my eyes. Schwarz deserves nothing less. He needs to be home with his family."

So on Thursday March 7th, 2002 at the bail hearing I formally offered to put up my condominium as part of Schwarz's bond package. I remember when Ron Fischetti got up and said, "Your honor, on the question of bail, my client doesn't have the assets to post bail, but we have with us former Borough President Guy Molinari who has offered to put up his home as collateral."

The courtroom became silent as we listened to the prosecutors whispering amongst themselves, "Don't take it, don't take it, it won't look good." Sure enough, the prosecutors said, "No, it's not necessary." They instead agreed to Schwarz's mother and aunts to put up their homes as security for his $1 million bond.

His freedom was the direct result of the aggressive "Free Chuck Schwarz" campaign spearheaded by his wife. On that date, he left the court and was embraced by his loving and supportive family. I went to sleep that night at peace with myself knowing that Schwarz, an innocent man, who spent almost four harrowing years in solitary confinement in federal prison, was back where he belonged, with his family.

Yet the prosecutor from hell, Alan Vinegrad, would continue his psychotic unscrupulous obsession to convict an innocent man by any means necessary. In June of 2002 Schwarz was tried for a third time in Brooklyn Federal Court. This time Schwarz was charged with perjury for claiming he did not lead Louima into the bathroom during the second trial and the original civil rights charges from the first trial in which prosecutors alleged Schwarz held Louima down during the assault.

Since I had retired from being borough president and resumed practicing law, I was able to go to the courtroom almost every day to support him and his family during the trial. It was a difficult and physically painful experience since I was suffering from tremendous crippling back pain as a direct result of the auto accident almost thirty-five years before. It was grueling for me to stay in the courtroom for the whole session, but I did, because I felt so bad for Schwarz. It was clear to me that Schwarz was overwhelmed and had no idea what was happening to him due to the years he spent in prison. He would never be able to accept his situation. He could not comprehend how the cowardly Eric Turetzky could repeatedly lie on the stand to save his own career. When Schwarz testified, he was insistent that he never took Louima to the bathroom. He told the jury how he processed Louima at the 70th Precinct desk and then gave the arrest to Volpe when Sergeant Fallon ordered him to. Schwarz then walked outside the precinct building and searched the police car that he had transported Louima in for illegal contraband.

Then the unthinkable happened during the trial. Thomas Weise, the officer who was actually in the bathroom, decided not to testify on the advice of his attorney Joseph Tacopina. Weise's testimony would have corroborated Schwarz's testimony. If Wiese had testified that it was he who had escorted Louima to the bathroom, there would be no way the jury would convict Schwarz. Yet it would be testimony the jury would tragically never hear. Finally, when Volpe testified that it was Weise not Schwarz in the bathroom, Volpe's testimony was impeached when the prosecutors introduced a tape recorded while Volpe was in prison. In that tape Volpe told his father that he wanted time off his sentence to testify. The tape destroyed any credibility Volpe had.

So again, tragically, on July 16th the jurors convicted Schwarz of one count of perjury and deadlocked on the remaining counts. Federal Judge Reena Raggi, who replaced Judge Nickerson after he died, set a date in September for a re-trial on the deadlocked counts.

On Saturday night at 9:00 p.m. September 21st, 2002, two days before Schwarz's fourth trial was scheduled to begin, Schwarz accepted a plea bargain in which he would serve five years for his conviction on the perjury charge alone and in return the prosecutor would drop the assault charge and the case would finally be over. It was an incredibly difficult decision for Schwarz and his family to make but based on the uncertainty of the outcome of a new trial and the clear vindictiveness of the prosecution this nightmare would never end for the Schwarz family. In an effort to put an end to the entire ordeal it only made sense to take a plea.

The most unusual part of the plea agreement was a "gag order" placed on Schwarz, his wife, and attorneys during Schwarz's incarceration. The "gag order" barred them from claiming publicly that Schwarz was innocent of the charges and he was prohibited from publicly discussing the merits of the case. One of the key elements of the plea agreement that Schwarz was defiant on was the fact that he had absolutely nothing to do with the assault on Louima. He would never admit to something he did not do. If Schwarz's side adhered to the agreement, a thirteen-month sentence reduction would be applied upon Judge Raggi's approval.

Schwarz and his team kept their end of the bargain. However, when it came time for Schwarz to be released early in March of 2006, Judge Reena Raggi refused to enforce the agreement and re-sentenced Schwarz to the original five-year sentence. Even though I was initially disappointed in the plea agreement, especially the part of the gag order, I knew then that Schwarz's lawyers gave him the best advice. A plea deal was the only way Chuck Schwarz would be done with the case once and for all. Between Judge Nickerson and Raggi, they had effectively tried to kill an innocent man. Yet after the five years Schwarz was finally free.

I had hoped that when Schwarz was finally released from prison, we could have had a press conferences where Schwarz would say, "I'm innocent. I spent five years in jail for something that I didn't do, etc." But the terms of the plea agreement silenced him. So I, as his voice, stated unequivocally that the vindictive persecutor Alan Vinegrad convicted an innocent man. Abner Louima was brutalized by one man alone: Justin Volpe. Schwarz was collateral damage from a prosecution gone rabid. Again I roar loud and clear for the world to hear **"CHUCK SCHWARZ IS AN INNOCENT MAN."**

The lives of the Schwarz family have not been easy after his release but the determination to overcome adversity runs in the veins of the Schwarz family. After his release I would always be there to assist Chuck and his family in any way possible. I will always look back and be grateful for all the courageous supporters who had the tenacity to speak up on behalf of an innocent man. Today Chuck and Andra have a beautiful son, they are remarkable people and I wish them a long, healthy life.

People have to understand that right now, even as this book is being written, when we don't support good police officers who are wrongfully prosecuted, the whole system will eventually break down and every citizen will suffer. Being a police officer is a tough enough job to begin with, but having been involved with several cases such as Joseph Occhipinti's, the "Feerick Four," and the Schwarz case the same pattern always emerges. Honest police officers are indicted, tried, convicted, and sent to jail for something they did not do. How can we let this happen? We have a duty to support the law enforcement component of our city, state, and indeed the federal government. When we fail to do that, we fail in our basic responsibilities.

CHAPTER 50

You Gotta Go with Your Gut

On October 2nd, 1999, I was standing at Mayor Giuliani's side in the Blue Room of City Hall when Rudy formally announced that he was endorsing Texas Governor George W. Bush's presidential campaign. During the preceding eight months I was a major recruiter to generate Republican politicians who would formally endorse George W. Bush's presidential bid.

Surprisingly within a few short weeks of Mayor Giuliani's endorsement I would have a complete change of mind. I decided to place principles above politics. After a month of soul searching, and many things that turned me off during my association with members of the Bush campaign, I changed my mind. Although I was very close with the Bush family, I came to believe that Senator John McCain gave the Republican Party the best chance of having a Republican president elected. McCain was the candidate who was best able to continue the legacy of leadership of George Bush, Sr. and Ronald Reagan and lead the nation into the next millennium

A key thing that influenced my decision was George W. Bush's chief strategist for his 2000 presidential bid, Karl Rove. Rove would call me up and dictate what I needed to do in New York State. By this time, I had tremendous political campaign experience. In fact, I was an expert on New York Republican politics.

It was the first time in a campaign that somebody who had no idea about New York State politics was telling me what my role was to be. I didn't like the way Rove talked to me and ordered me to do certain things. I said to Karl, "I've never had anybody talk to me like this, Karl." His response was very abrupt, "Well, I'm talking to you like this now. If you want to be on our team, this is what you're going to have to do." I didn't think this was the type of person who should be organizing Bush's campaign. I saw Rove as a poor communicator who could easily piss off people.

At the same time, I began to hear my constituents were being more and more supportive of John McCain. I spoke to friends and Staten Islanders in general and the majority of them indicated that they liked John McCain. I thought to myself, "Well if I listen to what I'm being told, then I should be supporting John McCain, not George W. Bush." I knew it was going to be a close election.

The school of thought is that when you elect a president, it is critical that you try to elect someone from the same party, in this case the Republican Party, because of shared principles, like less government involvement, no tax increases, military support, and things of that nature. Most importantly with McCain was that I saw an experienced senator, a military hero who had spent five years as a POW, and an honest "straight talker" when I looked in his eyes.

There were other factors that contributed to my decision. I was having a lot of disagreements with Governor George Pataki at the time on a variety of issues. I publicly stated that he had a difficult time making decisions and taking a position. Political insiders anonymously stated to the press that they thought that I made my decision because I was mad that I had been "shoved aside" in the Bush campaign in New York, and that Bush did not come to Staten Island when he visited New York City several weeks before my endorsement of McCain.

Nevertheless, there were other issues which changed my mind on such a crucial race. I told the press that I would not support or endorse somebody because somebody else may have snubbed me. At the time I firmly believed that Pataki was guiding Bush's New York State campaign strategy. Pataki was pushing Bush to name Charles Gargano, Pataki's Economic Development Director, as Bush's New York Campaign Chair. I made it abundantly clear that Gargano was an untrustworthy individual. It bothered me a lot that he would even be considered. Because of that a lot of political insiders took it as a given that my decision was based on my animosity toward Pataki at the time. In addition, I was furious with Governor George Pataki's inaction in regards to the imprisonment of former Lieutenant Patricia Feerick who was in solitary confinement in a Rikers Island Jail serving a disgraceful two-year prison sentence since September 21st. I had sent five written requests for gubernatorial clemency and/or a pardon on Pat's behalf and each fell on deaf ears. I had not even received the courtesy of a written response. Was I annoyed? You betcha. Especially since I was Pataki's New York City Campaign chief in 1994 and was a key reason why he was elected to governor in the first place.

I remember telling the press that, "It would be discourteous not to respond if it was just a private citizen writing, but not to respond to someone serving in a representative capacity? Feerick is going to be eligible for parole after she serves a minimum of sixty days, so if the governor is going to have an impact on this situation, he's going to have to intervene now."

I was present at 111 Centre Street on September 21st when Pat surrendered to the court to start her sentence and it broke my heart. She had left her newborn son at home and was now confined in the most notorious jail in the nation, Rikers Island, for doing her job.

During the course of my reevaluation of who I would endorse in the presidential election, I called up Senator McCain. I had served with John McCain in the House of Representatives before he moved over to the Senate. I said, "John, I'm thinking of endorsing you." John was ecstatic and said, "Oh my God, I'm going to hop a plane right now. I'll fly to Staten Island right away."

And I said, "No, no, no. I'm not there yet, but I just wanted to let you know that it's something in the mix and I'm thinking about it. I'll make a decision about it probably in the next week or so." Senator McCain said, "Well please let me know. I'll come over right away."

In the end I was drawn to McCain by a growing admiration for his independence and willingness to take on tough issues, such as campaign finance overhaul and his stellar record in the military and time spent as a prisoner of war. As we were both war veterans I owed him that much. In my judgment, John McCain offered the Republican Party a better opportunity to elect a Republican that would benefit this country.

Several days later I called Senator McCain up and said, "Alright, John, I've made my decision. I am going to endorse you." It was the toughest political decision I ever made because I was so close to the Bush family, but in my opinion it was the right decision. The only person I consulted regarding this massive decision was myself. Of course this dramatic choice would change the relationship that I enjoyed with the Bush family, but I admired John McCain. He is a great American, he has always served his country steadfastly, and most of all he is a free thinker, that's for sure.

On October 18th, 1999 John McCain flew into New York and we formally made the announcement at the Manhattan Vietnam War Memorial. I told the press that while I was analyzing the race and watching it, I saw this decorated Navy pilot who was held captive in North Vietnam and I was struck by his character. It was like an epiphany. At the time I said, "Despite all odds, my overwhelming respect for a candidate like John McCain demands that I rise to endorse him."

Just like that, off we went and started aggressively campaigning in New York State. At the time he asked me to co-chair his New York

State campaign which I agreed to do. I opened up an office in Staten Island not far from Borough Hall. During lunch hours and what-not, I would go to that office and make phone calls and coordinate the campaign. Since nearly all of the elected Republican officials in New York State were supporting George Bush, I assembled a team of mostly political neophytes people that hadn't been involved in politics before.

Within a week of breaking ranks with the Republican Party by endorsing Senator John McCain on October 26th, 1999, Governor Pataki miraculously granted Pat Feerick clemency. I was actually shocked that he did it especially after our feuding. It was common knowledge that Governor Pataki rarely invoked his power to offer clemency yet in this instance he boldly toppled the explosive case that seared the police department for a decade by commuting Feerick's two-year sentence. It was his first mid-year commutation in in almost two years. That made it more unusual, since normally his clemencies were announced just before Christmas.

I was at the end of the Hazen Street Bridge in Queens waiting with her husband, Joe, the President of the Lieutenants Benevolent Association Tony Garvey, and dozens of supporters for Pat as she was escorted off Rikers Island to freedom. I told the press that, "this is a tragedy, and that's why I stuck by her, Drug dealers convicted this lady who was a star in the Police Department. I'm going to fight to clear her name. This case has definitely created a source of tension between me and Governor Pataki. I have nothing but praise at this time for George Pataki in finally releasing her."

Pat hugged Tony Garvey and me, and said, "I owe my freedom to both of you. You were relentless in your pursuit of freeing me. I will never forget your efforts on my behalf. I can finally move forward in my life." It was a dramatic emotional reunion as Pat embraced her husband Joe and they headed straight home where her three-month-old son, Joseph, and four-year-old son, John, anxiously awaited the return of their mother.

At the time Pataki stated, "Her clemency represents my firm belief that under all the circumstances including the misdemeanor nature of the offenses and her otherwise exemplary record the request by this highly decorated officer and mother of two children deserves to be granted." I slept well that night knowing that Pat was where she belonged: home.

By December, the McCain presidential campaign was in full force. I actually recruited Pat Feerick as one of my political neophytes to be a delegate out in Nassau County. True to her work ethic she jumped right into the process. She was not scarred by her imprisonment; actually she was reborn when she came out. She believed that John McCain was a true American hero with tremendous character. Pat collected signatures, distributed leaflets and worked the phones. She threw herself into the task with zeal as with the other volunteers we had assembled. She gave the campaign 100% and I was proud of her efforts.

The campaign itself was an uphill battle from the beginning. It was totally grassroots. I knew that even to get on the ballot you had to pass tremendous hurdles. I told the press that, "The process we have in New York State is deliberately skewed in favor of the political establishment. We all know that."

So we had to hustle aggressively to get on the ballot. In New York State at that time you had to collect signatures of 1,000 voters, or 5% of the party members whichever was less in each of the 31 congressional districts in the state. Bush's campaign would challenge many of the signatures in an attempt to not have McCain's name on the ballot just as they continued to challenge everything the McCain campaign was doing. It was another David and Goliath scenario. I loved when McCain started referring to Pataki as "Comrade Pataki," and William Powers, who was Republican Party State Chairman, as "Comrade Powers," in a reference to them trying to keep him off the New York ballot.

By the end of December, we had to file a lawsuit in Brooklyn Federal District Court to force McCain's name on to the March 7th primary ballot. It was a strong strike against the byzantine Republican ballot access rules. To me it was machine politics at its worst. In the court case titled "Molinari V. Powers" we moved for a preliminary injunction to declare the entire Republican-selected ballot access scheme unconstitutional and asked to place delegate candidates pledged to support Senator McCain on the ballot in each of New York's 31 congressional districts.

On February 2nd, John McCain won a landslide victory over Gov. George W. Bush in New Hampshire's presidential primary, handing Bush a significant loss in their first head-to-head contest. McCain accumulated 49% of the vote, compared to Bush's 31%. In his victory speech, McCain characterized his win as a triumph of the little guy over Washington's powerful special interests.

Immediately after John's landslide victory, on February 4th the court case was settled when they agreed to place McCain's name on all 31 congressional districts. It was a great victory. McCain was ecstatic that he would be on the ballot. Pataki, who was behind the initial decision to aggressively fight the placing of McCain's name on the ballot essentially bowed to the inevitable. Judge Edward R. Korman tossed out parts of the complex ballot law and put all GOP hopefuls on the ballot as long as they had delegates slated. Judge Korman stated in his opinion, "I accepted the stipulation only after independently concluding that the scheme, both in its totality and by virtue of two of its individual but related elements, places an undue burden on the right to vote under the First Amendment."

Obviously, there was a tremendous amount of pressure to produce, but I knew that when I jumped on board McCain's campaign, we all knew it was an uphill battle with little monetary support. I remember a conference phone call that I received from the entire McCain camp immediately before the primary. Lindsay Graham, Fred Thompson, and the whole gang were talking about Super Tuesday, March 7th. We had to win New York in order to become the candidate. The topic of that conversation was, "Well, Molinari, how does it look?"

For the first time in my political career I could not give a definitive answer. There were too many hurdles to make an accurate prediction. The campaign volunteers had given their heart and soul to John McCain, but the lack of money and Republican political support was absent in New York State making our task insurmountable.

On Super Tuesday March 7th, 2000 the results started rolling in. Sixteen states held primaries on Super Tuesday. It was the largest presidential primary election day in U.S. history. Although we did extremely well in New York State, unless you have a majority plus one, the Republican overall winner takes all the delegates in New York State.

I was shocked at the fact that we did win 26 seats. We beat many elected officials who were well-known names. When all was said and done Bush won 67 delegates of the state's 93. As a testament to her determination, Pat Feerick was elected a delegate for the 3rd congressional district in Nassau County and would have the honor of attending the thirty-seventh Republican National Convention to be held in Philadelphia, Pennsylvania at the end of July. Personally, I was proud of Pat, considering where she was not six months earlier.

Senator McCain won the primaries in Vermont, Connecticut, Massachusetts, and Rhode Island. But Bush won in states like California, New York, and Ohio. McCain recognized that there was little hope of overcoming Bush's delegate lead after Super Tuesday so he withdrew from the race on March 9th, 2000.

History showed that George W. Bush almost lost the election. The country didn't know for almost three weeks after the election who our next president was going to be. The result of the election hinged on a mandatory recount in Florida based upon the infamous hanging/dimpled/pregnant chad voting card controversy and subsequent court litigation. On December 13th, 2000 after the Supreme Court ruled in favor of George W. Bush Jr., Al Gore conceded victory. "Bush 43" was finally declared the victor.

Obviously attending the Republican Convention of 2000 was much different than the one in 1996. At the convention, all the

McCain delegates dutifully and respectfully supported the presidential candidacy of George W. Bush. The sting of losing the primary would be sharper, since this would be my last national political campaign as an elected public official.

Senator McCain came out of that battle, yet he continues on a daily basis to serve all of us and this great country of ours, even after all of the problems that he has been through. He's no youngster, and he still suffers from the injuries that were inflicted on him when he was captured and held as a prisoner of war and tortured for almost six years in a Vietnamese prison. He is a great American, and I admire the man tremendously.

CHAPTER 51

9/11 & My Final Year of Public Service

My final year as borough president was a real roller coaster ride. If it were up to me I would have loved to stay on, but due to term limits I was required to pass the torch and retire. I was conflicted because as much as I loved what I was doing, my wife's health was in serious decline and it would be easier to fall back into the life of a successful lawyer and care for my wife without all the 24/7/365 of the world of politics. There would be more quality family time in the long run, something that politics had interfered with for many years.

So once I decided that there would be no further public office aspirations for myself, one of my goals was to confirm that my replacement would ensure that my policies continued. The obvious choice was James Molinaro since he had been by my side for many years. Molinaro had expressed the desire to succeed me many times, so this was his opportunity. Molinaro also told me that he would continue the path that I had paved for the benefit of Staten Islanders. With that I made a commitment that Jimmy Molinaro, one of my best friends and political allies at the time would succeed me as Staten Island borough president.

In the world of politics, things rarely go smoothly. In February of 2001 Chairwoman Leticia Remauro of the Staten Island Republican Party unexpectedly endorsed Republican Assemblyman Robert Straniere as the party candidate for my replacement. I was surprised that she made the decision without consulting me. Everyone knew that Molinaro had served as my deputy borough president for my entire tenure, and it only made sense that he would follow in my steps and continue what I began. The reason Remauro gave me for Straniere's endorsement was that Molinaro was a registered Conservative, whereas Straniere was a registered Republican.

From an outsider's perspective it may sound logical but regarding Staten Island politics, their decision was illogical. I knew that Molinaro was a much better successor than Straniere and I was going to make sure that Staten Island knew it as well. The way the political machine worked, I knew the only way Molinaro could get on the Republican line of the ballot was if it came from Albany.

Since I had earnestly helped newly elected Governor Pataki get into office, I decided to make a trip to Albany and request that Governor Pataki help secure a Wilson-Pakula certificate for Molinaro. The Wilson-Pakula certificate would allow Molinaro to run on the Republican Party line for the borough presidency even though he was a registered Conservative, not a Republican.

On a brisk winter day in February 2001, Molinaro and I took that desolate three hour ride up to Albany in order to improve Molinaro's chances of being elected. When we arrived in Albany we met with Governor Pataki and his Chief of Staff John Cahill to discuss Molinaro receiving a Wilson-Pakula certificate. At this meeting I personally made a strong impassioned pitch to Governor Pataki for Molinaro to get the certificate. I explained to Governor Pataki that Molinaro needed to be on two lines of the ballot to win. Once

I made my pitch it was time to return to the Island and continue aggressively campaigning for Molinaro.

Fortunately, in May the Republican Party dropped their support for Straniere when it became unclear if Straniere actually lived on Staten Island or in Manhattan. At that time, the Staten Island Republican Party endorsed Molinaro. Now Molinaro would be running on the conservative and Republican lines. So, in the long run, I got exactly what I wanted in order to ensure Molinaro's success in his quest to be borough president. During the next several months I continued working hard on Molinaro's campaign as well as fulfilling my responsibilities as outgoing borough president.

Soon enough the all-important primary day was upon us: Tuesday September 11th, 2001. It is a day that is eternally etched in New York City's history. It was a beautiful crystal clear day when the primary polls opened at 6:00 am. For me the day began as a typical hotly contested primary election that was coming to its climax. I anticipated that by the end of the day the borough president's primary race against Assemblyman Bob Straniere would wind up in Molinaro's favor. In addition, I wanted billionaire media mogul Mike Bloomberg's first bid for public office as mayor of New York to be successful. I had worked on his campaign as well and I knew he would be good for New York City.

After Molinaro voted in his own district, he wanted to accompany me as I cast my vote in my district. Any publicity was good publicity on Election Day and I agreed. We went to P.S. 53 in Bay Terrace together so that I could vote.

On the way to vote I had heard a blip on the radio that a plane had crashed into the North Tower of the World Trade Center around 8:45 am. I remember when we entered the school to vote, a gentleman by the door said, "Mr. Molinari did you hear that a plane just hit the World Trade Center?" I said, "I heard something like that before I left the house. Do you know if it was a small plane?" He said, "I think so, but I'm not sure."

Although it was an unusual event, in a city full of skyscrapers and tremendous air traffic, once in a blue moon a plane would strike a building accidently as a result of engine failure, weather disturbances, etc. It was always a tragic event, but until that day, it had never been a deliberate one.

At approximately 9:05 a.m. after I cast my vote as I was exiting the building the same gentleman said, "Mr. Molinari, another plane just hit the World Trade Center." The shock of that statement blew my mind. I would come to learn later that the second plane had intentionally crashed into the South Tower of the World Trade Center at 9:03 a.m. I tried to comprehend what possibly could have occurred to have two separate planes hit the Twin Towers within minutes of each other. It was clear that something was very, very wrong. As borough president, I needed to find out immediately what happened. I could only conclude that there was little doubt in my mind that it was anything other than a deliberate act of terrorism.

Molinaro and I immediately drove to the 122nd precinct on Hylan Boulevard since I was told that borough hall had been closed down. When I arrived at the precinct I was brought into a room where retired Staten Island Borough Commander Toscano "Tony" Simonetti and former Police Commissioner Richard Condon were. I asked them what they heard since they were watching television and I assumed that they had to know more than I did.

It was kind of a surreal setting as I was waiting for relevant information. Simonetti was sitting in a chair calmly peeling an apple and giving slices to those of us that were in the room. I wasn't about to sit there and eat apples while terrorists were crashing commercial jets into the World Trade Center. I had a responsibility to my constituents and I needed to do something and in hurry.

Immediately after the attack telephone communications throughout the area, specifically cell phone service became almost nonexistent due to the magnitude of the event. Everyone was trying to contact loved ones, which caused an overloading of the circuits. Surprisingly I was able to finally reach Ed Burke who was at Borough

Hall. He confirmed that Borough Hall had been closed as a security measure. I told him I was coming down and he would have to make sure I could gain entrance.

As I crossed the island, the South Tower of the World Trade Center collapsed at 9:58 a.m. and the North Tower followed at 10:28 a.m. It was the most devastating event I had ever personally witnessed. It was clear that thousands if not tens of thousands of people had perished in our beloved city. Downtown Manhattan was the financial center of the world, and was always extremely crowded location during the workweek and it was a Tuesday.

I will never forget the view from Borough Hall. It was incredibly sad to see lower Manhattan simmering in ashes. The magnificent world renowned skyline of Manhattan veiled by the unforgettable twin towers was forever changed due to the fanatical actions of the world's most evil person, Osama Bin Laden.

At the time I was receiving phone calls from NYPD detective Jimmy Reyes who had been in contact with the New York City Office of Emergency Management (OEM). Detective Reyes advised me that they believed at a minimum 750 firemen were killed with the collapse of the two towers. It was impossible to imagine that any kind of tragedy could have killed that many firemen. 750 firefighters were more than most fire departments in any city in our country had. The New York City Fire department was devastated.

New York City came to a grinding halt on that day as a result of the attack. The city was locked down. Gov. George Pataki promptly suspended the elections and said a new primary would take place in two weeks. No one cared, including me. Everyone suspended their campaigns. Almost every candidate lost a friend, volunteer, supporter, or family member that day. We all knew that our main priority was for us to regroup from the devastating tragedy and pull together like the great city that New York is.

Initially I was advised that Manhattan was going to send the remains of the deceased over to Staten Island to be identified at the Richmond County Bank Ballpark. I directed Deputy Borough

President Molinaro to immediately go to the site and work with the New York City Medical examiner's office to organize the effort. In the meantime, I attended to the critical emergency situations on the Island. Staten Island University Hospital lost their electricity while they were in the middle of critical surgeries. They appealed to me to help resolve the situation and I did. I was in contact with the Director of OEM Richard Sheirer to help resolve other critical issues as well. We set up areas for the Red Cross and other agencies that were necessary to deal with Staten Island residents who had suffered a loss.

As the hours went by I asked Molinaro how many casualties were at the site. I remember Molinaro saying, "I don't know what's happening, but we don't have any casualties here." I thought that this was very strange. The mind works funny when something like this happens. Nobody knew what was going to happen next. With my military background, I was as prepared as you could be since I knew there were a number of things that had to be done.

When the dust had settled we were faced with the painfully grim realization that there were hardly any recoverable bodies. Many of the bodies had evaporated. Most people as well as I had never heard of that before. When the massive buildings collapsed, the bodies were incinerated. It was bizarre, and it was one of those difficult things for everyone to understand at the time and I still think it is. After years of searching the rubble, the majority of remains were never recovered and sadly the number of bodies that were recovered from the rubble was small. It remains a perverted contrast to the carnage and devastation of which we all witnessed. The tragedy of 9/11 left a permanent void for many families of the deceased since they never got to bury their loved ones' remains.

By 5:20 p.m. 7 World Trade Center had collapsed as well. Inside was the OEM. As we all know, that was the office that was specifically set up for disasters. Fortunately, no one was killed since there was ample time to evacuate.

During the initial hours after the attack there was understandable chaos. There were all kinds of rumors that were completely false: some for the better, some for the worse. But as the real information was received everyone started to understand the true scope of this enormous tragedy. It was hard for everyone, including myself, to fathom how this event could happen in our country with all our technology and our great military forces. Yet, two of the largest buildings in the world were destroyed by terrorists. When all was said and done the death toll in New York City on 9/11 was 2,763. Historically it was the deadliest incident for firefighters and law enforcement officers in the history of the United States; 343 firefighters and 71 police officers were killed.

Immediately prior to 9/11 Rudy Giuliani was somewhat unpopular amongst the electorate; however, the leadership that he demonstrated at the time of the attack and thereafter was remarkable. Despite my differences with the man, I would give him the highest praise possible for the leadership skills that he exhibited at that time. It didn't matter what this man did or didn't do before the World Trade Center attack; when the public was desperate for help, solace, and other kinds of assistance, he was there. Most of all he gave the city hope when hope was needed. The people began to love and adore the mayor again. His reception by the public thereafter was glowing.

We all remember seeing Mayor Giuliani walking down the streets after the attack guiding the city through this tragedy. Yet no one knew at the time that he had almost died during 9/11. Immediately after the attack, Mayor Giuliani went to Ground Zero. He ran into Father Mychal Judge, the FDNY chaplain, immediately before Father Judge went into the North Tower to be with his beloved firefighters. I remember Rudy telling me that his last words to Father Judge were, "Father Myke, pray for us!" He told me that Father Mychal responded, "I always do! I always pray for you!" At the time Rudy was on the way to 75 Barclay Street, where the city had set up a makeshift command center. It was only a short period of time after Father Mychal Judge went into the North Tower when the South Tower came down and Father Judge was killed by debris. Father Judge's body was the first one that was recovered and recorded as a casualty on that date. As for Giuliani, he became trapped in 75 Barclay Street when the South Tower collapsed. He missed dying by a hair.

When I heard about the heartbreaking death of Father Judge, I immediately thought of the last time I saw him. On August 28th, 2001 twenty-seven year-old New York City Firefighter Michael Gorumba, a husband and father, was killed in the line of duty while fighting a fire on Staten Island.

As soon as we heard there was a seriously injured fireman, Mayor Giuliani, Father Judge, and I all rushed to St. Vincent's Medical Center on Staten Island. Unfortunately, there was nothing we could do. When we arrived at the hospital, Michael had passed away. At least we could offer all the resources the city had available to the family for the rest of their lives. Michael had given his life for the city and we owed him nothing less.

In retrospect it was odd when I met Rudy Giuliani and Father Judge at the hospital. I overheard Father Judge saying to Giuliani, "Is Guy okay? He doesn't look well." And Rudy responded, "No, Guy's okay. He just has a problem with pain, but he's alright." Father Judge showed such concern about me that it was hard to fathom that within two weeks after this heroic firefighter lost his life, Father Mychal Judge would join him in heaven. Father Judge was a well-loved priest who epitomized the holiness of the Catholic Church. I will always see him as a true Saint. He devoted his entire life to saving the world. There is nothing more I can say.

So, Giuliani demonstrated to me at the time, and I'm sure to everybody else, that he was a courageous man, and he did everything expected of a mayor. When the city faced its darkest hours, Rudy's actions demonstrated to the world that New York City would still be the center of the world.

The day after the attack, Mayor Giuliani picked me up by helicopter and we flew over downtown Manhattan to survey the damage. We saw the unbelievable sights down below and we just looked at each other and kept shaking our heads in disbelief. The enormity of what transpired could only be understood and appreciated if you actually went on the site. As I walked the smothering site, the air was thick and full of toxins and other aggravating substances. I thought I should put a mask on but I noticed that the majority of the people working there, firemen and otherwise, didn't have masks on. They were digging furiously for survivors without thought of personal health. As long as there was the slimmest of possibilities that they could find a survivor they would not stop. So I thought it would look funny for me to put on a mask if I was only going to be there for a couple of hours.

When I got back to Staten Island I received a phone call from Mayor Giuliani asking my permission to use the Fresh Kills landfill to help find the remains of the deceased among the wreckage from the buildings. He told me that the landfill would be designated a crime scene. Giuliani knew we fought tooth and nail to get the dump closed, but this was a situation where Staten Island would be able to help our devastated city, so of course the only answer was "Yes."

On the night of September 12th the first trucks began arriving at the landfill with debris from Ground Zero. Over the next ten months an intense effort would be conducted to recover human remains, personal items and forensic material. Thousands upon thousands of civil servants, forensic specialists, and ordinary citizens would devote their time to help recover remains of their fellow countrymen and women.

The following day I walked by myself for several blocks near the World Trade Center site. Again it was an unbelievable sight that I will always remember. The streets were vacant. The only people you could see were men and women in uniform, the majority of them with weapons, walking the streets.

New York City suffered not only the pain and anguish of losing loved ones, but also faced the challenge of trying to put their lives back together. I myself attended over 65 funerals of residents of Staten Island who had perished on 9/11. Many of the masses I attended were at the mayor's request since there were many cases where the mayor couldn't attend a funeral because there was another one going on the same time elsewhere. On one day I attended four masses, as I'm sure the mayor did as well. The people who were murdered needed to be recognized by the world as the heroes they all were, and that's what everyone did day in and day out.

Although the city was full of sorrow, the citizens were coming together in a way that the world could never have imagined. The resilience of New Yorkers was admired worldwide and the stereotype of the cold, uncaring New Yorker was gone forever.

I remember Mayor Giuliani saying that Staten Island lost more people proportionally than any other section of the city. I directed my staff that any family member who lost somebody should be brought into my inner office. I would have a one-on-one meeting with each of them and offer whatever support we could. One incident that sticks out in my mind was a young woman who came to Borough Hall with three children. She said that she didn't have any relatives or friends. She didn't know how to write a check. Her husband's remains were never recovered and she didn't know how to face tomorrow. It was a terrible thing to listen to this poor lady. I had my office contact retired police officers who volunteered to adopt someone like this lady on a temporary basis so that they could walk them through the things that they needed done in the ensuing days and weeks to help them survive the tragedy. Again it was a difficult time to try to determine what we needed to do for the people who lost their loved ones.

On Tuesday September 25th, just three short weeks after 9/11, I did have cause to celebrate. Molinaro hammered Straniere by a 2 to 1 margin in the Republican primary. It was a landslide. Molinaro would go against Democratic City Councilman Jerome X. O'Donovan in the general election. Additionally, Michael Bloomberg defeated former Congressman Herman Badillo to become the Republican nominee for the mayoral election against Mark Green. So in the midst of tragedy, life moved on and it was a good day for Staten Island Republicans.

I was at Ground Zero on Thursday October 18th, 2001 when all the civil service personnel present lined up because the Vice President was going to address the workers. Dick Cheney was a personal friend of mine. As he went through the ranks, when he spotted me, he came over to where I was and held my hand. We were speechless but I think the expression in our eyes conveyed the message that we wanted to convey to each other. To see him at a time like this was something that brought back memories of the time that I was in Korea in combat. I had experiences with military battles and their aftermath and I'm sure that it helped me deal with this attack, but I also knew that people who didn't have that kind of military background would probably find it much more difficult to react in the right way, if there is in fact a right way. I just didn't know.

When I think about what happened and I think about being a Marine in combat, it seems like this was more difficult to deal with. You didn't have a squad, company, regiment, or a battalion under attack - you had the entire City of New York under attack. We had no idea whatsoever what would happen next. Would the city ever recover? Would there be further attacks? Would people be able to fly again in the skies over New York? Would they be willing to?

While I hope we never experience anything like 9/11 again, it certainly forced us to reach out and try to provide whatever assistance we could. Certainly New York City provided a great deal of assistance and I'm proud to say that I was part of that City Administration called upon to help the public at the worst time in New York City's history. I'm also proud of New York City, its citizens, and the way they responded. There was just so much help that was being provided to the survivors by volunteers.

On November 6th, 2001, Michael Bloomberg defeated Mark Green and became the 108th mayor of the City of New York. Additionally, Molinaro won the general election with over 50%

of the vote as compared to 43% to his Democratic opponent. On January 1st, 2002, I stood proudly at James P. Molinaro's side when he was sworn in as Staten Island borough president. On that day I became a private citizen for the first time in over twenty-five years. To say the least it was a strange feeling, a sort of emptiness since I felt that I could do much more for the city, especially after the tragic events of 9/11.

But looking back I had a wonderful career and I lived a politician's dream. The boy from Midland Beach actually got to live his dream of being the "King of Midland Beach."

EPILOGUE

ALTHOUGH I WANTED TO END THE BOOK WITH MY exit from public office, there are two areas that I believe the public would want me to address and they are both difficult ones. The first involves the end of my relationship with my lifelong friend, James Molinaro. The second involves my good friend, Michael Grimm. So, being the humble public servant that I am, please let me explain…

Many people wonder today why Guy Molinari and Jimmy Molinaro no longer talk. It is an issue that goes to the heart and soul of my belief in political integrity. I stood by Molinaro through all his ups and downs in life yet he disappointed me sorely when he publicly attacked my close friend, Dan Donovan for making a hard, yet clearly ethical decision regarding a criminal case involving Molinaro's grandson. So, if we're being honest with ourselves, the kiss of death in our relationship revolved around the arrest of Molinaro's grandson.

Molinaro's grandson was arrested and charged with attempted murder, assault, and weapons charges regarding a brawl that occurred between a group of teenagers behind P.S. 52 in Dongan Hills that resulted in the stabbing of fourteen year-old Richard Orloski.

At the time, Dan Donovan was the district attorney of Staten Island and he had no choice but to recuse himself from the prosecution due to the appearance of impropriety—he had been Molinaro's Deputy Borough President for three years and was a personal friend. Molinaro had actually encouraged Dan to run for D.A. since Dan had previously worked for the Manhattan district attorney's office.

Unfortunately, tragedy continued for Molinaro when On April 29th, 2006 his forty-year-old son, Stephen, died of a drug overdose. For years Molinaro had tried to help his son overcome drug addiction. In the past Stephen had overdosed on drugs and had been hospitalized. It was a terrible thing for a father to witness a son being destroyed by drug addiction. I remember Jimmy showing me pictures of his son in the hospital hooked up to machines. Jimmy took the pictures so that he could show them to Stephen when he got out of the hospital to remind him of how close he had come to death. His son entered rehab at least two times but it was never successful. There is nothing worse for a parent than to bury their own child. No one can deny that it is every parent's nightmare. At the time of Stephen's death, our relationship was very strained due to the Dan Donovan controversy, but we still talked and of course I supported him during this difficult time.

Unfortunately, the nightmare continued for Molinaro, but it was not of his doing. His grandson was again arrested two more times within the next several months for misdemeanor crimes. By the end of 2006, his grandson negotiated a plea bargain avoiding jail time. Steven was put on probation for one year and was told to stay away from the victims. At the time of the plea deal, the judge told Steven that if he violated the terms of probation, she would throw the book at him, making him serve the full five-year sentence.

On May 22nd, 2007 one of the victims, Mark Veras, filed a complaint against Steven. Veras said that he saw Steven drive by his house in a car. As a result, Steven was arrested and prosecuted for violation of the terms of his probation. I thought, as well as many others believed at the time, that the case against Steven was extremely flimsy and he would definitely be found not guilty. At trial, witnesses testified that Steven was nowhere near the victim at the time and that Steven was in school. Witnesses also testified that the car that Steven allegedly drove by Veras' house was in an auto repair shop being repaired. For some inexplicable reason, the jury found Steven guilty of violating terms of his probation. It was a shocking verdict because the witnesses' testimony was so divergent. The judge then made good on her promise to prosecute Steven. He was sent to prison for five years. I feel terrible that this happened to Molinaro and his grandson, but Dan Donovan had nothing to do with it.

Prior to 2006, as you can see, Molinaro and I were like brothers. We were friends for close to forty years. When his wife, Carol, was alive she was best friends with my wife. We were over each other's house all the time. Carol was a wonderful wife who loved to have family over on Sunday and on holidays. Many times I would go over with my family and we would spend the day laughing and trading stories. I got to watch the Molinaro family grow up.

As a grandparent, I understand that the arrest of your grandchild has to be a devastatingly emotional time. Yet from the day that Dan Donovan recused himself from the case, Molinaro has never spoken to Dan. I could live with that, but Jimmy would not let it go. Molinaro went after Dan with a vendetta. He tried to destroy Dan Donovan, a man whom I consider a true friend.

From my perspective, our relationship ended on Tuesday, October 23rd, 2007. Molinaro spent $7,000 and placed a full-page ad titled "Justice Denied: The Steven Molinaro Case" in the *Staten Island Advance*. The ad vehemently attacked Dan Donovan with the purpose of ensuring that he would not be reelected. Immediately after the ad ran, Molinaro formally endorsed Dan's opponent, Democrat Michael Ryan. It broke my heart to see this behavior from a man whom I had considered one of my best friends.

When I saw the ad I flipped out. After all, I hired Dan as my Chief of Staff in 1996. Once I hired him, I directed everything through him. Dan has tremendous integrity and is extraordinarily thorough and efficient. He was my right-hand-man. I didn't have to say anything more than, "Dan, I want you to get so-and-so, and ask him to do whatever." I never had to follow up with him because I knew it was as good as done. He was excellent in the performance of his duties. Hence when I saw the ad, I saw it as a shot at not only my administration, but my family, if you will. I was infuriated and at that point the relationship between us was severed.

Molinaro was relentless with his hate campaign against Donovan. It was mean to the core. I thought that I knew Molinaro better, but apparently I did not.

Fortunately, righteousness prevailed and Donovan won the District Attorneys' election in 2007 and in 2011. Molinaro again endorsed the same Democratic rival Michael Ryan in these elections. As a testament to Dan's integrity and perseverance, Dan Donovan now holds the congressional seat that I held for ten years, and my daughter held for over seven years, and I could not be prouder. To this day I treasure the relationship I have with my protégé, Dan Donovan. I am proud of the accomplishments he has made and the job he has done for Staten Island. He is a true American, born to serve our borough and country, and a man of impeccable integrity that can never be questioned. He can make the tough decisions that many cannot. That is the type of politician our country yearns for.

Even now I know that every ethical lawyer will tell you that the close relationship Jimmy Molinaro had with Dan Donovan left Donovan with no choice but to recuse himself. But, in Molinaro's mind, he expected Dan to help his grandson out behind the scenes and that's not something that Dan Donovan would ever do. It is a terrible position to be placed in, but in law, ethics rules.

I only hope that someday Molinaro will be honest with himself and recognize that Donovan made the only move he could. Dan did not create the issue but he dealt with it professionally, fairly, and ethically.

THE PERFECT RACE

IN 2009, MICHAEL MCMAHON WAS THE FIRST DEMOCRAT TO hold the 13th Congressional District since my election in 1981, a span of almost thirty years. McMahon replaced Republican Vito Fossella who did not seek reelection after he was arrested for DUI. After his arrest, Vito Fossella publically acknowledged that he had an extra-marital affair resulting in an out of wedlock child. The loss of this congressional seat was a big blow to the Republican Party since it was the only Republican Congressional seat in all of New York City.

As I was over eighty years old, I thought that it was time for me to quit. Continuing to be heavily involved in the world of Staten Island politics took too much of a physical toll on me. That all changed, somewhat remarkably, when I received a phone call from a former employee, and personal friend, Carmela "Chickee" Piazza. My friend, Todd Ciaravino, asked Chickee to call me. Chickee told me that there was a fellow named Michael Grimm who was attempting to reach me without success. He was interested in running for the congressional seat currently occupied by McMahon. It was not going to be an easy race because McMahon was a popular Democrat.

I kind of laughed at her, and said, "Everybody wants to run for Congress. Who is he?" She said, "Well, I don't know him that well, but he seems like a good man; somebody that would make a fine candidate."

I disagreed, but then she went on to say that Grimm was in the Marine Corps. Since he was a Marine, I told Chickee to tell Grimm to make an appointment with my secretary and I would meet him. At that point I was about two weeks away from endorsing a Brooklyn Republican named Michael Allegretti at the bequest of the party. I wouldn't have to work terribly hard because Allegretti was not a Staten Islander.

A few days later, Grimm came to my office. I remember saying to him, "Who the hell are you?" Grimm said, "I'm Michael Grimm and I want to run for Congress." I waved him off by shooing him away with my hand. I said, "I'm retired, I really don't do that anymore. Everybody wants to run for Congress."

I then walked back into my office and shut the door. There was a knock on my door just as I was sitting down. I screamed out, "Are you still here?"

Grimm said, "Yes, sir. I'm still here." I said, "I thought I told you I don't do that anymore?" Grimm said, "Well, sir, I'm a United States Marine."

I said quizzically, "You're a marine?" Grimm said, "Yes, sir. I served in combat in the first Gulf War." That's when I said, "Well, if you're a marine, you automatically get fifteen minutes of my time." Grimm sat down and the rest is history.

Grimm went over his background and when he was finished I was quite impressed. I liked the fact that he was given a combat battlefield promotion, since I received the same promotion during the Korean War, so I knew it was a rare thing. I then found out that he graduated from my law school, New York Law. I could not ignore these coincidences. I felt that I was destined to take him under my wing. I also admired the fact that he worked for the FBI. He seemed like a driven, hard-working man dedicated to public service, somewhat akin to myself.

By the time we were done with our conversation I said to Grimm "Now, hold on here. If all this stuff about you is true, I need to reevaluate who I endorse." I explained to Grimm there were several factors to consider. McMahon was not just an incumbent, but he was also a City Councilman for ten years, so he was not a new politician; he was someone who was involved in Staten Island politics for a very long time and came from a political family. His wife was a judge, and his sister was Deputy Mayor under Bloomberg. He was also very well-funded. He had a ton of money.

I asked Grimm, "Do you know a lot of people with money? Michael Allegretti comes from a wealthy family. He's already raised about $250,000 because his family knows a lot of wealthy people. So you, Michael Grimm, do you have these connections?"

Grimm said, "No, sir. Most of my friends are cops, firemen, and government type people. I don't know a lot of people with money. I've grown up humble, I've been in government service most of my life. I do not come from money."

Although it was not what I wanted to hear, I still liked his answer. We discussed that he needed to be a household name for people on Staten Island, so that he could have a lot of supporters willing to help the campaign and do the grunt work. Grimm told me no, but only because he spent the last six years assigned deep undercover working for the FBI. He said most of his neighbors didn't even know his real name. They thought he was an international lawyer who leaves for eighteen months to two years at a time to go practice law overseas.

At that point I laughed and said, "Now let me get this straight: you don't have any money; you don't know anybody with money; and you're starting out with zero votes and zero help on the ground as far as volunteers."

Grimm said, "Well, sir, that's not 100% accurate." I looked at him sternly and said, "What do you mean? What am I missing?"

Grimm said, "Well, sir, you're right that I don't have money and don't know anybody with money, and I have zero votes. Actually, I just arrested eighteen Staten Islanders, so considering them and their families, we're in the negative column."

I laughed and said, "Okay. I'll ask you the pivotal question. You don't have any of these resources, and it takes money to win, why do you think you can win?"

With that Grimm laid out his plan on how he could win. He went through the different groups of constituents that would vote for him starting with veterans. Staten Island has the largest population in New York City per capita of veterans, so as a veteran, Grimm knew they would vote for him. The same was true with small business owners, cops, and firemen because he was formerly law enforcement, and he was a 9/11 first responder as well.

I liked what Grimm had to say. I then told him, "Before I make any decisions, I want to get two other opinions." That's when I consulted my law partner Bob Scarmadella. I asked Bob to do me a favor and sit down with this Grimm guy, and then let me know what his impression was. Afterward Bob told me he thought Grimm was a very presentable man, articulate, and good-looking. He thought Grimm had the making of a good candidate. In addition to Bob, I called up Mike Long, Chairman of the New York State Conservative Party. I knew that in order to win this race it was imperative that we had the endorsement of the Conservative Party. So I asked Mike to interview Grimm, and he agreed.

Since the race involved a Congressional District that has two boroughs, Staten Island and Brooklyn, the Staten Island Conservative Party could endorse a candidate however they could not choose one. That was Mike Long's responsibility. At the time, the leading candidate was Allegretti.

After Mike Long interviewed Grimm I called him up and asked him what he thought. He said he was impressed by this Michael Grimm guy. Well, if Long supported him, I supported him. He looked like he might make a fine candidate even though he was lacking two key components: namely money and friends.

Before we formally endorsed Grimm he had to pass one final test. Mike Long and I agreed that if Grimm couldn't raise any money before December 31st, then we would have to go with Allegretti. Even though Grimm was a good candidate, no one would know it if Grimm could not raise money. I told Grimm and he answered that he would raise as much as the $250,000 the Allegretti campaign had. I laughed when he said it, since Grimm never raised money before. I thought that goal would be impossible because of the Jewish holidays and the Christmas season. Raising money during that time is nearly impossible.

Miraculously, Grimm did incredibly. He raised over $300,000 by the end of the year. I was blown away by his determination. I told Grimm his results were amazing and I believed we had ourselves a race. I then called Mike Long, told him how much money Grimm had raised, and we both agreed to support Michael Grimm's candidacy. So, that was the start of the impossible dream.

I was completely pissed to hear that Vito Fossella orchestrated the Staten Island Republican Committee's endorsement of Michael Allegretti along with State Senator Andrew Lanza, Assemblyman Lou Tobacco, and GOP chairman John Friscia. They supported a Brooklyn candidate over a Staten Islander because they all believed that McMahon would win and then Fossella could come back and run against McMahon in the 2013 election. Obviously it was going to be an uphill battle for Grimm to win.

From the beginning, people questioned a primary between Michael Allegretti and Grimm. They though it was a waste of money. I told Grimm that a primary was a good thing for a first time unknown candidate: if you're an entrenched incumbent, a primary doesn't help you. Many people disagreed with me, but there is no question in my mind that Grimm never would have beaten Mike McMahon without a primary.

We had to work twice as hard to win the Republican primary election. So Grimm was out there working relentlessly while McMahon, who did not have a primary, wouldn't care since the race for him wasn't until November. So, Grimm was out there working hard, building support, and getting name recognition.

It was good news that Grimm would not debate McMahon right away. He would get to practice on Allegretti. This was a huge plus. Grimm's first debate occurred because he needed the endorsement of the Molinari Republican Club, which I founded, but was now run by Bob Scarmadella. Scarmadella said that Grimm had to have a debate in order to get their endorsement. I told Bob that Grimm was out there working hard on the streets and just was not ready. Although I was right, he wasn't completely ready, he surprised us all with his adaptability.

In the first half of the debate I cringed because he was so stiff, and really nervous. Grimm's prep for the debate fell short of what he needed as a political novice. Fortunately, half way through the debate, Michael Allegretti made a comment about Grimm having illegitimate children. It was something that Allegretti's campaign had up their sleeve. When Allegretti asked Grimm about having children, Grimm jokingly said, "Well, Mr. Allegretti, maybe you could introduce me to them someday because I've never met them. As far as I know, I don't have any children."

Allegretti was embarrassed, and from that moment on Grimm was relaxed and at the top of his game. Had Grimm not had a primary his first debate would have been against McMahon, who was a much more seasoned debater and politician. McMahon was head and shoulders above Allegretti and it would have been a disaster for Grimm. So the primary was a great stepping stone in preparation for the actual election. Grimm could make some slight mistakes in the primary, but we knew that we couldn't have any mistakes in the general election. We had to run a perfect race.

Grimm wound up crushing Allegretti in every single district in Staten Island as well as Brooklyn. Grimm beat him by over forty points. It was one of the biggest landslides ever. Grimm even crushed Allegretti in Allegretti's own home election district. It was unbelievable how well Grimm did. The people loved him. We gained a tremendous amount of momentum. Plus, with such a huge victory it was easier to raise money since people knew his name.

One of the reasons I think we were so successful, and why it was the perfect race was that, as two Marines, we were able to work together with a trust that only one Marine could have for another. I gave Michael the marching orders and he marched. Throughout the campaign, Michael never once questioned my judgment. If I told him to go out and shake 400 hands at such-and-such a location, the answer was always, "Yes, sir," and it was never 400 hands, it would be 450 or 500. Michael would follow my advice to the letter. If I came up with an idea for the press, Michael would type it up at two o'clock in the morning and then email it out to the press. Unsuccessful campaigns mull it over 'til death and ultimately the opportunity is lost, especially with press. It was an extreme loyalty, flexibility, tireless devotion, and constant attention to details that made the difference.

The highlight of the campaign was the final debate that took place, delivering the kiss of death for McMahon. I told Grimm to take the gloves off and be aggressive with McMahon. No more poking just throw punches. McMahon nervous based off how prior debates had gone that for the final debate, McMahon recruited Grimm's ex father-in-law, Grandmaster Jhong Uhk Kim, a well-known figure in Staten Island, his ex-brother-in-law, and ex-wife, Susan Kim Piazza to sit in the front row wearing McMahon stickers.

On the night of the debate I noticed that they moved Grimm's podium- instead of being cornered with respect to the center of the stage, Grimm's podium was moved over so that he was directly in front of his ex-wife. Now, of course McMahon did this in an effort to shake Grimm up and throw him off his game. In reality, it had no effect on Grimm whatsoever. By all accounts, if you were to ask most people who were at the debate, they would say that Grimm won handily.

During the applause at the end, McMahon, being an experienced politician, walked over to the moderators and shook their hands. Instead, Grimm made a bee-line off the stage right to his ex-family. He hugged his ex-brother-in-law, shook hands with Grandmaster Kim, and as he got to his ex-wife, he said, "It's so nice to see you. You're as beautiful today as the first day I met you." And he meant it as a sincere compliment. Unbeknownst to Grimm a news reporter was standing behind him. The reporter heard what Grimm said, and printed his statement in the paper.

The headline the next day reported that McMahon tried to pull a dirty trick by bringing the Kim family, yet the whole thing blew up in McMahon's face. The fact of the matter was Grimm's ex-brother-in-law and his ex-wife were just doing what their father asked them to do. There was no question that this blunder cost McMahon a couple of thousand votes. It was the talk of the town and Grimm's campaign peaked the following week. Staten Islanders don't like dirty tricks, and Grimm came off as the classy individual. That was it! A political campaign can change in one day and this was the pivotal moment that allowed Grimm to win the overall election. The campaign immediately picked up momentum and we could see the difference in the polling. The public saw Grimm's dedication and determination and knew he would devote his life to Staten Island.

As with any election, when politicians see that a specific candidate will win, they jump on the bandwagon. They are insignificant endorsements since they were not there from the beginning. Such was the endorsement of then City Councilman James Oddo a week before the election. As far as we were concerned, Oddo could toss his endorsement down the toilet. Grimm rose from the trenches with loyal followers and did not need a last minute half-hearted endorsement from a man who could not make the right decision earlier. The only politician who was with Grimm from the beginning was City Councilman Vinny Ignazio. A man with a heart and drive.

On Election Day all the political gurus usually pile into a room that's reserved for a candidate and his followers waiting for the returns. At the end of election night in 2010, there were still four districts outstanding. Two appeared to be in friendly territory and two in enemy territory. The elected officials turned to me told me not to announce yet because two of the districts are bad and the board of elections shut down their operations and wouldn't be open again till the following day. I was floored. I wondered if we'd have to come back the following day and pick up where we left off. That was ridiculous. So I said, "What are you going to do with all these supporters? You've got a thousand people down there. I've studied the results and am very upset with the fact that you are taking a position that is flawed."

Then something happened that made me livid. When my back was turned, these gurus put Grimm in a private room and tried to convince him not to announce a victory. At one point, I was looking to see where he was since I couldn't find him. I opened a door to another room and saw that they had shanghaied him. As a matter of fact, they cited a couple of legal cases where it blew up in the candidate's face. I knew enough about politics to be able to determine the probable result of those four districts. I knew it would be a disaster if we didn't declare that night.

I was angry and I said, "I don't give a damn what any of you say, I've had enough. I'm the campaign manager. I'm satisfied that we have a win. We're sitting on a few thousand votes. Even under the worst of circumstances I firmly believe we have a win. I'm going downstairs now and I'm going to announce victory and let the chips fall where they may." I turned around and walked toward the stairway. As I approached the stairs I heard Grimm give the Marine Corps grunt sound and he yelled, "I'm with you, sir."

We walked down the stairs, everybody was applauding, clapping, we were all smiles, and we declared victory. As I expected, McMahon swiftly gave a graceful concession to Michael Grimm.

We would have looked like terrible politicians had we followed the elected officials' recommendations. It was a triumphant night.

Although I wanted to stay and enjoy the well-deserved celebration I slipped out shortly thereafter because I was unable to stand anymore. As I left, I looked up at the stage, saw Grimm, and I was happy. I knew that the 13th Congressional District had just elected a fine young man who would serve his constituents honorably and diligently.

So in 2011, in an extremely close race, Michael Grimm was elected to the Congress of the United States as a Representative for New York's 13th Congressional District. He received 51.3% of the vote compared to 48% of the vote for McMahon. He sat in the seat previously occupied by myself, and my daughter. As it was in my time he was the only Republican representing a significant portion of New York City.

He was reelected for a second term in 2013 to the same district which was renumbered the 11th Congressional District. He won with 52.2% of the vote as compared to 46.8% of the vote by his challenger Mark Murphy. Throughout his tenure he has vigorously fought for issues that mattered most for his constituents.

His biggest accomplishment involved actively leading efforts to pass the Superstorm Sandy Relief Bill. On October 29th, 2012 a significant portion of Staten Island was destroyed by the devastating effects of Superstorm Sandy. Michael had relentlessly fought for our community so that Staten Island and Brooklyn were able to rebuild stronger than before. Michael did not orchestrate his efforts from behind a desk; he was front and center with his constituents immediately after the disaster. He was relentless in ensuring that he was able to help the thousands of his constituents directly affected by Sandy. This is the type of congressman you need to represent you. Leadership is shown by how one reacts to crisis, and Michael reacted flawlessly.

Michael reminds me of myself when I was a congressman. His work and moral ethics are remarkable. He is like a son or a younger brother to me. I love him, what he represents, and I will do whatever

I can to enable him to continue his political career. 'Til my last breath I will fight for him.

Now for my final words on the attempted political assassination of my cherished friend, loyal marine, and devoted congressman, Michael Grimm….

THE WITCH HUNT

It broke my heart to see the relentless political beating bestowed upon Michael Grimm, from the minute he won his first election. The disgraceful selective prosecution of the sole New York City Republican Congressman from Staten Island and Brooklyn must be exposed for what it is: a political witch-hunt orchestrated by the malicious Democrats. It is common knowledge that the Democratic majority is always demonically and systematically plotting how to take another Republican seat by any means necessary, and this is a perfect example. As we go to print, the house Republicans have charged that the Democrats illegally utilized the IRS to target conservative Republicans.

The biased investigation against Grimm allegedly concerned campaign finance violations. After years of investigation and spending taxpayer's dollars, the U.S. Attorney General's office came up empty handed. So, the politically motivated Democratic federal prosecutor's office kept investigating Grimm so that they might be able to save face. This is the same government where the IRS selectively targeted the Tea Party. The disgraceful abuse of authority is plain for all to see.

The privacy of a grand jury investigation in searching for the truth was important to our founding fathers. Yet the grand jury investigation concerning Grimm involved malicious leaks and strong arm tactics. I am sure our founding fathers are turning over in their graves because of distortions that federal prosecutors under the direction of Loretta Lynch and Todd Kaminsky have made out of the grand jury proceeding. They have butchered and fouled up the sanctimony of the very proceeding.

In Grimm's case, the government kept up their politically motivated persecution, but after nearly three years, they came up empty handed. Ultimately he was indicted for paying workers off-the-books at a health food restaurant where he was a minority owner. This had nothing to do with his time in Congress, since it occurred before he was elected. Normally when somebody else did what Grimm was accused of, the IRS would come to you with a bill indicating what you owe. These issues are routinely handled with civil or administrative action typically resulting in fines from the Department of Labor or the IRS. If you cannot work it out, then it would proceed as a civil case. That's what the Government is interested in normally: money.

As a result of what happened to Grimm, I believe that every Republican restaurant owner involved in politics should be on pins and needles hoping that the same thing does not happen to them. No other restaurant owner in the history of New York had ever been hit with felony charges and jail time for such an offense

After a selective targeted investigation, Grimm's attorneys told him on Friday April 25th, 2014 that he had been indicted and was to surrender on Monday April 28th for arraignment at Brooklyn Federal District Court. I will never forget that day. My nephew was visiting me from Alaska with his wife and daughter. Just as they were getting ready to leave, Grimm called me to tell me that he was coming over. I was glad because I wanted him to meet my relatives. He said he would, but he needed to talk about something important, too.

So, there we were in the living room, having a normal conversation. I would never have guessed the bomb that Grimm was going to drop. My relatives joked with Grimm, asking him a bunch of questions about Congress. After about half an hour they left and I went to the bathroom.

When I came out of the bathroom, I heard Grimm say, "Sir, I'm going to be indicted on Monday." I immediately looked up and I saw him sitting in the living room, his head hung low in grief, cupped by his hands. You have to know the guy to realize the impact that it had upon him was much greater than the average person. I told Grimm that we needed to sit down and talk about it to figure out what steps we had to take. As true marines, we would be going into the greatest battle of his life together. Then he started going over the facts. There we were: two congressmen, the elder retired and the young freshman whose whole career could be destroyed. His whole life was turned upside down. He was facing a trial. He could go to jail.

On Monday, April 28th, 2014 Grimm was arraigned on a twenty count federal indictment that had absolutely nothing to do with the initial investigation of campaign finance violations. As a testament to Grimm's devotion to his constituents, immediately after his arraignment Robert Ollis, father of Army Staff Sgt. Michael Ollis who was killed in the line of duty in Afghanistan on August 28th, 2013 during Operation Enduring Freedom stood loyally at Grimm's side during the press conference. As Grimm helped Robert Ollis during his darkest hours when he learned of his son's death in Afghanistan, Ollis stood by Grimm during his darkest hours. To have a man who suffered such a grave loss willing to stand up at a time like that for Michael speaks volumes.

Immediately after Grimm's arraignment, one of the lead Democratic prosecutors who pursued the criminal case, Assistant U.S. Attorney Todd Kaminsky, resigned and stated he was running for the 20th Assembly District in New York State located in Long Beach. When I heard this I flipped out. It boggled my mind that this bastard could attempt to ruin a true American hero's life, and the next day turn around and run for public office himself.

Could the entire country be blind to the fact that Kaminsky was specifically targeting Grimm because he had political aspirations to run for office on the Democratic Party line? Conflict of interest? You bet. Appearance of impropriety? You bet. It is obvious that Kaminsky used the resources of the federal prosecutor's office and the power of the justice department to ultimately facilitate his own and the Democratic Party's political aspirations in the wrongful prosecution of Republican Michael Grimm.

So, what is it all really about? Well, in my opinion, the Democrats in this country, specifically the present administration, are crooked. They're bad, particularly in areas like New York State. There is no question in my mind that the Democrats targeted him. He was targeted by the Clinton Democratic machine, spearheaded by her good friend, Senator Chuck Schumer. Senator Schumer is one of the sharpest yet most devious politicians in Washington. I served with him, I was elected to the assembly and congress the same year that he was. Schumer and I worked together to save public housing in New York City. I got to know him really well. Although his personality comes off as a boring slug, innately he is always scheming to benefit himself. I truly believe that Schumer saw Grimm as a threat to him in a future senatorial race. Also I believe that Congressman Steve Israel, who is in charge of all the congressional Democratic races in the country, saw Michael as a threat as well. Together, with a politically corrupt administration, anything is possible when evil minds get together.

There are numerous stories about how this administration has used the Internal Revenue Service to do its political bidding. It is disturbing to watch the political favoritism that abounds in the criminal justice system, particularly our federal system. In essence it amounts to the vindictive discriminatory prosecution of some and turning a blind eye to others. In my strong opinion, the only difference is a ruthless double standard held by the Democrats in power.

Today when I watch the Democratic presidential election coverage, my body writhes in agony, not from my physical condition, but from the intense mental stress created by the fact that Hilary Clinton is presently looking to become President of the United States. Can you imagine the audacity? Disgustingly, Clinton is the presumptive Democratic presidential candidate. You must ask yourself if this lying, divisive, and clearly deceitful individual is what our country needs.

The most troublesome part of her background involves the obvious selective criminal immunity she receives from our allegedly impartial justice system. She has become the 21st Century "Teflon Dame." For some inexplicable reason, all the reported criminal acts she has been accused of during her tenure as a politician, and there have been many, she has always evaded prosecution.

It is clear that Clinton covered up Benghazi. Our representatives in Benghazi were butchered, due to the criminal malfeasance of Hillary and the Obama Administration, yet they remain unscathed. She used an unsecure personal email account for top secret communications regarding national security in her role as Secretary of State, and then knowingly deleted the evidence. Now she wants to be president, and it appears she is to be given another free pass.

Why does this drive me crazy? Because as the blistery winter days slowly passed, I prayed for my good friend, Michael Grimm, who was incarcerated in a federal prison at taxpayers' expense for a ridiculous civil crime.

Grimm is the true victim. Congressman Michael Grimm is a war hero who was almost killed in combat, received a battlefield promotion, was a decorated federal agent, and was loved by his former constituents. And the sin of Michael Grimm is that as a novice restaurateur he made a mistake that essentially all restaurants do. He hired undocumented aliens to work in his restaurant. Yet, no one has ever been politically destroyed or criminally prosecuted as Grimm has. The Democrats will out and out target and crucify a Republican while ignoring their own sins.

I ask you to look out your window and think who cuts your lawn, cleans your dishes in restaurants, shovels your snow, renovates our houses, watches your children, and does a multitude of jobs that many Americans do not want or do not have the time to do. None of us are without sin including, Hillary Clinton, yet Michael Grimm went to prison.

Now let's look at how Hillary frolics around our country professing she should be the next president, knowing that she has a rancid history of deceit buried by her beloved Democratic party. Drop the Democratic "Teflon Shield" and let her answer for her crimes. I look forward to the day that she is indicted for her misdirected political aspirations.

The righteous path is almost never the easy path in politics. Michael has always followed that path. After watching what happened to Michael I firmly believe that any Republican congressperson from Staten Island will always have a target on their back, and that is why we have to aggressively stop the political prosecution of our Republican party. We must demand equal prosecutions for all and end these politically motivated witch-hunts.

Even during his indictment, Grimm fought nonstop to retain his seat and was successful. The people of Staten Island backed up the man who fought for them during their direst time – Super Storm Sandy. In early 2014, he sponsored the Homeowner Flood Insurance Affordability Act over strenuous objections from his own party leadership. After an arduous battle, it passed the house and ultimately became law. It was a tremendous benefit to Staten Island residents adversely affected by Super Storm Sandy. As he was there for them, Staten Islanders were there for Grimm. Staten Island is synonymous with "People Power" when it comes to doing the right thing. Michael was reelected on November 5th, 2014 despite his indictment.

On December 23rd, 2014, after much soul searching, negotiations with the government, and the desire to get this behind him, Michael pleaded guilty to one felony count that he paid restaurant staff off the books at the restaurant Healthalicious.

Sadly, after initially vowing to retain his seat, Michael announced on December 30th, 2014, that he would resign from Congress effective January 5th, 2015. It was the right thing to do for his constituents. On May 5th, 2015, Daniel M. Donovan, my former Chief of Staff, and a man whom I dearly love, won the special election to replace Michael. We ensured that Staten Island would be cared for by a passionate, dedicated, Republican.

After months of anguish on July 17th, 2015, Grimm was sentenced to an unprecedented eight months in prison for tax evasion beginning September 22nd, 2015, in Pennsylvania's McKean Federal Correctional Institution. He was released on April 27th, 2016.

The people should ask how much the biased Attorney General's Office spent on this malicious investigation, prosecution, and incarceration of an American hero. Millions! For what? To destroy a man who has served his country and his constituents honorably and diligently. To the people who wonder why our country has such an exorbitant debt, just look at this case. Staten Island needed a politician like Grimm who had the political spine to do the right thing, especially during tragic events like Super Storm Sandy.

It's sad to say that I continue to witness so many incidents where mistakes were being made against public servants, specifically law enforcement officer, who in my opinion are the cream of the crop. In the end the only one conclusion I can make is that there is always some ulterior motive and political aspiration on the part of the prosecutors in these erroneous cases.

Michael was and always will be the number one hero for Sandy victims all over our state. No elected officials on Staten Island or Brooklyn worked as hard as Michael Grimm to assist Storm Sandy victims. Those who lost so much due to the onslaught of Super Storm Sandy would do anything that they can for him. Michael did not lead from an office in the aftermath of Sandy he went to the frontline of the devastation and worked with distraught homeowners one by one. That is the Michael Grimm Staten Islanders and Brooklynites know and admire.

I will always see Michael as the hero he is: the twenty year-old marine who volunteered and survived a potential suicide mission for our country; the man who earned a degree in accounting and later, law; the man who worked deep undercover for five years for the FBI as a special agent to expose corruption on Wall Street; the young, politically unconnected man who rose to congressman in one short year; the man who toiled tirelessly for his Staten Island constituents after Super Storm Sandy when the government abandoned our city; the man who dedicated his entire life to public service of our country and the City of New York.

It will be my dream to see Michael become the servant of Staten Island in some political capacity again. This is what he was born to do. In his own words, Michael Grimm is, "The man who will always run toward the line of fire to serve the people and my country." Public service and a love for our great country are in his blood, and there is still so much for Michael to do. I will do everything in my power to ensure his resurrection.

So let's get to it!

ABOUT THE AUTHORS

Guy Molinari was born in the Lower East Side of New York City. His family moved to Staten Island during the Great Depression. After serving honorably in the Marine Corps during the Korean War, he became a lawyer and he then followed in his father's footsteps and began a lifelong commitment to politics. He served as a New York State assemblyman from 1975 to 1980, a United States congressman from 1981 to December 1989, and Staten Island Borough President from 1989 until 2001.

While providing for his constituents' needs, Molinari was also instrumental in the successful election campaigns of President Reagan, Bush 41, Mayor Rudy Giuliani, and many other public officials. He fought relentlessly to ensure safe air travel, to address toxic waste environmental issues, and to continue the fight for democracy throughout the world. He orchestrated the final closure of the largest garbage dump in the world: the Fresh Kills Landfill.

Patricia Feerick-Kossmann met Molinari over twenty years ago, when he relentlessly fought for justice after Pat while a NYPD Lieutenant and three of her officers were unjustly convicted of an illegal search in a politically motivated prosecution. Molinari successfully gained clemency for Pat. They have remained loyal friends since that time and this book is a testament to that enduring friendship.

CPSIA information can be obtained
at www.ICGtesting.com
Printed in the USA
LVOW12*0857090217
523715LV00001BA/10/P

9 781684 091706